# OLE DB Consumer Templates

MW01017230

# OLE DB Consumer Templates
## A Programmer's Guide

Pierre Nallet

Addison-Wesley

Boston • San Francisco • New York • Toronto • Montreal
London • Munich • Paris • Madrid
Capetown • Sydney • Tokyo • Singapore • Mexico City

Many of the designations used by manufacturers and sellers to distinguish their products are claimed as trademarks. Where those designations appear in this book, and we were aware of a trademark claim, the designations have been printed in initial capital letters or in all capitals.

The author and publisher have taken care in the preparation of this book, but make no expressed or implied warranty of any kind and assume no responsibility for errors or omissions. No liability is assumed for incidental or consequential damages in connection with or arising out of the use of the information or programs contained herein.

The publisher offers discounts on this book when ordered in quantity for special sales. For more information, please contact:

Pearson Education Corporate Sales Division
One Lake Street
Upper Saddle River, NJ 07458
(800) 382-3419
*corpsales@pearsontechgroup.com*

Visit us on the Web at *www.awl.com/cseng/*

*Library of Congress Cataloging-in-Publication Data*
Nallet, Pierre
        OLE DB consumer templates : a programmer's guide / Pierre Nallet.
            p.   cm.
        ISBN 0-201-65792-9 (alk. paper)
        1. Database management.   2. OLE (Computer file)   I. Title.
QA76.9.D3 N32 2000
005.75'8--dc21                                                          00-059357

Text printed on recycled paper

1  2  3  4  5  6  7  8  9  10–MA–04  03  02  01  00
*First printing, October 2000*

# Contents

# Preface

OLE DB, OLE DB consumer templates? Why should you care? At first, when a new technology emerges, the first reaction is confusion: Why do we need something new? What does it do? How does it work? Is it worth my time?

OLE DB is one of many data access technologies. The field of data access technology is very crowded, one example being Microsoft's ODBC. Usually when there are many competing technologies, it is a sign of tradeoffs. One technology might be easy to use but slow; another might be fast but not portable; another might be portable but difficult to use; and so forth. OLE DB does better than any of the other technologies in many areas: It is based on COM, it is very modular and efficient, it covers many aspects of data access, and it is supported by many data vendors. In fact, this explains why Microsoft uses OLE DB inside its SQL Server and for distributed queries. However, OLE DB has one drawback: complexity. Writing a simple program or component with OLE DB is similar to writing a graphical user interface (GUI) application using the Windows API: It takes lots of (not so simple) code to perform a simple task.

This is where the OLE DB consumer templates come in: They are a high-level, high-performance C++ library on top of OLE DB. In short, the OLE DB consumer templates are to database programming what ATL is to GUI programming. One of the great benefits of this approach is that you can choose the level you are working at. You can use the template library and stay at a high level of abstraction, but you also have access to all the lower-level details.

There are two ways to look at what OLE DB can offer:

- If you are a database programmer, you probably know first-hand the drawbacks of letting people access the database directly. You need some kind of intermediate protective layer. A set of COM components is a good choice for accomplishing this, and the OLE DB consumer templates are a good tool for gluing the components and the database together.

- If you are a C++ developer, you might need persistence support. Databases are one of many choices. One of the traditional drawbacks of storing data in a database is that the database is complicated for the programmer to manage. The OLE DB consumer templates, however, provide a straightforward approach for C++ programmers.

At first, I was happy being a simple OLE DB consumer templates programmer. As time passed, however, I realized that there was no in-depth documentation of this library and no book devoted to it. I had to explore this library by myself.

Furthermore, I realized that the OLE DB consumer templates did not cover all facets of OLE DB, so I started writing small extensions that would cover additional aspects of OLE DB or offer different options. I grouped them together in one library that I called the OLE DB extensions. When I thought about releasing the code, it became obvious that the OLE DB extensions were bigger than the OLE DB consumer templates and hence needed some documentation. As a result, I decided to write this book to explain both the OLE DB consumer templates and the OLE DB extensions.

When starting with OLE DB, you have two options: One, you can start at the lower level with Microsoft's OLE DB SDK and then go up a more abstract level. Two, you can start at the C++ level with the OLE DB consumer templates and go down to the SDK level when needed.

This book presents OLE DB programming using the templates, not the SDK. Microsoft provides detailed documentation of OLE DB, so there is no point in replicating that effort here. However, this book is designed to be more or less self-contained. If there is a concept of the SDK that needs to be understood, I'll spend some time on it. In other words, you won't have to turn to the SDK documentation too frequently. This does not mean that you should not refer to the OLE DB SDK; the SDK remains the best the reference to use.

Dealing with OLE DB is a little bit like using COM. At first, you wonder why you need to deal with this complex technology. But once you have used it for some time, you will wonder how you could have programmed without it. In between, several events need to occur. First, you should understand, through experience, the motives behind the technology; when you understand why something exists, it is easier to understand how it works. Second, you need to think that it is easy—easy to understand and easy to use.

The OLE DB consumer templates will facilitate this transition because you can use them progressively. Performing simple tasks is straightforward. Then you can increasingly explore the numerous options that the library offers. In other words, your understanding of the OLE DB consumer templates can grow with your needs.

The goal of this book is to take you along this learning path and to help you develop efficient, scalable, manageable database applications.

## THE FUTURE OF OLE DB

OLE DB is an evolving technology. While this book is based on version 2.5, it is likely that a new version will be released before or right after this book appears on the shelves. Actually, OLE DB 2.6 is already available with SQL Server beta 2. OLE DB 2.6 introduces streams as a result of commands, which is useful for returning an XML stream instead of a rowset. The OLE DB for Data Mining specification is also close to the final stage of development.

What is next? OLE DB will continue to follow the needs of the marketplace. Look for complex row support, more XML support, and more command languages.

## LOGISTICS

What do you need to be able to run the OLE DB consumer templates on your computer? First, you need a C++ compiler—Visual C++ 6.0 or later. Visual C++ comes with the OLE DB consumer templates files and a default OLE DB setup.

It also would be a good idea to download the latest platform SDK from *http://msdn.microsoft.com/*. Finally, the OLE DB extension files and the examples discussed in this book are available at *http://www.com-object.com/oledbtemplates*. Note that some examples require the Windows Template Library (WTL), which is part of the SDK platform.

# Acknowledgments

Writing a book is a little bit like writing an application. It looks easy but many things can go wrong. Many people helped me along the way.

I would like to thank Bob Beauchemin for the help he provided. While preparing his course, "Essential OLE DB and ADO," for DevelopMentor, Bob acquired a thorough understanding of OLE DB, its objects and interfaces, and the different provider implementations available. He shared his insights with me and caught many mistakes. In fact, it would take too much space to enumerate his contributions.

Thanks to Lyn Robison who encouraged me to write this book, and then reviewed it, and to Hubert Divoux who reviewed this manuscript.

The folks at Addison-Wesley provided me with all the help I needed when I needed it. Thanks to Marisa Meltzer, Jenie Pak, Marilyn Rash, and Michael Slaughter.

Finally, I would like to thank my wife Darcy for making me believe I was almost finished even before I had written the first page. Somehow, it made things easier.

# 1

# Windows DNA and COM

COM, OLE DB, ADO, DNA, DNS—the development world is full of acronyms. New ones come up constantly, making it a challenge to stay up to date. This chapter answers the question "Where does OLE DB fit?" by describing the big picture.

## DISTRIBUTED INTERNET APPLICATIONS

How does the Internet change the programming model? First, Web sites do not know how many users they will get, so it is better to be able to scale to a large number of users. Second, there is obviously a need to separate the client machine and the server machine. Some scenarios require a fat client while others work better with a thin one. Third, Internet applications need to be flexible.

A good idea for the Internet is usually a good idea for the corporate world as well. But what direction should you take? There are many options, but this book will focus on those provided by the Microsoft architecture.

DNA stands for Distributed Internet Applications architecture. It is a framework proposed by Microsoft for building a new generation of applications for both the Web and intranets. It follows the principles described here.

- *The best of Windows.* Windows offers rich services. Would you rather reuse them or rewrite them from scratch? To develop and deploy great DNA applications, programmers need to use the capabilities of Windows to their fullest. Such capabilities include security, transactions, components, and directory services. Because Windows offers all of these services as part of its operating system, programmers do not have to worry about deploying, managing, and upgrading them.

1

- *The best of the Internet.* The days when you could develop a business application without thinking about the Internet are over. Organizations and individuals want the worldwide reach the Internet provides. DNA employs the Internet as a full-time platform.

- *Compatibility.* Organizations do not want to start from scratch each time a new technology comes around. Instead, they want to continue with their current systems and extend them with the new technology functionality. This means in particular that new components need to interoperate with legacy systems. They should also be able to interoperate with components from other vendors. Thus, new applications are built around standard formats, protocols, and interfaces coming from the Internet and from Windows.

## THE WINDOWS DNA ARCHITECTURE

Windows DNA is not rocket science. It is a common-sense, proven architecture that incorporates the notion that applications should be divided into three layers.

Those layers, or tiers, are presentation, business logic, and data, as shown in Figure 1-1 and described as follows:

- The *presentation tier* is responsible for the user interface. This includes displaying information on the screen as well as receiving input from the user (mouse, keyboard, etc).

- The *business logic tier* is the heart of the system. It implements the business operations and rules.

- The *data tier* manages all of the persistent data of the application.

This partitioning enables greater flexibility than that provided by the traditional client–server model.

Note that the tree tiers are logical only, not physical. They might run on the same machine, or one tier might span several machines or several processes.

### The Presentation Tier

The presentation tier implements information display and user interaction.

**Figure 1-1** DNA Diagram

**Table 1-1**  DNA Presentation Technologies

| Technology | Domain | Portability | Functionality |
|---|---|---|---|
| HTML | Internet | Any Web browser | Text/image display |
| Scripting | Internet | Browser with scripting | Basic interaction |
| Dynamic HTML | Internet | Internet explorer | Basic interaction |
| ActiveX components | Windows | COM | Rich |
| Windows API | Windows | Windows | Very rich |

Windows DNA offers a broad range of presentation services, enabling the developer to choose the right technology for an application (see Table 1-1). Some components are Internet based, others Windows based. The former offer the best portability, while the latter offer maximum functionality. As a rule, the more portable a technology, the less functionality it supports.

The choice is not necessarily either/or. You can use different presentation services together. For example, a product such as Microsoft Outlook, a Win32 API product, uses ActiveX components and embedded dynamic HTML.

## The Business Logic Tier

The business logic tier is the heart of any application. It defines application-specific behavior and algorithms. It is difficult to say what the business logic does because its functions depend on the application. For example, a Web store might have concepts like product, order, and payments, while a scientific application might have concepts like matrix and optimization. In any case, the business logic tier does not deal with the storage of persistent data or its presentation. It is a bridge between the presentation and the data tiers.

Even though the business logic applies to many domains, Windows comes with a set of services that can be useful in many scenarios, summarized in Table 1-2.

**Table 1-2**  Windows Business Logic Services

| Technology | Description |
|---|---|
| Component services | Services related to COM: transactions, security, concurrency, etc. |
| Messaging services | Message queuing services |
| Web services | Development of Web sites (Internet or intranet): IIS and ASP |

## The Data Tier

Two components compose the data tier: Microsoft's universal data access and XML.

*Universal data access* provides any Windows client access to a variety of data sources, particularly relational, hierarchical, and multidimensional data. It allows programmers to focus on the business logic rather than the specifics of a given data source. Universal data access contains three parts:

- *Open DataBase Connectivity* (ODBC), the legacy standard for accessing relational data
- *OLE for Data Bases* (OLE DB), a set of Component Object Model (COM) interfaces for high-performance data access to diverse sources of data
- *ActiveX Data Objects* (ADO), a simplified layer on top of OLE DB targeted mainly to Visual Basic, Java, and scripting programs

Chapter 2 describes universal data access in more detail.

*Extensible Markup Language* (XML) is the Internet standard for structured information. Its functions include

- Delivering data on non-Windows clients
- Delivering data for local processing and presentation
- Storing hierarchical data
- Transferring data from server to server while keeping format problems under control
- Exchanging information between Web sites

XML has some connections with universal data access. For example, it is possible to transform an OLE DB rowset into an XML stream and vice versa. In addition, one can use XML for services such as the *Simple Object Access Protocol* (SOAP), which provides a standard for method calls on remote Web sites. Finally, data store products offer rich integration with XML.

Table 1-3 summarizes the components of the data layer.

## DNA Summary

DNA is a common-sense architecture for today, not a hypothetical bet for the future. Its tiers offer many options, some of them complementary. It allows developers to choose the approach that solves their problems.

Putting all the DNA pieces together, we obtain the diagram in Figure 1-2.

**Table 1-3** The Data Layer Components

| Technology | Domain | Description |
| --- | --- | --- |
| ODBC | Microsoft universal data access | Legacy access to SQL databases |
| OLE DB | Microsoft universal data access | COM-based data access to a wide variety of data sources |
| ADO | Microsoft universal data access | Simplified version of OLE DB targeted at Visual Basic, Java, and scripting |
| XML | Internet standard | Text format for data transfer |

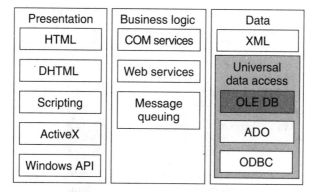

**Figure 1-2** DNA Elements

# DNA SCENARIOS

An effective way to understand DNA is to test it with a few key scenarios.

## The Client–Server Architecture

Before DNA, the prevailing model was client–server. Briefly, the client–server model consists of a client, which handles presentation, and a server, which holds data. It is unclear and open to debate as to where the business logic should reside. In a sense, DNA is a "clean" client–server model in which the business logic is separate from *both* the client/presentation and the server/data. Whether it physically resides on the server or client or even on another machine is application specific.

## The Web

The most basic way to build a Web application is to have ASP dynamically generate Web pages. Since Active Server Pages (ASP) is VB-like, ADO is a good choice for accessing the data layer. The presentation part can consist of HTML pages that mix HTML, DHTML, and client-side scripting (Figure 1-3).

As such a project grows, it can become harder to manage scripting and ADO because they are weakly typed. A solution is to replace scripting with ActiveX components and access the data with OLE DB (Figure 1-4). However, the resulting system is more complex to develop and suitable only for larger projects.

If the user interface becomes more sophisticated, a browser and a page-based system might become insufficient for the presentation layer. The solution here is to replace the browser with a Windows-based application (Figure 1-5). If the application runs on an intranet, the user interface can access the COM objects with distributed COM. If the application runs on the Internet, you can use the DCOM HTTP transport over the Internet or a solution such as SOAP.

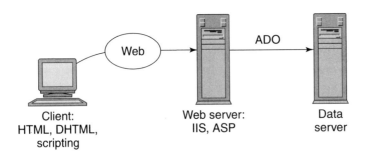

Client:
HTML, DHTML,
scripting

Web server:
IIS, ASP

Data
server

**Figure 1-3** Web Scenario 1

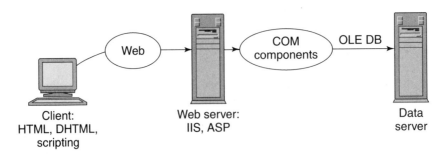

Client:
HTML, DHTML,
scripting

Web server:
IIS, ASP

Data
server

**Figure 1-4** Web Scenario 2

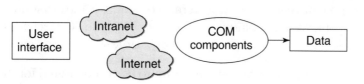

**Figure 1-5** Web Scenario 3

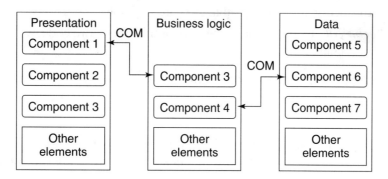

**Figure 1-6** DNA Application Components

## COMPONENT OBJECT MODEL

Using Windows DNA means taking advantage of Windows and the Internet and partitioning applications in three tiers. This is a practical approach that is not unreasonably complex or futuristic. A logical question is how these partitioned elements talk to each other. When the element is Internet based, there is a standard such as HTML or XML, but what about all the other elements (Figure 1-6)? For many components, the answer is COM—the foundation of DNA and of OLE DB in particular.

Before diving into the data tier of DNA, it might be a good idea to review a few characteristics of COM. If you are a COM beginner, you might want to get a book that explains the details. If you are already a COM expert, the next section will refresh your memory, as well as emphasize a few points that are important for OLE DB.

### Reuse

Today, developers are under pressure to deliver applications that do more and do it better and faster. Of course, they must deal with time and resource constraints. The only way to get around these constraints is to reuse components written and tested by someone else.

"Component reuse" is a fuzzy term. For some, it means source code reuse through a copy/paste operation or some type of include file mechanism. However, source code reuse is not very successful on a large scale for several reasons:

- *Economic.* Usually programmers want to be compensated for their work. By giving their source code away, they have little control over how their work will be reused and therefore little power over their revenues.
- *Practical.* Code reuse is not always straightforward. In particular, it often introduces name conflicts that are hard to resolve.
- *Technical.* By definition, code reuse introduces more code, which means fatter executables.

The solution resides in the other sense of "component reuse"—binary reuse.

## Challenges

When individual vendors from around the world write components at different times without knowing what the others are doing, enabling the components to talk with each other reliably is not easy.

Developers face five challenges when writing reusable components:

- *Performance.* Reusing components should not result in less efficient systems.
- *Interoperability.* Components need a simple and efficient way to interact with each other regardless of who developed them.
- *Upgrade.* Developers need a way to update a particular component without having to update the entire system. A component upgrade should be backward compatible.
- *Language independence.* We hear about "language wars." However, languages come, evolve, and go, and, as a result, systems usually employ a combination of computer languages. Components should therefore be able to use other components regardless of the language they have been written in.
- *Location transparency.* Some components run on the same process, others write in a different process or on a different machine. The developer should not have to know where the component actually runs.

## The COM Solution

COM is the combination of two concepts. The first is a binary standard, under which reuse occurs with binary—that is, compiled—components. This solves the language independence problem because COM is not based on any one language, although many languages can generate COM components.

The second concept is a complete separation of interface and implementation. Of course, languages such as C++ allow you to separate interface (.h file) and implementation (.cpp file). However, only COM provides an effective, practical, and systematic way to do this on a large scale.

## Interfaces

Objects have an interface and an implementation. The interface answers the question "What does this object do?" (Figure 1-7). The implementation answers the question "How does this object do it?"

COM defines an interface as a collection of semantically related methods. Precisely, an interface is an array of function pointers that specifies a strongly typed contract between software components. By convention, interfaces start with "I". Usually, they are declared in the Interface Definition Language, or IDL (.IDL file).

Many object-oriented approaches use interfaces. However, COM is special in two ways. First, it does not define how to do the implementation. In fact, the implementation can be in many languages such as C++, Basic, or Java. Second, COM objects can support several interfaces. As a convention, COM components are represented in a rectangle and their interfaces are represented by a small circle (Figure 1-8).

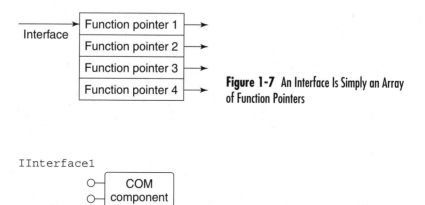

**Figure 1-7** An Interface Is Simply an Array of Function Pointers

**Figure 1-8** COM Component and Interfaces

IUnknown is an interface defined by COM that is special in two aspects:

- All COM components are required to support it.
- All interfaces inherit from it.

`IUnknown` has three methods:

```
virtual    HRESULT    QueryInterface(IID& iid, void** ppvObj) = 0;
virtual    ULONG    AddRef() = 0;
virtual    ULONG    Release() = 0;
```

As the name suggests, `QueryInterface` is used to retrieve another interface supported by the component, where `iid` identifies the requested interface and `ppvObj` holds the returned interface. If the requested interface is not supported, `QueryInterface` returns an error.

A later section will explain `AddRef` and `Release`.

## COM Classes

The definition of a component interface is not sufficient. You also need to specify the component implementation. A COM class does this.

To create a COM component, you simply call the `CoCreateInstance` API function.

```
WINOLEAPI CoCreateInstance(REFCLSID rclsid, LPUNKNOWN pUnkOuter,
    DWORD dwClsContext, REFIID riid, LPVOID FAR* ppv);
```

where `rclsid` is an identifier that identifies the COM class and `ppv` holds the requested interface.

## COM Instances

As in C++, instances live and die. Unlike C++, COM defines a standard and easy instance management mechanism.

COM objects internally hold a reference count. In the creation of a COM object, the reference count is set to 1. When `AddRef` is called, the reference count is incremented; when `Release` is called, it is decremented. If the reference count reaches 0, the object assumes that there are no valid references on it and destroys itself. In other words, the programmer is responsible for calling `AddRef` when getting an additional reference on a COM interface and calling `Release` when finished with it.

While this model is simple, elegant, and effective, it is also error prone. If the programmer forgets to call `AddRef` when necessary, the COM object can be released prematurely. If the programmer forgets to call `Release`, the COM object will stay alive indefinitely. The section on ATL explains how to avoid errors with COM smart pointers.

## GUIDs

In C++, classes and variables are identified by a name such as `CMyClass` or `m_MyVariable`, which is just fine until you have a name clash. Name clashes occur when two distinct classes have the same name or when two variables have the same name in a given scope. If a project has one or just a few programmers, it is fairly easy to resolve the clash by renaming one of the entities or by using mechanisms such as namespaces. However, if a project involves many programmers, possibly from different companies in different countries, resolving name clashes is a challenge. Moreover, as the system grows, name conflicts become more likely.

To deal with name clashes, COM uses Global Unique Identifiers (GUIDs), which are simply binary 128-bit identifiers. There are so many possibilities for the values of a GUID that conflicts are highly improbable—so improbable, in fact, that we will consider them impossible.

GUIDs are used in many different places. For example, they can identify a COM interface or a COM class. A GUID that identifies a COM interface is called an interface identifier (IID); one that identifies a COM class is called a class identifier (CLSID). GUIDs can be used to identify other entities. OLE DB in particular uses GUIDs in several places.

When working in C++, it is convenient to map a GUID with a C++ variable. For example, if the interface IMyInterface has the GUID {D9542ED2-705E-11d3-8B2B-00105A13D8B9}, we define the variable IID_IMyInterface as

```
DEFINE_GUID(IID_IMyInterface
0xd9542ed2, 0x705e, 0x11d3, 0x8b, 0x2b, 0x0, 0x10, 0x5a, 0x13, 0xd8, 0xb9);
```

From there, we use IID_IMyInterface for the GUID of IMyInterface.

## COM+ and Attributes

With Windows 2000 comes COM+, which is an upgrade of COM. "COM 2000" would have been my choice for a name because it underlines that it is a new version of COM in the same way the new version of Windows is "Windows 2000."

COM+ objects have declarative attributes. Roughly, these describe the context in which instances should run—for example, whether in process or out of process, in what transaction, or with what concurrency. CoCreateInstance checks the attribute of the component and sets up the appropriate context. Thus, if it is in process, COM will load the DLL and request the instantiation. Otherwise, COM will create a separate process and load the DLL there. The same applies for transactions, security, concurrency, and other attributes.

COM+ is a new and useful technology that would take a whole book to describe. Find such a book and take a look at it because it will have a profound impact on software development under Windows. COM+ does not greatly affect OLE DB because OLE DB objects do not care about the COM+ context. The job of the OLE DB object is to get data, which it can do in process or out of process, synchronously, or from a queued component. One major exception is the trans-actional context, as an OLE DB data object can be intimately associated with a transaction. Chapter 12, on transactions, will explain this in more detail.

## The Benefits of COM

We reviewed the challenges that face programmers when developing compo-nents. Here is how COM solves these problems

### Performance

A function call on one of an in-process COM component's interfaces is nothing more than an indirect function call through two pointers. In other words, a COM call is comparable to a C++ virtual method call. It is slightly slower than a direct function call, and the compiler cannot perform any inlining for it. However, the speed is acceptable in most cases.

For an out-of-process COM component, a COM function call is much slower. Its speed also depends on whether the component runs on the same machine.

### Upgrades

Interfaces are immutable, which means that once published, they should never be changed. This might look like a drawback, but it is a considerable strength. A smooth component upgrade does not require that the client of the component be upgraded as well.

When you upgrade a component, you usually add or improve functionality. A natural way to improve existing features without changing the interface is to provide a new implementation of the interface (Figure 1-9). In this case, any client will interact with the new version of the component the same way it did with the old one.

However, if you add features, you will probably need to support at least one additional interface. This is the case if the new feature is not related to any exist-ing feature (Figure 1-10).

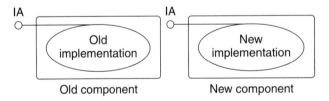

**Figure 1-9** Old and New Components, Same Interface

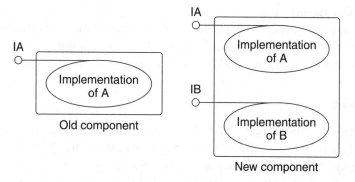

**Figure 1-10** The New Component Supports an Additional Interface, IB

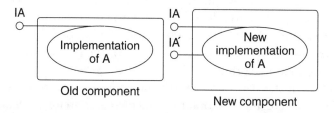

**Figure 1-11** The New Component Supports an Upgraded Interface

Sometimes, the old interface, say, IA, is not appropriate and needs to be replaced by, say, IA'. The COM approach is to provide a new component that will support both IA and IA'. An "old" client would use IA, unaware that there is a new interface. A "new" client would use IA' (Figure 1-11).

### Computer Language Independence

In COM an interface is just an array of functions. Therefore, any language that supports function pointers can easily implement a COM object. Such languages include C++, Visual Basic, and Java among others. C++ is a natural candidate for COM because it provides full support for pointers, virtual function tables, and structures. On the other hand, Visual Basic and Java are great contenders for a subset of COM objects—those that support dual interfaces.

### Location Transparency

A COM server can be implemented in process or out of process on the same machine or on a different machine. COM knows where components are and how to create them and deals with all the plumbing. From a programmer's point of view, there is almost no visible difference.

### Reuse of Components

Reuse comes in several forms in COM. The most obvious method is to hold a pointer to the interface of a COM instance. This is very similar to holding a pointer to a C++ instance. The second method, aggregation, is more subtle.

## COM Aggregation

C++ supports inheritance, in which the descendant class incorporates, or inherits, the functionality of the parent class. Optionally, the descendant class can redefine the inherited methods, and it can inherit several base classes. COM does not support inheritance, but provides a mechanism that has some similarities: *aggregation*.

Aggregation is one of the more advanced COM techniques and one that many COM programmers can do without. However, since OLE DB relies heavily on aggregation, it is important to fully understand it.

COM aggregation relates to the aggregation of two instances that each play a particular role. One is the inner object (instance); the other is the outer object. Here is how aggregation works.

First, a client instantiates an outer instance and requests a given interface (Figure 1-12). Once created, the outer instance creates an inner instance (Figure 1-13) and passes itself as the outer argument of `CoCreateInstance`.

```
WINOLEAPI CoCreateInstance(REFCLSID rclsid, LPUNKNOWN pUnkOuter,
    DWORD dwClsContext, REFIID riid, LPVOID FAR* ppv);
```

In the call of `CoCreateInstance`,

- `rdlcid` is the `CLSID` of the inner object.
- `pUnkOuter` is the `IUnknown` interface of the outer instance.
- `riid` is `IID_IUnknown`; the outer object requests the `IUnknown` interface of the inner instance.

Note that the inner object should not call `AddRef` on the outer object because it is considered part of the object.

Things get a bit complicated for the inner object here because it has to behave as the private instance of the outer object and also has to look like the same

**Figure 1-12** Aggregation, Step 1

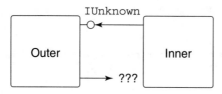

**Figure 1-13** The Outer Instance Creates an Inner Object

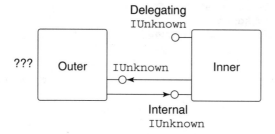

**Figure 1-14** The Inner Instance Supports Two `IUnknown` Interfaces

instance from a client of outer. Therefore, the inner object does something that is otherwise forbidden: It implements two `IUnknown` interfaces.

One `IUnknown` interface will be for the use of the outer instance only, enabling it to call `QueryInterface`, `AddRef`, and `Release` internally. We will call this interface *internal* `IUnknown`. The other `IUnknown` interface will simply delegate all its calls to the outer `IUnknown` interface, which we will call the delegating interface. At creation time, the inner object returns its internal `IUnknown` interface because it knows it is part of an aggregate.

The internal and delegating `IUknown` interfaces are illustrated in Figure 1-14. From now on, the outer instance will keep a reference on the inner internal `IUnknown` and the inner instance will keep a reference on the `IUnknown` interface of the outer object.

Let's suppose that the outer instance supports an interface that we will call `IOuter` and that the inner instance supports an interface called `IInner`. The implementation of `QueryInterface` of the outer `IUnknown` will look like

```
// pseudo code
QueryInterface(REFIID riid, LPVOID * ppvObj)
{
    if (riid == IID_IOuter)
        // return the implementation of outer
    else
        inner->QueryInterface(riid, ppvObj);
```

```
                   // return the delegating unknown
}
```

The implementation of `QueryInterface` of the internal `IUnknown` will look like this:

```
// pseudo code
QueryInterface(REFIID riid, LPVOID * ppvObj)
{
   if (riid == IID_IInner)
      // return the implementation of inner
   else if (riid == IUnknown)
      // return the delegating unknown
}
```

The outer instance can get a reference on the delegating `IUnknown` by calling

```
inner->QueryInterface(IID_IUnknown, ..);
```

The implementation of `QueryInterface` of the delegating `IUnknown` will look like this:

```
// pseudo code
QueryInterface(REFIID riid, LPVOID * ppvObj)
{
      if (riid ++ IID_IUnknown)
            // return delegating IUnknown interface pointer
      else
            return outer->QueryInterface (riid, ppvObj);
}
```

After creating the inner instance, the outer object needs to return the requested interface. If the requested interface is `IUnknown`, the outer will return the delegating interface of the inner object. As a result, the `IUnknown` interface of the outer instance will be visible only to the inner instance and the internal `IUnknown` of the inner instance will be visible only to the outer instance (Figure 1-15).

When the client requests an interface to `IOuter`, the delegating `IUnknown` forwards the call to the outer `IUnknown`, which returns `IOuter`. When the client requests an interface to `IInner`, the delegating `IUnknown` forwards the call to the outer `IUnknown`. Since the outer object does not support this interface, it forwards the call to the internal `IUnknown`, which then returns `IInner` (see Figure 1-16).

When the client has an interface to, let's say, `IOuter` and then requests an interface to `IInner`, the following happens. First, the implementation of `IOuter::QueryInterface` is probably the same kind of interface as the outer `IUnknown::QueryInterface`. Since, `IInner` is not implemented by the outer instance, it passes the request to the internal `IUnknown`. The internal `IUnknown` then returns the `IInner`.

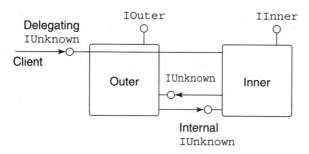

**Figure 1-15** The Delegating `IUnknown` Interface Appears as the `IUnknown` Interface of the Aggregate from the Client Point of View

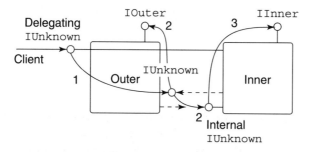

**Figure 1-16** `QueryInterface` from `IUnknown`

The following happens when the client has an interface to `IInner` and requests an interface to `IOuter`. The implementation of `IInner::QueryInterface` is the same as the delegating `IUnknown`. The `IUnknown` forwards the requests to the outer `IUnknown`, which returns the `IOuter` interface. Figure 1-17 shows a round trip between `IOuter` and `IInner`. For clarity, the figure has an arrow from

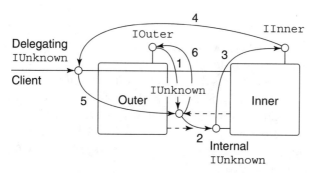

**Figure 1-17** `QueryInterface` between `IInner` and `IOuter`

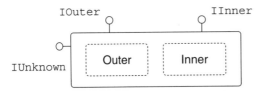

**Figure 1-18** The Aggregate from the Client Perspective

`IInner` and `IOuter` to their implementation of the `QueryInterface` event if there is no actual change of the interface.

What is the bottom line? From the client perspective, there are three interfaces (`IUnknown`, `IOuter`, and `IInner`) that appear to refer to the same object (Figure 1-18).

## USING COM OBJECTS WITH ATL

Using COM objects directly is error prone: Each time you use a COM object, you need to call `AddRef` and then `Release` when you are finished. If you forget to call `AddRef` when you should, the COM object will probably be released prematurely, leading to an access violation later. If you forget to call `Release`, the COM object stays alive indefinitely.

ATL provides a class that eases the use of COM objects: `CComPtr`. `CComPtr` is defined as

```
Template <class T>
class CComPtr
{
/// functions
   T* p
};
```

`CComPtr` is a simple but very powerful class. In most cases, a raw interface pointer can be replaced by a COM pointer.

A COM pointer implements the concept of smart pointers for COM objects. In other words, it calls `AddRef` and `Release` for you. In addition, it provides some COM-specific functions. The following paragraphs demonstrate how to perform simple tasks with `CComPtr`.

`CComPtr` integrates `CoCreateInstance` so that it is easy to create a COM instance directly from a `CComPtr`:

```
CComPtr<IMyInterface> spMyInterface;
hr = spMyInterface.CoCreateInstance(CLSID_MyClass /*optional
parameters*/);
```

If you receive a standard interface pointer, it is possible to assign it to a COM interface pointer. CComPtr will take care of calling AddRef for you.

```
IMyInterface* other;
CComPtr<IMyInterface> spMyInterface = other;
SpMyInterface = other;
```

If you assign a CComPtr to NULL, the CComPtr will automatically call Release. Alternatively, you can call Release directly.

```
{
    CComPtr<IMyInterface> spMyInterface;
    /// work with spMyInterface
    spMyInterface = NULL; // method one
    spMyInterface.Release() //method two
}
```

CComPtr can typecast itself into a interface pointer. As a result, if some method accepts an interface pointer, it is possible to pass a CComPtr as well, provided it corresponds to the valid interface.

```
HRESULT DoSomething(IMyInterface * param);
//
CComPtr<IMyInterface> spMyInterface;
DoSomething(spMyInterface);
```

Functions sometimes accept a pointer to an interface pointer. It is possible to pass a pointer to a CComPtr only if the CComPtr points to a NULL.

```
HRESULT c(IMyInterface** param);
CComPtr<IMyInterface> spMyInterface;
GetInterfacePointer(&spMyInterface);
GetInterfacePointer(&spMyInterface);///may cause an error!
```

CComPtr makes it easier to query the COM interface. You just have to call QueryInterface and CComPtr will deduce the interface identifier.

```
CComPtr<IInterface1> spInterface1;
CComPtr<IInterface2> spInterface2;
hr = spInterface1.CoCreateInstance(…);
hr = spInterface1.QueryInterface(&spInterface2);
//or
hr = spInterface1.QueryInterface(IID_IInterface2,
reinterpret_cast<void**>(&spInterface2));
```

Calling a method on a COM interface is similar to calling a method on an interface pointer.

```
CComPtr<IMyInterface> spMyInterface;
// Get the interface pointer
hr = spMyInterface->CallMethod(argument1, argument2, ...);
```

## COM COMPONENT ENCAPSULATION

By now, you must understand the power of components supporting multiple interfaces. When using COM objects, you need to choose a language. In this book, C++ will be the language of choice because the OLE DB consumer templates are a C++ library. There are three ways to use a COM object from C++. The first method is to call functions against a raw interface. The second technique involves CComPtr, as described in the previous section.

This section presents the third method: encapsulating the COM component into a C++ class. One issue is that a COM component usually supports several interfaces while a C++ class has only one interface.

Let's suppose that IA has two functions, a1() and a2(); IB has one function, b(), and IC has one function, c().

The C++ class should have an interface like

```
Class CMyClass
{
   HRESULT Create();
   HRESULT a1();
   HRESULT a2();
   HRESULT b();
   HRESULT c();
};
```

There are two techniques for the implementation of the CMyClass.

The first method is to hold a pointer to each interface (see Figure 1-19). In other words, the class would have three class members:

```
CComPtr<IA> m_spIA;
CComPtr<IB> m_spIB;
CComPtr<IC> m_spIC;
```

The Create method would look approximately like the following:

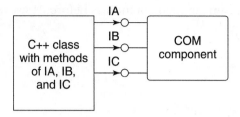

**Figure 1-19** COM Object Encapsulation, First Method

```
// pseudo code!
HRESULT Create(..)
{
   m_spIA.CoCreateInstance(CLSIDComponent);
   m_spIA.QueryInterface(&m_spIB);
   m_spIA.QueryInterface(&m_spIC);
}
```

The implementation of the other methods would simply be

```
// pseudo code, would need some ATLASSERT
HRESULT ia1()
{
   return m_spIA->a1();
}
HRESULT ia2()
{
   return m_spIA->a2();
}
HRESULT ib()
{
   return m_spIB->b();
}
HRESULT ic()
{
   return m_spIC->c();
}
```

The second technique to implement the C++ class is to hold an interface pointer on only one interface, say IA, and to query other interfaces as needed.

Concretely, the class has only one class member: CComPtr<IA> m_spIA. The Create method becomes:

```
MM
HRESULT Create(..)
{
   return m_spIA.CoCreateInstance(CLSIDComponent);
}
```

al() and a2() have the same implementation as before. However, b() and c() need some adjustment, as here.

```
// pseudo code
HRESULT b()
{
    CComPtr<IB> spB
    HRESULT hr = m_spA.QueryInterface(&spB)
    if (FAILED(hr))
        return hr;
    return spb->b();
}
```

c() would have a similar implementation (see Figure 1-20). Both methods have advantages and disadvantages.

The first method consumes more memory and can get interface pointers on interfaces that will not be used. On the other hand, the method calls are faster because there is no need to call QueryInterface. The second method uses only one class member and does not request only the necessary interfaces; however, it uses QueryInterface in many method calls.

The OLE DB consumer templates use an intermediate approach. As a rule, the OLE DB consumer templates hold only one interface pointer. However, when an additional interface is likely to be used frequently, the class will hold an additional interface pointer.

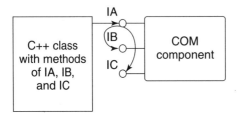

**Figure 1-20** COM Object Encapsulation, Second Method

## SUMMARY

This chapter presented the big picture: Windows DNA and COM. The next chapter will focus on the data part and OLE DB in particular.

# 2 Universal Data Access

This chapter introduces one of the components of Windows DNA, *universal data access* (UDA), and focuses on one of its components, *OLE DB*. It also introduces the *OLE DB consumer templates*.

The world of data has witnessed quite a few changes in recent years. One of them is that database management systems (DBMS) have become a commodity. Even though DBMSs have been around for some time, only recently have they become easy and relatively cheap to build. Just as it is possible to set up a Web site in a bedroom, it is now possible to set up a terabyte database there as well. Microsoft has even released a free database engine for Windows: Microsoft Data Engine (MSDE).

Another change is the multiplication of data and database types. In the old days, a typical database stored text and numbers. Now, it also stores multimedia content, special data types, and so forth. At the same time, data is usually stored in a specific data store such as SQL databases for relational data, mail servers for email messages, directory services for enterprise information, OLAP servers for multi-dimensional data, and so forth.

A third change, and one of the most fascinating, is, of course, the rise of the Internet. In just a few years, the Internet has become a major source of the data all of us rely on for everyday tasks such as online shopping or Web searches. Indeed, it can be much easier to find information on the Internet than in a corporate database. On the server side, this translates into a high number of potential users.

# UNIVERSAL DATA SERVER

To respond to these changes, several database vendors implement the "universal data server" strategy. Simply put, a universal data server supports many data types, can scale to a high number of users, and supports a high volume of data. The ultimate vision is that of organizations being able to centralize all of their data on one server.

Figure 2-1 shows the universal data server architecture. The universal data server has several benefits:

- Because it is centralized, it reduces management costs. This includes factors like centralized security management, centralized hardware and backup, and so forth.

- Because the content is in one place, the server can perform optimization that would be difficult to achieve with multiple data stores.

- The server can provide unified models for services such as security or transaction.

Not surprisingly, database-centric vendors favor this strategy, but the universal data server can be challenging for several reasons.

First, this approach requires you to transfer data from legacy systems to a new database, which is obviously risky for critical data. It also means that the legacy processes that use the data need to be rewritten to access it in the new database. This is usually the most problematic aspect of the conversion. In fact, this explains why so many organizations still use old systems and formats.

If you start from scratch, you will not have this conversion problem. However, you will have to find a database that provides support for the data types and data access types you need. In some cases, this will be very easy. In other cases, it will

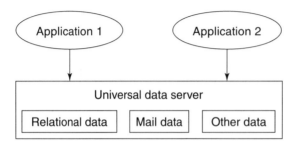

**Figure 2-1** Universal Data Server Architecture

be difficult. Even if you can overcome these challenges, the universal data server approach will still have shortcomings.

First, its centralized nature means that its management will be centralized. Although this is a system manager's dream, it does not necessarily go with the culture of an organization. A typical organization is made up of several autonomous divisions that might want to keep control over the format of and access to their data.

Second, it locks you in with the database provider, which is obviously in the best interest of the provider but can represent a serious risk for you since software companies are not infallible.

## UNIVERSAL DATA ACCESS IN DETAIL

Microsoft provides an alternative, universal data access (Figure 2-2). Instead of focusing on the uniformity of the data, that is, storing it all in one place, UDA focuses on the uniformity of data access so that you can access diverse data stores with the same interface regardless of where the data comes from.

It is important to understand that UDA is more a standard than a product. It cannot do much without the underlying data store. Think of it not as a competitor to traditional DBMS but as a complement, offering solutions to the shortcomings of the universal data server approach.

UDA decouples development from the underlying database. This means that developers and users do not need to commit to a particular database vendor. It also means that you do not necessarily have to transfer your data to a new data server but can keep it in a legacy data store and access it through modern interfaces.

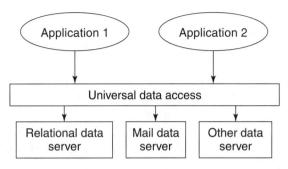

**Figure 2-2** Universal Data Access Architecture

UDA allows you to access several data sources almost as flawlessly as if they were only one. This is important if you use data servers from several vendors. It also allows scenarios where the data is spread across several entities of an organization but appears as if it were consolidated in one place.

Spreading the data across multiple servers can present drawbacks. Because the data is not in one place, it is harder to manage. For example, since each server can have its own security system, it is harder to administer the different access policies. Note, however, that directory services can help solve this problem.

Different physical servers can also increase network traffic and influence performance. In addition, they make optimizations across servers difficult.

Understand that choosing universal data access does not force you to give up a universal server strategy. The two can cooperate. Universal data access can help you migrate from one vendor to another and allows more flexibility. For example, you can have most of your data on a universal server and access the remaining data the same way with universal data access.

# UDA COMPONENTS

The following are the three components of UDA.

- ODBC
- OLE DB
- ADO

In short, ODBC is a legacy data access API for SQL data, OLE DB is a COM-based set of interfaces to access any data, and ADO is a high-level layer on top of OLE DB. The following sections examine these three technologies.

## Open DataBase Connectivity

In the same way Windows DNA is an evolutionary architecture that comes from DDE and OLE, ODBC is the historic foundation of UDA.

### ODBC and Data Access under Windows

When the SQL standard was in its infancy, numerous data access interfaces began to proliferate. At that time, Microsoft embraced a vendor-independent database API called *Open DataBase Connectivity* (ODBC). This was an SQL-based API, which made it naturally attractive for SQL programming. Being a standard, it attracted numerous ODBC providers, also called drivers, and many tools.

As time passed, Microsoft extended the features supported by ODBC so that it is now a well-established standard.

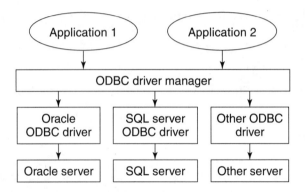

**Figure 2-3** ODBC Architecture

### Architecture

ODBC contains a set of standard functions, which an ODBC driver implements in a DLL. It also comes with a driver manager—a component that manages the different ODBC drivers installed on the machine. When a client application wants to access a database server, it first asks the ODBC driver for the corresponding driver. The client application then calls the ODBC functions against the loaded driver. Figure 2-3 summarizes the ODBC architecture.

One complaint from programmers is that ODBC is slow. However, since ODBC is just a standard, its performance depends on the underlying driver. In many cases, ODBC driver performance is comparable to that of the native API.

### ODBC Shortcomings

ODBC targets only SQL data. Today, however, a large amount of data resides not in relational databases but in other server types such as OLAP or mail.

Also, because ODBC came before COM, it does not take advantage of its modular architecture. This means that the driver has to implement all of the ODBC functionality. It also means that much binary code is going to be duplicated, making the system bigger and harder to manage. For example, every ODBC driver needs an SQL parser and a cursor engine. Why not have them in the operating system instead of duplicating them in each ODBC driver?

## OLE DB

A simple way to understand OLE DB is to see it as a new ODBC based on COM. It introduces a new vocabulary, in which, for example, a driver becomes a *provider* and a client becomes a *consumer*.

OLE DB is different from ODBC in three ways:

- OLE DB supports multiple types of providers, not just SQL data providers.
- OLE DB is based on COM.
- OLE DB offers a new architecture.

The following sections will explore these differences.

### OLE DB Provider Types

One can divide OLE DB data providers into the following three categories.

- Tabular
- Multidimensional
- Hierarchical

### *Tabular Providers*

Tabular providers are made up of a set of tables. Usually, tables can have relations, in which case we talk about relational providers. Microsoft Access, SQL Server, and Oracle are relational providers. Not all tabular providers support SQL, but all SQL providers are tabular providers. In other words, it is possible to build a tabular provider that uses another access method such as a custom language or direct access to tables and views. Figure 2-4 shows a table from a tabular provider.

Because ODBC is targeted to SQL providers, its scope is limited to only a portion of tabular providers. The providers not covered by ODBC are discussed in the next two sections.

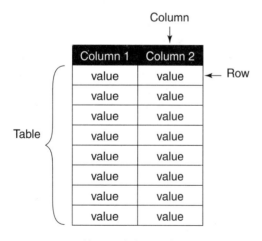

**Figure 2-4** A Table in a Tabular Provider

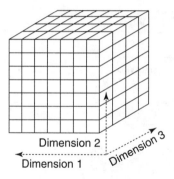

**Figure 2-5** A Cube from a Multidimensional Provider

## Multidimensional Providers

A relational table can be viewed as a two-dimensional rectangle with rows and columns. *Multidimensional* (or *OLAP*) *providers* introduce the more general concept of the *cube*. Unlike the relational table, a cube can have more than two dimensions. In fact, most cubes can easily have three or four. Figure 2-5 shows a cube from a multidimensional provider.

OLE DB version 2.0 introduced support for multidimensional providers, which Chapter 15 explains how to access.

## Hierarchical Providers

Look at your personal data, and ask yourself if it is all stored in a series of relational databases or piled up in a series of files and emails on your hard drive. The answer is probably both. Indeed, relational databases are great for storing well-organized data, but they are not practical for other data types. Hierarchical providers, introduced in OLE DB version 2.5, are very similar to the file system, with equivalents to a folder or a file. They are great for a file system (local or Internet), but they are also practical for email messages or contacts. Figure 2-6 illustrates hierarchical providers, which Chapter 16 will explain in more detail.

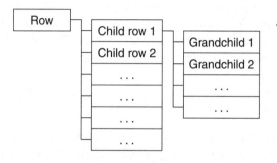

**Figure 2-6** Rows in a Hierarchical Provider

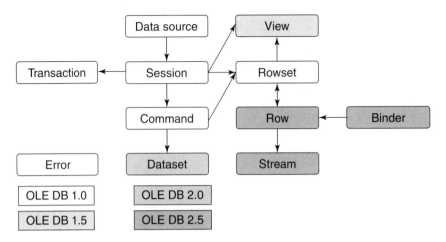

**Figure 2-7** OLE DB Types

## OLE DB Types

The OLE DB types are illustrated in Figure 2-7. At the root of OLE DB is the *data source* type. The data source offers many options for specifying where the data is.

The *session* type corresponds to an actual connection to the data store. Optionally, the session can run in the context of a *transaction*.

The *rowset* type is a central concept. Not surprisingly, a rowset represents a set of rows with columns. You can open a rowset directly against a session or through a *command*.

The *view* type represents a view of a rowset. Views are handy for sorting and filtering operations on the client side.

While the rowset concept is fine for tabular data, multidimensional providers also need a *dataset* type. In short, a dataset is a multidimensional rowset.

The *row* type represents a row for hierarchical providers. While it would seem intuitive to have a row object for nonhierarchical providers, this is not the case.

The *binder* type provides a way to open a row from a URL. The *stream* type defines a way to read a stream from rows, or BLOBs (see Chapter 11), in rowsets.

Finally, all OLE DB types can create *errors*.

## OLE DB and COM

### *Performance*

Similar to that of ODBC, the performance of OLE DB does not make much sense by itself. What matters is the performance of each individual provider. Chapter 1 explained the performance of a COM object. OLE DB providers are implemented as a DLL, and OLE DB components are activated in process. Executing a method on an OLE DB object is as fast as calling a virtual function on a C++ object. OLE DB does not mandate that OLE DB providers use COM for their implementation, and many do not. The only requirement is that OLE DB objects expose a set of interfaces, which in practice translates into the performance limitation of a virtual function call. Because OLE DB is newer than ODBC, OLE DB providers tend to have less optimization than their ODBC counterparts. However, this will be less and less true as time goes on.

### *Flexibility with Multiple Interfaces*

Chapter 1 explained that a COM object could support multiple interfaces. OLE DB objects are no different and, in fact, usually support many interfaces. For each type, OLE DB defines a set of interfaces; some are mandatory and others are optional. An OLE DB command, for example, should always support the `ICommand` mandatory interface, which has the `Execute` method. Optionally, a command can have parameters, in which case it supports the `ICommand WithParameters` optional interface.

Providers can also define and support their own proprietary interfaces, enabling consumers to access proprietary features. Obviously, once the consumer assumes that the object supports provider-specific interfaces, the code is no longer portable.

### A New Architecture

One of the drawbacks of ODBC is that it makes writing high-quality drivers difficult. OLE DB makes this a little easier by providing reusable services, which perform different tasks that are usually common to many providers. For example, OLE DB provides a cursor service that can transform a simple forward-only rowset into a full-fledged rowset.

Using OLE DB services has two benefits. First, because they are already implemented and tested, developers can build their providers quickly and more reliably. Second, if a better version of a service comes around, the provider can automatically take advantage of it.

OLE DB offers two kinds of services: *service components* and *service providers*. The difference between the two is somewhat fuzzy, so I will apply my own definition. A service component implements some improvements for a given OLE DB component. For example, the cursor service implements additional functionality for a rowset object. A service provider applies to an entire provider. It can be viewed as an OLE DB provider that uses another OLE DB provider as its backend.

## Service Components

How can OLE DB provide service components? The answer is aggregation, which "merges" two components so that they appear as one from the client perspective. When aggregated, the outer object is the OLE DB service and the inner object is the provider's object.

As an example, suppose that the data source component needs resource pooling to scale for a large number of users. Instead of each provider implementing its own resource pooling mechanism, OLE DB implements the mechanism once and distributes it with the operating system. In this way a consumer has the choice between a stand-alone data source and a data source aggregated with pooling, as shown in Figure 2-8.

OLE DB comes with three service components:

- Resource pooling, which scales resources to a large number of users.
- Transaction enlistment, which integrates transactions with a COM+ transaction or Microsoft transaction server.
- Client cursor, which provides rich functionality to a rowset, including bidirectional cursors, find operations, views, and so forth.

## Data Shaping Service

One of the challenges in developing database applications is dealing with relations. Typically, the developer will have to handle keys and multiple queries and rowsets, which is not necessarily difficult but can certainly be repetitive. In OLE DB this repetitive work is regrouped into one component: the *data shaping service*, which works in concert with any regular OLE DB provider. The data shaping service is responsible for parsing a distinctive language, called the *shape language*, and generating queries to the underlying OLE DB provider. In return, the provider returns a set of rowsets, which the shaping service is responsible for organizing and presenting to the provider in the form of a hierarchy, as shown in Figure 2-9.

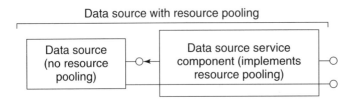

**Figure 2-8** Aggregation of a Data Source with a Data Source Service Component

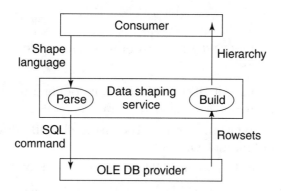

**Figure 2-9** Data Shaping Architecture

Note that the consumer does not see the underlying OLE DB provider. From the consumer point of view, the data shaping service appears to be doing all the work even though the underlying OLE DB provider exerts most of the effort.

## OLE DB Providers

The *Microsoft Data Access Components* (MDAC) come with a series of OLE DB providers. Of course, these are the most popular: Microsoft Access, Microsoft SQL Server, and Oracle. It also comes with non-SQL data stores such as Microsoft directory services, Microsoft indexing services, and Microsoft OLAP. The most significant provider is the OLE DB provider for ODBC, which bridges the gap between OLE DB and ODBC. In other words, it is possible to access all ODBC data stores, including future ones, through OLE DB.

Figure 2-10 summarizes the different OLE DB providers.

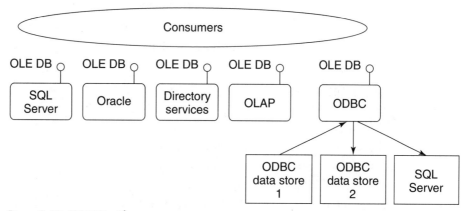

**Figure 2-10** OLE DB Providers

## ODBC versus OLE DB

Is OLE DB a replacement for ODBC? The answer is yes and no, for the following reasons:

- ODBC is an integral part of UDA. Microsoft will continue to support and enhance it as long as there is a demand in the marketplace.
- OLE DB comes with an ODBC provider. Therefore, all ODBC drivers can be used either directly of through OLE DB.
- ODBC targets only SQL data, while OLE DB targets all kinds of data.
- OLE DB is based on COM, whereas ODBC is based on raw API.

The equivalences of ODBC and OLE DB are listed in Table 2-1.

## OLE DB Versions

A common joke about Microsoft products is that they are good after version 3. This cannot be said about OLE DB, whose version 2.5, shipped with Windows 2000, is already very mature and extensive.

It is difficult to summarize the different versions because they correspond to a release time, not necessarily to a consistent set of features. Moreover, new releases of OLE DB provide improvements that are hard to categorize. Nevertheless, the following list is an attempt at a rough summary of the main versions of OLE DB.

- Version 1.0 contains the main interfaces for accessing relational databases. It provides enough functionality for most applications.
- Version 1.5 introduced two concepts: chapters and views. Chapters identify a subset of the rows of a rowset. Views allow operations on rowsets on the consumer side, including sorting and filtering.
- Version 2.0 introduces support for multidimensional data stores.
- Version 2.5 introduces support for hierarchical data stores.

**Table 2-1**  ODBC to OLE DB

| ODBC | OLE DB |
| --- | --- |
| ODBC driver | OLE DB provider |
| ODBC client | OLE DB consumer |
| C functions | COM interfaces |
| SQL data only | Various data stores |
| Monolithic drivers | Database components |

As of when this book is being written, Microsoft is preparing OLE DB 2.6 and SQL Server 2000. OLE DB 2.6 is still in beta and is not covered here. It introduces native support for XML, including retrieving data as an XML stream instead of a traditional rowset and specifying queries with XML or XPath instead of SQL. The Web site of this book will show you how to use OLE DB 2.6. Fortunately, this part of OLE DB is small and easy to use.

## ActiveX Data Object

Even though OLE DB is a great technology, it has its drawbacks. For example, it is too sophisticated for beginners or casual programmers. Also, it uses low-level techniques such as custom interfaces, structures, pointers, and explicit memory management. Languages such as Visual Basic and Java that do not support these features cannot use it.

These drawbacks could drive away many developers. To avoid this, Microsoft provides the *ActiveX Data Object* (ADO) library. ADO is a COM library on top of OLE DB that exposes only high-level objects. Because it is automation-based, it uses dual interfaces. Hence, it can be accessed by both compiled and interpreted languages, which makes it attractive to developers using Visual Basic, Java, and scripting languages such as VBScript and JavaScript.

### Architecture

ADO is very similar to older Microsoft technologies, *Data Access Objects* (DAO) and *Remote Data Objects* (RDO). This section is a brief overview of its main objects:

- Connection
- Command
- Recordset
- Error
- Parameter
- Field

ADO's architecture is shown in Figure 2-11.

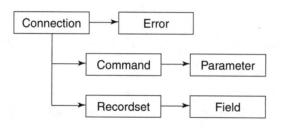

**Figure 2-11** Simplified ADO Architecture

The *connection* object represents a session on a data source, which you usually use as a root object. It allows you to specify the location of the data source, customize connection options, and perform transactions. Once you have your connection object open, you can create other objects on it.

Typically, you create a *command* object on your connection. This object represents a command or query on the data source. You can specify the text of the command and execute it. The command text syntax is based on the data source that underlies it. Usually, this is SQL but it can be another language.

The command can contain a collection of *parameters*. If the underlying data source supports commands with parameters, this collection contains as many parameter objects as the command needs. Otherwise, the parameters should be ignored.

The *recordset* object represents a set of records. It can be returned upon command execution if the underlying data source supports commands. A recordset can also be opened with a table name. The data contained in a recordset can be accessed through a set of *fields*, each of which represents a column.

ADO's recordset offers a rich set of features. Of course, it allows fetching and scrolling operations. It also has sophisticated options for specifying the cursor location (client or server) and provides rich functionality such as filtering.

The *error* object contains error information. The field and parameter objects do not have any equivalent OLE DB objects.

## When to Use ADO

As a simplified version of OLE DB, ADO is, needless to say, less powerful than OLE DB. It is significantly slower in certain areas and does not provide the same functionality. However, it can be "good enough" in many cases, especially in small projects.

Where is ADO less efficient? First, it is a layer on top of OLE DB, so it usually involves a double indirection in the calls. In most cases, however, this is negligible. Its main inefficiency is in the data exchange between the COM object and the C++ object. With OLE DB, the COM object writes the data directly to the C++ memory. With ADO, the programmer has to access a collection of fields, which is much slower because it involves as many calls as columns. In addition, fields hold a variant, which involves additional overhead.

ADO objects have an additional drawback: They support only one interface, making it difficult to access specialized interfaces.

Choosing between ADO and OLE DB is not always easy because both are great technologies. When making the choice, you have to ask the following questions:

- What language will be used?
- What kind of programmers are involved?
- How big is the project, how quickly does it need to be delivered?
- What are the performance constraints?

For example, if a team of Visual Basic developers needs to deliver a small project fast, ADO is a good choice. On the other hand, if a team of expert C++ programmers needs to deliver a top-performance job, OLE DB is the one to have.

If you cannot make up your mind, you can have ADO and OLE DB in the same project, using the ADO–OLE DB bridge. For example, it is possible to transform an OLE DB rowset into an ADO recordset and vice versa.

## OLE DB TEMPLATES

Writing OLE DB providers and consumers is hard. Microsoft provides the *OLE DB templates*, a C++ library for OLE DB, to make things easier. The OLE DB templates are composed of two distinct sublibraries: the *OLE DB provider templates* for writing OLE DB providers and the *OLE DB consumer templates* for writing OLE DB consumers. This book will explore the OLE DB consumer templates only.

The first chapter explained what makes the COM approach so much better than the traditional C++ library approach. So why a C++ library? OLE DB provides great control over its objects but it can be difficult to use this control correctly. The OLE DB consumer templates facilitate the development of consumer code. As the name suggests, the OLE DB consumer templates use the C++ template, something that COM does not support. At first, they can seem confusing; however, once you are used to them, you will not be able to program without them. In addition, COM and OLE DB use COM types such as `BSTR`. The OLE DB consumer templates provide convenient mapping of these types to the usual C++ types such as `char *` or `WCHAR*`. Finally, the OLE DB consumer templates help you manage both C++ and COM memory.

Perhaps the best way to convince you is with a simple example using OLE DB directly and the OLE DB consumer templates. In this scenario, we want to open a table called "testtable" with an SQL command. This table contains only one column, a, of type `integer`. The table is on a server called `SERVERNAME` in a database called `databasename`. Once we open the table, we want to fetch each row.

### Using Raw OLE DB

The class `Ctesttable` will hold the value. It is defined as

```
class Ctesttable
{
public:
   LONG m_a;
};
```

The following code shows how to perform the different operations with raw OLE DB. It is long and you are not supposed to read it carefully. It is here only to show how difficult it is.

```
HRESULT PerformActionWithRawOLEDB()
{
   HRESULT hr = S_OK;
   USES_CONVERSION;

   DBPROPSET dbinit;

   DBPROP Props [5];
   dbinit.cProperties = 5;
   dbinit.rgProperties = Props;
   dbinit.guidPropertySet = DBPROPSET_DBINIT;
   for (int iii = 0; iii < 5; iii ++)
   {
      Props[iii].colid = DB_NULLID;
      Props[iii].dwOptions = DBPROPOPTIONS_REQUIRED;
   }
   Props[0].dwPropertyID = DBPROP_AUTH_INTEGRATED;
   Props[0].vValue.vt = VT_BSTR;
   Props[0].vValue.bstrVal = SysAllocString(OLESTR("SSPI"));

   Props[1].dwPropertyID = DBPROP_INIT_CATALOG;
   Props[1].vValue.vt = VT_BSTR;
   Props[1].vValue.bstrVal = SysAllocString(OLESTR("databasename"));

   Props[2].dwPropertyID = DBPROP_INIT_DATASOURCE;
   Props[2].vValue.vt = VT_BSTR;
   Props[2].vValue.bstrVal = SysAllocString(OLESTR("SERVERNAME"));

   Props[3].dwPropertyID = DBPROP_INIT_LCID;
   Props[3].vValue.vt = VT_I4;
   Props[3].vValue.iVal = 1033;

   Props[4].dwPropertyID = DBPROP_INIT_PROMPT;
   Props[4].vValue.vt = VT_I4;
   Props[4].vValue.iVal = 4;

   CComPtr<IDBInitialize>  m_spInit;
   {
      CLSID   clsid;
      hr = CLSIDFromProgID(T2COLE("SQLOLEDB.1"), &clsid);
      if (FAILED(hr))
         return hr;

      m_spInit.Release();
      hr = CoCreateInstance(clsid, NULL, CLSCTX_INPROC_SERVER,
         IID_IDBInitialize, (void**)&m_spInit);
      if (FAILED(hr))
         return hr;
```

```
        CComPtr<IDBProperties>   spProperties;
        HRESULT                  hr;

        hr = m_spInit->QueryInterface(IID_IDBProperties,
            (void**)&spProperties);
        if (FAILED(hr))
            return hr;

        hr = spProperties->SetProperties(1, &dbinit);
        if (FAILED(hr))
            return hr;
        hr = m_spInit->Initialize();
    }
    if (FAILED(hr))
        return hr;


    CComPtr<IOpenRowset> m_spOpenRowset;
    {
        CComPtr<IDBCreateSession> spSession;

        // Check we have connected to the database
        ATLASSERT(m_spInit != NULL);

        hr = m_spInit->QueryInterface(IID_IDBCreateSession,
            (void**)&spSession);
        if (FAILED(hr))
            return hr;

        hr = spSession->CreateSession(NULL, IID_IOpenRowset,
            (IUnknown**)&m_spOpenRowset);
    }

    if (FAILED(hr))
        return hr;
    Ctesttable test;
    CComPtr<ICommand> m_spCommand;
    HACCESSOR HAccessor;
    CComPtr<IRowset> Rowset;
    {
            // Check the session is valid
        ATLASSERT(m_spOpenRowset != NULL);

        CComPtr<IDBCreateCommand> spCreateCommand;
        HRESULT hr = m_spOpenRowset->QueryInterface(
            IID_IDBCreateCommand, (void**)&spCreateCommand);
        if (FAILED(hr))
        return hr;

        hr = spCreateCommand->CreateCommand(NULL, IID_ICommand,
            (IUnknown**)&m_spCommand);
        if (SUCCEEDED(hr))
        {
            CComPtr<ICommandText> spCommandText;
            hr = m_spCommand->QueryInterface(&spCommandText);
```

```
            if (SUCCEEDED(hr))
                hr = spCommandText->SetCommandText(DBGUID_DEFAULT,
                    T2COLE("select  b from testtable"));
        }

        if (FAILED(hr))
            return hr;

        {
            HRESULT     hr;
            DBPARAMS    *pParams;

            pParams = NULL;

            hr = m_spCommand->Execute(NULL, IID_IRowset, NULL,
                NULL, (IUnknown**)&Rowset);
            if (FAILED(hr))
                return hr;

            CComPtr<IAccessor> spAccessor;
            hr = Rowset->QueryInterface(&spAccessor);
            if (SUCCEEDED(hr))
            {
                DBBINDING*  pBindings = NULL;
                ULONG       nColumns;
                nColumns = 1;
                ATLTRY(pBindings = new DBBINDING[nColumns]);
                if (pBindings == NULL)
                    return E_OUTOFMEMORY;
                ZeroMemory(pBindings, sizeof(DBBINDING));
                pBindings[0].cbMaxLen = sizeof(int);
                pBindings[0].dwPart = DBPART_VALUE;
                pBindings[0].obValue = (int)(&test.m_a) - (int)
                    (&test);
                pBindings[0].wType = DBTYPE_I4;
                pBindings[0].iOrdinal = 1;
                if (FAILED(hr))
                    return hr;

                hr = spAccessor->CreateAccessor(DBACCESSOR_ROWDATA,
                    nColumns, pBindings, sizeof(CtesttableAccessor),
                    &HAccessor, NULL);
                delete [] pBindings;
            }
        }
    }

    if (FAILED(hr))
        return hr;
    {

        hr = Rowset->RestartPosition(NULL);
        if (FAILED(hr))
            return hr;
```

```
    }
    HROW m_hRow = NULL;
    while (hr == S_OK)
    {
        ULONG ulRowsFetched = 0;

        if (m_hRow != NULL)
        {
            hr = Rowset->ReleaseRows(1, &m_hRow, NULL, NULL, NULL);
            m_hRow = NULL;
        }

        HROW* phRow = &m_hRow;
        hr = Rowset->GetNextRows(NULL, 0, 1, &ulRowsFetched,
            &phRow);
        if (hr != S_OK)
            return hr;

        hr = Rowset->GetData(m_hRow, HAccessor, &test);
        if (FAILED(hr))
        {
            ATLTRACE2(atlTraceDBClient, 0, _T(
                "GetData failed - HRESULT = 0x%X\n"),hr);
            if (m_hRow != NULL)
            {
                hr = Rowset->ReleaseRows(1, &m_hRow, NULL, NULL,
                    NULL);
                m_hRow = NULL;
            }
        }
    }
    return hr;
}
```

## Using the OLE DB Consumer Templates

As we just saw, the conceputally simple task of opening a table is hard to implement. The OLE DB consumer templates simplify the implementation greatly.

We first define an accessor class that contains the binding between the database and the C++ object:

```
class CtesttableAccessor: public Ctesttable
{
BEGIN_COLUMN_MAP(CtesttableAccessor)
    COLUMN_ENTRY(1, m_a)
END_COLUMN_MAP()

DEFINE_COMMAND(CtesttableAccessor, _T(" \
    SELECT \
        a \
        FROM dbo.testtable"))
```

```
    void ClearRecord()
    {
        memset(this, 0, sizeof(*this));
    }
};
```

The following code shows the same scenario using the OLE DB consumer templates. It is shorter and much more readable.

```
HRESULT PerformActionsWithOLEDBConsumerTemplates()
{
    HRESULT hr = S_OK;
    CDataSource db;
    CDBPropSet   dbinit(DBPROPSET_DBINIT);

    dbinit.AddProperty(DBPROP_AUTH_INTEGRATED, OLESTR("SSPI"));
    dbinit.AddProperty(DBPROP_INIT_CATALOG, OLESTR("databasename"));
    dbinit.AddProperty(DBPROP_INIT_DATASOURCE, OLESTR("SERVERNAME"));
    dbinit.AddProperty(DBPROP_INIT_LCID, (long)1033);
    dbinit.AddProperty(DBPROP_INIT_PROMPT, (short)4);
    hr = db.Open(_T("SQLOLEDB.1"), &dbinit);

    if (FAILED(hr))
        return hr;

    CSession Session;
    Session.Open(db);
    if (FAILED(hr))
        return hr;
    CCommand<CAccessor<CtesttableAccessor>, CRowset> test;
    hr = test.Open(Session);
    if (FAILED(hr))
        return hr;
    hr = test.MoveFirst();
    while (hr == S_OK)
    {
        hr = test.MoveNext();
    }
    return hr;
}
```

## The OLE DB Template Extensions

As the rest of this book will show, using the OLE DB consumer templates is a real pleasure. Even so, while using them, I noticed that they do not cover everything, nor do they fit all needs. For these reasons I started to develop OLE DB consumer template extensions, and as time passed these extensions covered more and more. The OLE DB extensions are a free library that you can find on the Web site of this book. When possible, I will use the standard templates here. However, when an aspect is not covered, I will turn to the extensions.

The OLE DB extensions have three goals:

1. They fill gaps left by the OLE DB consumer templates.
2. They show alternative methods.
3. They provide some reusable code.

When writing an application, be careful which library you use. Obviously, Microsoft does not support the OLE DB extensions. As it releases new versions of the consumer templates, my intention is to update the extensions so that they use the OLE DB consumer templates as much as possible. The goal is not to redo what Microsoft does or to provide a competing version.

## SUMMARY

Microsoft provides a flexible and efficient approach to data access: universal data access, of which OLE DB is the cornerstone. If you want optimum performance for your C++ application, use OLE DB, not ADO. OLE DB is hard to use without the OLE DB consumer templates. This book will now dive into this library.

# **3** The OLE DB Wizard

Though much easier to use than "raw" OLE DB interfaces, the OLE DB consumer templates can be intimidating at first. To help, Microsoft Visual Studio provides a "wizard" that generates OLE DB template classes from a database table or a stored procedure. The wizard is good introduction to the OLE DB template classes, and, like other wizards, it is a good way to produce code quickly. However, once the code is generated, you might have to maintain it. Therefore, you should also understand the generated code.

This chapter will

- Explain how to use the wizard.
- Explain how to understand the generated code.
- Explain how to use the generated code.
- Explain what improvements can be made.
- Give a brief introduction to the OLE DB consumer templates.

## IS THE WIZARD A GOOD THING?

With just a few clicks, the wizard can generate a great deal of bug-free code. However, this code can be worrisome to use. Moreover, it is not always clear what can and what cannot be changed. Unlike other wizards (such as regular MFC wizards) the OLE DB wizard goes only one way—there is no reverse engineering mechanism. You use the wizard to generate code, and once the code is generated, there is no way to get the wizard back.

This approach has two benefits. First, the wizard does not have to insert any wizard-specific code. The Microsoft Foundation Classes (MFC) wizard needs to insert pieces like "//{{AFX_MSG_MAP" to differentiate the wizard code from the programmer's code. In contrast, the OLE DB wizard can generate "clean" code. The other benefit is that there is no incentive to keep the code "wizard compatible"; the code can evolve freely from its original state.

The OLE DB wizard does not cover all of the OLE DB consumer templates but only the main scenarios: opening a table, an SQL query, or a stored procedure. It does not cover multidimensional or hierarchical data or complex SQL queries.

## USING THE WIZARD

The OLE DB template wizard is functional only for ActiveX Template Library (ATL) projects and certain MFC projects (executables, controls, and regular DLLs). If a project does not support the OLE DB wizard, it will pop up the dialog in Figure 3-1. Since OLE DB templates are part of ATL, it is natural to use them in an ATL project.

### Creating an ATL Project

To create an ATL project, follow these steps, illustrated in Figures 3-2 and 3-3.

1. Select "File" and "New . . ." in the main menu. The "New" dialog will pop up.
2. Choose "ATL COM AppWizard" in the "Projects" tab and type the name of your project in the "Project name" box. Click "OK."
3. Choose the server type. The OLE DB consumer templates can be used from an EXE, a DLL, or a service.

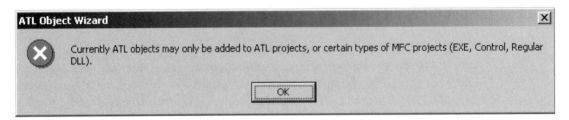

**Figure 3-1** Warning Dialog for Projects That Do Not Support the Wizard

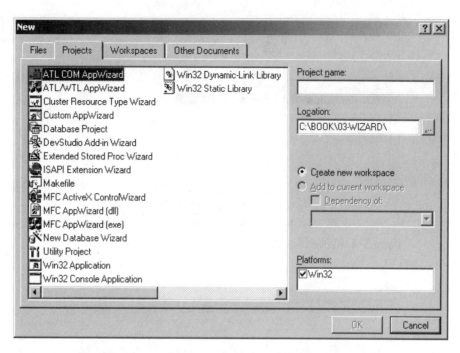

**Figure 3-2** "New" Dialog

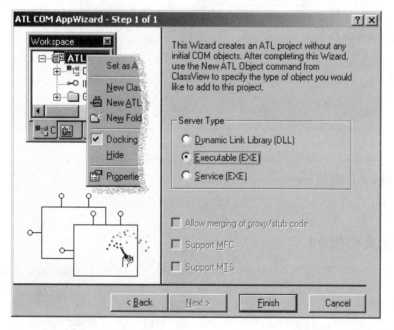

**Figure 3-3** ATL COM AppWizard—Step 1

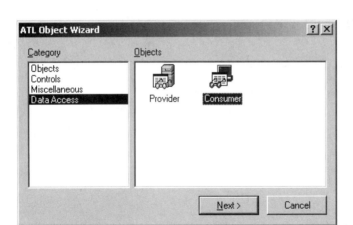

**Figure 3-4**  ATL Object Wizard

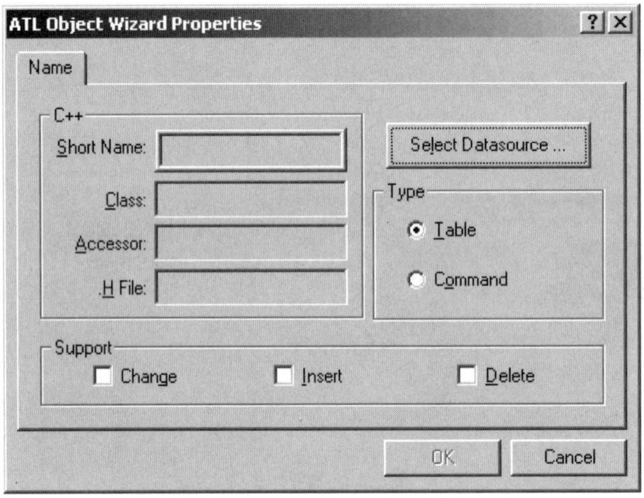

**Figure 3-5**  OLE DB Consumer Templates Wizard

## Invoking the Wizard

To use the OLE DB consumer templates, select "Insert" and "New ATL object . . ." in Visual Studio's main menu. The ATL Object Wizard dialog displays the collection of ATL wizards. Then select "Data Access" and "Consumer." Click "Next" (Figure 3-4). The OLE DB consumer templates wizard appears (Figure 3-5), proposing three choices:

- "Select Datasource . . ." allows you to choose the data source and the table to open.
- "Type" allows you to choose the method to get the data (Table or Command).
- "Support" allows you to choose the level of data update support (Change, Insert, or Delete).

### Selecting the Data Source

The first step in selecting the data source is to choose the OLE DB data source using the data source dialog (Figure 3-6). This dialog offers four property pages: "Provider," "Connection," "Advanced," and "All."

The first property page allows you to choose the type of OLE DB provider. For now, we will choose the OLE DB Provider for SQL Server, which provides native support for MS SQL Server. To go to the next page, press the "Next" button to simply click on the "Connection" tab.

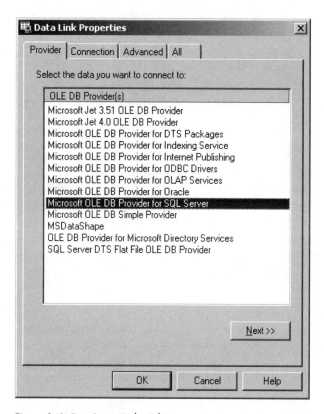

**Figure 3-6** Data Source Dialog Tab 1

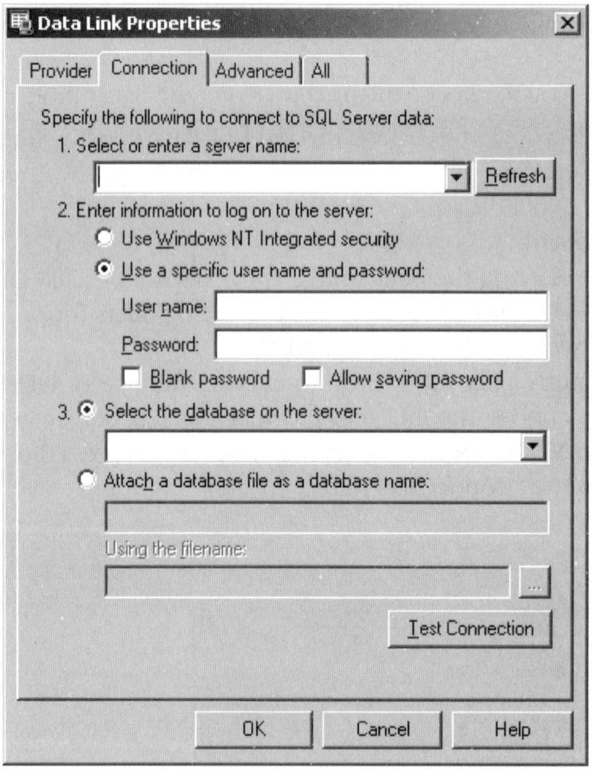

**Figure 3-7** Data Source Dialog Tab 2

The second property page (Figure 3-7) allows you to choose the most commonly used properties. It is provider specific, which means that the choices offered depend on the type of provider chosen in the first step.

The third property page (Figure 3-8) offers advanced properties. Usually, the default values are fine. The fourth and last property page (Figure 3-9) offers a recapitulation of the chosen properties.

### Selecting the Table

Once the data source is established, the next step is choosing the table. In our example, we choose Mytable, as shown in Figure 3-10 on page 52. By default, the wizard uses the table name for the short name and the file name (Figure 3-11, page 52).

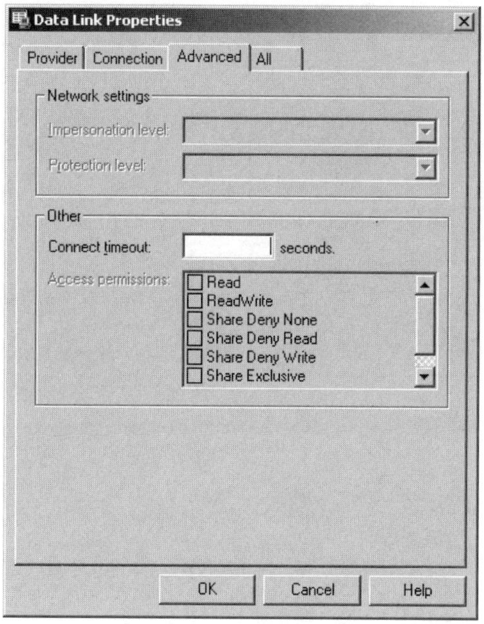

**Figure 3-8** Data Source Dialog Tab 3

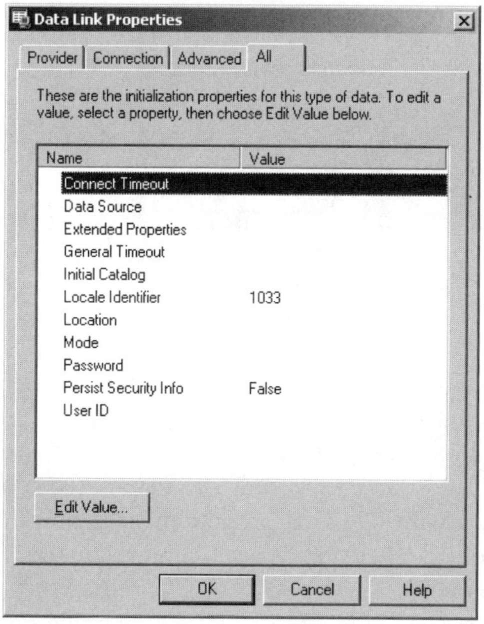

**Figure 3-9** Data Source Dialog Tab 4

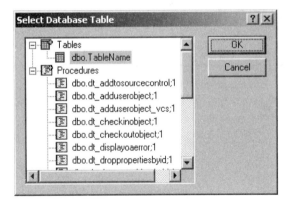

**Figure 3-10** Table Selection Dialog

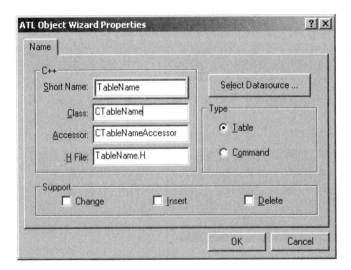

**Figure 3-11** OLE DB Consumer Templates Wizard

## GENERATED CODE

The generated code is of three types. The first type is static—it does not depend on the wizard at all and will always be the same. The second type comes from the database—it depends on the wizard but the programmer has only indirect control over it. The third type depends directly on what was entered in the wizard, and the user has complete control over it.

In the following section, I will highlight the code depending on the degree of control the user has. The code presented is formatted to fit the dimensions of this book. The actual code might appear in a different format but the semantics remain the same.

```
This is repetitive code, it does not change
This code is deducted from the database. The user has some control
on it.
This code comes straight from the wizard. The user has complete
control on it.
```

The first time you insert an OLE DB object with the wizard, the wizard includes the OLE DB include file in the main `include` file: **stdafx.h**:

```
#include <atldbcli.h>
```

This is a one-time-only action; it does not have to be included again.

## Opening a Table

If you chose "MyTable," the wizard will generate code using the CMyTable class and with the file name we chose, MyTable.H. The code consists of two classes: **CMyTableAccessor**, which should be used for implementation, and **CMyTable**, which is for clients. Each has distinct responsibilities: **CTableNameAccessor** defines the class members and the binding to the underlying table. **CMyTable** opens the connection to the database and opens the rowset on the table.

**CMyTableAccessor** first defines one class member per table column. In our case, the code has two class members:

```
public:
    LONG m_Column1;
    TCHAR m_Column2[11];
```

Next, the class needs to specify which class member corresponds to which column. In OLE DB, columns are identified by their ordinal, starting at 1. Thus, the first column will have ordinal 1, the second ordinal 2, and so forth. The accessor class defines the binding this way:

```
BEGIN_COLUMN_MAP(CMyTableAccessor)
    COLUMN_ENTRY(1, m_Column1)
    COLUMN_ENTRY(2, m_Column2)
END_COLUMN_MAP()
```

Lastly, a canned function initializes the class members.

```
    void ClearRecord()
    {
        memset(this, 0, sizeof(*this));
    }
```

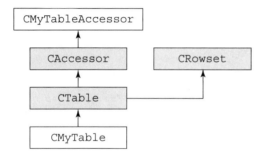

**Figure 3-12** Inheritance between `CMyTable` and `CMyTableAccessor`

Since we chose the Table option in the wizard, `CMyTable` inherits from `CTable`:

```
class CMyTable : public CTable<CAccessor<CMyTableAccessor> >
```

It turns out that `CTable` inherits from `CAccessor` and `CAccessor` inherits from its template parameter `CMyTableAccessor`. As a result, `CMyTable` inherits from `CMyTableAccessor`. It also inherits from class `CRowset` (Figure 3-12).

Class `CMyTable` has these three methods: `Open`, `OpenDataSource`, and `OpenRowset`. `Open` is a simple method: It tries to connect to the database and, if successful, tries to open the rowset:

```
HRESULT Open()
{
    HRESULT hr;

    hr = OpenDataSource();
    if (FAILED(hr))
        return hr;

    return OpenRowset();
}
```

`OpenDataSource` attempts to connect to the database. For this method, the wizard collects information from the data source dialog and generates the properties and `ProgID`:

```
HRESULT OpenDataSource()
{
    HRESULT      hr;
    CDataSource  db;
    CDBPropSet   dbinit(DBPROPSET_DBINIT);

    dbinit.AddProperty(DBPROP_AUTH_INTEGRATED,OLESTR("SSPI"));
    dbinit.AddProperty(DBPROP_INIT_CATALOG, OLESTR("wizard"));
    dbinit.AddProperty(DBPROP_INIT_DATASOURCE,
        OLESTR("SERVER"));
```

```
    dbinit.AddProperty(DBPROP_INIT_LCID, (long)1033);
    dbinit.AddProperty(DBPROP_INIT_PROMPT, (short)4);
    hr = db.Open(_T("SQLOLEDB.1"), &dbinit);
        if (FAILED(hr))
        return hr;

    return m_session.Open(db);
}
```

OpenRowset simply forwards the call to the **CTable** method:

```
HRESULT OpenRowset()
{
    return CTable<CAccessor<CMyTableAccessor> >::Open(
        m_session, _T("dbo.MyTable"));
}
```

The full code for **CMyTable** and **CMyTableAccessor** is the following:

```
// MyTable.H : Declaration of the CMyTable class

#ifndef __MYTABLE_H_
#define __MYTABLE_H_

class CMyTableAccessor
{
public:
    LONG m_Column1;
    TCHAR m_Column2[11];

BEGIN_COLUMN_MAP(CMyTableAccessor)
    COLUMN_ENTRY(1, m_Column1)
    COLUMN_ENTRY(2, m_Column2)
END_COLUMN_MAP()


    // You may wish to call this function if you are inserting a
    // record and wish to initialize all the fields, if you are
    // not going to explicitly set all of them.
    void ClearRecord()
    {
        memset(this, 0, sizeof(*this));
    }
};

class CMyTable : public CTable<CAccessor<CMyTableAccessor> >
{
public:
    HRESULT Open()
    {
        HRESULT        hr;

        hr = OpenDataSource();
```

```
        if (FAILED(hr))
            return hr;

        return OpenRowset();
    }
    HRESULT OpenDataSource()
    {
        HRESULT       hr;
        CDataSource db;
        CDBPropSet    dbinit(DBPROPSET_DBINIT);

        dbinit.AddProperty(DBPROP_AUTH_INTEGRATED,OLESTR("SSPI"));
        dbinit.AddProperty(DBPROP_INIT_CATALOG, OLESTR("wizard"));
        dbinit.AddProperty(DBPROP_INIT_DATASOURCE,
            OLESTR("SERVER"));
        dbinit.AddProperty(DBPROP_INIT_LCID, (long)1033);
        dbinit.AddProperty(DBPROP_INIT_PROMPT, (short)4);
        hr = db.Open(_T("SQLOLEDB.1"), &dbinit);
        if (FAILED(hr))
            return hr;

        return m_session.Open(db);
    }
    HRESULT OpenRowset()
    {
        return CTable<CAccessor<CMyTableAccessor> >::Open(
            m_session, _T("dbo.MyTable"));
    }
    CSession  m_session;
};

#endif // __MYTABLE_H_
```

## Opening a Command

Choosing a command instead of a table in the wizard generates code using the **CCommand** class. When we choose a command, we introduce two differences: First, the wizard needs to specify the text of the query in **CMyTableAccessor**

```
DEFINE_COMMAND(CMyTableAccessor2, _T(" \
    SELECT \
        Column1, \
        Column2 \
        FROM dbo.MyTable"))
```

Second, **CMyTable** inherits from **CCommand** instead of CTable:

```
class CMyTable2 : public
    CCommand<CAccessor<CMyTableAccessor2> >
```

## Adding Support for Changes

When we check one of the support check boxes, the wizard inserts these lines in the OpenRowset method:

```
CDBPropSet    propset(DBPROPSET_ROWSET);
propset.AddProperty(DBPROP_IRowsetChange, true);
propset.AddProperty(DBPROP_UPDATABILITY,
    DBPROPVAL_UP_CHANGE | DBPROPVAL_UP_INSERT |
    DBPROPVAL_UP_DELETE);
```

The first property, **DBPROP_IRowsetChange**, specifies that we want some support for changing the rowset. The second property, **DBPROP_UPDATABILITY**, specifies the support needed. In this particular case, **DBPROPVAL_UP_CHANGE, DBPROPVAL_UP_INSERT**, and **DBPROPVAL_UP_DELETE** are specified since all three operations are necessary.

The following is an example of a command with support for Insert, Delete, and Change.

```
// MyTable2.H : Declaration of the CMyTable2 class

#ifndef __MYTABLE2_H_
#define __MYTABLE2_H_

class CMyTableAccessor2
{
public:
    LONG m_Column1;
    TCHAR m_Column2[11];

BEGIN_COLUMN_MAP(CMyTableAccessor2)
    COLUMN_ENTRY(1, m_Column1)
    COLUMN_ENTRY(2, m_Column2)
END_COLUMN_MAP()

DEFINE_COMMAND(CMyTableAccessor2, _T(" \
    SELECT \
        Column1, \
        Column2 \
        FROM dbo.MyTable"))

    // You may wish to call this function if you are inserting a
    // record and wish to initialize all the fields, if you are
    // not going to explicitly set all of them.
    void ClearRecord()
    {
        memset(this, 0, sizeof(*this));
    }
};
```

```
class CMyTable2 : public
   CCommand<CAccessor<CMyTableAccessor2> >
{
public:
   HRESULT Open()
   {
      HRESULT        hr;

      hr = OpenDataSource();
      if (FAILED(hr))
         return hr;
      return OpenRowset();
   }
   HRESULT OpenDataSource()
   {
      HRESULT        hr;
      CDataSource db;
      CDBPropSet dbinit(DBPROPSET_DBINIT);

      dbinit.AddProperty(DBPROP_AUTH_INTEGRATED,OLESTR("SSPI"));
      dbinit.AddProperty(DBPROP_INIT_CATALOG, OLESTR("wizard"));
      dbinit.AddProperty(DBPROP_INIT_DATASOURCE,
         OLESTR("SERVER"));
      dbinit.AddProperty(DBPROP_INIT_LCID, (long)1033);
      dbinit.AddProperty(DBPROP_INIT_PROMPT, (short)4);
      hr = db.Open(_T("SQLOLEDB.1"), &dbinit);
      if (FAILED(hr))
         return hr;

      return m_session.Open(db);
   }
   HRESULT OpenRowset()
   {
      // Set properties for open
      CDBPropSet    propset(DBPROPSET_ROWSET);
      propset.AddProperty(DBPROP_IRowsetChange, true);
      propset.AddProperty(DBPROP_UPDATABILITY,
         DBPROPVAL_UP_CHANGE | DBPROPVAL_UP_INSERT |
         DBPROPVAL_UP_DELETE);

      return CCommand<CAccessor<CMyTableAccessor2> >::Open(
         m_session, NULL, &propset);
   }
   CSession    m_session;
};

#endif // __MYTABLE2_H_
```

## Using Stored Procedures

A stored procedure is very similar to a regular SQL command. The notable difference is the use of output parameters or return values. The parameter map can contain both in and out parameters. Before each parameter, the wizard specifies the parameter type with the macro. In the following example, the stored procedure has one parameter (`Parameter1`) and one return value.

```
// dboStoredProcedureName1.H : Declaration of the
     CdboStoredProcedureName1 class

#ifndef __DBOSTOREDPROCEDURENAME1_H_
#define __DBOSTOREDPROCEDURENAME1_H_

class CdboStoredProcedureName1Accessor
{
public:
    LONG m_RETURNVALUE;
    LONG m_Parameter1;
    LONG m_colColumn1;
    TCHAR m_colColumn2[11];

BEGIN_PARAM_MAP(CdboStoredProcedureName1Accessor)
    SET_PARAM_TYPE(DBPARAMIO_OUTPUT)
    COLUMN_ENTRY(1, m_RETURNVALUE)
    SET_PARAM_TYPE(DBPARAMIO_INPUT)
    COLUMN_ENTRY(2, m_Parameter1)
END_PARAM_MAP()

BEGIN_COLUMN_MAP(CdboStoredProcedureName1Accessor)
    COLUMN_ENTRY(1, m_colColumn1)
    COLUMN_ENTRY(2, m_colColumn2)
END_COLUMN_MAP()

DEFINE_COMMAND(CdboStoredProcedureName1Accessor, _T("{ ? = CALL
dbo.StoredProcedureName;1 (?) }"))

    // You may wish to call this function if you are inserting a
    // record and wish to initialize all the fields, if you are
    // not going to explicitly set all of them.
    void ClearRecord()
    {
        memset(this, 0, sizeof(*this));
    }
};

class CdboStoredProcedureName1 : public
CCommand<CAccessor<CdboStoredProcedureName1Accessor> >
{
public:
    HRESULT Open()
    {
        HRESULT          hr;

        hr = OpenDataSource();
```

```
        if (FAILED(hr))
            return hr;

        return OpenRowset();
    }
    HRESULT OpenDataSource()
    {
        HRESULT      hr;
        CDataSource  db;
        CDBPropSet   dbinit(DBPROPSET_DBINIT);

        dbinit.AddProperty(DBPROP_AUTH_INTEGRATED,OLESTR("SSPI"));
        dbinit.AddProperty(DBPROP_INIT_CATALOG, OLESTR("wizard"));
        dbinit.AddProperty(DBPROP_INIT_DATASOURCE,
            OLESTR("SERVER"));
        dbinit.AddProperty(DBPROP_INIT_LCID, (long)1033);
        dbinit.AddProperty(DBPROP_INIT_PROMPT, (short)4);
        hr = db.Open(_T("SQLOLEDB.1"), &dbinit);
        if (FAILED(hr))
            return hr;

        return m_session.Open(db);
    }
    HRESULT OpenRowset()
    {
        return CCommand<CAccessor<CdboStoredProcedureName1Accessor
            > >::Open(m_session);
    }
    CSession    m_session;
};

#endif // __DBOSTOREDPROCEDURENAME1_H_
```

## Improvements to the Generated Code

As mentioned before, the wizard does a reasonable job introducing you to the OLE DB consumer templates, but it is not a perfect solution. This section describes several improvements you can add to the generated code.

In many cases, you want to access several tables from the same data source. The problem with the wizard is that it will duplicate the data source code. Thus, if you decide to move your data source, you must update the code in multiple places. A better way might be to regroup the code for the data source in one place and inherit from it.

Another problem with the data source code is that the data source is opened without service components (Chapter 6 will explain the importance of service components). In general, it is better to open a data source with them. To do this, replace

```
hr = db.Open("SQLOLEDB.1", &dbinit);
```

with

```
hr = db.OpenWithServiceComponents("SQLOLEDB.1", &dbinit);
```

As the rest of the book will show, the OLE DB consumer templates offer much more than the wizard can. The wizard is an interesting tool for generating column binding and data source properties, but there is no reason to try to keep your code close to the wizard code.

## THE MFC WIZARD

Microsoft provides a wizard for MFC projects. Since the principles behind it are the same as those behind the OLE DB wizard, there is no need to explain how to use it. However, if you go from one to the other, you might notice a couple of differences. First, the MFC wizard opens the data source with service components. Second, after getting the rowset, it automatically moves to the first row. Except for these two details, the generated code is very similar.

## OLE DB CONSUMER TEMPLATE CLASSES OVERVIEW

The classes generated by the wizard provide a good entry point to the OLE DB consumer template classes. This section will explore the code in the order of a typical execution. Before going further, you might want to jump to Appendix A (advanced C++ techniques) and check that you understand these techniques.

The first method generated by the wizard is **Open**. **Open** performs two actions: **OpenDataSource** and **OpenRowset**.

**OpenDataSource** uses three classes. The first, **CDataSource**, encapsulates an OLE DB data source object. This object specifies where the data store is. Chapter 6 explores data sources in more detail.

The second class, **CDBPropSet**, sets the properties of the data source. It contains a set of OLE DB properties. OLE DB uses property sets for many objects. Chapter 5 explains how property sets are used.

The third class, **CSession**, encapsulates the OLE DB session object, which sits between the data source object and the other OLE DB objects. The main purpose of sessions is to provide support for transactions. Chapter 12 gives more details on this class.

**OpenRowset** uses **CDBPropSet** like **OpenDataSource**. However, its implementation is a bit more complex because it uses inherited methods, requiring us to go into the overall architecture.

## Table Command Rowset Accessor Architecture

The core of the OLE DB consumer templates is a group of classes that are subtly dependent on each other. Though somewhat complex for beginners, this architecture will prove very powerful and flexible once mastered.

The core classes are never used alone but always in combination. When manipulating data, you should ask four questions:

- Command or table?
- How many rowsets?
- What navigation?
- What binding?

The following sections explore these questions.

### Command or Table?

With OLE DB, you can either open a table or execute a command as the wizard suggests. Opening a table is the simplest way to get data. An OLE DB table represents an entire relational table. In this case, you should use **CTable**.

A command is an object that has an execute method. Usually it has a text, which in most cases is an SQL command. In such cases, you should use **CCommand**.

### How Many Rowsets?

Some commands do not return any rowset. For example, INSERT INTO XXX VALUES ... inserts rows in a table but does not return anything. Other commands, such as SELECT * FROM XXX WHERE ..., return one rowset containing the selected rows. If the selection does not contain any row, the command will return an empty rowset. In other cases it will return several rowsets. For example, SELECT * FROM XXX ; SELECT * FROM YYY returns one rowset per select, two in this case.

For OLE DB, the question of how many rowsets can have two answers: "one or less" or "two or more." If we have two or more rowsets, we need a mechanism to go from one to another if there is only one rowset. This becomes unnecessary because you do not need an iteration mechanism.

Use the **CMultipleResults** class when there are multiple results. Use the **CNoMultipleResults** class otherwise. Note that since a table always returns exactly one rowset, it does not support multiple results.

### What Navigation?

Once you have a rowset, you will want to navigate its rows either sequentially or by jumping from one to another. Once on a given row, you might want to exchange data with the underlying data store. These functions are performed by the three rowset classes provided by the OLE DB consumer templates: **CRowset**, **CBulkRowset**, and **CArrayRowset**. Each essentially provides the same functionality with variations.

If the command does not have any rowset, there is no need for rowset support. In that case use **CNoRowset**, which, as the name suggests, does not provide any rowset functionality. Obviously, it makes no sense to use **CNoRowset** with **CMultipleResults**.

### What Binding?

When exchanging data, you need to specify how the different columns relate to C++ memory. For example, a rowset might have columns A and B, while a corresponding object might have class members m_a and m_b. the accessor classes define the binding between C++ memory and the underlying rowset.

The OLE DB consumer templates provide four accessor classes:

- **CAccessor<T>**
- CDynamicAccessor
- CDynamicParameterAccessor
- CManualAccessor

Each provides a different binding mechanism. Chapter 9 explores accessors in more detail.

When there is no rowset, there is no need for an accessor. As the name implies, **CNoAccessor** is the class to use in this case. **CNoRowset** and **CNoAccessor** should be used in conjunction.

## Putting Classes Together

Once you know which classes you need, you assemble them with a template parameter. If you choose a table, the type will be

```
CTable<AccessorClass, RowsetClass>
```

If you choose a command, the type will be

```
CCommand < AccessorClass, RowsetClass, NoMultipleResultsClass>
```

There are many possible combinations. Here are a few:

```
CTable<CDynamicAccessor, CRowset>;
CCommand<CDynamicParameterAccessor, CBulkRowset, CMultipleResults>;
CCommand<CNoAccessor, CNoRowset, CNoMultipleResults>;
```

Many combinations will not compile. For example, it is not possible to combine **CNoAccessor** and **CRowset**.

## CAccessorRowset

At the raw OLE DB level, a rowset represents a series of rows with columns. As mentioned before, the OLE DB consumer templates distinguish the binding part of the rowset from the navigation part. Binding relates to columns; navigation relates to rows. When accessing an OLE DB rowset object, we need to specify both, as illustrated in Figure 3-13.

Class **CAccessorRowset** represents the combination of a rowset and an accessor. It is the most central class of the OLE DB templates, and so it is necessary to understand it to understand the OLE DB templates themselves. The casual programmer does not need to use this class directly.

**CAccessorRowset** is a good example of a class inheriting from its template parameters. Its first purpose is to bring together the accessor class and the rowset class. It is declared as follows and illustrated in Figure 3-14.

```
template <class TAccessor = CNoAccessor, class TRowset = CRowset>
class CAccessorRowset :
    public TAccessor,
    public TRowset
```

**Figure 3-13** Accessor and Rowset Classes

**Figure 3-14** `CAccessorRowset` Inheritance

The accessor and the rowset class are not symmetrical. That is, the rowset usually needs some access to the accessor but the accessor does not need to know about the rowset.

The constructor of **CAccessorRowset** binds the accessor with the rowset:

```
CAccessorRowset()
{
    // Give the rowset a pointer to the accessor
    SetAccessor(this);
}
```

**SetAccessor** is a method inherited from the rowset template argument. It allows the rowset to keep a pointer on the accessor. An empty class such as **CNoRowset** will do nothing. In all other cases, the rowset will set its **m_pAccessor** class member:

```
void    SetAccessor(CAccessorBase* pAccessor)
{
    m_pAccessor = pAccessor;
}
```

The net result is something like what is shown in Figure 3-15.

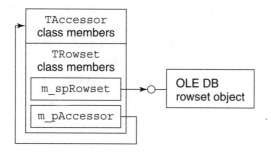

**Figure 3-15** The Rowset Points to the Accessor

## Closing CAccessorRowset

Closing **CAccessorRowset** means closing the accessor and the rowset.

```
void Close()
{
    if (GetInterface() != NULL)
    {
        ReleaseAccessors(GetInterface());
        TAccessor::Close();
        TRowset::Close();
    }
}
```

**GetInterface**, inherited from the TRowset type, returns the interface pointer to the OLE DB rowset object. If it is NULL, there is no rowset and no accessor. Otherwise, it performs three actions:

- ReleaseAccessors(GetInterface()) is inherited from TAccessor. TAccessor needs a pointer to the rowset object to release any accessor handles. Since TAccessor does not keep a reference on the COM object, it takes the rowset object from TRowset as an argument.
- TAccessor::Close(); releases any internal structure from TAccessor.
- TRowset::Close(); releases the interface pointer to the rowset object.

At destruction time, CAccessorRowset calls Close:

```
~CAccessorRowset()
{
    Close();
}
```

## SUMMARY

This chapter presented the wizard and a brief overview of the OLE DB consumer templates. The next chapters will go into more detail on these topics. Chapter 4 will explain how to handle errors and interpret them. Chapter 5 will explore OLE DB properties. Chapter 6 will examine data sources. Chapters 7 through 10 will explain tables, commands, rowsets, and accessors. Chapters 11 through 16 will deal with more advanced concepts for particular providers.

# 4 Errors and Error Mechanisms

Databases are a little different from other programming domains because they are far from any graphical interface. In general, it is not possible to provide graphical feedback, such as a message box, when an error occurs. As a database developer, you are responsible for transmitting as much useful error information as possible to the user or system administrator. Thus, you must understand OLE DB's error mechanism.

In the old days of C programming, the standard was for functions to return a status code, such as

```
ERROR_CODE MyFunction (..);
```

With C++ came *exceptions,* which are clearly more elegant and better enable programmers to handle errors effectively.

However, exceptions have the drawback of being local to the process and the machine. For example, it is not possible to throw a C++ exception on one process and catch it on another. This is fine in a one-machine and one-process environment, but it becomes problematic in a distributed environment and is against the whole philosophy of COM.

COM has two mechanisms for handling errors. First, virtually all COM methods return an error code called HRESULT that resembles the old C function error code. After an error occurs, it is possible to learn more about it through a COM object that contains information about past errors.

# HRESULT

With COM, virtually all methods return an HRESULT, which is simply a 32-bit structure that contains all the success failure information about a method. It is defined as follows:

```
typedef LONG HRESULT;
```

An HRESULT actually contains three pieces of error information. The *severity* indicates whether the method executed successfully. When set, an error has occurred; otherwise, the method has executed successfully. The *facility* indicates which group the code belongs to. In most cases, it will be FACILITY_ITF, which means that the meaning of the code depends on the underlying interface. The *error code* describes what actually happened. You can access the different pieces with the macros

- HRESULT_SEVERITY (HRESULT hr)
- HRESULT_FACILITY (HRESULT hr)
- HRESULT_CODE (HRESULT hr)

The following macros will tell you whether an HRESULT corresponds to a success or a failure:

- FAILED (HRESULT hr)
- SUCCEEDED (HRESULT hr)

In practice, there are three main cases. One, if FAILED (hr) is true, or if SUCCEEDED (hr) is false, the method failed. For example, if the method was a denied permission, DB_SEC_E_PERMISSIONDENIED would be returned. Two, if FAILED (hr) is false, or if SUCCEEDED (hr) is true but is not S_OK, the method succeeded but produced some warnings—for example, DB_S_ROWLIMIT EXCEEDED. Three, if S_OK is returned, the method executed successfully without warnings.

## Interpreting HRESULT

The OLE DB Software Development Kit (SDK) provides extensive information about the HRESULTs each OLE DB method can return and their exact meanings. When a method returns an error, the most accurate way to understand what happened is by tracing which method of which interface is involved. Armed with this information, you can consult the OLE DB SDK documentation for more details.

The error lookup program that comes with Visual Studio documentation also provides an easy way to find the meaning of an HRESULT. Another alternative is the FormatMessage API function, which looks up the error description of a given HRESULT for a given module. If the HRESULT corresponds to a standard COM error, the function will automatically find the module in the system. However, if the HRESULT corresponds to an OLE DB error, you have to pass the MSDAERR.DLL OLE DB error module explicitly.

For more information about FormatMessage, consult the Microsoft SDK.

The following example shows how to trace the description of an HRESULT.

```
HRESULT TraceHresult (HRESULT hr)
{
   LPCTSTR lpMsgBuf;
   HMODULE hModule = LoadLibrary ("C:\\Program Files\\Common Files\\
      SYSTEM\\ole db\\MSDAERR.DLL");
   if (FormatMessage (FORMAT_MESSAGE_ALLOCATE_BUFFER |
      FORMAT_MESSAGE_FROM_HMODULE | FORMAT_MESSAGE_FROM_SYSTEM,
      hModule, hr, MAKELANGID(LANG_NEUTRAL, SUBLANG_DEFAULT),
      (LPTSTR) &lpMsgBuf, 0, NULL))
   {
      OutputDebugString(lpMsgBuf);
      LocalFree((HLOCAL)lpMsgBuf);
   }
   FreeLibrary(hModule);
   return S_OK;
}
```

For example, the following code:

```
TraceHresult(DB_E_CANCELED);
TraceHresult(E_NOINTERFACE);
```

will generate the following output:

```
The change was canceled during notification; no columns are changed
No such interface supported
```

## HRESULT in Practice

When writing a COM component, you call a series of methods, each of which returns an HRESULT. Your code will look like this:

```
HRESULT CMyComponent::MyMethod()
{
   HRESULT hr = S_OK;
   hr = Object1->Method1(..);
   if (FAILED(hr))
      return(hr);
   hr = Object2->Method2(..);
```

```
    if (FAILED(hr))
        return(hr);
    hr = Object2->Method2(..);
    if (FAILED(hr))
        return(hr);
    return hr;
}
```

As you can see, this type of programming can be quite repetitive. To avoid it, use the CHECK_RESULT macro defined as

```
#define CHECK_RESULT(_expr_) \
{HRESULT _hr_ = _expr_; if (FAILED(_hr_)) return _hr_;}
```

Using this macro, the code becomes

```
HRESULT CMyComponent::MyMethod()
{
    CHECK_RESULT (Object1->Method1(..))
    CHECK_RESULT (Object2->Method2(..))
    return Object3->Method3(..);
}
```

Obviously, this programming style is more compact. On the other hand, it is slightly more difficult to debug.

## ERROR INFO AND ERROR RECORDS

When the HRESULT does not provide enough information, it is possible to obtain additional details through the error info objects.

### Tracing Errors

Obtaining error info objects is not straightforward. The easiest way is to trace them using a OLE DB consumer template function. In this case, the error information will appear in the debug window of Visual Studio.

The trace function is declared as

```
inline void AtlTraceErrorRecords(HRESULT hrErr = S_OK)
```

Use this function after an error occurs. For example,

```
HRESULT CMyComponent::MyMethod()
{
    HRESULT hr = Object1->Method1(..));
    if (FAILED(hr))
        AtlTraceErrorRecords (hr);
    returned
}
```

The implementation of `AtlTraceErrorRecords` depends on the compilation options. In nondebug mode, it does nothing.

HRESULTs are fine for Visual C++ developers, but they are not suitable for, say, Visual Basic developers. For them Microsoft introduced the automation error mechanism, which allows programmers to set and get thread-wide error information. This information is nothing more than a COM object that supports the `IErrorInfo` interface. Here is what occurs when a client calls a method that causes an error:

1. The client calls a method on the server object.
2. The server object realizes that it cannot perform the requested action.
3. The server object creates a COM object that supports `IErrorInfo` and calls the `SetErrorInfo` API function.
4. Since the server object is unable to perform the requested action, it returns an error code.
5. When the client object receives the return code, it notices that an error occurred through the HRESULT. It then calls the `GetErrorInfo` API function and retrieves the error object created by the server object.
6. The client calls methods on the error object to get more details on the error and releases the object when finished with it.

Figure 4-1 illustrates this process.

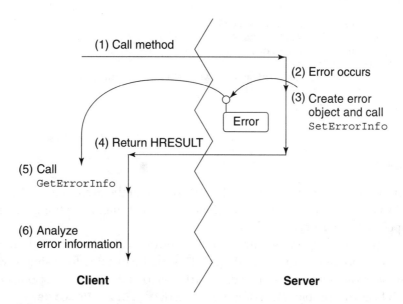

**Figure 4-1** Error Info Mechanism

There are several important points to make here. First, there is only one error object per thread. Therefore, if there was already an error object just before the call to SetErrorInfo, it will be lost. Second, calling GetErrorInfo resets the global error info object to NULL. When you call it, you should keep the returned object since there is no way to get it back; calling GetErrorInfo again will return NULL.

## IErrorInfo

GetDescription provides a textual description of the error. For example, if you attempt to open a table that does not exist, you might get the following description:

```
"Invalid object name 'invalid_table'."
```

GetSource returns a string that represents the class that raised the error. Alternatively, Microsoft could have returned a CLSID. GetGUID identifies the interface that defines the error. A better name might have been GetIID. GetHelpFile and GetHelpContext provide the name of the help file and the help context. IErrorInfo was defined before HTML and it really shows here. Nowadays, a URL would be more appropriate.

A typical use of the error info object would be

```
// something went wrong
{
    CComPtr<IErrorInfo> ErrorInfo;
    GetErrorInfo (0, &ErrorInfo);
    BSTR bstrDescription;
    BSTR bstrSource;
    ErrorInfo->GetDescription (&bstrDescription);
    ErrorInfo->GetSource(&bstrSource);
    // will need to free the strings
}
```

## IErrorRecords

Until now, there was nothing OLE DB specific in the error mechanism—any type of COM application would have done the same thing. Everything will be OLE DB specific from now on.

The most important limitation of the error mechanism is that there is only one error information object per thread. This can be just fine for a simple Visual Basic application, but it can be a severe restriction for anything more sophisticated. OLE DB fixes this problem by adding one interface: IErrorRecords.

IErrorRecords makes two improvements. First, it contains a series of error records, not just one. Each record is simply a COM object that supports the IErrorInfo interface. Second, each error record contains basic error information and custom error information. Basic information is that which is frequently requested; custom information is a COM object that returns error information that does not fit into the traditional error information structure.

IErrorRecords has six methods:

- GetRecordCount gets the number of records it contains.
- GetErrorInfo gets the error info object for a given record index (the record index is zero based).
- GetBasicErrorInfo gets the basic error information for a given record index.
- GetCustomErrorObject gets the custom error object for a given record index.
- AddErrorRecord adds a new error record. This method is used primarily by providers.
- GetErrorParameters returns the parameters that caused the error.

Figure 4-2 summarizes the difference between error info, error records, and custom error information.

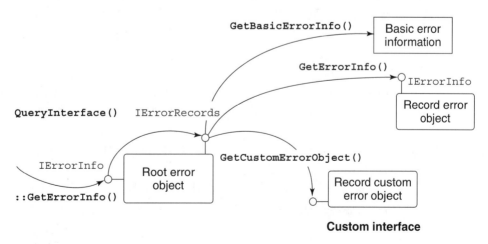

**Figure 4-2** Error Info and Error Records

## Using the OLE DB Classes

The OLE DB consumer templates provide only one class: *CDBErrorInfo*. You initialize an instance of CDBErrorInfo by calling GetErrorRecords:

```
HRESULT GetErrorRecords(ULONG* pcRecords)
```

where pcRecords receives the number of records. One of the confusing aspects is that CDBErrorInfo does not keep the number of records internally; the user of the class needs to know this. A better design would have had the number of records as a class member of CDBErrorInfo.

Internally, CDBErrorInfo holds a pointer to both the IErrorInfo and the IErrorRecords:

```
// Implementation
    CComPtr<IErrorInfo>     m_spErrorInfo;
    CComPtr<IErrorRecords>  m_spErrorRecords;
```

GetErrorRecords first attempts to get the pointer on IErrorInfo. If successful, it then tries to get the pointer on IErrorRecords; if not successful, it sets the content of pcRecords to 1. The pointer to the IErrorInfo interface will be considered as the unique error record. Otherwise, spErrorRecords holds the interface pointer to IErrorRecords and pcRecords receives the actual record number.

Once you open CDBErrorInfo successfully, the next step is to get all the error information it contains by calling

```
HRESULT GetAllErrorInfo(ULONG ulRecordNum, LCID lcid, BSTR*
    PbstrDescription, BSTR* pbstrSource = NULL, GUID* pguid=NULL,
    DWORD* pdwHelpContext = NULL,BSTR* pbstrHelpFile = NULL)const
```

GetAllErrorInfo has two different behaviors depending on whether the error info object supports the IErrorRecords interface.

If the object does not support IErrorRecords (Figure 4-3), the object will use m_spErrorInfo as the error record and ignore both ulRecordNum and lcid. GetAllErrorInfo then calls the different methods on m_spErrorInfo.

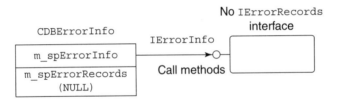

**Figure 4-3** Case 1: No Support for **IErrorRecords**

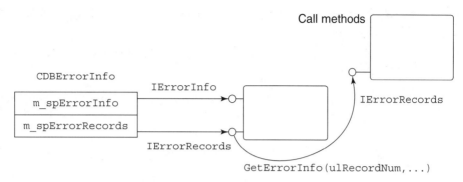

**Figure 4-4** Case 2: Support for `IErrorRecords`

If the error object does support `IErrorRecords`, it first gets the error info object from `IErrorRecords` and then calls the different methods on it. Figure 4-4 illustrates this case.

## Getting the Basic Error Information

Each error record contains basic information, represented by the `ERRORINFO` structure.

```
typedef struct   tagERRORINFO
    {
    HRESULT hrError;
    DWORD dwMinor;
    CLSID clsid;
    IID iid;
    DISPID dispid;
    }   ERRORINFO;
```

The term `ERRORINFO` is somewhat misleading because the structure it represents is disconnected from the `IErrorInfo` interface. Think of it as additional information to that in the error info object. It could have been a COM object supporting an imaginary `IBasicErrorInfo` interface; however, having a structure simplifies programming.

- `hrError` is the HRESULT that caused the error. It can be helpful in tracing the different HRESULTs for the different records. The first record will have the HRESULT that caused the original error. The last one will have the HRESULT returned to the client. In between, the provider can choose to change `hrError`.

- `clsid` and `iid` are the class ID and interface ID, respectively, of the instance that created the error.
- `dwMinor` and `dispid` are optional provider-specific codes. In many cases, they are both zero.

Consumers are able to obtain the basic error information by calling the `GetBasicErrorInfo` method.

```
HRESULT GetBasicErrorInfo(ULONG ulRecordNum,
    ERRORINFO* pErrorInfo) const
```

`ulRecordNum` represents the record index, and `pErrorInfo` receives the basic error information.

## Getting a Custom Error Object

When error info and basic error are not enough, you can use a custom error object. This is simply a COM object that supports some provider-specific interface. Consumers get it by calling the `GetCustomErrorObject` method.

```
HRESULT GetCustomErrorObject (
    ULONG        ulRecordNum,
    REFIID       riid,
    IUnknown **  ppObject);
```

where

- `ulRecordNum` is the record index.
- `riid` is the interface identifier of the requested interface.
- `ppObject` receives the interface pointer.

One of the custom interfaces is `ISQLErrorInfo`—an interface for SQL providers. It has one function:

```
HRESULT GetSQLInfo (
    BSTR *   pbstrSQLState,
    LONG *   plNativeError);
```

`pbstrSQLState` receives a 5-character string defined by the ANSI SQL standard that describes the error. `plNativeError` receives some provider-specific error code.

## Tracing Custom Information

AtlTraceErrorRecords does a good job tracing errors, but it does not trace the most common custom error information interface: ISQLErrorInfo. For this reason, the OLE DB extensions provide AtlTraceErrorRecordsEx, an enhancement of AtlTraceErrorRecords that does what AtlTraceErrorRecords does and also attempts to get the ISQLErrorInfo interface and trace its information. It is implemented as follows.

```
inline void AtlTraceErrorRecordsEx(HRESULT hrErr = S_OK)
{
    CDBErrorInfo ErrorInfo;
    ULONG        cRecords;
    HRESULT      hr;
    ULONG        i;
    CComBSTR     bstrDesc, bstrHelpFile, bstrSource;
    GUID         guid;
    DWORD        dwHelpContext;
    WCHAR        wszGuid[40];
    USES_CONVERSION;

    // If the user passed in an HRESULT then trace it
    if (hrErr != S_OK)
        ATLTRACE2(atlTraceDBClient, 0,
          _T("OLE DB Error Record dump for hr = 0x%x\n"), hrErr);

    LCID lcLocale = GetSystemDefaultLCID();

    hr = ErrorInfo.GetErrorRecords(&cRecords);
    if (FAILED(hr) && ErrorInfo.m_spErrorInfo == NULL)
    {
        ATLTRACE2(atlTraceDBClient, 0,
          _T("No OLE DB Error Information found: hr = 0x%x\n"), hr);
    }
    else
    {
        for (i = 0; i < cRecords; i++)
        {
            hr = ErrorInfo.GetAllErrorInfo(i, lcLocale, &bstrDesc,
                &bstrSource, &guid, &dwHelpContext, &bstrHelpFile);
            if (FAILED(hr))
            {
                ATLTRACE2(atlTraceDBClient, 0,
 _T("OLE DB Error Record dump retrieval failed: hr = 0x%x\n"), hr);
                return;
            }
            StringFromGUID2(guid, wszGuid, sizeof(wszGuid) /
                sizeof(WCHAR));
            LPOLESTR IidSymbol;
            SymbolStringFromIID(guid, &IidSymbol);
```

```
            ATLTRACE2(atlTraceDBClient, 0,
                _T("Row #: %4d Source: \"%s\" Description: 11\"%s\"
Help File: \"%s\" Help Context: %4d GUID: %s %s\n"),
                i, OLE2T(bstrSource), OLE2T(bstrDesc),
                OLE2T(bstrHelpFile), dwHelpContext,OLE2T(IidSymbol),
                OLE2T(wszGuid));
            CoTaskMemFree(IidSymbol);
            bstrSource.Empty();
            bstrDesc.Empty();
            bstrHelpFile.Empty();
            if (ErrorInfo.m_spErrorRecords)
            {
                ERRORINFO BasicErrorInfo;
                hr = ErrorInfo.GetBasicErrorInfo(i,&BasicErrorInfo);
                if (FAILED(hr))
                    ATLTRACE2(atlTraceDBClient, 0,
                        _T("No basic error information\n"));
                else
                    TraceBasicErrorInfo(&BasicErrorInfo);
                CComPtr<ISQLErrorInfo> spSQLErrorInfo;
                hr = ErrorInfo.GetCustomErrorObject(i,
                    IID_ISQLErrorInfo, (IUnknown **)&spSQLErrorInfo);
                if (FAILED(hr) || !spSQLErrorInfo)
                    ATLTRACE2(atlTraceDBClient, 0,
                        _T("No SQL error information\n"));
                else
                {
                    CComBSTR strSQLState;
                    LONG NativeError;
                    spSQLErrorInfo->GetSQLInfo(&strSQLState,
                        &NativeError);
                    ATLTRACE2(atlTraceDBClient, 0,_T("SQL error
information: SQLState:%n , NativeError: %i\n"),
                        W2T(strSQLState), NativeError);
                }

            }

        }
        ATLTRACE2(atlTraceDBClient, 0,
            _T("OLE DB Error Record dump end\n"));
    }
}
```

The following example shows the output of `AtlTraceErrorRecordsEx`.

```
ATL: Row #:    0 Source: "Microsoft OLE DB Provider for SQL Server"
Description: "Invalid object name 'invalid_table'." Help File:
"(null)" Help Context:    0 GUID: IID_ ICommand {0C733A63-2A1C-11CE-
ADE5-00AA0044773D}
```

```
ATL: Basic error info: hrError: 0x80040e37, dwMinor: 208, clsid:
CLSID_SQLOLEDB {0C7FF16C-38E3-11D0-97AB-00C04FC2AD98} , iid:
IID_ICommand {0C733A63-2A1C-11CE-ADE5-00AA0044773D} , dispid: 0

ATL: SQL error information: SQLState: , NativeError: 208
```

## ErrorInfo Support

One of the difficulties with the COM error mechanism is that any object can create an error, but not all objects actually do create errors. For example, if you call a method and get an error HRESULT, should you try to get the associated error information? If you do get it, does it correspond to the error that just occurred or to a past error? The ISupportErrorInfo interface provides an unambiguous answer to both questions.

The OLE DB objects that could create errors should support the ISupportErrorInfo interface. This interface has only one method:

```
HRESULT InterfaceSupportsErrorInfo (REFIID riid);
```

where riid represents the identifier of the interface that might create errors. If InterfaceSupportsErrorInfo returns S_OK, all interface methods will create error information if it fails. Conversely, if InterfaceSupportsErrorInfo returns S_FALSE, calling a method on this interface will never produce a new an error information object. Be careful, as S_FALSE is considered a success code (SUCCEEDED(S_FALSE) is true); it does not mean that the object "successfully" creates errors.

For example, say an object supports two interfaces, IA and IB. When a client calls a method on IA, the object might create an error. However, an error object will never be created when a client calls a method on IB. Thus, SupportError Info(IID_IA) should return S_OK while SupportErrorInfo(IID_IB) should return S_FALSE.

This information is static, which means that SupportErrorInfo will have the same behavior for the lifetime of the object. You can get it by calling the OLE DB extensions function SupportErrorInfo:

```
template <class Q>
HRESULT SupportErrorInfo(Q* p)
```

You might write something like

```
ICommand* pCommand;
//...get the command
HRESULT hr = SupportErrorInfo(pCommand);
```

## Putting Things Together

When a client calls a method on some object, it should check the return code:

```
HRESULT hr = SomeObject->SomeMethod();
if (FAILED(hr))
{
```

If hr is an error code, the first step is to check whether the object created an error object:

```
if (SupportErrorInfo(SomeObject) == S_OK)
{
```

The client can then get more information with the CDBErrorInfo class. First, the client should get the number of error records:

```
CDBErrorInfo    ErrorInfo;
ULONG cRecords;
ErrorInfo. GetErrorRecords(&cRecords);
```

If there are any records, the client can iterate through the list to get the information contained in the error object for each one,

```
for (i = 0; i < cRecords; i++)
{
   hr = ErrorInfo.GetAllErrorInfo(i, lcLocale, &bstrDesc,
       &bstrSource, &guid, &dwHelpContext, &bstrHelpFile);
```

the basic error information,

```
ERRORINFO BasicErrorInfo;
hr = ErrorInfo.GetBasicErrorInfo(i, &BasicErrorInfo);
```

or some custom error object

```
CComPtr<ISQLErrorInfo> spSQLErrorInfo;
hr = ErrorInfo.GetCustomErrorObject(i, IID_ISQLErrorInfo,
    (IUnknown **)&spSQLErrorInfo);
   }
  }
 }
```

# SUMMARY

This chapter presented the different ways to get error information. While HRESULTs can give some indication of what went wrong, OLE DB offers more options. Calling `AtlTraceErrorRecords` is the simplest way to access this information.

   The next chapter will present the OLE DB properties. From there, we will be able to attack the core classes.

# 5 OLE DB Properties

Most OLE DB objects support OLE DB properties. These are not like any other COM properties, so it is a good idea to review them before we review the objects themselves. The property mechanism is the same for all OLE DB objects.

This chapter will examine the properties in OLE DB, focusing on

- What makes OLE DB properties "special"
- The property architecture
- How to set, get, and enumerate properties

## THE NOTION OF PROPERTY

A property is defined as the quality or trait belonging to and peculiar to an object. This definition is very broad and allows flexibility in implementation. In C++, for example, a property can be implemented either as a member variable or as a pair of member functions. The following sample exhibits a class with two properties.

```
class CMyClass
{
   type Property1;
   void SetProperty2(type value);
   type GetProperty2() const;
};
```

With COM, interfaces support only functions, not member variables. In the following example, the COM interface supports two properties. Property1 is read/write while Property2 is read only:

```
Interface IMyInterface : IDispatch
{
   [propget,id(1), HRESULT Property1([out, retval] short *pVal);
   [propput,id(1), HRESULT Property1([in] short newVal);
   [propget,id(2), HRESULT Property2([out, retval] short *pVal);
};
```

This approach is traditional in the COM world, especially when using Visual Basic tools. It is easy to understand and code. However, one of its drawbacks is that it does not allow setting several properties in one function call.

Setting several properties at once offers benefits. First, it reduces the number of COM function calls, which, although not of much consequence in a "same machine" scenario, can make a substantial difference when the server is located on a different machine. Second, the interfaces are simple. If there were one method for setting a property and one for getting a property, the number of methods would be twice the number of properties. Since there are many properties, this would make the number of methods unmanageable. In addition, some objects call for a set of properties at creation time, which obviously requires some notion of property set.

## Properties and Property Sets

A property set contains a set of property. Inside the property set, a property identifier (property ID) uniquely identifies the property. Its type, DBPROPID, is defined as

```
typedef DWORD DBPROPID;
```

Properties can have various types. For example, a user name is of type string while a timeout is of type integer. As a result, each property value is contained in a VARIANT.

## Property Set GUIDs

One of the goals of OLE DB is to allow providers to define their own additional features, including properties. The folks at Microsoft do not pretend to know all the possible properties of OLE DB objects, so individual providers need to declare their own custom properties and consequently create their own identifiers. This represents a challenge: How can we make sure that property IDs are unique? If only one company wrote all OLE DB properties, we could imagine a central database of all property IDs. However, individual providers do not have any reliable way of knowing what the others are doing.

**Table 5-1**  Property Set GUIDs Defined by OLE DB

| GUID | Description |
| --- | --- |
| DBPROPSET_COLUMN | Rowset properties that apply to columns |
| DBPROPSET_DATASOURCE | Data source properties |
| DBPROPSET_ DATASOURCEINFO | Data source information properties |
| DBPROPSET_DBINIT | Data source initialization properties |
| DBPROPSET_INDEX | Index properties |
| DBPROPSET_ROWSET | Rowset properties |
| DBPROPSET_SESSION | Session properties |
| DBPROPSET_TABLE | Table properties |
| DBPROPSET_TRUSTEE | Trustee properties |
| DBPROPSET_VIEW | View properties |

As in similar cases in COM, the solution resides with GUIDs. Each property set has a unique GUID; the property IDs are unique within the property set only. In other words, the GUID plays the same role as that of a namespace in C++.

OLE DB defines a collection of property set GUIDs. The property sets apply to a particular OLE DB object for a given operation, and they contain only properties defined by OLE DB. Properties specific to a given provider will always be part of another property set.

Table 5-1 summarizes the property sets defined by OLE DB.

## Property Groups

Each property applies to a given object or concept. For example, one property might apply to the rowset object while another might be used for initializing a data source. Although the property set is useful implementation information, it is not practical for knowing what object or concept its property applies to. Indeed, the property set GUID does not uniquely identify what the property applies to because several property sets can be used for a given operation.

This is where *property groups* come in. Each property also belongs to a one and only one property group. Even though the name sounds similar, a property group has nothing to do with a property set. It simply represents the OLE DB object or concept the property applies to. For example, if a property is part of the

**Table 5-2** Property Groups

| Group | Description |
| --- | --- |
| DBPROPFLAGS_COLUMN | Applies to a column |
| DBPROPFLAGS_DATASOURCE | Applies to a data source object |
| DBPROPFLAGS_DATASOURCECREATE | Applies to data source creation |
| DBPROPFLAGS_DATASOURCEINFO | Gives information about data sources |
| DBPROPFLAGS_DBINIT | Used to initialize a data source |
| DBPROPFLAGS_INDEX | Applies to an index |
| DBPROPFLAGS_ROWSET | Applies to a rowset |
| DBPROPFLAGS_SESSION | Applies to an index |
| DBPROPFLAGS_TABLE | Applies to a table |
| DBPROPFLAGS_VIEW | Applies to a view |

property group DBPROPFLAGS_DATASOURCE, it applies to the data source object, but whether it is part of the property set identified by DBPROPSET_DATASOURCE or another provider-specific property set is not specified.

The property groups defined by OLE DB are contained in Table 5-2. Note that the property group does not necessarily correspond to an OLE DB object. For example, there is a property group for columns but OLE DB does not define any column object.

Moreover, the data source initialization property group corresponds only to the initialization of a data source. That is, we use properties from this group for initializing a data source, but they are not valid once initialization is complete.

## Property Operations

The four property operations are

- Set properties
- Get properties
- Enumerate properties
- Get property information

They will be explained in the sections that follow.

## SETTING PROPERTIES

A property set contains properties that have the same GUID. When setting properties, you might need properties coming from different property sets—in other words, an array of property sets.

OLE DB objects that support setting properties have a method that looks like

```
HRESULT Method(DBPROPSET* pPropSet = NULL, ULONG nPropertySets=1)
```

where pPropSet is an array of property sets and nPropertySets is the number of property sets in it.

## DBPROPSET

The DBRPROPSET structure represents one property set. It is defined as follows

```
typedef struct tagDBPROPSET {
   DBPROP *    rgProperties;
   ULONG       cProperties;
   GUID        guidPropertySet;
} DBPROPSET;
```

where

- rgProperties is a pointer to an array of DBPROP.
- cProperties is the number of DBPROP in rgProperties.
- guidPropertySet is the GUID common to all properties.

Figure 5-1 on the next page represents an array of the DBPROP property sets.

## DBPROP

Each DBPROP structure represents one property in a property set:

```
typedef struct tagDBPROP {
   DBPROPID        dwPropertyID;
   DBPROPOPTIONS   dwOptions;
   DBPROPSTATUS    dwStatus;
   DBID            colid;
   VARIANT         vValue;
} DBPROP;
```

The most important fields are the property ID (dwPropertyID) and the value (vValue). Since the variant is of type VARIANT, it may need to be freed after use.

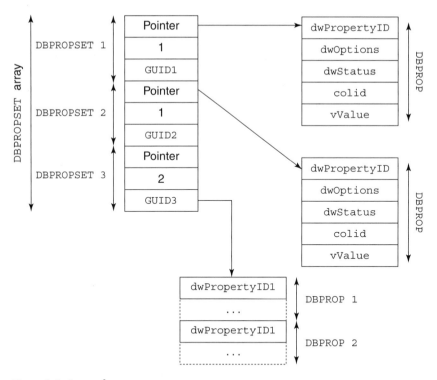

**Figure 5-1 Array of DBPROPSET**

This is always the consumer's responsibility. The other fields are less important. We will discover them as needed.

The methods to set properties usually have convenient default arguments: If you do not specify any argument, no property set will be passed. If you specify only the pPropSet argument, the method will assume that the property set array contains only one item.

## Using the Raw Structures

The standard method to set OLE DB properties entails the following six steps:

1. Determine the property IDs and the property set GUID of the properties you want to set.

2. Regroup the properties with the GUID inside property sets. At this stage, you know how many property sets you have and how many properties each property set contains.

3. Allocate an array of property sets (PROPSET). For each property set, set the GUID.

4. For each property set, allocate an array (DBPROP) and set the fields.

5. Pass the property set array to the SetProperty or Open method of the object.

6. Free all the variants and all the structures.

Note that even if you want to set only one property, you still have to allocate a property set array.

The following example shows how to set two properties from one property set using the OLE DB structures directly.

```
DBPROPSET PropSet;
DBPROP Props [2];
PropSet.guidPropertySet = DBPROPSET_DBINIT;
PropSet.cProperties = 2;
PropSet.rgProperties = Props;
Props[0].colid = DB_NULLID;
Props[0].dwOptions = DBPROPOPTIONS_REQUIRED;
Props[0].dwPropertyID = DBPROP_AUTH_INTEGRATED;
Props[0].dwStatus = DBPROPSTATUS_OK;
Props[0].vValue.vt = VT_BSTR;
Props[0].vValue.bstrVal = SysAllocString(OLESTR("SSPI"));
Props[1].colid = DB_NULLID;
Props[1].dwOptions = DBPROPOPTIONS_REQUIRED;
Props[1].dwPropertyID = DBPROP_AUTH_INTEGRATED;
Props[1].dwStatus = DBPROPSTATUS_OK;
Props[1].vValue.vt = VT_BOOL;
Props[1].vValue.boolVal = VARIANT_FALSE;

CDataSource DataSource;
HRESULT hr = DataSource.Open(_T("SQLOLEDB.1"), &PropSet);
VariantClear(&Props[0].vValue);
VariantClear(&Props[1].vValue);
```

As noted, the client is responsible for freeing all values by calling VariantClear. In this example, the client does not have to free the structures because they are allocated on the stack.

## CDBPropSet

Managing DBPROPSET and DBPROP can be difficult and error prone. For this reason, the OLE DB consumer templates provide classes that facilitate the property set manipulation. CDBPropSet is an encapsulation of DBPROPSET. It is defined as

```
class CDBPropSet : public tagDBPROPSET
```

CDBPropSet does not add class members, only methods. As a result, you can use a it anywhere you would use DBPROPSET.

CDBPropSet introduces several improvements. First, it resizes the array of properties dynamically; you do not have to do this statically. Second, it sets the variant type of the value automatically. Third and most important, it releases all the variants automatically.

When using an instance of CDBPropSet, you first need to set the GUID of the property set. You can do this either with the constructor or with the SetGUID method.

The interesting method is AddProperty, which adds a property from two arguments:

```
bool AddProperty( DWORD dwPropertyID, type Value );
```

where dwPropertyID is the property ID of the property to add and Value is the value of the property. AddProperty accepts numerous types for Value. When needed, the value will be converted into a VARIANT-compatible value and the variant type will be set automatically. Table 5-3 summarizes the types accepted by AddProperty and their VARIANT counterparts.

AddProperty returns true if it succeeds and false otherwise. For example, it can fail if it is out of memory or if it is passed a NULL string.

CDBPropSet makes the life of the programmer significantly easier. Here is the previous example rewritten with it:

```
CDBPropSet MyDBPropset(DBPROPSET_DBINIT);
MyDBPropset.AddProperty(DBPROP_INIT_DATASOURCE, "NAME");
MyDBPropset.AddProperty(DBPROP_INIT_MODE, (long)0);
```

**Table 5-3** C++ Types and Variant Types

| C++ Type | Variant Type |
| --- | --- |
| VARIANT | Same as the type in the variant |
| LPCTSTR | VT_BSTR |
| LPCWSTR | VT_BSTR |
| bool | VT_BOOL |
| BYTE | VT_UI1 |
| short | VT_I2 |
| long | VT_I4 |
| float | VT_R4 |
| double | VT_R8 |
| CY (currency) | VT_CY |

If the properties belong to several property sets, you must use an array of CDBPropSet and set the property GUIDs by hand. The following code sample shows how to use an array of two property sets with two properties in one and one property in the other.

```
CDBPropSet PropSets [2];
PropSets[0].SetGUID(DBPROPSET_DBINIT);
PropSets[0].AddProperty(DBPROP_AUTH_INTEGRATED, OLESTR("SSPI"));
PropSets[0].AddProperty(DBPROP_AUTH_PERSIST_SENSITIVE_AUTHINFO,
    false);

PropSets[1].SetGUID(DBPROPSET_DBINIT);
PropSets[1].AddProperty(SSPROP_INIT_AUTOTRANSLATE, true);

CDataSource DataSource;
HRESULT hr = DataSource.Open(_T("SQLOLEDB.1"), PropSets, 2);
```

If the properties are in the same property set, it is not necessary to use an array of CDBPropSet; you can pass the CDBPropSet address. Usually, the default number of property sets is one. Therefore, you do not need to pass it when you have only one property set. In the following example, there is only one property set containing two properties.

```
CDBPropSet PropSet (DBPROPSET_DBINIT);
PropSet.AddProperty(DBPROP_AUTH_INTEGRATED, OLESTR("SSPI"));
PropSet.AddProperty(DBPROP_AUTH_PERSIST_SENSITIVE_AUTHINFO,
    false);

CDataSource DataSource;
HRESULT hr = DataSource.Open(_T("SQLOLEDB.1"), &PropSet);
```

CDBPropSet has two drawbacks. The first is that each time you add a property, the whole property array is reallocated. Each AddProperty method calls Add, which is an implementation method. Let's have a look at the Add method:

```
bool Add()
{
   rgProperties = (DBPROP*)CoTaskMemRealloc(rgProperties,
     (cProperties + 1) * sizeof(DBPROP));
   if (rgProperties != NULL)
   {
     rgProperties[cProperties].dwOptions =
        DBPROPOPTIONS_REQUIRED;
     rgProperties[cProperties].colid     = DB_NULLID;
     rgProperties[cProperties].vValue.vt = VT_EMPTY;
     return true;
   }
   else
     return false;
}
```

The second drawback is that it always sets the property option to "required" and the column ID is always DB_NULLID. If you want to use optional properties and column properties, you will need another class, as we will see later.

## Setting One Property

If you want to set only one property, dealing with a property set can be burdensome. Another option is to call the SetProperty method:

```
template <class T>
HRESULT SetProperty(const GUID& guid, DBPROPID propid, T Value)
```

where guid and propid identify the property and Value contains the property's value.

SetProperty is defined as follows:

```
template <class T>
HRESULT SetProperty(const GUID& guid, DBPROPID propid, T Value)
{
    CDBPropSet PropSet (guid);
    PropSet.AddProperty(propid, Value);
    return SetProperties(&PropSet);
}
```

The types possible for values are the same ones that are possible for CDBPropSet::AddProperty.

In the following example, the property CURRENTCATALOG in the data source property set is set to "CatalogName".

```
hr = DataSource.SetProperty(DBPROPSET_DATASOURCE,
    DBPROP_CURRENTCATALOG, "CatalogName");
```

SetProperty is easy to use. However, it does not offer any way to diagnose errors.

## Required and Optional Properties

It is possible to specify if a property to be set is optional or required. The property option is of type DBPROPOPTIONS and can have one of the values DBPROP OPTIONS_REQUIRED and DBPROPOPTIONS_OPTIONAL.

The property option has an influence when an object method is unable to set the property. If the property is required, the method will fail and return an error such as DB_E_ERRORSOCCURRED. It will not set any other property. Conversely, if the property is optional, the method will return a success code such as DB_S_ERRORSOCCURRED and ignore the property. If the property set contains other properties, the method will attempt to set them.

By default, CDBPropSet sets all properties as required. There are two ways to specify optional properties. The first method is to use the raw OLE DB structures. Instead of setting dwOptions to DBPROPOPTIONS_REQUIRED, set it to DBPROPOPTIONS_OPTIONAL. Otherwise, the code is the same.

The second method is to use an OLE DB extensions class: CDBPropSetEx. CDBPropSetEx inherits from CDBPropSet. The two are similar in every respect except their AddProperty methods. AddProperty here is similar to the one in CDBPropSet, but it accepts two additional arguments: the property option and the property column (see the next section for property columns).

```
bool AddProperty(DWORD dwPropertyID, type Value,
   DBPROPOPTIONS dwOptions = DBPROPOPTIONS_REQUIRED,
   DBID colid= DB_NULLID)
```

Because the default parameters match the implementation in CDBPropSet, you can replace CDBPropSet with CDBPropSetEx without any incompatibility.

The following example shows how to set an optional property:

```
CDBPropSetEx PropSet (DBPROPSET_DBINIT);
PropSet.AddProperty(DBPROP_AUTH_PERSIST_SENSITIVE_AUTHINFO,
   False, DBPROPOPTIONS_OPTIONAL);
```

## Column Identifiers

OLE DB defines objects that have columns, such as tables or indexes. However, it does not define any column object. When you want to set a property that applies to only one column, you need to indicate which column. As a result, all OLE DB properties contain a column identifier of type DBID (colid in the DBPROP structure). In most cases, the column identifier does not have any significance and should be set to DB_NULLID. Note that CDBPropSet sets the column identifier to DB_NULLID automatically.

Providers can offer different ways to identify a column: with a name, with a GUID, with an integer, or with a combination of these. The DBID structure contains all of these identifiers and a switch that indicates which to use. It is defined as

```
typedef struct  tagDBID
{
   union
   {
      GUID guid;
```

```
        GUID *pguid;
        /* Empty union arm */
    } uGuid;
    DBKIND eKind;
    union
    {
        LPOLESTR pwszName;
        ULONG ulPropid;
        /* Empty union arm */
    }   uName;
}   DBID;
```

Note that eKind is the switch.

The following example shows how to set a DBID to a given name:

```
dbid.eKind = DBKIND_NAME;
dbid.uName.pwszName = T2W(aName);
```

There are two ways to set the column identifier of a property: the raw OLE DB structures and CDBPropSetEx:

```
PropSet.AddProperty(DBPROP_COL_NULLABLE,
    False, DBPROPOPTIONS_REQUIRED, dbid);
```

## Custom Property Classes

Knowing and remembering which property ID corresponds to which property GUID can be a problem. The OLE DB extensions provide one custom class per OLE DB property set. These classes provide methods in the form

```
bool AddXXX(type Value)
{
    return AddProperty(DBPROP_XXX, Value);
}
```

where XXX is a property and type is the type associated with property XXX. For example, the code in the Setting Properties section can be replaced with

```
CInitializationPropSet PropSet;
PropSet.AddIntegrated(_T("SSPI"));
PropSet.AddPersistSensitiveAuthInfo(false);

CDataSource DataSource;
HRESULT hr = DataSource.Open (_T("SQLOLEDB.1"), &PropSet);
```

Table 5-4 contains the property set GUID defined by OLE DB and the corresponding OLE DB extension classes.

**Table 5-4** Property Set GUIDs and Custom Classes

| GUID | OLE DB Extension Class |
|------|------------------------|
| DBPROPSET_COLUMN | CColumnPropSet |
| DBPROPSET_DATASOURCE | CDataSourcePropSet |
| DBPROPSET_DBINIT | CIinitializationPropSet |
| DBPROPSET_INDEX | CIndexPropSet |
| DBPROPSET_ROWSET | CRowsetPropSet |
| DBPROPSET_SESSION | CSessionPropSet |
| DBPROPSET_TABLE | CTablePropSet |
| DBPROPSET_VIEW | CViewPropSet |

## Checking the Property Status

The property status dwStatus indicates whether a property was set properly and is of type DBPROPSTATUS. If everything went all right, the status is DBPROP STATUS_OK. Another status indicates that something went wrong.

Table 5-5 shows the different values of DBPROPSTATUS.

**Table 5-5** Property Status

| Symbol | Description |
|--------|-------------|
| DBPROPSTATUS_OK | Property was set properly |
| DBPROPSTATUS_BADCOLUMN | Column was invalid |
| DBPROPSTATUS_BADOPTION | Option was invalid |
| DBPROPSTATUS_BADVALUE | Value or type was invalid |
| DBPROPSTATUS_CONFLICTING | Value conflicted with another property |
| DBPROPSTATUS_NOTSET | Property optional and was not set |
| DBPROPSTATUS_NOTSUPPORTED | Object does not support this property |
| DBPROPSTATUS_NOTSETTABLE | Property is read only |
| DBPROPSTATUS_NOTALLSETTABLE | Property applied to all columns but could not be applied to one of them |

### Tracing Properties

A quick way to check the property status is to call the `AtlTracePropertySets` OLE DB extensions function, which, as the name suggests, traces any error in an array of property sets; it does nothing if there is no error.

`AtlTracePropertySets` is declared as follows:

```
inline HRESULT AtlTracePropertySets (DBPROPSET* PropertySets,
    ULONG PropertySetsCount = 1)
```

where `PropertySets` is an array of property sets and `PropertySetsCount` is the number of property sets in `PropertySets`.

In the following example, the property set has two errors:

- The type of the password is boolean; it should be a string.

- `INVALID_PROPERTY` is an invalid property ID.

```
CDBPropSet Propset[1];
Propset[0].SetGUID(DBPROPSET_DBINIT);
Propset[0].AddProperty(DBPROP_AUTH_USERID, "hello");
Propset[0].AddProperty(DBPROP_AUTH_PASSWORD, false);
Propset[0].AddProperty(INVALID_PROPERTY, (short)4);
CDataSource DataSource;

HRESULT hr = DataSource.Open(_T("SQLOLEDB.1"), Propset, 1);
if (FAILED(hr))
   AtlTracePropertySets(Propset, 1);
```

This example will output the following:

```
ATL: Bad Property in Property Set # 0, Property # 1, PropertyID = 9 ,
Status = 2 (Bad value)
ATL: Bad Property in Property Set # 0, Property # 2, PropertyID = 255 ,
Status = 1 (Not Supported)
```

## GETTING PROPERTIES

The first step in getting properties is to specify the ones desired. Objects that get properties have a method that looks like

```
HRESULT STDMETHODCALLTYPE GetProperties(
   ULONG cPropertyIDSets,
   DBPROPIDSET *rgPropertyIDSets,
      ULONG *pcPropertySets,
      DBPROPSET **prgPropertySets);
```

where `rgPropertyIDSets` is an array of `DBPROPIDSET` that contains the IDs of the properties to retrieve (`cPropertyIDSets` is the number of items in `rgPropertyIDSets`). The provider then allocates and fills up an array of property sets and returns it in `prgPropertySets` so that `pcPropertySets` contains the number of items in `prgPropertySets`.

## DBPROPIDSET

`DBPROPIDSET` represents a set of `DBPROPID`. It is defined as

```
typedef struct tagDBPROPIDSET {
   DBPROPID *    rgPropertyIDs;
   ULONG         cPropertyIDs
   GUID          guidPropertySet;
} DBPROPIDSET;
```

where

- `rgPropertyIDs` is a pointer to an array of `DBPROPID`.
- `cPropertyIDs` is the number of `DBPROPID` in `rgPropertyIDs`.
- `guidPropertySet` is the `GUID` common to all properties of the set.

Figure 5-2 illustrates an example with two property ID sets: The first `DBPROPIDSET` specifies three properties (property IDs 1, 2, and 3); the second `DBPROPIDSET` specifies only one. In return, the provider allocates an array of `DBPROPSET` similar to the array of `DBPROPRIDSET` passed: It has the same number of sets, each with the same properties. The structures allocated by the provider are in gray.

There are six steps to getting OLE DB properties:

1. Determine the property IDs and the property set `GUID` of the properties you want.

2. Regroup the properties with the same property set `GUID` inside property ID sets. At this stage, you know how many property sets you have and how many properties each property set contains.

3. Allocate an array of `property  ID` sets. For each property set, set the `GUID` and the property ID array.

4. Pass the `property ID` set array to the `GetProperties` method of your object.

5. Use the property set array returned.

6. When finished, free the property set.

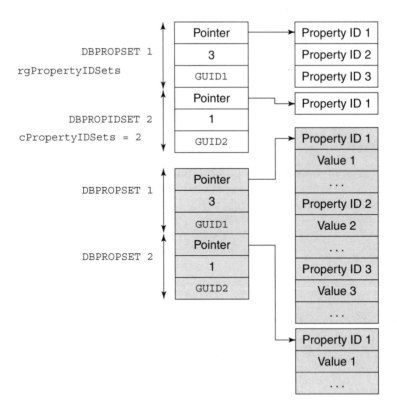

**Figure 5-2** Getting Property Structures

The following example illustrates how to get properties:

```
DBPROPIDSET PropIDSet;
PropIDSet.guidPropertySet = DBPROPSET_DATASOURCEINFO;
// Set the GUID of the property ID set
PropIDSet.cPropertyIDs = 2;
DBPROPID PropertyIDs [2];
PropIDSet.rgPropertyIDs = PropertyIDs;
// Set the property ID array
PropertyIDs[0] = DBPROP_ACTIVESESSIONS;
PropertyIDs[1] = DBPROP_ABORTPRESERVE;
ULONG PropSetCount;
DBPROPSET * PropSets;
hr = DataSource.GetProperties(1, &PropIDSet, &PropSetCount,
        &PropSets);
// work with PropSets.
// PropSets needs to be freed, see next section.
```

## CDBPropIDSet

Even though `DBPROPIDSET` is not that hard to use, the OLE DB consumer templates provide a class that facilitates its use: `CDBPropIDSet`, defined as

```
class CDBPropIDSet : public tagDBPROPIDSET
```

`CDBPropIDSet` does not add any new class members and can be used wherever a `DBPROPIDSET` is needed. It has two methods:

- A contructor that accepts the property set `GUID` as an argument.
- An `AddPropertyID` method that automatically resizes the `PROPID` array and updates the `PROPID` count.

The following code shows how to use `CDBPropIDSet`:

```
CDBPropIDSet MyDBPropIDSet(DBPROPSET_DBINIT);
MyDBPropIDSet.AddPropertyID(DBPROP_ACTIVESESSIONS);
MyDBPropIDSet.AddPropertyID(DBPROP_ABORTPRESERVE);
```

## Memory Management

The OLE DB provider allocates the property set array, and it is the responsibility of the consumer to free it by

- Releasing each variant for each property
- Freeing each property set
- Freeing the property array set

If you work with raw OLE DB structures, you can to do this by hand as follows:

```
for (ULONG i = 0; i < PropSetCount; i++)
{
   for (ULONG j; j < PropSets[i].cProperties; j++)
   {
      VariantClear(&(PropSets[i].rgProperties[j].vValue));
   }
   CoTaskMemFree(PropSets[i].rgProperties);
}
CoTaskMemFree(PropSets);
```

You can also use a function that is provided by the OLE DB extensions: `FreePropertySets`. The destructor of `CDBPropSet` already takes care of releasing the variants and frees its array of properties. `FreePropertySets` leverages this destructor and then frees the array.

```
inline HRESULT FreePropertySets(DBPROPSET * Sets,
   ULONG SetCount = 1)
{
   CDBPropSet * Sets2 = (CDBPropSet *)Sets;
   for(ULONG i = 0; i < SetCount; i++)
   {
      Sets2[i].~CDBPropSet();
   }
   CoTaskMemFree(Sets);
   return S_OK;
}
```

The code to get properties then becomes

```
CDBPropIDSet PropIDSet(DBPROPSET_DATASOURCEINFO);
PropIDSet.AddPropertyID(DBPROP_ACTIVESESSIONS);
PropIDSet.AddPropertyID(DBPROP_ABORTPRESERVE);
ULONG PropSetCount;
CDBPropSet * PropSets;
hr = DataSource.GetProperties(1, &PropIDSet, &PropSetCount,
reinterpret_cast<DBPROPSET**>(&PropSets));
FreePropertySets(PropSets, PropSetCount);
```

## Getting One Property

Dealing with all the property sets can be cumbersome, especially if you want only one. In this case, you can call the GetProperty method.

```
HRESULT GetProperty(const GUID& guid, DBPROPID propid, VARIANT*
   pVariant) const
```

where

- guid is the GUID of the property set.
- propid is the property ID of the property.
- pVariant receives the value of the property.

   The following sample demonstrates the use of GetProperty.

```
CComVariant variant;
hr = DataSource.GetProperty(DBPROPSET_DATASOURCEINFO,
   DBPROP_ACTIVESESSIONS, &variant);
```

Note that you do not have to release the variant explicitly if you use a class such as CComVariant. However, if you use a VARIANT, you might need to do so.

# ENUMERATING PROPERTIES

In the previous section, we examined how to get properties from sets of property IDs, that is, from those already known. However, you might want *all* of the properties for a given property set. OLE DB allows this for all properties supported by a given object. The mechanism is very similar to getting properties. However, instead of the usual property GUID, you use *enumeration* GUIDs.

When a DBPROPIDSET contains an enumeration GUID, all the properties are returned. The provider does not even look at the property ID that you pass. Contrary to a "regular" property GUID, the enumeration GUID allows the property set returned to contain more properties than specified in the property ID set.

Table 5-6 contains the enumeration GUIDs defined by OLE DB. Despite the name similarity, the enumeration GUIDs are *not* property set GUIDs; they relate to property groups.

For example, DBPROPSET_DBINITALL regroups all data source initialization properties. Many of these properties will probably come from the DBPROPSET_DBINIT property group, but others might come from some provider specific data source initialization property set. The bottom line is that one enumeration GUID can produce several property sets.

**Table 5-6** Enumeration GUIDs

| Symbol | Description |
| --- | --- |
| DBPROPSET_COLUMNALL | Returns all column properties |
| DBPROPSET_CONSTRAINTALL | Returns constraint properties |
| DBPROPSET_DATASOURCEALL | Returns all data source properties |
| DBPROPSET_DATASOURCEINFOALL | Returns all data source information properties |
| DBPROPSET_DBINITALL | Returns all data source initialization properties |
| DBPROPSET_INDEXALL | Returns all index properties |
| DBPROPSET_ROWSETALL | Returns all rowset properties |
| DBPROPSET_SESSIONALL | Returns all session properties |
| DBPROPSET_TABLEALL | Returns all table properties |
| DBPROPSET_TRUSTEEALL | Returns all trustee properties |
| DBPROPSET_VIEWALL | Returns all view properties |

The following example demonstrates how to get all the properties for the data source information property group.

```
CDBPropIDSet PropIDSet(DBPROPSET_DATASOURCEINFOALL);
ULONG PropSetCount;
CDBPropSet * PropSets;
hr = DataSource.GetProperties(1, &PropIDSet, &PropSetCount,
reinterpret_cast<DBPROPSET**>(&PropSets));
FreePropertySets(PropSets, PropSetCount);
```

As for the regular properties, the array of `CDBPropSet` needs to be freed with `FreePropertySets` after use.

Again, since the provider can include provider-specific property sets, there is no guarantee that the number of `CDBPropSets`, will be one.

## Enumerating Errors

When the setting of properties returns an error, the standard procedure is to check the error status. OLE DB offers an alternative with the `DBPROPSET_PROPERTIES INERROR` property set. In fact, this is not a regular property set because there is no corresponding property that belongs to it. Instead, it regroups all the properties that caused an error. Note that you should use this GUID just after an error occurs, since other method calls might cause the underlying object to clear the properties in error. The following example shows how to get such properties:

```
CDBPropIDSet PropIDSet(DBPROPSET_PROPERTIESINERROR);
ULONG PropSetCount;
CDBPropSet * PropSets;
hr = DataSource.GetProperties(1, &PropIDSet, &PropSetCount,
reinterpret_cast<DBPROPSET**>(&PropSets));
FreePropertySets(PropSets, PropSetCount);
```

## GETTING PROPERTY INFORMATION

The property information regroups all the information *about* a given property. It is static, which means that it does not depend on the value of the property or the object; it relates to the provider, not the object itself. In a sense, the property information is all the meta-information of a property (description, type, etc.). For example, the textual description of the rowset property `DBPROP_ABORTPRESERVE` is "Preserve on Abort," and its type is Boolean. These two pieces of information do not depend on the underlying rowset or whether the rowset actually preserves the rows after an abort.

Consequently, you do not get the property information for the object to which the property applies but rather for the data source that created it. For example, if you want the property information of DBPROP_ABORTPRESERVE for a given rowset, you should first get the data source that created the rowset and then get the property information from it. (See Chapter 6 for more information about data sources.)

CDataSource does not support property information explicitly. However, the OLE DB extensions provide an extended version that does—CDataSourceEx. Getting property information is very similar to getting property values:

```
HRESULT GetPropertyInfo(ULONG cPropertyIDSets,
    const DBPROPIDSET  rgPropertyIDSets[],
    ULONG *            pcPropertyInfoSets,
    DBPROPINFOSET **   prgPropertyInfoSets,
    OLECHAR **         ppDescBuffer)
```

where rgPropertyIDSets is an array of property ID sets (the number of items in which is represented by cPropertyIDSets). In response, the data source object allocates and fills up an array of property information sets and returns it in prgPropertyInfoSets (pcPropertyInfoSets thus contains the number of items in prgPropertyInfoSets).

The tricky argument is ppDescBuffer; this is a buffer that contains the description strings of the property information. It is not to be used directly; however, you are responsible for freeing it once you are done with the property information.

Before describing how to use this method, it is necessary to explore the different structures.

## DBPROPINFOSET

DBPROPINFOSET follows the same model as the other set structures: It is a set of DBPROPINFO:

```
typedef struct tagDBPROPINFOSET {
    DBPROPINFO *    rgPropertyInfos;
    ULONG           cPropertyInfos;
    GUID            guidPropertySet;
} DBPROPINFOSET;
```

## DBPROPINFO

DBPROPINFO contains the information about one property. It is defined as follows:

```
typedef struct tagDBPROPINFO {
    LPOLESTR        pwszDescription;
```

```
    DBPROPID        dwPropertyID;
    DBPROPFLAGS     dwFlags;
    VARTYPE         vtType;
    VARIANT         vValues;
} DBPROPINFO;
```

The *property description*, of type `LPOLESTR`, is a string describing the property. It is principally for uniquely describing connection strings. These strings can be useful for building user interfaces, but they are not localized.

The *property type*, of type `VARTYPE`, represents the type of the property. The OLE DB *property flags* specify

- The property group the property belongs to (see the section on property flags for more information on property groups).

- The read/write flags

- Whether the property is required

The following are the two possible read/write flags:

- `DBPROPFLAGS_READ`: OLE DB methods can read this property.

- `DBPROPFLAGS_WRITE`: OLE DB methods can write this property.

Some properties are read only, but usually a property that can be written can be read as well. Therefore, the property flag contains either `DBPROPFLAGS_READ` or `DBPROPFLAGS_READ | DBPROPFLAGS_WRITE`. It also can contain one of the following:

- `DBPROPFLAGS_REQUIRED`: The property is required.

- `DBPROPFLAGS_NOTSUPPORTED`: The provider does not support this property.

- `DBPROPFLAGS_COLUMNOK`: The property can apply to columns.

`vValues` is a variant containing a list of possible values of the associated property. It applies only to properties that have a limited number of possible values and is usually empty.

The following sample code shows how to get the property information of two properties.

```
DBPROPIDSET PropIDSet;
PropIDSet.guidPropertySet = DBPROPSET_DATASOURCEINFO;
DBPROPID PropIDs [2];
PropIDSet.cPropertyIDs = 2;
PropIDSet.rgPropertyIDs = PropIDs;
PropIDs[0] = DBPROP_ACTIVESESSIONS;
PropIDs[1] = DBPROP_ACTIVESESSIONS;
   ULONG PropertyInfoSetsCount;
```

```
DBPROPINFOSET * PropertyInfoSets;
OLECHAR * Strings;
hr = DataSource.GetPropertyInfo(1, &PropIDSet, &PropertyInfoSetsCount,
    &PropertyInfoSets, &Strings);

for (ULONG i = 0; i < PropertyInfoSetsCount; i++)
{
    for (ULONG j; j < PropertyInfoSets[i].cPropertyInfos; j++)
    {

VariantClear(&(PropertyInfoSets[i].rgPropertyInfos[j].vValues));
    }
    CoTaskMemFree(PropertyInfoSets[i].rgPropertyInfos);
}
CoTaskMemFree(PropertyInfoSets);
CoTaskMemFree(Strings);
```

## CDBPropertyInfoSet

Using `DBPROPINFOSET` directly can be difficult because you have to manage the memory by hand. The OLE DB extensions provide an encapsulation of `DBPROPINFOSET`: `CDBPropertyInfoSet`, which essentially plays the same role for `DBPROPINFOSET` that `CDBPropSet` does for `DBPROPSET`.

The following sample shows how to get the property information of two properties:

```
CDBPropIDSet PropIDSet(DBPROPSET_DATASOURCEINFO);
PropIDSet.AddPropertyID(DBPROP_ACTIVESESSIONS);
PropIDSet.AddPropertyID(DBPROP_DATASOURCENAME);
ULONG PropertyInfoSetsCount;
CDBPropertyInfoSet * PropertyInfoSets;
CAutoMemory<OLECHAR *, CComMemoryModel<OLECHAR*> > Strings;
hr = DataSource.GetPropertyInfo(1, &PropIDSet, &PropertyInfoSetsCount,
(DBPROPINFOSET ** )&PropertyInfoSets, &Strings);
ATLTRACE(PropertyInfoSets[0].rgPropertyInfos[0].pwszDescription);
ATLTRACE("\n");
ATLTRACE(PropertyInfoSets[0].rgPropertyInfos[1].pwszDescription);
FreePropertyInfoSets(PropertyInfoSets, PropertyInfoSetsCount);
```

## SUMMARY

This chapter presented the OLE DB property mechanism. In particular, it showed how to get properties, set properties, enumerate property information, and get property information.

We are now ready to move on to the different OLE DB objects.

# **6** Data Sources and Sessions

When creating an OLE DB application, the first step is to specify the data you are working on. That is, you have to know where the data is. This might seem obvious at first, but it is not always easy. Indeed, there are many ways to specify the location of the data store and how to access it. For example, the data store might reside in a file, on a given SQL Server or Oracle Server, in an MS Access database, or on the Internet.

- If it is in an SQL Server database, you will need at least a server name and an authentication method.
- If it is in an Access database, you will need a file name, a user name, a password, and a mode to open the database.
- If it is on the Internet, you will need a URL.

In fact, data location is so diverse that it has its own object: the *data source* OLE DB object, which is encapsulated by the OLE DB consumer templates class `CDataSource`.

By itself, the data source cannot do much. It needs a *session* object to open other OLE DB objects whose main purpose is to connect to the data store and support transactions. The class `CSession` encapsulates the session object.

The objective of this chapter is to review the data source object in detail. In particular, we will see how to

- Open a data source programmatically
- Use connection strings
- Use the data source dialogs

- Enumerate the data source types
- Examine service components
- Examine session basics

## SOME HISTORY

This section examines the data sources before OLE DB.

### Proprietary Database

If you use a proprietary database, you call a function like this:

```
HCONNECTION API Connect(char* ServerName, char*UserName,
    char* Password, UINT Mode)
```

This approach has two drawbacks. First, it is not portable, but works only on one type of database server. Second, you need to pass the name of the physical server, the user name, and the password. One solution is to hard-code this information: Each time you move the server or change login information, recompile your application. Another solution is to store this information outside the application or to request it from the user with some kind of dialog. However, data providers do not usually provide native support for this.

A third solution is to avoid the problem altogether by adding a level of indirection.

### ODBC

Open DataBase Connectivity (ODBC) provides this level of indirection with the *ODBC Data Source Administrator*, which stores the information required to access your data as a list of data sources. The programmer need only do something equivalent to

```
Connect (DSNName);
```

where the DSN is the name of the data source.

As a result, it is possible to change information about a data source at the Data Source Administrator level rather than at the application level. And it is possible to manage the data source through the ODBC Data Source Administrator dialog. Figure 6-1 shows this dialog, which you can get by clicking on the ODBC icon in the control panel.

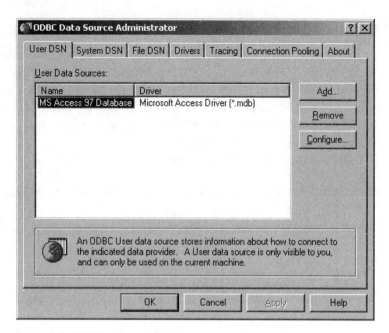

**Figure 6-1** ODBC Data Source Administrator

The benefit of this approach is that the data sources are specified at the system level rather than at the application level, allowing you to configure them outside the application. If the data source changes, you do not need to recompile.

The OLE DB data source has all the benefits of the ODBC data source and adds its own improvements. First, since OLE DB is based on COM, its data source object is a COM object. Second, the OLE DB data source can be transformed into a string that can be saved to a file, making it easy to transfer. Finally, you do not have to throw away your ODBC data sources: They can still be referenced by an OLE DB data source.

## OPENING A DATA SOURCE PROGRAMMATICALLY

Opening a data source consists of creating the data source COM object with a given CLSID and setting the data source properties. There are many Open methods for the data source, but ultimately they always get a CLSID and a set of properties. This section explains the different methods.

## ProgID and CLSID

In the COM section, we saw that a class identifier (CLSID) is a 16-byte unique identifier of a COM class. For example, CLSID_MSDASQL is the class ID of the OLE DB provider for ODBC. A ProgID is another way to specify a COM class. It is a human-readable string that is mapped to a CLSID. "MSDASQL," for example, is the ProgID of the OLE DB provider for ODBC. While the CLSID is guaranteed to be unique, there is no similar guarantee for ProgIDs.

To convert a CLSID to a ProgID, call

```
HRESULT CLSIDFromProgID (LPCOLESTR lpszProgID, LPCLSID pclsid );
```

To convert a ProgID to a CLSID, call

```
WINOLEAPI ProgIDFromCLSID(
   REFCLSID clsid ,//CLSID for which the ProgID is requested
   LPOLESTR * lplpszProgID //Address of output variable that
     // receives a pointer to the requested ProgID string
);
```

CDataSource makes the programmer's life easier by accepting either a ProgID or a CLSID. If you pass a ProgID to an Open method, it will convert it to a CLSID and call the Open method that accepts a CLSIDs.

## Opening a Data Source with User Name and Password

If you come from another database API, the most natural way to open a data source is with four properties:

* Name
* User name
* Password
* Initialization mode

The OLE DB consumer templates provide two functions:

```
HRESULT Open(const CLSID& clsid, LPCTSTR pName,
   LPCTSTR pUserName = NULL, LPCTSTR pPassword = NULL,
   long nInitMode = 0)

HRESULT Open(LPCTSTR szProgID, LPCTSTR pName,
   LPCTSTR pUserName = NULL, LPCTSTR pPassword = NULL,
   long nInitMode = 0)
```

pName is the name of the server. Its exact meaning depends on the provider. For an ODBC provider, pName is the name of the ODBC data source, which appears in the ODBC Data Source Administrator dialog. For an Access database, pName represents the database's file name.

User name and password are self-explanatory. If you pass NULL (the default value), the property will not be set.

The mode nInitMode can be a combination of zero or more items, as shown in Table 6-1. If you pass zero for the mode, the mode property will not be set, as zero is the default. The initialization is useful mainly for desktop databases such as Microsoft Access. Other databases usually ignore this property.

The following sample shows how to open a data source from name, user name, and password:

```
CDataSource DataSource;
DataSource.Open("MSDASQL", Name, UserName, Password, Mode);
//or
DataSource.Open(CLSID_MSDASQL, Name, UserName, Password, Mode);
```

Server name, user name, password, and mode are four properties of the data source. Opening a data source with server name, user name, password, and mode is nothing other than Open checking a data source and setting these four properties. But there are many other properties. To verify this, have a look at the code of CDataSource::OpenWithNameUserPassword on the next page.

**Table 6-1** Initialization Modes

| Symbol | Value | Meaning |
|---|---|---|
| DB_MODE_READ | 0x01 | Read-only |
| DB_MODE_WRITE | 0x02 | Write-only |
| DB_MODE_READWRITE | 0x03 | Read/write (DB_MODE_READ \| DB_MODE_WRITE) |
| DB_MODE_SHARE_DENY_READ | 0x04 | Prevents others from opening in read mode |
| DB_MODE_SHARE_DENY_WRITE | 0x08 | Prevents others from opening in write mode |
| DB_MODE_SHARE_EXCLUSIVE | 0x0c | Prevents others from opening in read/write mode (DB_MODE_SHARE_DENY_READ \| DB_MODE_SHARE_DENY_WRITE) |
| DB_MODE_SHARE_DENY_NONE | 0x10 | Neither read nor write access can be denied to others |

```
HRESULT OpenWithNameUserPassword(LPCTSTR pName,
    LPCTSTR pUserName, LPCTSTR pPassword, long nInitMode = 0)
    {
        ATLASSERT(m_spInit != NULL);
        CComPtr<IDBProperties>  spProperties;
        HRESULT hr;

        hr = m_spInit->QueryInterface(IID_IDBProperties,
            (void**)&spProperties);
        if (FAILED(hr))
            return hr;

        // Set connection properties
        CDBPropSet propSet(DBPROPSET_DBINIT);

        // Add Datbase name, User name and Password
        if (pName != NULL)
            propSet.AddProperty(DBPROP_INIT_DATASOURCE, pName);

        if (pUserName != NULL)
            propSet.AddProperty(DBPROP_AUTH_USERID, pUserName);

        if (pPassword != NULL)
            propSet.AddProperty(DBPROP_AUTH_PASSWORD, pPassword);

        if (nInitMode)
            propSet.AddProperty(DBPROP_INIT_MODE, nInitMode);

        hr = spProperties->SetProperties(1, &propSet);
        if (FAILED(hr))
            return hr;

        // Initialize the provider
        return m_spInit->Initialize();
    }
```

### dsedit

This book comes with an online example called dsedit that shows how to open and edit a data source. Try it out by choosing the menu item "Data source" and then "Open user password." Figure 6-2 shows the dialog that will pop up at that point. Choose your provider in the provider combo box, then type the server name, user name, password, and mode.

## Opening a Data Source from a Set of Properties

The data source object has initialization, data source, and data source information properties. As the name suggests, the initialization properties are used when opening the data source. The data source and data source information properties apply when the data source is already opened. For now, only initialization properties are useful (Table 6-2).

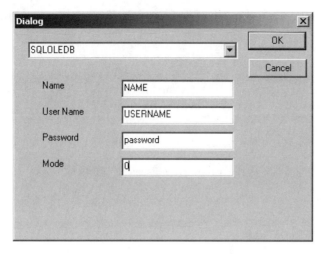

**Figure 6-2** Opening a Data Source with Name, User Name, and Password

**Table 6-2** Basic Initialization Properties

| Symbol | Meaning |
|---|---|
| DBPROP_INIT_DATASOURCE | Name of the data source |
| DBPROP_AUTH_USERID | User name |
| DBPROP_AUTH_PASSWORD | Password |
| DBPROP_INIT_MODE | Open mode |

Two functions allow you to open a data source with a set of properties:

```
HRESULT Open(const CLSID& clsid, DBPROPSET* pPropSet = NULL,
   ULONG nPropertySets=1)

HRESULT Open(LPCTSTR szProgID, DBPROPSET* pPropSet = NULL,
   ULONG nPropertySets=1)
```

We saw the properties listed in Table 6-2 in the previous section. This section will explore some others that are commonly used. Providers do not support all properties but only those that are relevant to them.

In the case of an SQL Server or other similarly "serious" data stores, you will need to specify both the name of the machine hosting the database and the name of the database on it. DBPROP_INIT_DATASOURCE represents the name of the machine, while DBPROP_INIT_CATALOG represents the name of the SQL database.

As an example, the following code opens the SQL database `"database"` on server `"SERVER"`.

```
CDBPropSet   dbinit(DBPROPSET_DBINIT);
dbinit.AddProperty(DBPROP_AUTH_USERID, OLESTR("username"));
dbinit.AddProperty(DBPROP_AUTH_PASSWORD, OLESTR("password"));
dbinit.AddProperty(DBPROP_INIT_CATALOG, OLESTR("database"));
dbinit.AddProperty(DBPROP_INIT_DATASOURCE, OLESTR("SERVER"));
CDataSource MyDataSource
MyDataSource.Open (_T("SQLOLEDB.1"), &dbinit);
```

In addition, OLE DB offers the properties listed in Table 6-3.

**Table 6-3** Other Initialization Properties

| Symbol | Description |
| --- | --- |
| DBPROP_AUTH_CACHE_AUTHINFO | Cache authentication |
| DBPROP_AUTH_ENCRYPT_PASSWORD | Encrypt password |
| DBPROP_AUTH_MASK_PASSWORD | Mask password |
| DBPROP_AUTH_PERSIST_ENCRYPTED | Persist encrypted |
| DBPROP_AUTH_PERSIST_SENSITIVE_AUTHINFO | Persist security info |
| DBPROP_INIT_IMPERSONATION_LEVEL | Impersonation level |
| DBPROP_INIT_LCID | Locale identifier |
| DBPROP_INIT_TIMEOUT | Connect timeout |
| DBPROP_INIT_ASYNCH | Asynchronous processing |

## Opening a Data Source with Incomplete Information

Sometimes, the set of properties that you pass is voluntarily incomplete. For example, you can pass the user name but intentionally forget the password or the name of the server. When you open the data source, you can request that the provider pop up a dialog asking for the missing information. The DBPROP_INIT_PROMPT property specifies this behavior. This property is of type `integer` and can have the values listed in Table 6-4.

You can also specify the parent of the dialog that the provider might prompt, which is represented by the DBPROP_INIT_HWND property. DBPROP_INIT_HWND is not required. If you do not set it, the dialog will not have a parent.

**Table 6-4** Prompt Constants

| Value | Meaning |
|---|---|
| DBPROMPT_PROMPT | Provider should always pop up a dialog, even if no information is missing; user can change any property |
| DBPROMPT_COMPLETE | Provider prompts a dialog only if some information is missing; user can edit any property |
| DBPROMPT_COMPLETEREQUIRED | Provider prompts a dialog only if some information is missing; user can edit only the missing properties |
| DBPROMPT_NOPROMPT | Provider does not prompt any dialog, even if some properties are missing; if some properties are missing, the data source won't be opened successfully |

## Security

OLE DB security entails authentication and protection. *Authentication* allows you to control who is looking at the data. *Protection* refers to the protection of the communication between the client and the data store.

### Authentication

The simplest way to authenticate a user is to pass a pair (user name and password). However, this approach has two drawbacks:

- If you hard-code the user name and password in your source code, you need to protect your source code. In addition, you have to know the user name and password at compile time.
- If you do not hard-code the user name and password in your source code, they must come from somewhere. Either the user will need to enter them in a dialog or they will need to be stored somewhere on disk. It can be burdensome for the user to enter his password each time he opens a data source. If the password is stored on disk, it will need to be protected. Either case can be problematic.

The solution is to avoid the user name and password altogether and use Windows NT/2000 integrated security.

When a user logs on to an NT/2000 machine, she must enter a login name and password. If the login/password pair is valid, she can start a Windows NT session. The service that grants or denies the Windows session is called a *security service provider* (SSP)—NTLM SSP and *Kerberos* are two examples. The interface that allows querying of the different security service providers is called *SSPI*. Once the Windows NT session starts, the user is authenticated. If the OLE DB provider also supports SSPI, it can communicate with the client to authenticate the user. All this is done without password exchange.

The property `DBPROP_AUTH_INTEGRATED` represents the name of the security service provider interface. If you use it, the provider will ignore the other authentication properties. Its value should be `"SSPI"`.

The following code shows how to use the integrated security property:

```
CDataSource db;
CDBPropSet dbinit(DBPROPSET_DBINIT);

dbinit.AddProperty(DBPROP_AUTH_INTEGRATED, "SSPI");
dbinit.AddProperty(DBPROP_INIT_CATALOG, OLESTR("database"));
dbinit.AddProperty(DBPROP_INIT_DATASOURCE, OLESTR("SERVER"));
hr = db.Open(_T("SQLOLEDB.1"), &dbinit);
```

This approach has many benefits; however, not all providers support it. Make sure your provider does. SQL Server supports integrated security.

### Protection and Encryption

It is possible to specify the level of protection and encryption between the client and the data store. While this protection exists at the COM level, providers do not necessarily communicate with the data store via COM. The property, `DBPROP_INITPROTECTION_LEVEL`, describes the COM protection level for non-RPC (and non-COM) communication. Its value is one of those listed in Table 6-5.

**Table 6-5** Protection Level Constants

| Symbol | Description |
| --- | --- |
| DB_PROT_LEVEL_NONE | None |
| DB_PROT_LEVEL_CONNECT | Authenticate caller at connection time |
| DB_PROT_LEVEL_CALL | Authenticate caller for each request |
| DB_PROT_LEVEL_PKT | Authenticate all network packets coming from the client |
| DB_PROT_LEVEL_PKT_INTEGRITY | Authenticate all network packets coming from client and check that they have not been changed in transit |
| DB_PROT_LEVEL_PKT_PRIVACY | Same as above and encrypt all packets |

## DATA LINKS AND INITIALIZATION STRINGS

In the previous section, we saw that a data source is defined by a CLSID and a set of properties. What if you want to store all this so that you can reuse it later? Of course, it is possible to write your own serialization method. However, OLE DB provides a better way: transforming the data source into a UNICODE string, which we call an *initialization string*. It is in UNICODE format rather than ANSI because it should be editable in any language. In a sense, an initialization string is similar to a URL.

This approach is a good one because it is standard—other applications will use the same storage format—and it is human readable—the format is understandable and editable by a user.

A *data link* is a file that contains an initialization string. Its file extension is .UDL. If you think about it, a data link is somewhat similar to a file shortcut: It is a file that contains the location of the information rather than the information itself.

The different versions of Windows and OLE DB do not have a standard way to create a data link: Some allow you to create one from the right-click menu in Windows Explorer; some do not. Thus, the surest way is to create an empty file and rename it with a .UDL extension.

If you click on the file, you get a *Data Link Properties dialog*, which helps you edit the data link. Figure 6-3 shows such a dialog.

Once the Data Link Properties dialog is closed, you can look at the file with a text editor such as Notepad. The content looks like this:

```
[oledb]

; Everything after this line is an OLE DB initstring

Provider=Microsoft.Jet.OLEDB.3.51;Persist Security Info=False;
   Data Source=C:\path\file.mdb
```

Note that some versions of Notepad do not support UNICODE, so when editing a data link, remember to use a UNICODE-compatible editor.

Call the OpenFromInitializationString method to open a data source from an initialization string:

```
HRESULT OpenFromInitializationString(
   LPCOLESTR szInitializationString)
```

Note that before you can call OpenFromInitializationString you have to close the data source. This is different from the other Open methods.

To get the initialization string from a data source already open, call

```
HRESULT GetInitializationString(BSTR* pInitializationString,
   bool bIncludePassword=false)
```

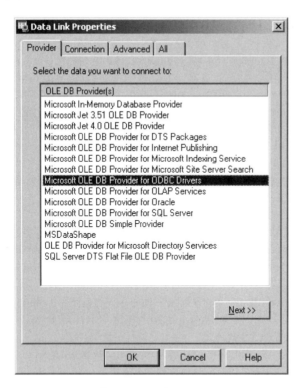

**Figure 6-3** Data Link Properties Dialog

where `bIncludePassword` specifies whether to include the password in the initialization string. Remember that the default is not to do so.

To open the data source from a data link, call `OpenFromFileName`:

```
HRESULT OpenFromFileName(LPCOLESTR szFileName)
```

The following example summarizes these three operations.

```
CDataSource DataSource;
DataSource.OpenFromInitializationString(MyInitString);
BSTR bstrInitString;
DataSource.GetInitializationString (&bstrInitString);
DataSource.OpenFromFileName(MyFileName);
```

The `DBPROP_INIT_PROVIDERSTRING` property specifies the initialization string. Use it for provider-specific properties.

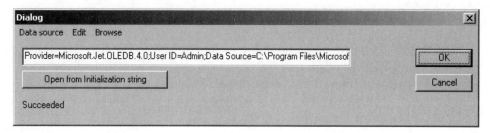

**Figure 6-4** dsedit Main Dialog

### dsedit

In the example, the connection string is systematically displayed in the edit control. If there is no data source, the text says "No data source" (Figure 6-4).

To open a data source from an initialization string in dsedit, enter the initialization string in the edit control and press "Open from Initialization string." The initialization string is displayed in the edit control when you open a data source with any method.

## Storing the Connection String

There are a couple of options for storing the connection string. The first (bad) idea is to hard-code it. This means recompiling the code each time a connection string changes.

The second solution is to store the connection string in a data link file. This offers more flexibility since it allows you to change the string without recompiling the code, but it, too, has drawbacks. First, reading the data link file can be too slow if you open the data source frequently. Second, you still have to manage the files and their location. Although this is doable, it is better avoided.

A third solution is to store the connection string in the registry, which means that a user is less likely to delete it inadvertently. When using the registry, the first task is to choose a key path. You need to make sure that each component accesses the right registry value and that there is no key path conflict. You also need to document where each component stores its connection string.

A way to avoid this is to use the *COM+ object construction string*, which is accessible to all instances of a given COM+ class. The COM+ catalog oversees the object construction string, so you do not have to manage any path. In addition, it offers a user interface to change the construction string. As a result, the administrator can change the data source location in the COM+ catalog. At creation time, the instance reads its construction string and opens the data source with it. The Web site for this book explains this in more detail.

## OPENING A DATA SOURCE INTERACTIVELY

In the previous sections, we looked at how to open a data source programmatically. This means that the developer decides how that will be done. Alternatively, you can allow the user to choose a data source with a dialog.

OLE DB comes with two kinds of dialog: a Data Link Properties dialog and an Organize Data Links dialog.

### The Data Link Properties Dialog

The Data Link Properties dialog interactively obtains the CLSID and builds the set of properties (Figure 6-5). The first tab selects the CLSID. The second and third tabs select the set of properties. The fourth tab shows all properties.

To open a data source with the Data Link Properties dialog, call

```
HRESULT Open(HWND hWnd = GetActiveWindow(),
  DBPROMPTOPTIONS dwPromptOptions= DBPROMPTOPTIONS_WIZARDSHEET)
```

If the user presses "Cancel," the method returns DB_E_CANCELED.

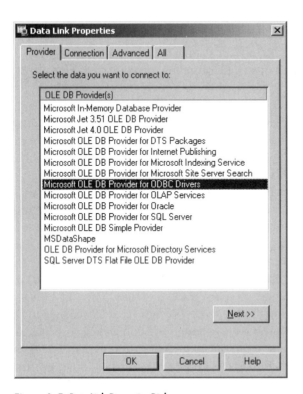

**Figure 6-5** Data Link Properties Dialog

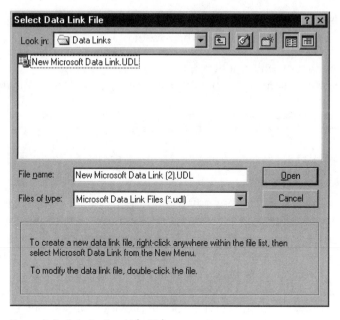

**Figure 6-6** Organize Data Links Dialog

## The Organize Data Links Dialog

The Organize Data Links dialog allows the user to select a data link (`.udl`) file and open the data source with the connection string it contains. This is illustrated in Figure 6-6. To open a data source with this dialog, call

```
HRESULT OpenWithPromptFileName(HWND hWnd = GetActiveWindow(),
    DBPROMPTOPTIONS dwPromptOptions = DBPROMPTOPTIONS_NONE,
    LPCOLESTR szInitialDirectory = NULL)
```

### dsedit
In the dsedit sample, select "Data source" and then "Open from dialog."

## SERVICE COMPONENTS AND RESOURCE POOLING

Until now, the creation of the data source object consisted of calling `CoCreate Instance` with the appropriate `CLSID`. In some cases, however, the functionality provided by the data source is not sufficient, and you must aggregate the data source with a service component. OLE DB provides three service components:

- *Resource pooling*, which applies to the data source object

- *Transaction enlistment*, which applies to the session object
- *Client cursor*, which applies to the rowset object

Note that transaction enlistment requires resource pooling.

To open with service components, call one of the following functions:

```
HRESULT OpenWithServiceComponents(const CLSID& clsid,
  DBPROPSET* pPropSet = NULL, ULONG nPropertySets=1)

HRESULT OpenWithServiceComponents(LPCTSTR szProgID,
  DBPROPSET* pPropSet = NULL, ULONG nPropertySets=1)
```

The DBPROP_INIT_OLEDBSERVICES property defines which service component should be used. It is a combination of the values listed in Table 6-6. If you want to use all service components, set the property to DBPROPVAL_OS_ENABLEALL.

If you do not set DBPROP_INIT_OLEDBSERVICES OLE DB run time will use a default combination of service components. This default value is stored in the OLEDB_SERVICES registry value below the registry key of the CLSID provider. Figure 6-7 shows the default services of the provider for SQL Server. In this case, the provider includes all services by default.

**Table 6-6** Service Component Constants

| Symbol | Meaning |
|---|---|
| DBPROPVAL_OS_RESOURCEPOOLING | Use resource pooling |
| DBPROPVAL_OS_TXNENLISTMENT | Use transaction enlistment |
| DBPROPVAL_OS_CLIENTCURSOR | Use client cursor |
| DBPROPVAL_OS_ENABLEALL | Use all service components |

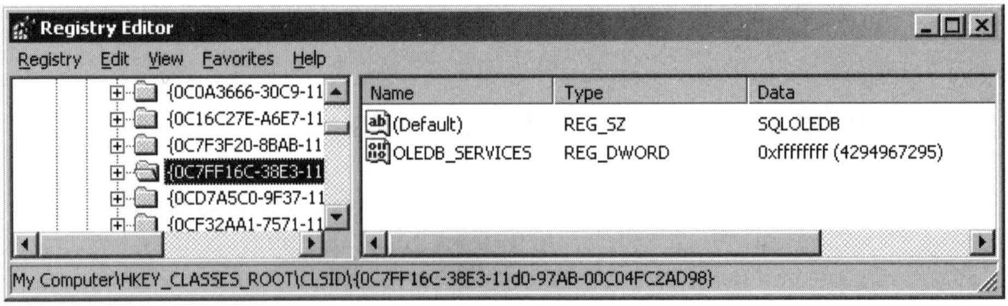

**Figure 6-7** Registry Value of the Provider for SQL Server

The two `OpenWithServiceComponents` methods are very similar to the "standard" `Open` method we examined. However, the implementation is different: Instead of directly calling `CoCreateInstance`, `OpenWithServiceComponents` first creates an object that supports the `IDataInitialize` interface and calls `CreateDBInstance` on it:

```
CComPtr<IDataInitialize> spDataInit;
HRESULT hr;

hr = CoCreateInstance(CLSID_MSDAINITIALIZE, NULL,
    CLSCTX_INPROC_SERVER, IID_IDataInitialize,
    (void**)&spDataInit);
if (FAILED(hr))
    return hr;

m_spInit.Release();
hr = spDataInit->CreateDBInstance(clsid, NULL,
    CLSCTX_INPROC_SERVER, NULL, IID_IDBInitialize,
    (IUnknown**)&m_spInit);
if (FAILED(hr))
    return hr;
// ..some more code
```

`CreateDBInstance` plays the same role as `CoCreateInstance`, except that it first creates a component manager and aggregates the data source objects. Figure 6-8 shows the difference between `Open` and `OpenWith ServiceComponents`. This is only an approximation since the actual implementation of `CreateDBInstance` is not documented by Microsoft. The actual implementation might differ, but the spirit is the same.

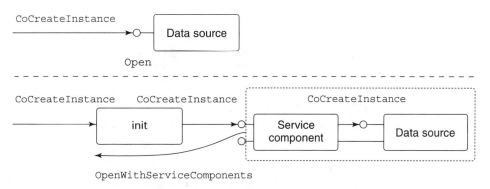

**Figure 6-8** `Open` versus `OpenWithServiceComponents`

The data source service component also manages the creation of the session service component. It intercepts the creation of the session object and, if another service component is not specified, it simply forwards it to the data source. However, if the transaction enlistment is specified, the data source service component first creates a session service component. Then it forwards the session creation to the data source and passes the session service component as an outer object. As a result, the session and the session service component are aggregated. Figure 6-9 summarizes this mechanism, which also applies to the rowset and the rowset client cursor service components.

The bottom line is that (1) you specify which service component to use when you create the data source, and (2) once the data source is created, you do not have to worry about it.

In general, it is better to use service components. It is somewhat unfortunate that the Open method does not use service components, since many programmers use it without even noticing that there is a service component version. The fact that the wizard generates code with Open does not help either. My personal preference would have been to have one Open method with service components and another, say, OpenWithNoServiceComponent, without them.

Note the following methods, which use service components:

- OpenFromFileName

- OpenFromInitializationString

- Open(HWND hWnd = GetActiveWindow(),...

- OpenWithPromptFileName

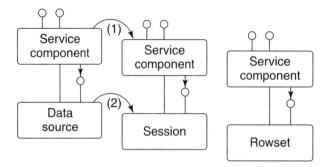

**Figure 6-9** Data Source, Session, and Rowset Service Component

## Resource Pooling

When using resource pooling, the unused resources are cached rather than systematically freed. What we are talking about here are transient objects that are expensive to create—for example, database connections, network connections, and large blocks of memory. In OLE DB, the most obvious resources are database connections and sessions.

Data source pooling (see Figure 6-10) works as follows:

1. The client requests a data source object from the provider. The resource pooling service intercepts the request and returns a proxy data source object. From the client point of view, the proxy acts like a regular data source object. However, there is no "real" data source object at this time.

2. When the client initializes the data source proxy, the resource pooling service looks for a data source object in its pool that corresponds to it. A data source corresponds if it has the same properties as those requested—for example, the server name and user ID. If no such object exists in the pool, a new "real" data source object is created. If there is such an object, the data source proxy uses it; the data source is removed from the pool.

3. When the data source proxy object is released, the "real" data source object is not destroyed but goes back to the resource pool.

4. Periodically, the resource pool inspects its cached objects. If they are not used for a certain period of time, they are released.

Resource pooling can be effective if you frequently create and destroy data sources that are expensive to create. In fact, if it is enabled, you can create and destroy data source objects without having to worry about performance. The data source pool will take care of that.

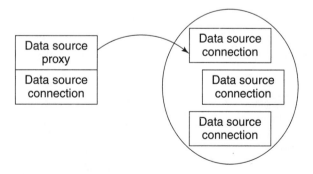

**Figure 6-10** Resource Pooling

### Closing a Data Source

The following method closes the data source:

```
void Close()
```

Note that you do not need to close the data source explicitly: Once the object is out of scope, the smart pointer will automatically release the data source object. Also note that you do not need to close the data source before reopening it, since most Open methods do this.

## ENUMERATORS

In the previous sections, we looked at how to open a data source when you know it already exists. However, how do you know what providers are installed on a machine in the first place?

This is where *enumerators* come in. They enumerate objects. The starting point of an enumeration is the *root enumerator*, which comes with MDAC. The root enumerator enumerates the different providers present on the machine, making it possible to open a data source for the one requested. It also enumerates *provider enumerators*, which enumerate some resource that is provider specific. For example, the ODBC provider enumerates the ODBC data sources present on the machine.

Figure 6-11 shows a root enumerator with two providers and one provider enumerator. The provider enumerator enumerates two items.

Enumerators are represented with two classes:

```
class CEnumeratorAccessor
class CEnumerator : public
        CAccessorRowset<CAccessor<CEnumeratorAccessor> >
```

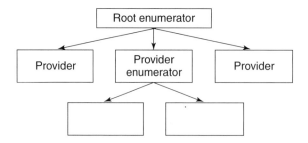

**Figure 6-11**  Enumerators and Data Sources

As you can see, an enumerator is also a rowset. Fortunately, only a minimal knowledge of rowsets is needed for now. They will be discussed in Chapter 8.

Figure 6-12 summarizes the inheritance of `CEnumerator`. In `CEnumerator`, `CEnumeratorAccessor` is an implementation class, so you will not have to use it directly. It introduces five attributes:

- `WCHAR m_szName[129]`: the name of the data source or enumerator.
- `WCHAR m_szParseName[129]`: the string passed to `IParseDisplayName` to obtain a moniker for the data source or enumerator. This is a string representation of the `CLSID`.
- `WCHAR m_szDescription[129]`: the description of the data source or enumerator.
- `USHORT m_nType`: the type of the enumerator or data source. It can be one of the values listed in Table 6-7.
- `VARIANT_BOOL m_bIsParent`: a variable indicating whether the enumerator is a parent enumerator, if the row is an enumerator. In other words, if `m_bIsParent` is `TRUE`, the attributes represent those of the enumerator itself. If it is `FALSE`, the attributes represent those of the current child object. This attribute is usually always `FALSE`, which means that it enumerates its children and does not include itself in the enumeration.

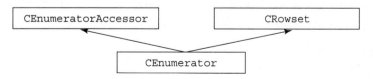

**Figure 6-12** `CEnumerator` Inheritance


**Table 6-7** Data Source or Enumerator Type Constants

| Symbol | Value | Meaning |
|---|---|---|
| DBSOURCETYPE_DATASOURCE | 1 | Object is a data source |
| DBSOURCETYPE_ENUMERATOR | 2 | Object is an enumerator |
| DBSOURCETYPE_DATASOURCE_MDP | 3 | Object is a multidimensional data source |

## The Root Enumerator

As mentioned before, the root enumerator is the starting point of an enumeration. To get one, call the `Open` method:

```
HRESULT Open(const CLSID* pClsid = &CLSID_OLEDB_ENUMERATOR)
```

The default parameter is the root enumerator `CLSID`. For example, to open the root enumerator, write

```
CEnumerator RootEnumerator
RootEnumerator.Open();
```

Then navigate the different rows of the enumerator.

## Enumerator Navigation

Rowsets are a powerful way to traverse lists of objects. However, only two methods are essential:

- `MoveFirst`: Move to the first child object.
- `MoveNext`: Move to the next object.

`MoveNext` returns `S_OK` if it successfully retrieves a new row. If there are no more rows, it returns `DB_S_ENDOFROWSET`. Be careful because `DB_S_ENDOFROWSET` is considered a "success." That is, `SUCCEEDED(DB_S_ENDOFROWSET)` is `TRUE`.

Thus, an enumeration of the children will look like this:

```
CEnumerator Enumerator;
// initialized Enumerator
HRESULT hr = Enumerator.MoveFirst();
while (hr == S_OK)
{
    // do something with Enumerator;
    hr = Enumerator.MoveNext();
}
```

Do not replace the loop condition with `while (SUCCEEDED(hr))`. If you do, you will get an infinite loop.

## Data Sources and Enumerators

One of the main purposes of enumerators is to open data sources. However, because they enumerate only the provider `CLSID`, it is also necessary to provide a set of properties. `CDataSource` provides an `Open` method that takes an enumerator and a set of properties:

```
HRESULT Open(const CEnumerator& enumerator,
   DBPROPSET* pPropSet = NULL, ULONG nPropertySets=1)
```

Internally, this method gets the OLE DB data source object from the enumerator information and sets the properties. A variation is to pass a name, user name, password, and mode that will eventually be converted into a set of properties:

```
HRESULT Open(const CEnumerator& enumerator, LPCTSTR pName,
   LPCTSTR pUserName = NULL, LPCTSTR pPassword = NULL,
   long nInitMode = 0)
```

The following shows how to use data sources against enumerators.

```
CEnumerator RootEnumerator
RootEnumerator.Open();
CDataSource DataSource1;
CDataSource DataSource2;
// Get the property set
// Open the data source on the first enumerated provider
RootEnumerator.MoveFirst();
DataSource1.Open(RootEnumerator, &PropSet);
// Open the data source on the second enumerated provider
RootEnumerator.MoveNext();
DataSource2.Open(RootEnumerator, &PropSet);
```

## Provider Enumerators

Open a provider enumerator with its parent as a parameter in `Open`.

```
HRESULT Open(const CEnumerator& enumerator)

CEnumerator RootEnumerator;
CEnumerator ProviderEnumerator;
// open the parent enumerator
ProviderEnumerator.Open(RootEnumerator);
```

### dsedit

In the dsedit example, choose the menu "Browse" and then "Enumerator." Figure 6-13 shows the Enumerator dialog.

Note that the root enumerator has a provider enumerator: the MSDASQL enumerator (MSDASQL is another name for ODBC), which enumerates the different types of ODBC data sources.

**Figure 6-13** Enumerators Dialog

## DATA SOURCE EXTENSIONS

We reviewed the class `CDataSource`. The OLE DB extensions include an extension to that class: `CDataSourceEx`.

### Saving the Connection String to a File

`CDataSource` allows you to open a data source from a `.udl` file containing a connection string. However, it does not allow you to save the connection string of a data source to a file. `CDataSourceEx` does allow this with the `WriteString ToStorage` method:

```
HRESULT WriteStringToStorage (LPCOLESTR pwszFileName, DWORD
    dwCreationDisposition = CREATE_NEW, bool bIncludePassword=false)
```

The parameters are self-explanatory.

### Editing a Data Source

`CDataSourceEx` allows you to edit a data source interactively through the Data Link Properties dialog:

```
HRESULT Edit(HWND hWnd = GetActiveWindow(), DBPROMPTOPTIONS
   dwPromptOptions = DBPROMPTOPTIONS_WIZARDSHEET,
   LPCOLESTR pwszszzProviderFilter = NULL)
```

This method is very similar to the Open method with a few differences:

- The data source needs to be open before you call Edit.
- The dialog is initialized with the data source type and the properties of the data source.
- If you press "Cancel," the method does not return S_OK. However, the data source is still open.

### dsedit

In the dsedit sample, choose "Edit" and then "Edit no browse." The dialog in Figure 6-14 will pop up.

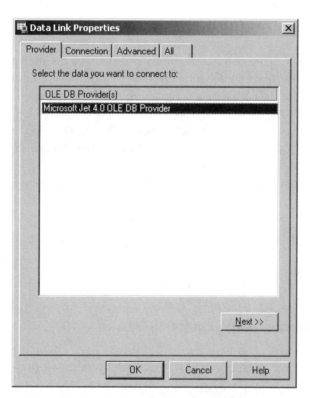

**Figure 6-14** Data Link Properties Dialog Editing a Data Source

## Getting the CLSID

A data source is determined by a CLSID and a set of properties. The OLE DB consumer templates enable you to get the properties but not the CLSID.

With CDataSourceEx it is possible to retrieve the CLSID with the following method:

```
HRESULT STDMETHODCALLTYPE GetClassID(CLSID *pClassID)
{
   CComPtr<IPersist> spPersist;
      // Check that we are connected
   ATLASSERT(m_spInit != NULL);
   HRESULT hr = m_spInit->QueryInterface(&spPersist);
   if (FAILED(hr))
      return hr;
   hr = spPersist->GetClassID(pClassID);
   return hr;
}
```

# SESSIONS

Data sources do not create command and rowset objects. An intermediate object between them and other OLE DB objects, called *session*, is required. The data source only specifies how to access the data; in contrast, the session represents an actual connection to the data store. Note, however, that data sources can create sessions ahead of time and cache them. The session object can support transactions. Even if you do not want to use transactions, you still need to create a session.

Data sources can create several sessions, but it is best to create only one per data source because some optimizations are valid only for the first session. The CSession class in the OLE DB consumer templates encapsulates the OLE DB session. A typical OLE DB consumer code looks like this:

```
CDataSource DataSource;
DataSource.Open (...);
CSession Session;
Session.Open(DataSource);
//Use Session to create other OLEDB objects.
```

Chapter 12 will treat sessions and transactions in more depth.

## SUMMARY

This chapter explained what a data source is and why it is important. It also reviewed the different ways to open a data source. One important point to remember is that the data source determines whether or not to use service components, which will be important for rowsets and transactions. Finally, we briefly examined the session. We are now ready to go forward with the other OLE DB objects.

# 7 Tables and Commands

OLE DB offers two methods for accessing data: *tables* and *commands*. Tables represent the simplest of the two. They correspond to tables in the underlying data store. When opening a table, you get all of its rows and columns in the order defined in the data store.

Commands are a bit more complex. In simple words, a command is an object that can be executed with an *execute* method. The action it performs can be specified by a command text, but another mechanism can be supported. In practice, however, commands support command texts; in most cases, they correspond to SQL statements. Optionally, commands can be prepared and have parameters. The section on commands will explain this in more detail.

## TABLE OR COMMAND?

When accessing data, the first decision is whether to use tables or commands. A table has these benefits:

- It is very easy to use. There is no SQL text involved, only a table name, so there is no risk that the text contains a syntax error. In addition, its implementation class, CTable, is very short and simple. As a result, it is very easy to debug.

- Opening a table might be faster than executing a command because there is no command text involved. Nor is there any OLE DB command object to create. However, this appearance of performance can be misleading because many OLE DB providers silently create and execute a command in the background. For example, if you open table X, the provider can execute command

`"SELECT * FROM X"`. In other words, performance depends on the underlying provider.

It also has drawbacks:

- There is no way to specify the order of the columns. The column will appear in the order declared in the underlying data store, which can lead to some surprises. For example, one programmer might write a component against a table with two columns, and during testing everything will seem all right. After deployment, however, the table might be recreated and the columns might be swapped. Although the swapping of columns is perfectly valid from the database perspective, it will break the component since the component is not aware that the columns have been swapped.

- A table represents *all* the rows of the underlying data store. The rows will appear in the order stored there. An OLE DB table does not provide any way to restrict or order the rows. However, it does provide the view object, which filters and sorts on an open rowset. Chapter 13 explains views in more detail.

The drawbacks can seem overwhelming. After all, why use a table in the first place? There are three possible reasons:

- You have control of the data store or you can use an accessor class that can access row values by column name. You can rely on the views for more advanced operations.
- You are lazy and tables are "good enough."
- The provider does not support commands, and there is no choice but to use tables.

If these do not apply to you, use commands instead as they are more sophisticated than tables:

- They can support rich command texts such as SQL statements.
- They can be prepared and unprepared.
- They can support parameters.
- They can support multiple results.

## TABLES

Class `CTable` encapsulates the notion of a table. It is defined as

```
template <class TAccessor = CNoAccessor,class TRowset = CRowset>
class CTable :
   public CAccessorRowset<TAccessor, TRowset>
```

The first task is to choose the accessor class (TAccessor) and the rowset class (TRowset). By default, the rowset class is CRowset, which is reasonable for a rowset type. Even though TAccessor has CNoAccessor as a default parameter, it does not make sense to use this default parameter because a table always needs an accessor. Moreover, using all the default template parameters as in

```
CTable <> test;
```

will generate the following compilation error:

```
c:\program files\microsoft visual
studio\vc98\atl\include\atldbcli.h(2818) : error C2664: 'SetAccessor'
: cannot convert parameter 1 from 'class ATL::CAccessorRowset<class
ATL::CNoAccessor,class ATL::CRowset> *const ' to 'class
ATL::CAccessorBase *'
```

The bottom line is that the TAccessor template parameter is not optional, while the TRowset template parameter is.

The OLE DB consumer templates provide several choices for the accessor and the rowset, which will be dealt with in the next chapters. For example, you might use the CTable class in the following ways:

```
CTable <CDynamicAccessor> Table1;
CTable <CDynamicAccessor, CBulkRowset> Table2;
CTable <CAccessor<CMyclass> > Table3;
CTable <CAccessor<CMyclass>, CBulkRowset> Table4;
```

## Opening a Table

Class CTable has only two methods, which are very similar to each other:

```
HRESULT Open(const CSession& session, LPCTSTR szTableName,
   DBPROPSET* pPropSet = NULL)
```

and

```
HRESULT Open(const CSession& session, DBID& dbid,
   DBPROPSET* pPropSet = NULL)
```

In the first method, the table is identified by its name. In the second, the table is identified by a DBID. Chapter 5 describes the DBID structure more fully.

The first Open method has the following three arguments:

- session represents the session on which to open the table. Obviously, it should already be opened; its m_spOpenRowset class member should be non-NULL.

- szTableName represents the name of the table to open.

- pPropSet represents an optional set of properties for the rowset to open. There is no property for the table itself. The properties relate to the rowset object. (Chapter 8 discusses rowset properties.)

The first Open method does not do much; it only converts the table name to a DBID and calls the second Open method:

```
HRESULT Open(const CSession& session, LPCTSTR szTableName,
    DBPROPSET* pPropSet = NULL)
    {
        USES_CONVERSION;
        DBID    idTable;

        idTable.eKind          = DBKIND_NAME;
        idTable.uName.pwszName = (LPOLESTR)T2COLE(szTableName);

        return Open(session, idTable, pPropSet);
    }
```

The second Open does the actual job:

```
HRESULT Open(const CSession& session, DBID& dbid,
    DBPROPSET* pPropSet = NULL)
    {
```

First, it gets the interface pointer to the rowset object. GetInterfacePtr is the method defined in the TRowset class that returns the interface pointer address; the pointer is opened by m_spOpenRowset->OpenRowset.

```
        // Check the session is valid
        ATLASSERT(session.m_spOpenRowset != NULL);
        HRESULT hr;

        hr = session.m_spOpenRowset->OpenRowset(NULL, &dbid, NULL,
            GetIID(), (pPropSet) ? 1 : 0, pPropSet,
            (IUnknown**)GetInterfacePtr());
```

If successful, it calls SetupOptionalRowsetInterfaces, a method inherited from TRowset, where it might get additional interface pointers on the rowset object.

```
        if (SUCCEEDED(hr))
        {
            SetupOptionalRowsetInterfaces();
```

It then checks _OutputColumnsClass::HasOutputColumns(), which is inherited from the accessor class. There is no reason for HasOutputColumns not to be true, since you cannot do much with a table if you do not get its rowset. `Bind` is inherited from `CAccessorRowset`. It gives the accessor class the chance to build its accessor handle.

```
    // If we have output columns then bind
    if (_OutputColumnsClass::HasOutputColumns())
        hr = Bind();
}

return hr;
}
```

Once the table is open, you will call the method inherited from the rowset or the accessor to navigate the rows and get the column values.

## COMMANDS

The OLE DB consumer templates come with two command classes: `CCommand` and `CCommandBase`. `CCommandBase` is a base implementation class; you do not use it directly. `CCommand` is the class you actually use. In theory, both classes can be combined into one, but having two classes improves the readability of the code.

Unlike tables, commands have their own OLE DB type. Figure 7-1 summarizes the OLE DB command interfaces. The mandatory interfaces are in bold; the optional interfaces are regular text.

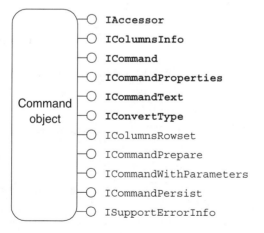

**Figure 7-1** Command Interfaces

`ICommand` is a central interface because it contains the `Execute` function. `ICommandText` and `ICommandProperties` set the command text and the command properties, respectively. `IAccessor` and `ICommandWithParameter` deal with parameters. Finally, `ICommandPrepare` supports command preparation.

CCommandBase keeps a reference on the OLE DB instance through the m_spCommand class member:

```
CComPtr<ICommand>    m_spCommand;
```

In addition, it implements some basic methods, shown in Table 7-1. It also keeps a reference on a parameter accessor with the m_hParameterAccessor class member (more on this in the section on parameters).

## CCommand

CCommand is the class you will use. It is declared as

```
template <class TAccessor = CNoAccessor, class TRowset =CRowset,
   class TMultiple = CNoMultipleResults>
class CCommand :
   public CAccessorRowset<TAccessor, TRowset>,
   public CCommandBase,
   public TMultiple
```

The first two template parameters are similar to the one for CTable. The third template parameter, TMultiple, indicates support for multiple results (more about this in the section on multiple parameters).

**Table 7-1** CCommandBase Methods

| Method Name | Description |
|---|---|
| CreateCommand | Create an OLE DB command object |
| Create | Create an OLE DB command object and set its command text |
| ReleaseCommand | Release the OLE DB command object |
| Prepare | Prepare the command |
| Unprepare | Unprepare the command |
| GetParameterInfo/ SetParameterInfo | Get and set parameter information—not used elsewhere |

Unlike tables, commands do not necessarily return a rowset: Simple commands do not return any result. For example, a command statement such as

```
UPDATE MyTable SET Column1 = 123
```

corresponds to simple commands. Simple commands do not need an accessor or a rowset.

The default template parameter for TRowset is CRowset. CCommand<>, therefore is equivalent to CCommand<CNoAccessor, CRowset>, which is not a valid combination of rowset and accessor. You must to specify the template parameters explicitly. The following shows an example of simple command:

```
CCommand <CNoAccessor, CNoRowset> Command;
hr = Command.Open(Session, UPDATE MYTABLE SET COLUMN1=123);
```

or

```
typedef CCommand <CNoAccessor, CNoRowset> CSimpleCommand;
CSimpleCommand Command2;
hr = Command2.Open(Session, UPDATE MYTABLE SET COLUMN1=123);
```

If the command returns a rowset, you use the template parameters, as in CTable.

## Opening a Command

Opening a command involves six steps:

1. Create the OLE DB command instance.
2. Set the command text.
3. Bind parameters if necessary.
4. Set the command properties.
5. Execute the command.
6. If there is a result, get the corresponding rowset and bind it.

Class CCommand has two Open methods. The first one is declared as

```
HRESULT Open(const CSession& session, LPCTSTR szCommand = NULL,
    DBPROPSET *pPropSet = NULL, LONG* pRowsAffected = NULL,
    REFGUID guidCommand = DBGUID_DEFAULT, bool bBind = true)
```

where

- session represents the session the command belongs to.
- szCommand represents the command text, if any.

- `pPropSet` represents the command and rowset property set.
- `pRowsAffected` receives the number of rows affected by the command.
- `guidCommand` identifies the language of the command text. By default, it is `DBGUID_DEFAULT`, the default text of the provider.
- `bBind` specifies whether to bind after the command is executed. If it is true, as is the usual case, and the inherited accessor supports binding, the command will call `Bind()`.

The second `Open` method is declared as

```
HRESULT Open(DBPROPSET *pPropSet = NULL,
    LONG* pRowsAffected = NULL, bool bBind = true)
```

The parameters have the same meaning as in the first `Open` method.

Although they have the same name, the two `Open` methods are quite different. The first method creates the COM object, sets the command text, and calls the second method. The second method binds the parameters, sets the properties, executes the command, and binds the returned the rowset if necessary. In other words, another name for the first `Open` could be `CreateAndExecute` while the second method could be called `Execute`.

Figure 7-2 illustrates the different steps in opening a command. The white items correspond to code in `CCommand`; the gray items are inherited.

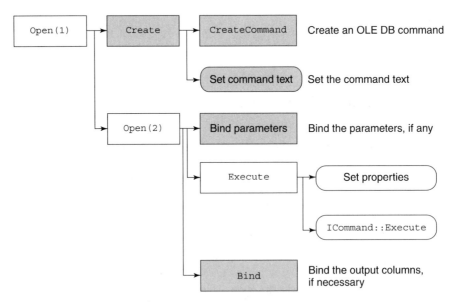

**Figure 7-2** Opening a Command

### Analysis of the First Open Method

The first Open method performs three actions:

- It gets the command text.
- It creates the underlying OLE DB command object.
- It calls the second Open method.

```
// Create a command on the session and execute it
HRESULT Open(const CSession& session, LPCTSTR szCommand = NULL,
   DBPROPSET *pPropSet = NULL, LONG* pRowsAffected = NULL,
   REFGUID guidCommand = DBGUID_DEFAULT, bool bBind = true)
{
   HRESULT hr;
   if (szCommand == NULL)
   {
   hr = _CommandClass::GetDefaultCommand(&szCommand);
   if (FAILED(hr))
   return hr;
   }
   hr = Create(session, szCommand, guidCommand);
   if (FAILED(hr))
      return hr;

   return Open(pPropSet, pRowsAffected, bBind);
}
```

As mentioned before, the Create method is inherited from CCommandBase. It creates the underlying COM object and sets its command text.

### Where Does the Command Text Come From?

If specified by the client, the command text is passed as is to the Create method. Otherwise, the command attempts to get it from _CommandClass::Get DefaultCommand. The global definition of the _CommandClass type is

```
typedef _CNoCommand        CommandClass;
```

As the name suggests, the _CNoCommand class does not have any command text. It is defined as

```
class _CNoCommand
{
public:
   static HRESULT GetDefaultCommand(LPCTSTR* /*ppszCommand*/)
   {
      return S_OK;
   }
};
```

It is possible to override the _CommandClass typedef with a typedef local to a class.

```
#define DEFINE_COMMAND(x, szCommand) \
    typedef x _CommandClass; \
    static HRESULT GetDefaultCommand(LPCTSTR* ppszCommand) \
    { \
        *ppszCommand = szCommand; \
        return S_OK; \
    }
```

In general, the accessor class uses this macro to define the command text.

### Command Dialects

While ODBC drivers support only SQL commands, OLE DB providers can understand command text of several dialects, each of which is identified by a unique GUID. Consumers can specify a dialect through the guidCommand parameter.

Table 7-2 shows the dialect GUIDs defined by OLE DB. Providers that support other dialects define their own GUIDs.

The interesting GUID is DBGUID_DEFAULT. When you pass it as a dialect GUID, you instruct the provider to interpret the command text with its default dialect. If the provider supports only SQL, DBGUID_DEFAULT is equivalent to DBGUID_SQL. Similarly, if the provider supports only MDX, DBGUID_DEFAULT is equivalent to DBGUID_MDX. In other words, DBGUID_DEFAULT is safe for providers that support only one dialect. However, it can lead to surprises with providers that support several. For example, if a provider supports both SQL and MDX, you need to know which dialect is the default. In such a case, it is always safer to designate the dialect explicitly.

**Table 7-2** Dialect GUIDs

| Dialect GUID | Description |
|---|---|
| DBGUID_SQL | Command uses the SQL dialect to interpret the command text |
| DBGUID_MDX | Command uses the MDX dialect to interpret the command text (see Chapter 15) |
| MDGUID_MDX | Synonymous to DBGUID_MDX |
| DBGUID_DEFAULT | Command uses its default dialect to interpret the command text |

By default, Open uses DBGUID_DEFAULT as a dialect GUID:

```
HRESULT Open(const CSession& session, LPCTSTR szCommand = NULL,
   DBPROPSET *pPropSet = NULL, LONG* pRowsAffected = NULL,
   REFGUID guidCommand = DBGUID_DEFAULT, bool bBind = true)
```

Until now all the examples used the default dialect. Nevertheless, you can specify the dialect explicitly as follows:

```
CCommand <CAccessor<CMyAccessor> > MyCommand;
hr = MyCommand.Open(Session, CommandText, NULL, NULL,
   DBGUID_MDX);
```

## Analysis of the Second Open Method

The second Open method performs three sequential tasks:

1. It binds parameters, if any.

2. It executes the command and gets the rowset result, if any.

3. It binds the rowset columns, if necessary.

Its implementation is as follows.

```
// Used if you have previously created the command
HRESULT Open(DBPROPSET *pPropSet = NULL,
   LONG* pRowsAffected = NULL, bool bBind = true)
{
   HRESULT      hr;
   DBPARAMS     params;
   DBPARAMS     *pParams;

   // Bind the parameters if we have some
   if (_ParamClass::HasParameters())
   {
      hr = BindParameters(&m_hParameterAccessor, m_spCommand,
         &params.pData);
      if (FAILED(hr))
         return hr;

      // Setup the DBPARAMS structure
      params.cParamSets = 1;
      params.hAccessor = m_hParameterAccessor;
      pParams = &params;
   }
   else
      pParams = NULL;

   hr = Execute(GetInterfacePtr(), pParams, pPropSet,
      pRowsAffected);
```

```
      if (FAILED(hr))
         return hr;

      // Only bind if we have been asked to and we have output
      // columns
      if (bBind && _OutputColumnsClass::HasOutputColumns())
         return Bind();
      else
         return hr;
}
```

This code can be confusing at first because it uses two types: _ParamClass and _OutputColumnsClass. _ParamClass specifies the level of parameter support. By default, it is the global definition

```
typedef _CNoParameters        ParamClass;
```

As the name suggests, _CNoParameters specifies support for no parameters.

```
class _CNoParameters
{
public:
   static bool HasParameters()
   {
      return false;
   }
   static HRESULT _GetParamEntries(ULONG*, DBBINDING*, BYTE*
      pBuffer = NULL)
   {
      pBuffer;
      return E_FAIL;
   }
};
```

The section on parameters will explain how to add parameter support.

_OutputColumnsClass specifies the level of support for output columns. By default, it has this global definition:

```
typedef _CNoOutputColumns     OutputColumnsClass;
```

_CNoOutputColumns specifies no support for output columns.

```
class _CNoOutputColumns
{
public:
   static bool HasOutputColumns()
   {
      return false;
   }
```

```
      static ULONG _GetNumAccessors()
      {
          return 0;
      }
      static HRESULT _GetBindEntries(ULONG*, DBBINDING*, ULONG,
          bool*, BYTE* pBuffer = NULL)
      {
          pBuffer;
          return E_FAIL;
      }
};
```

Accessors that have output columns redefine the _OutputColumnsClass type.

## Closing a Command

An instance of CCommand is the combination of two OLE DB objects: command and rowset. Thus, it has two Close methods:

- ReleaseCommand releases only the command object.
- Close closes only the rowset object, not the command object. It is inherited from CAccessorRowset.

### Releasing the Command Object

The destructor of CCommandBase closes the command object:

```
~CCommandBase()
{
    ReleaseCommand();
}
```

Since CCommand inherits from CCommandBase, any instance of it will close the OLE DB command object at destruction time. In addition, CreateCommand calls ReleaseCommand, so the first Open method calls ReleaseCommand as well. In short, there is no need for the programmer to call ReleaseCommand explicitly.

ReleaseCommand performs two actions: First, it releases the parameter accessor:

```
void ReleaseCommand()
{
    // Release the parameter accessor if necessary,
    // before releasing the command
    if (m_hParameterAccessor != NULL)
    {
```

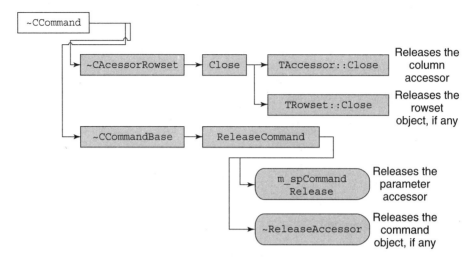

**Figure 7-3** CCommand Destructor

```
        CComPtr<IAccessor> spAccessor;
        HRESULT hr = m_spCommand->QueryInterface(&spAccessor);
        if (SUCCEEDED(hr))
        {
            spAccessor->ReleaseAccessor(m_hParameterAccessor,NULL);
            m_hParameterAccessor = NULL;
        }
    }
```

Second, it releases the interface pointer to the OLE DB command object:

```
    m_spCommand.Release();
}
```

Figure 7-3 illustrates the behavior of the destructor of CCommand.

### Summary of the Open and Close Methods

Table 7-3 summarizes the Open methods and their Close counterparts.

## Preparing a Command

On the provider side, opening an OLE DB command involves three steps:

**1.** The command gets the command text. At this stage, the command text can have syntax or semantic errors.

**Table 7-3** Open and Close Methods

| Open | Close |
|------|-------|
| CreateCommand | ReleaseCommand |
| Create | ReleaseCommand |
| BindParameters | ReleaseAccessor in ReleaseCommand |
| Open(const CSession& session, . . .) | Close and ReleaseCommand |
| Open(DBPROPSET *pPropSet, . . .) | Close |

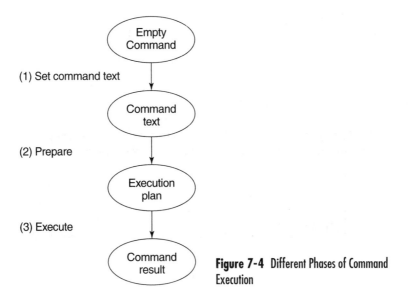

**Figure 7-4** Different Phases of Command Execution

2. The command parses the command texts and checks the syntax and semantics. If successful, the command builds an *execution plan*, which includes all the necessary information to execute the command in an optimal way. For example, it includes the indexes to use. This is the command preparation phase.

3. The command executes and eventually produces some result.

Figure 7-4 summarizes the command execution phases.

The execution plan can become quite complex. OLE DB does not give access to the execution plan but only the control over creating or deleting it. The SQL

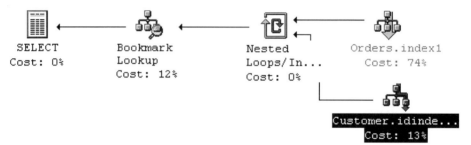

**Figure 7-5** An Execution Plan in SQL Server Query Analyzer

Server Query Analyzer tool that comes with SQL server 7.0 and later versions gives a good idea of what an execution plan is. Figure 7-5 shows an execution plan in SQL Server Query Analyzer.

Each step just discussed has a corresponding CCommand method:

- Create creates the OLE DB command object and performs step 1.
- Prepare performs step 2.
- Execute performs step 3.

If Prepare is not called before Execute, the provider will prepare the command before executing it. In other words, step 2 can be implicit.

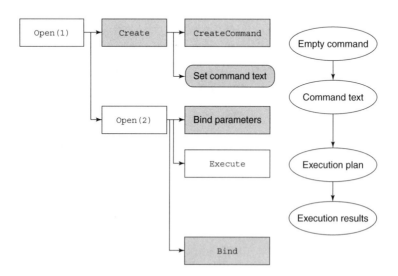

**Figure 7-6** Execution without Preparation

If we go back to the diagram of the Open method, we get Figure 7-6, in which the preparation is implicit. However, if we call Prepare, the preparation is explicit, as shown in Figure 7-7.

In the latter figure, the command is executed one time. The idea behind command preparation is that you can execute the command many times after one call to Prepare. This way, the cost of preparation is one time only and each subsequent execution is faster than an execution without Prepare.

The following example demonstrates the different steps to prepare a command and execute it several times.

```
CCommand <CNoAccessor, CNoRowset> Command;
Command.Create (MySession, CommandText);
Command.Prepare ();
Command.Open ();
Command.Open ();
```

If the command returns a rowset, it is necessary to call Close to release the rowset before executing the command again:

```
CCommand <CMyAccessor, CRowset> Command;
Command.Create (MySession, CommandText);
Command.Prepare ();
Command.Open ();
Command.Close ();
Command.Open ();
```

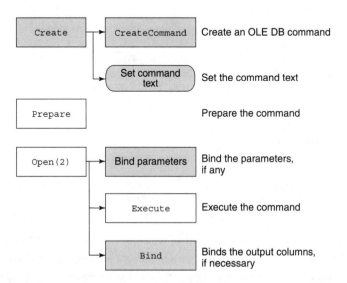

**Figure 7-7** Execution with Preparation

## Commands with Parameters

Providers can support commands with parameters, but they are not required to do so. The ICommandWithParameter is an optional interface.

Providers such as SQL server accept command texts like

```
SELECT * FROM MyTable where column = ?
```

In this case, the actual value of the parameter comes dynamically from the consumer code. An easy way to use commands with parameters is to define a parameter accessor (see Chapter 9). For example, an accessor class for the previous command text might be

```
CMyAccessor
{
    public:
        int m_Column;
    BEGIN_PARAM_MAP(CMyAccessor)
        COLUMN_ENTRY(1, m_Column)
    END_PARAM_MAP(CMyAccessor)
};
```

Commands with parameters work well with command preparation. They are also very useful in executing stored procedures.

While the BEGIN_PARAM_MAP macro is simple to use, it can be difficult to understand. It is defined as

```
#define BEGIN_PARAM_MAP(x) \
    public: \
    typedef x _classtype; \
    typedef x _ParamClass; \
    static bool HasParameters() { return true; } \
    static HRESULT _GetParamEntries(ULONG* pColumns, \
        DBBINDING *pBinding, BYTE* pBuffer = NULL) \
    { \
        ATLASSERT(pColumns != NULL); \
        DBPARAMIO eParamIO = DBPARAMIO_INPUT; \
        int nColumns = 0; \
        pBuffer;
```

The key instruction is

```
    typedef x _ParamClass; \
```

The global _ParamClass declaration is overridden by a local type declaration. Since x is the current class, _ParamClass becomes the current class. The rest is the implementation of the required methods HasParameters and GetParam Entries.

## Commands with Multiple Results

Until now, a command returned zero or one rowset. However, it can return more than one rowset, as in the following code. The first rowset corresponds to `Column1 = 1`; the second corresponds to `Column1 = 2`.

```
SELECT * FROM TableName WHERE Column1 = 1 ;SELECT * FROM
    TableName WHERE Column1 = 2
```

### Using Multiple Results

When a command returns several rowsets, the OLE DB approach is to iterate on the rowset list. When you execute the command, the `TRowset` rowset interface pointer points to the first rowset returned by the command. When you want a second rowset, you call `GetNextResult` and the rowset points to the second rowset, and so forth (see Figure 7-8).

The first step is to use `CMultipleResults` as the `TMultiple` template parameter. For example, you might declare a variable such as

```
CCommand<CAccessor<CTableNameAccessor>, CRowset,
    CMultipleResults> Command;
```

A command with multiple results is similar to one with one result. After opening the command, the rowset will point to the first rowset. Calling `GetNext Result` releases the current rowset and gets the next one. When there are

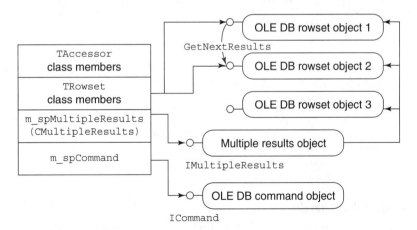

**Figure 7-8** Multiple Results

no rowsets left, GetNextResult returns DB_S_NORESULT. Note that this is a "success" code. The following example illustrates how to use multiple results.

```
hr = Command.Open(Session, _T("SELECT  * FROM TableName WHERE \
    Column1 = 1 ; SELECT  * FROM TableName WHERE Column1 = 2"));
// Navigate the first rowset
Command.MoveFirst();
Command.MoveNext();
// Get the next rowset
hr = Command.GetNextResult(NULL);
// do something
// iterate on the remaining rowsets
while (Command.GetNextResult(NULL) == S_OK)
{
    // do something
}
```

There is a glitch, however: When you call Close, it will release the rowset object but not the multiple results object. In addition, GetMultiplePtr Address, defined as

```
IMultipleResults** GetMultiplePtrAddress()
    { return &m_spMultipleResults.p; }
```

uses &m_spMultipleResults.p instead of &m_spMultipleResults. The difference is that it is valid even if m_spMultipleResults is non-NULL. As a result, there is no warning if you get an interface pointer to a new multiple results object before releasing the old one.

For example, the following code sample leaks memory:

```
CCommand<CAccessor<CTableNameAccessor>, CRowset,
    CMultipleResults> Command;
hr = Command.Open(Session, _T("SELECT  * FROM TableName WHERE \
    Column1 = 1 ; SELECT  * FROM TableName WHERE Column1 = 2"));
Command.Close();
Command.Open();
```

To avoid this, you need to explicitly release the interface pointer to the multiple object before reopening the command:

```
sor<CTableNameAccessor>, CRowset, CMultipleResults> Command;
hr = Command.Open(Session, _T("SELECT  * FROM TableName WHERE \
    Column1 = 1 ; SELECT  * FROM TableName WHERE Column1 = 2"));
Command.Close();
Command.m_spMultipleResults.Release();
Command.Open();
```

### Inside Multiple Results

The default multiple result support class is CNoMultipleResults. It is defined as

```
class CNoMultipleResults
{
public:
    bool UseMultipleResults() { return false; }
    IMultipleResults** GetMultiplePtrAddress() { return NULL; }
    IMultipleResults* GetMultiplePtr() { return NULL; }
};
```

By contrast, CMultipleResults is defined as

```
class CMultipleResults
{
public:
    bool UseMultipleResults() { return true; }
    IMultipleResults** GetMultiplePtrAddress()
    { return &m_spMultipleResults.p; }
    IMultipleResults* GetMultiplePtr()
    { return m_spMultipleResults; }

    CComPtr<IMultipleResults> m_spMultipleResults;
};
```

Having CMultipleResults, instead of the default CNoMultipleResults, as the template parameter has several consequences. First, UseMultipleResults returns true instead of false for CNoMultipleResults. Second, the command inherits the m_spMultipleResults class member, which is an interface pointer to a multiple results COM object. This object manages the list of returned rowsets. Inside the Execute method, the command checks whether it supports multiple parameters. If so, it attempts to set the m_spMultipleResults class member and get the first rowset. Otherwise, it gets the eventual rowset directly:

```
if (UseMultipleResults())
{
    hr = m_spCommand->Execute(NULL, IID_IMultipleResults,pParams,
        pAffected, (IUnknown**)GetMultiplePtrAddress());

    if (SUCCEEDED(hr))
    {
        hr = GetNextResult(pAffected, false);
    }
    else
    {
        // If we can't get IMultipleResults then just try to get
        // IRowset
        hr = m_spCommand->Execute(NULL, IID_IRowset, pParams,
            pAffected, (IUnknown**)GetInterfacePtr());
    }
}
else
{
```

```
hr = m_spCommand->Execute(NULL, GetIID(), pParams, pAffected,
    (IUnknown**)ppRowset);
if (SUCCEEDED(hr))
    SetupOptionalRowsetInterfaces();
```

# COMMAND EXTENSIONS

The OLE DB extensions provide one extension for `CCommand`: `CCommandEx`, which introduces two extensions:

- Support for several parameter accessors per class
- Support for multiple parameter sets

The following two sections explain these extensions.

## Commands with Multiple Parameter Accessors

Until now, we were using at most one parameter accessor per class. However, there are times when this is not practical. Consider the following example of a "customer" table with at least two columns:

- `Id` represents some kind of internal database identifier.
- `name` represents the name of the customer.

In some cases, you will want to retrieve the customer information given the `Id`. In other cases, you will want to do it by `name`.

The first solution is to create one accessor class per access. In this example, we might start by declaring a class containing only the class members:

```
class CustomersClassMembers
{
public:
    int m_Id;
    WCHAR m_Name [33];
};
```

The first accessor class retrieves customers by `Id`:

```
class CCustomerAccessorById: public CustomersClassMembers
{
public:

BEGIN_COLUMN_MAP(CCustomerAccessorById)
    COLUMN_ENTRY(1, m_Id)
    COLUMN_ENTRY(2, m_Name)
END_COLUMN_MAP()
```

```
BEGIN_PARAM_MAP(CCustomerAccessorById)
   COLUMN_ENTRY(1, m_Id)
END_PARAM_MAP()
DEFINE_COMMAND(CCustomerAccessorById, _T(" \
   SELECT \
      Id, \
      Name \
      FROM Customer WHERE Id = ?"))
};
```

DEFINE_COMMAND defines a command with Id as a parameter (" WHERE Id = ?").
BEGIN_PARAM_MAP defines a parameter map with m_Id as a unique parameter.
   We might then define a class CCustomerById:

```
class CCustomerById : public CCommand<CAccessor<
   CCustomerAccessorById> >
```

Similarly, a second accessor class accesses customers by name:

```
class CCustomerAccessorByName: public CustomersClassMembers
{
public:

BEGIN_COLUMN_MAP(CCustomerAccessorByName)
   COLUMN_ENTRY(1, m_Id)
   COLUMN_ENTRY(2, m_Name)
END_COLUMN_MAP()

BEGIN_PARAM_MAP(CCustomerAccessorByName)
   COLUMN_ENTRY(1, m_Name)
END_PARAM_MAP()
DEFINE_COMMAND(CCustomerAccessorByName, _T(" \
   SELECT \
      Id, \
      Name \
      FROM Customer WHERE Name = ?"))
};
```

And we might define a class CCustomerByName.
   The advantage of this method is that it is very readable and therefore easy to
debug. However, it requires many classes to perform a relatively simple task.
   There are many other ways to avoid having multiple accessor classes—
for example, using a dynamic accessor instead of a static accessor (dynamic
accessors are explained in Chapter 9). The OLE DB extensions solution is to
regroup the parameter accessor and the command text into local classes—
CAccessbyIdAccess and CAccessbyNameAccess in this example:

```
class CCustomerMultiAccessor
{
public:

    int m_Id;
    WCHAR m_Name [33];

BEGIN_COLUMN_MAP(CCustomerMultiAccessor)
    COLUMN_ENTRY(1, m_Id)
    COLUMN_ENTRY(2, m_Name)
END_COLUMN_MAP()

    class CAccessbyIdAccess: public CAccessorBase
    {
    public:
        BEGIN_PARAM_MAP_EX(CAccessbyIdAccess,
            CCustomerMultiAccessor)
            COLUMN_ENTRY(1, m_Id)
        END_PARAM_MAP()
        DEFINE_COMMAND(CAccessbyIdAccess, _T(" \
            SELECT \
            Id, \
            Name  \
            FROM Customer WHERE Id = ?"))
    };
    CAccessbyIdAccess AccessbyId;
    class CAccessbyNameAccess: public CAccessorBase
    {
    public:
        BEGIN_PARAM_MAP_EX(CAccessbyNameAccess,
            CCustomerMultiAccessor)
            COLUMN_ENTRY(1, m_Name)
        END_PARAM_MAP()
        DEFINE_COMMAND(CAccessbyNameAccess, _T(" \
            SELECT \
            Id, \
            Name  \
            FROM Customer WHERE Name = ?"))
    };
    CAccessbyNameAccess AccessbyName;
};
```

The local class defines the parameter accessor and the command text, but has no class member itself. The trick is to access the class member of the parent class. The BEGIN_PARAM_MAP_EX macro accepts two parameters; the first is the type of the local class and the second is the type of the parent class:

```
#define BEGIN_PARAM_MAP_EX(internal, external) \
    public: \
    typedef external _classtype; \
```

```
typedef internal _ParamClass; \
static bool HasParameters() { return true; } \
static HRESULT _GetParamEntries(ULONG* pColumns, \
   DBBINDING *pBinding, BYTE* pBuffer = NULL) \
{ \
   ATLASSERT(pColumns != NULL); \
   DBPARAMIO eParamIO = DBPARAMIO_INPUT; \
   int nColumns = 0; \
   pBuffer;
```

Defining the local classes explicitly can still be a burden. The OLE DB extensions provide two macros to automate the process:

- BEGIN_ACCESS starts the declaration of the local class.
- END_ACCESS terminates the declaration and declares the access function.

```
#define BEGIN_ACCESS(_accessname_) \
   class C##_accessname_##Access : public CAccessorBase \
   { \
      public: \
         typedef C##_accessname_##Access _self_;

#define END_ACCESS(_accessname_) \
   }; \
   C##_accessname_##Access _accessname_;
```

Our class then becomes

```
class CCustomerMultiAccessor2
{
public:

   int m_Id;
   WCHAR m_Name [33];

BEGIN_COLUMN_MAP(CCustomerMultiAccessor2)
   COLUMN_ENTRY(1, m_Id)
   COLUMN_ENTRY(2, m_Name)
END_COLUMN_MAP()

   BEGIN_ACCESS(AccessbyId)
      BEGIN_PARAM_MAP_EX(_self_, CCustomerMultiAccessor2)
         COLUMN_ENTRY(1, m_Id)
      END_PARAM_MAP()
      DEFINE_COMMAND(_self_, _T(" \
         SELECT Id, Name FROM Customer WHERE Id = ?"))
   END_ACCESS(AccessbyId)
   BEGIN_ACCESS(AccessbyName)
      BEGIN_PARAM_MAP_EX(_self_, CCustomerMultiAccessor2)
         COLUMN_ENTRY(1, m_Name)
```

```
        END_PARAM_MAP()
        DEFINE_COMMAND(_self_, _T(" \
            SELECT Id, Name FROM Customer WHERE Name = ?"))
    END_ACCESS(AccessbyName)
};
```

CCommandEx has two OpenEx methods that play the same role as the Open methods in CCommand. However, they also accept the type of the class that holds the parameter. When opening the command, it is possible to specify the type of the accessor to use. For example, to open the customer by Id, you write

```
CCommandEx<CAccessor< CCustomerMultiAccessor2> , CRowset> Command;
hr = Command.OpenEx(Session,Command.AccessbyId);
```

## Commands with Multiple Parameter Sets

Until now, commands were executed with one set of parameters. However, OLE DB has room for several parameter sets. In fact, the OLE DB structure that describes the parameter sets is defined as

```
struct DBPARAMS {
    void *        pData;
    ULONG         cParamSets;
    HACCESSOR     hAccessor;
};
```

In this structure, cParamSets represents the number of parameter sets. The OLE DB consumer templates always set this field to 1, but it is possible to set it to a greater value. In this case, the data store will execute the command once per parameter set. For example, if you want to insert a series of rows, the traditional method is to define an accessor class such as

```
class CMyAccessor
{
public:
    TCHAR m_a[11];
    LONG m_b;
BEGIN_PARAM_MAP(CMyAccessor)
    COLUMN_ENTRY(1, m_a)
    COLUMN_ENTRY(2, m_b)
END_PARAM_MAP()

DEFINE_COMMAND(CMyAccessor, _T(" \
    INSERT INTO table1 \
     (a, b) \
    VALUES (?, ?)"))
};
```

The next step is

```
CCommand<CAccessor<CMyAccessor> > Command;
// set m_a and m_b
hr = Command.Open (..);
```

We could repeat this for inserting multiple columns. Note, however, that this method requires a round trip for every inserted row.

The alternative is to define two classes. The first defines the parameters:

```
class CMyAccessor
{
public:
   TCHAR m_a[11];
   LONG m_b;
BEGIN_PARAM_MAP(CMyAccessor)
   COLUMN_ENTRY(1, m_a)
   COLUMN_ENTRY(2, m_b)
END_PARAM_MAP()

DEFINE_COMMAND(CMyAccessor, _T(" \
   INSERT INTO table1 \
   (a, b) \
   VALUES (?, ?)"))
};
```

The second contains an array of parameters:

```
class CMyAccessor
{
public:
   CParameters  parameters [100];

PARAMETER_SET_COUNT(Cdbotable1Accessor, 100)

};
```

The PARAMETER_SET_COUNT macro specifies the number of parameter sets, which is 100 in this example. The idea is to then insert all parameters at once. In fact, this is relatively easy with the CCommandEx class:

```
CCommandEx<CAccessor< CMyAccessor> , CNoRowset> Command;
hr = Command.OpenEx(Session,Command.parameters[0]);
```

## SUMMARY

This chapter introduced tables and commands. Tables are easy to use, but commands offer many options. It is likely that one of the command options will fit your needs.

If you do not want to retrieve data, you already know most of what you need at this point. However, if you want to get data from the data store, it is necessary to understand rowsets and accessors, which are discussed in the next two chapters.

# 8 Rowsets

As we saw in Chapter 7, opening tables and commands in many cases returns a rowset. This chapter on rowsets will accomplish the following:

- Explain why we need a rowset object.
- Explore the different rowset classes.
- Explain bookmarks.
- Describe the rowset properties.
- Give details on the client cursor service component.
- Explain how to find rows in a rowset.

## ROWSET OBJECTS

Conceptually, a *rowset* is a set of *rows*, each of which contains a set of values in *columns* or *fields*. The definition of the columns of a row is the same for each row. In standard C++, a rowset would be just an array of rows. For example, if a row were defined as

```
class MyRow
{
   int value1;
   char value2 [10];
};
```

The corresponding rowset would be defined as

```
typedef MyRow [] MyRowset;
```

With OLE DB, the problem is a little more complex because the rowset data comes from the server but is manipulated by the client. Usually, it is not wise to *systematically* transfer the entire rowset from server to client, as it can contain numerous rows and the client might be interested in only a few of them. Additionally, there is a possibility that the rowset contains too many rows to fit in the the client's memory. For these reasons, a standard C++ array would not be appropriate. As an alternative, OLE DB provides a rowset COM object, which has a mechanism for retrieving only a subset of the rows. For example, OLE DB rowsets can retrieve one or several rows and then scroll from row to row.

Figure 8-1 summarizes the rowset type and its interfaces. The mandatory interfaces are in bold; the optional interfaces are regular text. As you can see, the OLE DB type defines quite a few interfaces. In fact, it supports more interfaces than represented by the figure, which shows only the most significant and organizes them in logical groups. It will take four chapters to cover all the functionality.

This chapter will focus on the first group: row management. This includes how to get and release rows, how to fetch and scroll on them, and how to define and use bookmarks—an efficient way to go to a specific row. The chapter will also explain how to find rows and rowset properties.

Chapter 9 will explore how to get column information and access column values. Chapter 10 will explore how to get and set column values. Finally, Chapter 13 will deal with more advanced concepts, chapters and views.

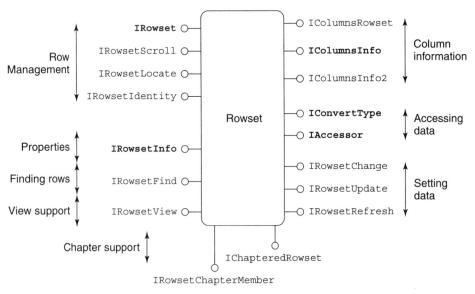

**Figure 8-1** Rowset Type

# ROWSET CLASSES

Before we go further, it is important to understand that rowsets are part of an architecture. With the OLE DB consumer templates, you do not use the rowset classes directly but as a part of a command or a table. For example, you will use a command such as

```
CCommand<CDynamicAccessor, CRowset>
```

or a table such as

```
CTable<CDynamicAccessor, CBulkRowset>
```

Classes `CCommand` and `CTable` do not encapsulate the OLE DB rowset object. Instead, they provide a way to get it. The accessor class and rowset classes (for example, `CDynamicAccessor` and `CRowset`) together encapsulate the OLE DB rowset object: The rowset class deals with rows; the accessor class, with columns. Here we focus on the rowset classes; the next chapter will focus on the accessor classes.

The OLE DB consumer templates provide four rowset classes:

- `CRowset` is the most basic class and in most cases will be sufficient for your needs. Unless specified otherwise, this chapter describes the method of `CRowset`, which is also the default template parameter of `CTable` and `CCommand`. For example, writing

```
CCommand<CDynamicAccessor, CRowset>
```

is equivalent to writing

```
CCommand<CDynamicAccessor>
```

- `CBulkRowset` offers the same functionality as `CRowset`, but provides some optimizations in retrieving several consecutive rows.

- `CArrayRowset<T>` makes possible the transfer of the content of the rows to the client; subsequently it behaves like an array of rows.

- `CNoRowset` should be used when a command does not return a rowset. This class includes just enough functionality to compile as a template parameter. Its functions do nothing.

The OLE DB extensions also offer two new classes:

- `CRowsetEx` offers supports for properties and OLE DB chapters. Chapters, discussed in Chapter 13, represent a group of rows in a rowset.

- CRowsetFind implements find operations. This chapter will present find operations in a later section.

## ROWSETS AND ROWS

An OLE DB rowset is a COM object that contains rows. You might imagine that a row is a COM object as well, but, this is not the case for tabular providers. Although OLE DB defines a row COM object, rowsets other than hierarchical providers (see Chapter 16) do not use it. They use a different mechanism, for two reasons. First, getting rows should be fast even if there are many rows; a COM object is typically too slow for this. Second, the lifetime of a row is included in the lifetime of the rowset; in other words, a rowset releases all its rows at destruction time. Since a COM object controls its lifetime, a row implemented as a COM object could stay alive after the rowset object had been destroyed.

Rows are defined by a handle of type HROW:

```
typedef ULONG HROW;
```

Like COM objects, rows have a reference count that can be incremented and decremented. At the raw OLE DB level, the IRowset interface has methods to increment and decrement the reference count associated with a row handle:

```
virtual HRESULT STDMETHODCALLTYPE AddRefRows(
    ULONG cRows,
    const HROW rghRows[ ],
    ULONG rgRefCounts[ ],
    DBROWSTATUS rgRowStatus[ ]) = 0;
virtual HRESULT STDMETHODCALLTYPE ReleaseRows(
    ULONG cRows,
    const HROW rghRows[ ],
    DBROWOPTIONS rgRowOptions[ ],
    ULONG rgRefCounts[ ],
    DBROWSTATUS  rgRowStatus[ ]) = 0;
```

At destruction time, a rowset object releases all its row handles regardless of their reference count. Conversely, a row with a reference count greater than 1 will not prevent the destruction of the associated rowset. In a sense, rows are second-class COM citizens.

### Row Management

Dealing with row handles is not necessarily simple. Consequently, the OLE DB consumer templates classes internally hold a row handle, which they use each time you perform an operation that requires one, such as getting column values.

I call the corresponding row the *current row*; however, the rowset class can also hold additional row handles for efficiency. I call all of these rows the *active rows*. Evidently, the current row is an active row. Two functions manage the row reference counts of the active rows:

```
HRESULT AddRefRows()
```

increments the reference count of all active rows;

```
HRESULT ReleaseRows()
```

decrements them.

The OLE DB consumer templates manage the row reference count, so the programmer does not have to worry about it.


## Row Count and Position

The most natural question about a rowset is how many rows it holds. The OLE DB answer to this question is not straightforward.

First, OLE DB knows only an *approximate number* of rows. Indeed, it is possible that somebody is deleting and inserting rows while you traverse the rowset. Imagine, for example, that you open a table that contains 100 rows. If you request the number of rows, the data store should answer 100, but as you start fetching rows, somebody inserts a new one, making the row count 101. Thus, when you reach row 100 there will still be one more to read.

Second, this feature is buried in another more complex method:

```
HRESULT GetApproximatePosition(const CBookmarkBase* pBookmark,
    ULONG* pPosition, ULONG* pcRows)
```

For now, we will ignore the first two parameters and set them to NULL. The third parameter, pcRows, holds a pointer to the number of rows.

To get the number of rows, write

```
CRowset MyRowset;
ULONG NumberOfRows;
hr = MyRowset.GetApproximatePosition(NULL, NULL, &NumberOfRows);
```

It is also possible to move to a given ratio of the rowset with the following method:

```
HRESULT MoveToRatio(ULONG nNumerator, ULONG nDenominator,
    bool bForward = true)
```

where nNumerator/nDenominator represents the ratio where the current row should go. In other words, the index of the current row becomes approximately

```
CurrentRowIndex = NumberOfRows * nNumerator / nDenominator
```

bForward specifies whether to fetch forward or backward.

The following example shows how to go to the row on the first quarter, on the second decile, and on a specific row index:

```
CRowsetMyRowset
MyRowset.MoveToRatio(1, 4)
MyRowset.MoveToRatio(2, 10)
ULONG RowCount;
GetApproximatePosition(NULL, NULL, &NumberOfRows);
MyRowset.MoveToRatio(SpecificRowIndex, NumberOfRows);
```

## Cursor Movement

OLE DB rowsets define two kinds of cursor movement: *fetching* and *scrolling*. Fetching moves the row cursor and gets rows handles; scrolling moves the cursor without getting row handles. The OLE DB consumer templates use both movements.

All rowsets can fetch and scroll forward, but not all can fetch or scroll backward. Table 8-1 summarizes the two properties that specify the backward capabilities. CRowset and CBulkRowset define five cursor movement methods, summarized in Table 8-2. HRESULT MoveNext(LONG lSkip, bool bForward) is the most interesting method because it calls the actual implementation; other cursor movements call it.

bForward specifies whether to fetch forward or backward. It should be negative only if the DBPROP_CANFETCHBACKWARDS property is true. lSkip represents the algebraic number of rows to scroll before fetching. If it is zero,

**Table 8-1** Backward Properties

| Property | Type | Description |
| --- | --- | --- |
| DBPROP_CANFETCHBACKWARDS | Boolean | Specifies whether a rowset can fetch backward |
| DBPROP_CANSCROLLBACKWARDS | Boolean | Specifies whether a rowset can scroll backward |

**Table 8-2** Cursor Movements

| Method | Description |
| --- | --- |
| HRESULT MovePrev() | Moves to the previous row; if already at the first row, stays at the first row |
| HRESULT MoveNext() | Moves to the next row; if already at the last row, stays at the last row |
| HRESULT MoveNext(LONG lSkip, bool bForward) | Moves to the next row |
| HRESULT MoveFirst() | Moves to the first row |
| HRESULT MoveLast() | Moves to the last row |

MoveNext just fetches the next row; if it is positive, MoveNext scrolls forward lSkip rows and then fetches the next row; if it is negative, MoveNext scrolls backward and then fetches the next row. Therefore, lSkip should be negative only if the DBPROP_CANSCROLLBACKWARDS property is true.

If a rowset is at a given row index, i, what will the row index be after a call to MoveNext? The simplest way to answer this is to imagine that the cursor is *between* rows: First, it is shifted by lSkip rows during the scroll operation. Then, if bForward is true, it moves one row forward. Otherwise, it moves one row backward. The new row stays between the cursor before and after the fetch.

The following scenario will help us understand the parameters of MoveNext.

1. The rowset is created. The cursor is before the first row (Figure 8-2).

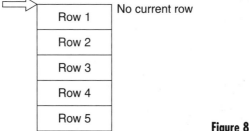

Figure 8-2 Before Fetching

2. During the call to MoveFirst, the cursor moves between the first and second rows, which means that the rowset holds the value of the first row (Figure 8-3).

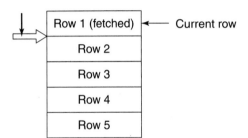

**Figure 8-3** After `MoveFirst()`

3. During a call to `MoveNext (0, true)`, the cursor moves between the second and third rows. Consequently, the rowset holds the values of the second row (Figure 8-4).

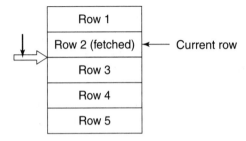

**Figure 8-4** After Another `MoveNext()`

4. During a call to `MoveNext (1, true)`, the cursor scrolls between the third and fourth rows because of the scroll and then between the fourth and fifth rows because of the fetch. Consequently, the rowset holds the value of the fourth row (Figure 8-5).

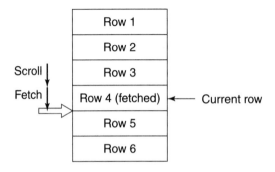

**Figure 8-5** After `MoveNext(1, true)`

**5.** During a call to MoveNext (0, false), the cursor moves between the third and fourth rows. Consequently, the rowset holds the value of the fourth row (Figure 8-6).

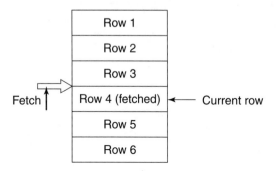

**Figure 8-6** After MoveNext(0, false)

**6.** During a call to MoveNext (1, false), the cursor first scrolls one row backward and then fetches one row backward. Consequently, the rowset holds the value of the fourth row (Figure 8-7).

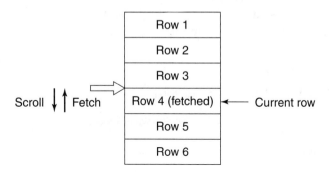

**Figure 8-7** After Another MoveNext(1, false)

Therefore, the row index after the call to MoveNext() depends on the value of bForward during the previous call to MoveNext().

```
if (bForward)
{
    if (bPreviousForward)
        NewRowIndex = PreviousRowIndex + lSkip + 1;
    else
        NewRowIndex = PreviousRowIndex + lSkip;
}
```

```
else
{
   if (bPreviousForward)
      NewRowIndex = PreviousRowIndex + lSkip;
   else
      NewRowIndex = PreviousRowIndex + lSkip - 1;
}
```

MoveNext() is defined simply as

```
HRESULT MoveNext()
{
   return MoveNext(0, true);
}
```

MovePrev is defined as

```
HRESULT MovePrev()
{
   return MoveNext(-2, true);
}
```

Thus, it requires the DBPROP_CANSCROLLBACKWARDS property to be true.

MoveFirst and MoveLast internally call IRowset::RestartPosition(). This method should succeed but can be slow. The DBPROP_QUICKRESTART property indicates if RestartPosition should be quick or not.

MoveLast also uses negative scrolling. Table 8-3 summarizes the different methods and their requirements.

**Table 8-3** Cursor Movement Methods and Requirements

| Method | Requirements |
| --- | --- |
| HRESULT MoveNext() | None |
| HRESULT MovePrev() | DBPROP_CANSCROLLBACKWARDS must be true |
| HRESULT MoveNext(LONG lSkip, bool bForward) | DBPROP_CANSCROLLBACKWARDS is true if lSkip is less than zero |
| | DBPROP_CANFETCHBACKWARDS must be true if bForward is false |
| HRESULT MoveFirst() | DBPROP_QUICKRESTART should be true for good performance |
| HRESULT MoveLast() | DBPROP_QUICKRESTART should be true for good performance |
| | DBPROP_CANSCROLLBACKWARDS must be true |

## Row Identity

As you go through the list of rows, it is important to know what they correspond to. In particular, it is essential to know whether two row handles correspond to the same actual row. If they are binary equal, they do. However, the reverse is not true: It is possible to have two distinct row handles that correspond to the same row in the same way two distinct file handles can refer to the same file.

To compare row handles, use this function:

```
HRESULT IsSameRow(HROW hRow) const
```

IsSameRow returns S_TRUE if hRow relates to the current row and S_FALSE if not. This comparison is valid only if the row handles come from the same rowset.

# BOOKMARKS

Usually when you take a break from your reading, you use a bookmark to know where to resume. On top of being easy to use, bookmarks offer the benefit of returning immediately to a page: There is no need to poke around to find the page. Like books, rowsets use bookmarks as a convenient way to return quickly to a row.

Before you go further, it is important to understand the difference between a row handle, a row index, and a bookmark. They all refer to a given row, but they differ in how you use them.

A row handle is used to identify a row while a bookmark is used to get to a row quickly and so contains the information needed to do this. A row handle, on the other hand, does not necessarily have information to get to a given row quickly. Row handles and bookmarks differ in their internal structures. An OLE DB bookmark is a variable-length opaque binary value, which you should not try to interpret. A row handle is a 4-byte structure. OLE DB does not have any specific type of row index—it is just the position of the row in the rowset. Row handles sometimes match the row index, but you should not count on it.

Table 8-4 summarizes the differences between row handles, bookmarks, and row indexes.

**Table 8-4** Row Handles, Row Indexes, and Bookmarks

| Characteristic | Row Handle | Row Index | Bookmark |
|---|---|---|---|
| Can get you quickly to a row | No | No | Yes |
| Size | 4 bytes | 4 bytes | Varies |
| Number of open items | Defined by DBPROP_MAXOPENROWS | No limit | No limit |
| Opaque | Yes | No | Yes |

Not all rowsets support bookmarks. The DBPROP_BOOKMARKS rowset property specifies bookmark support with a TRUE value (supported) and a FALSE value (not supported).

A bookmark is defined by a length and a buffer containing the binary value. The OLE DB templates come with two bookmark classes:

- CBookmarkBase, an implementation class used as a method argument in the rowset classes. You will not use this class directly.

- CBookmark, the class you will use.

CBookmark is defined as

```
template < ULONG nSize = 0 >
class CBookmark : public CBookmarkBase
```

where nSize represents the bookmark size in bytes. For example, to declare a bookmark of size 4, write

```
CBookmark<4> MyBookmark;
```

CBookmark has a template specialization defined as follows:

```
template < >
class CBookmark< 0 > : public CBookmarkBase
```

CBookmark<0> is used when the size of the bookmark is not fixed to allocate the buffer dynamically. You can use it in two ways: you pass the length of the buffer at construction time,

```
UINT Size;
CBookmark<> MyBookmark (Size);
```

or you set the buffer directly:

```
CBookmark<> MyBookmark;
BYTE* Bytes = new BYTE[Size];
MyBookmark.SetBookmark(Size, Bytes);
```

In either case, CBookmark manages the memory buffer.

Rowset classes allow you to get to a given row quickly with the MoveToBookmark method:

```
HRESULT MoveToBookmark(const CBookmarkBase& bookmark, LONG lSkip = 0)
```

which will get you to the row at offset lSkip of the row specified by bookmark. For example, if lSkip is zero, MoveToBookmark will go to the row specified by bookmark; if it is 1, MoveToBookmark will go one row after bookmark; and if it is −1, MoveToBookmark will go one row before bookmark.

## Bookmark Types

OLE DB defines numeric bookmark and key value bookmark types.

*Numeric bookmarks* are based on the row index or some other row identifier. This does not mean that the actual value of the bookmark is the row index but only that the bookmark uses the row index to compute its value. The length of the bookmark depends on the underlying database. In many cases, it will be 4 bytes but this can vary. Because it is based on the row position and not the row content, the bookmark will direct you to the same row even if the content has changed.

*Key value bookmarks* are based on a combination of column values that uniquely identifies a row. Obviously, a primary key is a good candidate for this. Key value bookmarks are possible only when a column combination can uniquely identify rows.

Do not attempt to interpret the content of a key value bookmark. Even though it might be possible to recognize the column values from the bookmark buffer, there is no guarantee that the provider will keep the same bookmark format.

Since a key value bookmark is based on column values, it might become invalid if some column values change. Therefore, it is recommended that you free the bookmark when you change column values and eventually get it back from the rowset.

The DBPROP_BOOKMARKTYPE rowset property indicates which bookmark type should be used: It can be one of the values DBPROPVAL_BMK_NUMERIC and DBPROPVAL_BMK_KEY. If you do not specify DBPROP_BOOKMARKTYPE, the OLE DB provider will choose the most appropriate type for you.

### Comparison of Bookmarks

The rows in the rowset are laid out in a certain order. In other words, a given row is either before or after another row. Bookmark comparison allows you to determine if a row associated with a given bookmark is before, after, or identical to another row associated with another bookmark.

The Compare method allows you to compare two bookmarks. It is defined as follows:

```
HRESULT Compare(const CBookmarkBase& bookmark1, const CBookmarkBase&
bookmark2, DBCOMPARE* pComparison) const
```

pComparison represents the result of the comparison, which can be one of the values in Table 8-5. In the case of DBCOMPARE_NE, the rowset knows that the bookmarks refer to distinct rows, but it is unable to determine which one comes first.

**Table 8-5** DBCOMPARE Values

| Symbol | Description |
|---|---|
| DBCOMPARE_LT | bookmark1 is before bookmark2 |
| DBCOMPARE_EQ | bookmark1 is equal to bookmark2 |
| DBCOMPARE_GT | bookmark1 is after bookmark2 |
| DBCOMPARE_NE | bookmark1 is not equal to bookmark2; rowset is unable to say which bookmark comes first |
| DBCOMPARE_NOTCOMPARABLE | bookmark1 and bookmark2 are not comparable; i.e., the rowset is unable to say anything about the relative position of the bookmarks. This can happen when one of the bookmarks is invalid |

**Table 8-6** DBPROP_ORDEREDBOOKMARKS Values

| Value of DBPROP_ORDEREDBOOKMARKS | Possible Values for Comparison of Valid Bookmarks |
|---|---|
| TRUE | DBCOMPARE_LT, DBCOMPARE_EQ, DBCOMPARE_GT |
| FALSE | DBCOMPARE_EQ, DBCOMPARE_NE |

You can fine-tune the bookmark comparison capabilities with DBPROP_ORDEREDBOOKMARKS. If this property is set to TRUE, the rowset should always be able to determine the order of two bookmarks, provided that they are valid. If it is set to FALSE, the rowset will only tell you whether the bookmarks are equal. Table 8-6 summarizes the possible values for comparison of valid bookmarks.

To speed up the comparison, it is sometimes possible to evaluate the value (content) of two bookmarks in order to compare them. You should perform bookmark value comparisons with respect to the type of bookmark values. Usually, the type is a sequence of bytes (DBTYPE_BYTES), and the comparison should compare the bytes.

The DBPROP_LITERALBOOKMARKS rowset property determines whether the content of bookmarks can be compared. If the bookmarks are ordered, their content can be compared to determine the relative order. If they are not ordered, their content can be compared only for equality. Table 8-7 summarizes this.

**Table 8-7** `DBPROP_LITERALBOOKMARKS` Values

|  | DBPROP_ORDEREDBOOKMARKS is TRUE | DBPROP_ORDEREDBOOKMARKS is FALSE |
|---|---|---|
| DBPROP_LITERALBOOKMARKS is TRUE | Bookmark values can be compared for equality and order | Bookmark values can be compared for equality only |
| DBPROP_LITERALBOOKMARKS is FALSE | Bookmark values cannot be compared | Bookmark values cannot be compared |

## Bookmark Position

A previous section presented the `GetApproximatePosition` method ignoring the first two parameters. As the name suggests, this method is useful to get the approximate position of a bookmark as shown in the following sample:

```
CRowset MyRowset;
CBookmark<x> MyBookmark;
ULONG BookmarkPosition;
MyRowset.GetApproximatePosition(&MyBookmark, &BookmarkPosition, NULL);
```

This method can be intriguing because it can get the position of a bookmark and the number of rows.

## Standard Bookmarks

OLE DB comes with a bookmark for the first row, a bookmark for the last row, and an invalid bookmark. The first two are self-explanatory. The third, invalid bookmark, represents a bookmark for an invalid row, such as one that has been deleted. A *key value* bookmark can also become invalid if the content of the underlying row has changed and the content bookmark does not correspond to any row.

The length of all standard bookmarks is `STD_BOOKMARKLENGTH`, which is equal to 1 byte:

```
#define STD_BOOKMARKLENGTH 1
```

Table 8-8 contains the values of the standard bookmarks.

**Table 8-8** Standard Bookmarks

| Symbol | Description |
|--------|-------------|
| DBBMK_INVALID | Value of the invalid bookmark |
| DBBMK_FIRST | Value of the first bookmark |
| DBBMK_LAST | Value of the last bookmark |

### Using Standard Bookmarks

Standard bookmarks can be used with content allocated either statically or dynamically. The following code shows how to use standard bookmarks in both cases:

```
CBookmark<STD_BOOKMARKLENGTH> InvalidBookmark;
BYTE byte = DBBMK_INVALID;
memcpy (InvalidBookmark.GetBuffer(), &byte,STD_BOOKMARKLENGTH);

CBookmark<> FirstBookmark;
byte = DBBMK_FIRST;
FirstBookmark.SetBookmark(STD_BOOKMARKLENGTH, &byte);
```

## ROWSET PROPERTIES

Like many OLE DB objects, OLE DB rowsets support properties. However, unlike other objects, it is not possible to change properties once the rowset is created; it is only possible to set them at creation time. Once the rowset is created, the properties can only be read. Getting rowset properties is not implemented in the OLE DB consumer templates classes. You need to use CRowsetEx for this.

### Setting Properties at Creation Time

The rowset properties are passed in the Open method of the command or table. For example, the following code shows how to open a command with properties:

```
CDBPropSet Properties(DBPROPSET_ROWSET);
Properties.AddProperty(DBPROP_CANFETCHBACKWARDS, true);
CCommand<CAccessor<CdboFetchScrollAccessor>, CRowset > MyCommand;
hr = MyCommand.Open(Session, "select * from TableName", &Properties);
```

Open has NULL as a default argument for the properties. Therefore, it is also possible to write

```
hr = MyCommand.Open(Session, "select * from TableName");
```

in which case the rowset will be created with default properties.

Some of the important properties include the COM interfaces that the rowset should support. Usually, these start with DBPROP_IRowset. For example, if you specify DBPROP_IRowsetLocate, the rowset creation will succeed only if the provider can create a rowset that supports the IRowsetLocate interface.

## Getting Properties

Once the rowset is created, CRowsetEx sets the OLE DB properties with two methods:

```
HRESULT GetProperties(ULONG ulPropIDSets, const DBPROPIDSET*
    pPropIDSet, ULONG* pulPropertySets, DBPROPSET** ppPropsets)
```

and

```
HRESULT GetProperty(const GUID& guid, DBPROPID propid, VARIANT*
    pVariant) const
```

GetProperties gets a set of properties, while GetProperty gets only one. The two methods are "regular" property methods (see Chapter 5).

The following sample demonstrates how to use GetProperties and GetProperty.

```
CCommand<CSomeAccessor, CRowsetEx > MyRowset;
// Open MyRowset
CDBPropIDSet PropertiesIDs(DBPROPSET_ROWSET);
PropertiesIDs.AddPropertyID(DBPROP_CANFETCHBACKWARDS);
CDBPropSet Properties[];
ULONG PropertyCount;
MyRowset.GetProperties(1, &PropertiesIDs, &PropertyCount,
    &Properties);
// Use Properties
//Free Properties
CComVariant Variant;
MyRowset.GetProperty(DBPROPSET_ROWSET, DBPROP_CANFETCHBACKWARDS,
    &Variant);
```

# BULK ROWSETS

Imagine that you consume one bottle of water a day. You can buy one bottle per day, every day, or you can buy a six-pack every six days. In other words, you can buy one by one or in bulk. Usually, buying in bulk is cheaper and saves trips to the store. However, there are limits to buying in bulk—for example, not enough storage space.

Rowsets and rows operate somewhat like this. When you retrieve consecutive rows, you have two options.

The first option is to retrieve rows one by one (Figure 8-8). This is the method used by CRowset, which keeps track of a unique row handle defined as

```
HROW                          m_hRow;
```

When you call MoveNext, CRowset releases the current row handle and gets a new one for the next row (Figure 8-9).

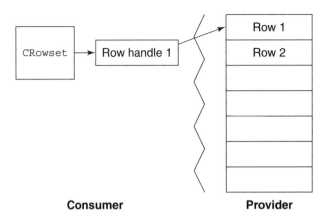

**Figure 8-8** CRowset at Row 1

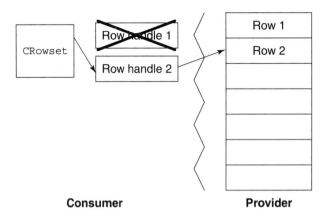

**Figure 8-9** CRowset at Row 2

Alternatively, you can you acquire row handles in bulk using CBulkRowset. CBulkRowset is almost identical to CRowset, with the difference in implementation only. Therefore, it is easy to switch from one to the other.

CBulkRowset keeps track of an array of row handles. It has the following class members:

```
HROW*   m_phRow; // Pointer to array of HROWs for each row in
                 // buffer
ULONG  m_nRows;       // Number of rows that will fit in the buffer
ULONG  m_nCurrentRows; // Number of rows currently in the buffer
ULONG  m_nCurrentRow;  // Index of the current row in the buffer
```

m_phRow is a cache array of m_nRows row handles. It is not always full; it cannot be, for example, when MoveNext reaches the end of the rowset. Only the first m_nCurrentRows items of m_phRow hold a valid row handle. Like CRowset, CBulkRowset has a concept of "current row." The current row handle is at position m_nCurrentRow in the row handle array. That is, the current row handle, m_hRow, is also m_phRow [m_nCurrentRow] .

By default, the number of row handles m_nRows is 10. It is possible to change this by calling

```
void SetRows(ULONG nRows)
```

For convenience, we will assume that m_nRows is 3 in the following paragraphs.

At the first call of MoveNext, CBulkRowset retrieves an array containing the first three row handles and sets the current row handle to the first array item. Figure 8-10 shows CBulkRowset at this stage.

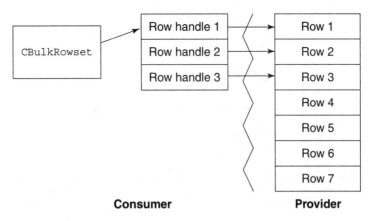

**Figure 8-10** CBulkRowset after the First MoveNext()

During the following calls to MoveNext, CBulkRowset updates the current row handle from the array, provided it is in the cache. This means that CBulkRowset gets the current row handle without requesting anything from the provider, which works fine until the third row handle, as shown in Figure 8-11.

At row 4, CBulkRowset needs to get some new row handles. First, it releases all those contained in the cache. Then it gets row handles for rows 4, 5, and 6 and sets the current row handle to row handle 4. Figure 8-12 shows the CBulkRowset object at this stage.

For simplicity, Figures 8-10, 8-11, and 8-12 show an example with three row handles in the cache. However, CBulkRowset can get any number of row handles. How many should you choose?

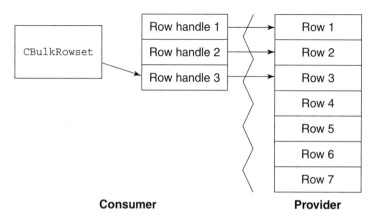

**Figure 8-11** CBulkRowset at Row 3

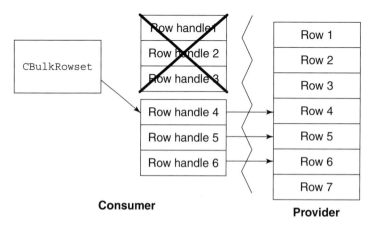

**Figure 8-12** CBulkRowset at Row 4

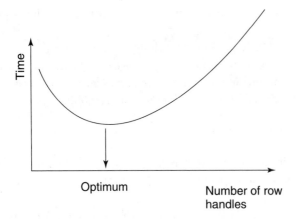

**Figure 8-13** Process Time/Number of Row Handles

First, `CBulkRowset` is attractive only when you work with consecutive rows. In other words, it provides better speed when you call `MoveNext` or `MovePrev`. However, it is not fast if you work with nonconsecutive rows—for example, when you call `MoveToBookmark` or `MoveToRatio`.

Second, keeping row handles alive can have a cost, so it is not always a good idea to set too large a number of them. One measure is the time necessary to fetch a rowset as a function of the number of rows in the cache. Usually, this measure has the shape shown in Figure 8-13.

As the number of row handles increases, the time decreases, as `MoveNext` performs fewer calls to `GetNextRows`. However, as the number of row handles increases further, it becomes harder for the provider to keep track of them. The gain of `GetNextRows` is offset by the performance loss due to the number of active row handles, so the time increases.

The curve thus presents an optimum, which evidently depends on the provider used.

## ROWSET ARRAYS

Conceptually, rowsets are just an array of rows. The `CArrayRowset` class allows programmers to access the rows as if the rowset were an array. It is defined as follows:

```
template <class T, class TRowset = CRowset>
class CArrayRowset :
   public CVirtualBuffer<T>,
   public TRowset
```

where `TRowset` represents the rowset class, for example, `CRowset` or `CBulkRowset`.

`CVirtualBuffer<T>` is an ATL class defined in `atlbase.h` that represents an array of `T` with a current item. `CArrayRowset` combines the features of the rowset and the virtual buffer. When creating `CArrayRowset`, it is possible to specify the capacity of the virtual buffer. By default, it is 100,000:

```
CArrayRowset(int nMax = 100000)
```

You should specify a capacity that is large enough for your needs. You will avoid many problems if the capacity is greater than the number of rows in the rowset.

At creation time, `CArrayRowset` does not hold any value. Optionally, you can call the `Snapshot` method to retrieve all the rows contained in the rowset.

The `[]` operator allows you to get the row at a given position. If the row has already been retrieved by `Snapshot`, `operator[]` merely gets the value in the virtual buffer; otherwise, it retrieves rows until it reaches the requested row.

`operator[]` is defined as follows:

```
T& operator[] (int nRow)
```

Note that `Snapshot` is optional. If you use it, all rows will be retrieved at once. If not, they will be retrieved on demand.

Also, `CArrayRowset` is different from `CBulkRowset`. `CBulkRowset` manages a buffer of row handles, while `CArrayRowset` manages a buffer of actual row

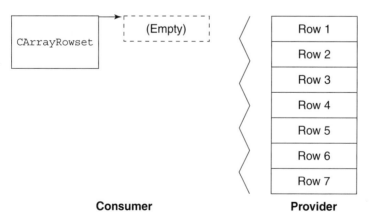

**Figure 8-14** `CArrayRowset` before the Call to `operator[]`

values. Once those values are retrieved there will be no OLE DB call to get them again.

Suppose that we have a `CArrayRowset` on which `Snapshot` has not been called. Its virtual buffer contains no item, as shown in Figure 8-14. When the user requests the values for the first row by calling `operator [0]`, `CArrayRowset` notices that the virtual buffer does not hold them and gets the values for row 1, as shown in Figure 8-15.

If the user then requests the sixth row by calling `operator [5]`, `CArray Rowset` will get the values of all rows until the sixth, as shown in Figure 8-16. `CArrayRowset` offers two benefits:

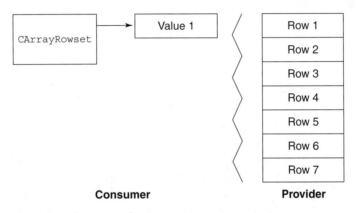

**Figure 8-15** `CArrayRowset` after the Call to `operator [0]`

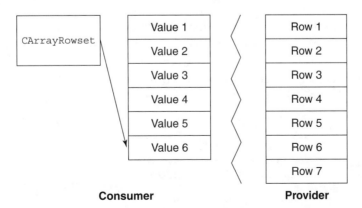

**Figure 8-16** `CArrayRowset` after the Call to `operator [5]`

- Once the values of a row are retrieved, getting them again does not involve any COM call. In other words, it is fast.
- It is very easy to use.

It also has the following drawbacks:

- It uses more memory than `CRowset`. The memory issue can be significant if `CArrayRowset` deals with a rowset with many rows.
- It might not be aware of changes made to the database if, for example, they occur after `Snapshot` is called.

## CLIENT CURSOR SERVICE COMPONENT

Writing an efficient rowset is not easy. Writing a rowset that supports backward fetching, find operations, and other advanced operations (see Chapter 13) is even more challenging. In fact, providers usually offer only the functionality of the underlying data store and do not add any extra features.

One of the goals of OLE DB is to provide a high level of features for many providers. As usual with OLE DB, the solution is a service component that aggregates with the native rowset and implements the additional interfaces.

The service component for the rowset object is the *client cursor service component*, and its use is optional. If the consumer chooses not to use it, the resulting rowsets will support few native features. If the consumer does use it, the resulting rowsets will be aggregated with a COM object that supports greater functionality. From the consumer point of view, the rowset object looks as if it implements all the functionality natively. Another benefit of this architecture is that the client cursor service component is more likely to be up to date than the different providers are.

For example, a simple provider might have rowsets that do not support advanced features such as finding rows and views. This translates into a rowset COM object that does not support `IRowsetFind` and `IRowsetView`. However, if the client curser service component is present, the rowset object is aggregated with it, as shown in Figure 8-17.

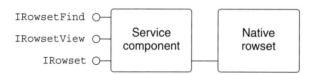

**Figure 8-17** Rowset with Service Component

Note that the service component implementation can introduce some caching mechanism on the client side. For example, when you request the `IRowsetFind` interface, the service component can cache the row values to perform the search. In other words, the client cursor service component can make the client fatter.

The decision on whether to use the service components comes at the data source level. In practice, it is not a bad idea to systematically request the service components, as here:

```
HRESULT hr;
CDataSource DataSource;
CDBPropSet   dbinit(DBPROPSET_DBINIT);
// add properties
hr = DataSource.OpenWithServiceComponents(_T("SQLOLEDB.1"),
    &dbinit);
```

See Chapter 6 for more information on data sources.

Once the data source specifies the client cursor service component, all of its rowsets will contain it. There is no specific code on the part of the rowset.

## FINDING ROWS

OLE DB offers three ways to find a particular row given the value of one of the columns.

- Using SQL commands with the form `select * from mytable where mycolumn = value` or with parameters, which is the most common way.
- Using the database indexes. With this method, the client accesses the index on the server, seeks a particular set of values, and retrieves the bookmark of the row. Then the client can scroll to the retrieved bookmark on the base table. (Chapter 13 discusses OLE DB indexes.)
- Searching the rowset on the client using the client cursor service components.

Note that the third method is very different from the other two:

- The find operation is on the client, not the server. Consequently, the client might end up retrieving the entire rowset before finding the right row. Also, the search can be on only one column.
- The processing will probably not take advantage of the databases indexes. In other words, the search will be sequential, not on a tree, and will be *slow* if the rowset contains many rows.

All of these statements might make the find feature seem worthless. However, it can be beneficial when used in conjunction with other mechanisms. For example, it is possible to issue an SQL statement and then perform a find operation on the resulting rowset. Also, the find is handy for performing searches on small rowsets without having to deal with SQL or indexes.

## A Find Example

Imagine that we have a table with two keys, which for simplicity are of type `integer`. Also suppose that two consecutive searches probably have the same first key. A real-world example might be that the first key is a customer identifier and the second is a product identifier. The process goes product by product, so two consecutive queries are likely to deal with the same product `identifier`.

A traditional approach is to fire an SQL statement each time a new row is needed:

```
SELECT * from table where product = ? and customer = ?
```

However, this is not optimal because it can lead to a high number of queries sent to the database. It may be preferable to cache the value of `product` for the last value. When a new row is needed, the component checks whether `product` has changed. If it has, a new query is executed. Then the component performs a find operation on the resulting rowset with `customer` as the search criterion.

Note that this scenario is efficient with the following conditions:

- `product` does not change too frequently, so not too many queries are executed.

- The resulting rowset is not too large, so the search operation is fast enough.

## Using the Find

Unfortunately, the OLE DB consumer templates do not support find. This feature is only part of the OLE DB extensions, which leads us to the OLE DB extensions rowset class `CRowsetFind`:

```
template <class T = CRowset>
class CRowsetFind: public T
```

`CRowsetFind` inherits from template parameter `T`, so you can combine it with `CRowset`, `CBulkRowset`, or another rowset class of your choice. Typically, you will just use the default:

```
CCommand<CMyAccessor, CRowsetFind<> > MyRowset;
```

`CRowsetFind` uses the `IRowsetFind` interface. When creating a rowset to use with the find features, you first need to set the `DBPROP_IRowsetFind` property to TRUE. This indicates to the provider that you require the `IRowsetFind` inter-face. If the provider is unable to create a rowset supporting `IRowsetFind`, it will not return any rowset at all.

If your provider does not support `IRowsetFind` natively, you can get around this problem by using the client cursor engine. To use the client cursor engine, you need to

1. Open the data source with service components. Chapter 6 explains which methods open with service components and which open without them.

2. Open the data source with the `DBPROPSET_DBINIT` data source initialization property, including the `DBPROPVAL_OS_CLIENTCURSOR` bits.

Once you do these two steps, every rowset created by the data source will support `IRowsetFind` if requested.

When you have the rowset, just call the `FindNextRow` method:

```
template <class VALUE>
HRESULT FindNextRow(VALUE v, ULONG iOrdinal, DBCOMPAREOP
    CompareOp = DBCOMPAREOPS_EQ, bool bBind = true, const
    CBookmarkBase* pBookmark = NULL, LONG lRowsOffset = 0)
```

where

- `v` is the value to find. Since the method is a template method, you can pass a value with any type recognized by OLE DB, including integer, boolean, and string. `FindNextRow` will automatically find the corresponding OLE DB type and create the right accessor for it.

- `iOrdinal` is the ordinal of the column the value should belong to. After this parameter, all other parameters have a default value that will fit most needs.

- `CompareOp` specifies the comparison operator to use for finding the row (see Table 8-9). By default, it is `DBCOMPAREOPS_EQ`, which means that the search finishes when the value in the row exactly matches the requested value.

- `bBind` specifies whether to get the values in the rowset if a row is found. In most cases, `bBind` will be `True`, the default value.

- `pBookmark` and `lRowsOffset` specify the position from which to start the search. If the bookmark is `NULL`, the search will start from the current cursor position and the current cursor will be moved to the found position if the search was successful. If it is not `NULL`, the search starts from the position at offset `lRowsOffset` from `pBookmark`. When the bookmark is not `NULL`, the cursor position does not change.

**Table 8-9** DBCOMPAREOPSENUM Values

| Symbol | Description |
|---|---|
| DBCOMPAREOPS_LT | Find the first value that is less than the searched value |
| DBCOMPAREOPS_LE | Find the first value that is less than or equal to the searched value |
| DBCOMPAREOPS_EQ | Find the first value that is equal to the searched value |
| DBCOMPAREOPS_GE | Find the first value that is greater than or equal to the searched value |
| DBCOMPAREOPS_GT | Find the first value that is greater than the searched value |
| DBCOMPAREOPS_BEGINSWITH | Find the first value that starts with the searched value—valid only for strings |
| DBCOMPAREOPS_NOTBEGINSWITH | Find the first value that does not start with the searched value—valid only for strings |
| DBCOMPAREOPS_CONTAINS | Match the first value that contains the search value—valid only for values bound as string data types |
| DBCOMPAREOPS_NOTCONTAINS | Find the first value that contains the searched value—valid only for strings |
| DBCOMPAREOPS_NE | Find the first value that is not equal to the searched value |
| DBCOMPAREOPS_IGNORE | Ignore the searched value; i.e., any comparison will be successful—equivalent to scrolling |
| DBCOMPAREOPS_CASESENSITIVE | Search is case sensitive—might be combined with other comparison operators |
| DBCOMPAREOPS_CASEINSENSITIVE | Search is case insensitive—might be combined with other comparison operators |

In this example, the rowset finds the value 3 for the first column:

```
HRESULT        hr;
CDataSource db;
CDBPropSet     dbinit(DBPROPSET_DBINIT);
dbinit.AddProperty(DBPROP_AUTH_INTEGRATED, OLESTR("SSPI"));
dbinit.AddProperty(DBPROP_INIT_CATALOG, OLESTR("db"));
dbinit.AddProperty(DBPROP_INIT_DATASOURCE, OLESTR("SERVER"));
hr = db.OpenWithServiceComponents(_T("SQLOLEDB.1"), &dbinit);
if (FAILED(hr))
    return hr;
CSession Session;
hr = Session.Open(db);
if (FAILED(hr))
    return hr;
CDBPropSet Properties(DBPROPSET_ROWSET);
Properties.AddProperty(DBPROP_IRowsetFind , true);
CCommand<CAccessor<CdboFetchScrollAccessor>, CRowsetFind<> >
    MyRowset;
hr = MyRowset.Open(Session, "select * from FetchScroll",
    &Properties);
if (FAILED(hr))
    return hr;
hr = MyRowset.FindNextRow(3, 1);
return hr;
```

## SUMMARY

This chapter presented the rowset object and its associated classes. Rowsets are powerful and flexible. They enable strategies to get rows that suit many different needs and situations. One of their powerful features is the client cursor service component, with which any "dumb" rowset can become fully featured.

Getting rows is not useful until one can access the associated column values. This is the subject of the next chapter.

# 9 Accessors

Rows are not very useful if we cannot access column data: We need to get the exchange data between the C++ object and the OLE DB rowset. This is where *accessors* come in.

Accessors are unique to OLE DB, and it is crucial to understand them in order to use the OLE DB consumer templates effectively because they are at the core of the library. For OLE DB beginners, accessors are difficult to apprehend because they have no equivalent in other database APIs. However, they are not difficult by themselves but just represent a new concept. The OLE DB consumer templates show their full power with accessors: The implementation is elegant, flexible, and efficient. Once you understand accessors, you will not be able to go back to traditional database APIs or products like ADO.

Briefly, an accessor describes the relation between the columns of a rowset and a C++ class. This chapter

- Explains the mechanism behind accessors.
- Describes the different kinds of accessors.
- Explains how to use assessors.

## OVERVIEW

The easiest way to describe accessors is to understand the problem that they solve. Let's imagine a rowset with three columns: A, B, and C. The corresponding C++ class has three class members: m_a, m_b, m_c. How can we specify which class member corresponds to which column? Figure 9-1 represents the rowset and the C++ object.

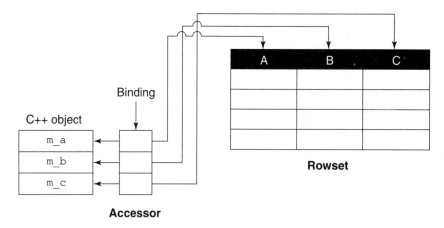

**Figure 9-1** An Accessor as a Collection of Bindings

There are many ways to solve this problem. A traditional method is to provide a function that gets the column value given a column ordinal or a column name. The code to get the class member values looks like

```
// pseudo code
m_a = GetColumnValue(Rowset, "A");
m_b = GetColumnValue(Rowset, "B");
m_c = GetColumnValue(Rowset, "C");
```

OLE DB's approach is quite different. An accessor is a collection of bindings, each of which identifies a class member and the corresponding column. For example, Figure 9-1 contains one accessor with three bindings. Bindings contain additional information useful in transferring data.

With a collection of bindings, the rowset can read and write the column values to the C++ object. There is no need for the C++ object to perform any iteration to exchange any data.

## Column and Parameter Accessors

There are two types of accessor: column accessors and parameter accessors. *Column accessors* transfer column data from a rowset as shown in the previous section. *Parameter accessors* play the same role for command parameters. For example, the following command needs an accessor with one parameter:

```
SELECT * FROM table where A = ?
```

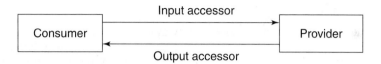

**Figure 9-2** Input and Output Accessors

## Input and Output Accessors

You can use accessors both ways: from the rowset or command parameter to the consumer object or the other way around. An input accessor goes from the provider object to the consumer object; conversely, an output accessor goes from the consumer object to the provider object. Figure 9-2 summarizes input and output accessors. Note that an accessor can be of both input and output types.

It is natural to imagine a column output accessor: The column data flows to the C++ class members. However, column accessors can also be used as input accessors to update a row in a rowset or to insert a new row. This offers an interesting alternative to UPDATE and INSERT statements (see Chapter 10).

It is also easy to imagine a parameter input accessor. However, parameter accessors can be used for output parameters as well. For example, if a stored procedure returns a result, this result will be an out parameter.

Common sense applies to accessors:

- If you do not bind a column, you will not be able to get its value.
- You can bind a column twice with different class members as long as you do not use it as an output accessor.
- When inserting or updating data, all columns that do not have any default value must be bound.

## Bindings

A binding *binds* a column or parameter with the consumer's memory. OLE DB defines three types that can be bound: fixed-length, variable-length, and very large.

A fixed-length type is one whose length is always the same. For example, a 4-byte integer is always 4 bytes long. The various fixed-length types include

- Integer types (1, 2, and 4 bytes, signed and unsigned)
- Real types (4 and 8 bytes)
- All date types

- Boolean types
- Other numeric types (such as currency)

A *variable-length* type, such as a string, does not have a fixed length. For the consumer, this means that passing a pointer is usually not sufficient to get and set a value. You also need the length of the value at the pointer's address. Variable-length types can be read at once. Therefore, the length should not be too large, which typically means less than a few kilobytes.

In some cases, the length of the data is too great for the value to be read in one shot, so it must be read in several iterations. We call these *very large* types. For example, images, sounds, or very large strings are considered very large objects. Chapter 11 will cover them in more detail.

The DBBINDING structure represents a binding. It is defined as

```
typedef struct tagDBBINDING {
    ULONG    iOrdinal;
    ULONG    obValue;
    ULONG    obLength;
    ULONG    obStatus;
    ITypeInfo * pTypeInfo;
    DBOBJECT * pObject;
    DBBINDEXT * pBindExt;
    DBPART    dwPart;
    DBMEMOWNER    dwMemOwner;
    DBPARAMIO eParamIO;
    ULONG    cbMaxLen;
    DWORD    dwFlags;
    DBTYPE    wType;
    BYTE    bPrecision;
    BYTE    bScale;
} DBBINDING;
```

where iOrdinal represents the ordinal of the column or parameter to which the binding applies. It goes from 1 to the number of columns. Zero is reserved for the self-bookmark.

## Data Parts

Data is composed of value, length, and status, any or all of which can be bound.

- *Value* is the actual value of the data—this is the simplest part to comprehend.
- *Length* is the length of the data in bytes, which for fixed-size types is always equal to the size of the type. This is useful for variable-length data like strings. For ANSI strings, the length does not include the terminal zero. For UNICODE strings, the length is twice the number of characters since each UNICODE character is composed of 2 bytes. For COM objects, the

length represents the size of the pointer to the COM interface—4 in a 32-bit architecture.

- *Status* is used to specify "special" values such as NULL or a default. As with OLE DB errors, it can indicate success (the value was successfully read or written, with or without warning) or failure. Success status starts with DBSTATUS_S*, failure status starts with DBSTATUS_E*. Table 9-1 lists the status constants.

dwPart indicates which part is being used. It is a combination of one or more 06symbols from Table 9-2. For example, if dwPart = DBPART_VALUE | DBPART_LENGTH, the value and length are used and the status is not.

When reading or writing data, the rowset receives a buffer and a list of bindings. When you specify the value, length, or status, you do not pass a pointer but

**Table 9-1** OLE DB Status Constants

| Symbol | Description |
| --- | --- |
| DBSTATUS_S_OK | Value is valid |
| DBSTATUS_S_ISNULL | Value is a NULL value |
| DBSTATUS_S_TRUNCATED | Value was truncated |
| DBSTATUS_E_BADACCESSOR | Accessor is invalid |
| DBSTATUS_E_CANTCONVERTVALUE | No conversion available between consumer and provider types |
| DBSTATUS_E_CANTCREATE | Provider could not create or allocate the value |
| DBSTATUS_E_DATAOVERFLOW | Data overflow |
| DBSTATUS_E_SIGNMISMATCH | Sign mismatch |
| DBSTATUS_E_UNAVAILABLE | Value was unavailable |
| DBSTATUS_S_DEFAULT | Value is the default value defined by the data store |
| DBSTATUS_S_IGNORE | Provider should ignore this value |
| DBSTATUS_E_BADSTATUS | Status is invalid |
| DBSTATUS_E_INTEGRITYVIOLATION | Value violated the constraint of the column |
| DBSTATUS_E_PERMISSIONDENIED | Provider does not have permissions on this column |
| DBSTATUS_E_SCHEMAVIOLATION | Value violated the schema's constraint of the column |

**Table 9-2** Part Flags

| Symbol | Description |
| --- | --- |
| DBPART_VALUE | Binding includes a value part |
| DBPART_LENGTH | Binding includes a length part |
| DBPART_STATUS | Binding includes a status part |

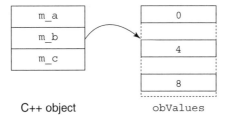

C++ object          obValues          **Figure 9-3** Bindings

an offset from the buffer start. This offset will be added to the pointer to the object you pass.

- obValue represents the offset of the value in your object in bytes. It is ignored if dwPart does not include DBPART_VALUE. You need to make sure that obValue is properly aligned for the processor architecture of your machine. For example, if the data is of type ULONG, it should be a multiple of 4 for 32-bit architectures.
- obLength represents the offset of the length in your object in bytes, which must be a multiple of 4. It is ignored if dwPart does not include DBPART_LENGTH.
- obStatus represents the offset of the status in your object in bytes, which must be a multiple of 4. It is ignored if dwPart does not include DBPART_STATUS.

Figure 9-3 represents the obValue fields in the example shown at the beginning of this chapter, supposing that all the class members are of type int. The first object value is zero because m_a is the first class member; the second object value is 4, the offset of m_b in our class, and so on. When getting and setting data, the rowset receives a pointer to the buffer (a pointer to our C++ object) and a series of bindings. The rowset is then able to reconstitute the class member addresses.

- pTypeInfo is not used yet. It should be set to NULL.

- pObject is used for BLOBs (see Chapter 11).

- pBindExt is not used yet. It should be set to NULL.

- dwMemOwner indicates if the memory is owned by the consumer or by the provider. The value of dwMemOwner is either DBMEMOWNER_CLIENTOWNED or DBMEMOWNER_PROVIDEROWNED. Memory ownership is discussed in more detail later in this chapter.

- eParamIO is used only for parameter bindings and can be one of the values in Table 9-3.

- cbMaxLen represents the length of allocated data values in bytes. It applies to variable-length data when the value part is used (dwPart includes DBPART_VALUE). When the provider writes the value in your data buffer, it truncates the data if the buffer is too small, and sets the status to DBSTATUS_S_TRUNCATED if the status is bound.

**Table 9-3** Parameter Type Flags

| Symbol | Description |
|---|---|
| DBPARAMIO_NOTPARAM | Accessor is not used for parameters. In most cases eParamIO is set to this value in row accessors to remind the programmer that it is ignored |
| DBPARAMIO_INPUT | Parameter is an input parameter |
| DBPARAMIO_OUTPUT | Parameter is an output parameter |

Note that cbMaxLen and obLength do not represent the same notion. obLength relates to the length of the actual data in the provider's rowset, while cbMaxLen represents the size of the data you allocated.

For strings, the length of the buffer includes the terminal zero. For example, if you allocate a buffer of five characters, you should set cbMaxLen to 5. If you retrieve the string abcde, the provider will attempt to write abcde\0, which has six characters. Therefore, it will write abcd\0 in your buffer, set the length to 5, and set the status to DBSTATUS_S_TRUNCATED. In short, you should allocate one character more than the maximum size of the data. This does not apply to DBTYPE_BYTES.

- dwFlags specifies the format in which the data is returned. Currently, only DBBINDFLAG_HTML is supported.

- wType represents the type of the consumer data, which does not have to match the type of the provider. If the provider and consumer types differ, OLE DB will attempt to perform the conversion. Appendix B enumerates the possible types and conversions.

- bPrecision represents the maximum precision to use when getting data and when wType is DBTYPE_NUMERIC. This is ignored when setting data, when wType is not DBTYPE_NUMERIC, or when the DBPART_VALUE bit is not set in dwPart.

- bScale represents the scale to use when getting data and when wType is DBTYPE_NUMERIC or DBTYPE_DECIMAL. As with bPrecision, this is ignored when setting data, when wType is not DBTYPE_NUMERIC or DBTYPE_DECIMAL, or when the DBPART_VALUE bit is not set in dwPart.

## Accessors as Collections of Bindings

At the OLE DB level, there is no distinction between an input accessor and an output accessor. If you do not bind a given column (if your accessor does not contain any binding with the ordinal of the given column), the information in it will not be passed to your C++ object. If you bind a given column several times (if your accessor contains several bindings with the ordinal of the given column), the information will be written twice.

The situation is different with parameters, which must get their value once and only once. Thus, if you attempt to bind the same parameter several times, the accessor will not know where to read from. Conversely, if you do not bind a parameter, its value will be indeterminate—a situation you definitely want to avoid.

Assessors are similar to rows: There is no COM object for an accessor. Rather, accessors are represented by a handle, HACCESSOR.

```
typedef ULONG HACCESSOR;
```

You create and manipulate accessors through the IAccessor interface. IAccessor does not represent an accessor but rather an object that can manipulate it. Table 9-4 contains its methods.

Creating bindings and accessors is nontrivial and error prone. This is why the OLE DB templates come with classes that make this task easier.

**Table 9-4** `IAccessor` Methods

| Method | Description |
|--------|-------------|
| AddRefAccessor | Adds a reference to an existing accessor |
| CreateAccessor | Creates an accessor from a set of bindings |
| GetBindings | Returns the bindings in an accessor |
| ReleaseAccessor | Releases an accessor |

# ACCESSOR CLASSES

The OLE DB consumer templates accessor classes facilitate the management of accessor handles. They include a buffer to read and write the data and a set of accessor handles that define the binding between the buffer and the rowset. All accessor classes inherit from `CAccessorBase`, which implements some common features.

## CAccessorBase

You will not need to use `CAccessorBase` directly. However, if you must write a function that takes any kind of accessor as one of its parameters, you should use `CAccessorBase` as the parameter type.

`CAccessorBase` has three class members. `m_nAccessors` holds the number of accessor handles while `m_pAccessorInfo` is an array of `m_nAccessors` items holding all the accessor information. Each item is an instance of `ATL_ACCESSOR_INFO`, where `_ATL_ACCESSOR_INFO` is defined as

```
struct _ATL_ACCESSOR_INFO
{
   HACCESSOR    hAccessor;
   bool         bAutoAccessor;
};
```

`hAccessor` is the accessor handle. `bAutoAccessor` specifies whether the accessor is an auto accessor. If so, the rowset will get the data for this accessor at each row movement. Otherwise, the rowset will not get any data for this accessor unless asked explicitly. (See Chapter 10 for more details.)

All descendants of `CAccessorBase` inherit this multi-accessor handle support. Some accessor classes support only a single accessor handle, in which case `m_nAccessors` will always be 1.

`CAccessorBase` also holds a data buffer (`m_pBuffer`). Its descendants are responsible for setting the buffer with the `SetBuffer` method. The clients of `CAccessorBase` get the buffer through the `GetBuffer` method.

## Distinguishing the Accessor Classes

The OLE DB consumer templates provide a wide range of accessor classes. When choosing a class, the first question is whether you know the columns of the underlying rowset. If you know this at compile time, you should use `CAccessor`, which binds columns and parameters statically.

If you do not know the columns of your rowset at compile time, you have the choice between `CDynamicAccessor` and `CDynamicParameterAccessor`. As the name suggests, `CDynamicAccessor` allocates the data buffer dynamically. `CDynamicParameterAccessor` is similar to `CDynamicAccessor` but also adds support for parameters

The OLE DB consumer templates also have an accessor class that provides low-level details: `CManualAccessor`, which, like `CAccessor`, gives the user the responsibility for allocating the memory buffer. `CManualAccessor` and `CAccessor` support column binding and parameter binding. In practice, `CManualAccessor` does not offer much benefit on top of the raw OLE DB structures, so it is not covered in this book.

Table 9-5 summarizes the different accessor classes and their characteristics.

**Table 9-5** Accessor Types

| Accessor Class | Buffer | Type | Support Parameter Binding |
|---|---|---|---|
| CAccessor | User | Static | Possible |
| CDynamicAccessor | OLE DB templates | Dynamic | No |
| CDynamicParameterAccessor | OLE DB templates | Dynamic | Yes |
| CManualAccessor | User | Dynamic | Possible |

### CNoAccessor

CNoAccessor is a "fake" accessor class: From the outside, it looks like an accessor, but it does nothing. Use it with commands that do not use any parameters or
return any rowset.

```
class CNoAccessor
{
public:
    // We don't need any typedefs here as the default
    // global typedef is not to have any parameters and
    // output columns.
    HRESULT BindColumns(IUnknown*) { return S_OK; }
    HRESULT BindParameters(HACCESSOR*, ICommand*, void**)
    { return S_OK; }
    void    Close() { }
    HRESULT ReleaseAccessors(IUnknown*) { return S_OK; }
};
```

CNoAccessor is interesting because it exposes the *required* methods of an
accessor:

- BindColumns is the opportunity for the accessor class to build the OLE DB
  column accessor handles.
- BindParameters is the equivalent method for parameter accessors. Accessor classes do not keep a reference on the accessor handle; it is passed to the
  command class through the HACCESSOR* parameter.
- Close releases any object, handle, or memory held by the accessor class.
- ReleaseAccessors releases all column accessors.

## USING CACCESSOR

The inheritance of CAccessor is defined as follows:

```
template < class T >
class CAccessor : public T, CAccessorBase
```

where T is a type declared by the user. At first, CAccessor can be difficult to
understand because it inherits from its template parameter. T defines the class
members and the bindings. CAccessor<T> then inherits the class members
of T and builds the accessor handles via the methods that are inherited from
CAccessorBase and the bindings inherited from T.

Figure 9-4 represents the inheritance diagram of CAccessor. T needs to define the column bindings and optionally the parameter bindings. The BindColumns implementation of CAccessor sets the buffer to itself:

```
HRESULT BindColumns(IUnknown* pUnk)
    {
    /// Some code
        SetBuffer((BYTE*)this);
```

As a result, the layout of the object appears as shown in Figure 9-5.

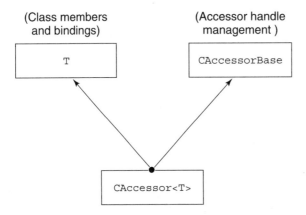

**Figure 9-4** CAccessor Inheritance

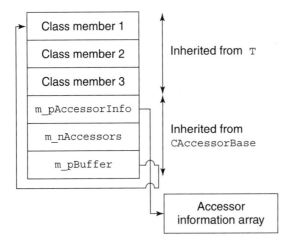

**Figure 9-5** CAccessor<T> Layout

## Column Binding Macros

OLE DB consumer templates use a set of macros to define bindings. The definition of column binding starts with

```
BEGIN_COLUMN_MAP(T)
```

where T is your class. It ends with

```
END_COLUMN_MAP()
```

The COLUMN_ENTRY macro helps you declare column bindings between the beginning and the end of the column map.

```
COLUMN_ENTRY(nOrdinal, data )
```

where

- nOrdinal is the ordinal of the column.
- data is a member of your class.

COLUMN_ENTRY is smart enough to deduce the OLE DB type from the C++ type of its data argument.

Table 9-6 summarizes the C++ types and the corresponding OLE DB types. For example, if the database contained a table with one column of type integer, the corresponding class would be

```
class CMyTable
{
   int m_column1
   BEGIN_COLUMN_MAP(CMyTable)
      COLUMN_ENTRY(1, m_column1)
   END_COLUMN_MAP()
};
```

Remember, unlike C arrays, the columns start at index 1, not zero; zero is reserved for bookmarks.

The binding macros are simple to use. However, much is done in the background by the OLE DB templates.

### Macro Internals

As you probably guessed, COLUMN_MAP and COLUMN_ENTRY and its variations work hand in hand.

COLUMN_MAP does two interesting things. First of all, it declares the type _OutputColumnsClass as the macro parameter, with the result that the global

**Table 9-6** C++ Types and OLE DB Types

| C++ Type | OLE DB Type |
| --- | --- |
| CHAR[] | DBTYPE_STR |
| WCHAR[] | DBTYPE_WSTR |
| signed char | DBTYPE_I1 |
| SHORT | DBTYPE_I2 |
| int | DBTYPE_I4 |
| LARGE_INTEGER | DBTYPE_I8 |
| BYTE | DBTYPE_UI1 |
| unsigned short | DBTYPE_UI2 |
| unsigned int | DBTYPE_UI4 |
| unsigned long | DBTYPE_UI4 |
| ULARGE_INTEGER | DBTYPE_UI8 |
| float | DBTYPE_R4 |
| double | DBTYPE_R8 |
| DECIMAL | DBTYPE_DECIMAL |
| DB_NUMERIC | DBTYPE_NUMERIC |
| IDispatch* | DBTYPE_IDISPATCH |
| GUID | DBTYPE_GUID |
| SAFEARRAY* | DBTYPE_ARRAY |
| DBDATE | DBTYPE_DBDATE |
| DBTIME | DBTYPE_DBTIME |
| DBTIMESTAMP | DBTYPE_DBTIMESTAMP |
| FILETIME | DBTYPE_FILETIME |
| DBFILETIME | DBTYPE_DBFILETIME |
| PROPVARIANT | DBTYPE_PROPVARIANT |
| DB_VARNUMERIC | DBTYPE_VARNUMERIC |

declaration of _OutputColumnsClass as _CNoOutputColumns is overridden in this class. Second, it defines a new declaration of _GetBindEntries:

```
inline static HRESULT _GetBindEntries(ULONG* pColumns,
   DBBINDING*pBinding, ULONG nAccessor, bool* pAuto,
   BYTE* pBuffer = NULL)
```

_GetBindEntries' pColumns parameter receives the number of columns. CAccessor can then allocate the appropriate number of bindings. If pBinding is not NULL, _GetBindEntries fills up the structures. The pBuffer argument is used to free any column value if necessary.

Since CAccessor supports multiple accessors, it is necessary to specify the accessor index in the accessor handle table. If there is only one accessor, this parameter will be zero. The section on multiple accessors gives more information on this topic.

The pAuto parameter determines whether the accessor is an auto accessor (more about this in the section on auto accessors later in this chpater). Eventually, each COLUMN_ENTRY macro is transformed into the _COLUMN_ENTRY_CODE macro, defined as

```
#define _COLUMN_ENTRY_CODE(nOrdinal, wType, nLength, nPrecision,
nScale, dataOffset, lengthOffset, statusOffset) \
    if (pBuffer != NULL) \
    { \
      CAccessorBase::FreeType(wType, pBuffer + dataOffset); \
    } \
    else if (pBinding != NULL) \
    { \
      CAccessorBase::Bind(pBinding, nOrdinal, wType, nLength, \
          nPrecision, nScale, eParamIO, \
          dataOffset, lengthOffset, statusOffset); \
      pBinding++; \
    } \
    nColumns++;
```

_COLUMN_ENTRY_CODE does three things:

- If the buffer is not NULL, it performs the necessary free operation.
- If the binding pointer is not NULL, it set its fields and increments it to position it for the next COLUMN_ENTRY macro.
- It increments nColumns. At the end of all column entries, nColumns will therefore hold the number of columns.

COLUMN_ENTRY is not the only macro that calls _COLUMN_ENTRY_CODE. The following section will explore others.

## Length and Status Binding Macros

It is usually a good idea to bind the status of a value. This tells you if your value was correctly read or written and if the value is NULL. It also allows you to set NULL and default values.

The COLUMN_ENTRY_STATUS macro binds the value and its status. The following example shows how to bind the status for column1:

```
      LONG m_column1;
      DBSTATUS m_column1_status;
//...
BEGIN_COLUMN_MAP(CTable1Accessor5)
      COLUMN_ENTRY_STATUS(1, m_column1, m_column1_status)
```

For variable-length data, it is also a good idea to bind the length with the COLUMN_ENTRY_LENGTH macro. The following example shows how to bind the length for column2:

```
      char m_column2 [51];
      ULONG m_column2_length;
//...
      COLUMN_ENTRY_LENGTH(2, m_column2, m_column2_length)
```

The following examples show how to bind both the status and the length for column2 with COLUMN_ENTRY_LENGTH_STATUS:

```
      char m_column2 [51];
      ULONG m_column2_length;
      DBSTATUS m_column2_status;

//...
      COLUMN_ENTRY_LENGTH_STATUS(2, m_column2, m_column2_length,
        m_column2_status)
```

Table 9-7 summarizes the column entry macros with length or status.

As you can see, the number of members in your class is multiplied by 2 or 3. This can make your class mode difficult to read because the namespace for your class members becomes crowded.

The OLE DB extensions offer three classes that resolve the class member naming problem:

- ValueStatus <T> contains both the value and the status.
- ValueLength <T> contains both the value and the length.
- ValueLengthStatus <T> contains the value, the length, and the status.

**Table 9-7** Main Binding Macros

| Macro | Description |
|---|---|
| COLUMN_ENTRY | Binds value |
| COLUMN_ENTRY_LENGTH | Binds value and length |
| COLUMN_ENTRY_STATUS | Binds value and status |
| COLUMN_ENTRY_LENGTH_STATUS | Binds value, length, and status |

To use `ValueStatus`, change your class member from

```
My_type m_member;
```

to

```
ValueStatus<My_type> m_member;
```

Change the binding from

```
COLUMN_ENTRY (ordinal, m_member)
```

to

```
COLUMN_ENTRY_STATUS_AUTO (ordinal, m_member)
```

The macro `COLUMN_ENTRY_STATUS_AUTO` will bind the value and the status automatically.

`ValueLength` and `ValueLengthStatus` are used the same way. Their binding macros are `COLUMN_ENTRY_LENGTH_AUTO` and `COLUMN_ENTRY_LENGTH_STATUS_AUTO`, respectively. In addition, `ValueStatus` has some convenient methods for getting and setting the value:

```
operator T*()
ValueStatus <T> operator =(T* other)
ValueStatus <T> operator =(T other)
```

The first method allows you to access the value as if it were a pointer. For example:

```
ValueStatus<LONG> m_value;
LONG* value_pointer = m_value;
```

where `value_pointer` contains the value if the status is okay. Otherwise, it is `NULL`. The two other methods allow you set the value.

If you pass a pointer, it will check whether it is `NULL`. If so, the operator sets the status to `DBSTATUS_S_ISNULL`. If not, it sets the status to `DBSTATUS_S_OK` and sets the value. If you pass a value, the status is set to `DBSTATUS_S_OK` and the value is set. For example, you can write

```
LONG* value_ptr = NULL;
my_accessor.m_column1 = value_ptr;
LONG value;
my_accessor.m_column1 = value
```

**Table 9-8** `COLUMN_ENTRY` Macros with Precision and Scale Support

| Macro | Description |
| --- | --- |
| COLUMN_ENTRY_PS | Same as COLUMN_ENTRY with precision and scale |
| COLUMN_ENTRY_PS_LENGTH | Same as COLUMN_ENTRY_LENGTH with precision and scale |
| COLUMN_ENTRY_PS_STATUS | Same as COLUMN_ENTRY_STATUS with precision and scale |
| COLUMN_ENTRY_PS_LENGTH_STATUS | Same as COLUMN_ENTRY_LENGTH_STATUS with precision and scale |

## Precision and Scale Macros

The OLE DB consumer templates provide a series of binding macros for types that require precision and scale. These are summarized in Table 9-8.

## Column Type and Size Macros

The `COLUMN_ENTRY` macro and its variations automatically determine the type of the variable through the `_OLEDB_TYPE` macro:

```
#define COLUMN_ENTRY(nOrdinal, data) \
    COLUMN_ENTRY_TYPE(nOrdinal, _OLEDB_TYPE(data), data)
```

`_OLEDB_TYPE` transforms the C++ type into the OLE DB type, as summarized in Table 9-6. Sometimes the type it returns is not satisfactory or correct. In this case, it is possible to bypass the `COLUMN_ENTRY` macro and indicate the type explicitly with `COLUMN_ENTRY_TYPE`.

`COLUMN_ENTRY_TYPE` is also able to find the size of the variable through the `_SIZE_TYPE` macro:

```
#define COLUMN_ENTRY_TYPE(nOrdinal, wType, data) \
    COLUMN_ENTRY_TYPE_SIZE(nOrdinal, wType, _SIZE_TYPE(data), data)
```

You can bypass this and specify the size of the variable by hand with the `COLUMN_ENTRY_TYPE_SIZE` macro.

## Auto Accessors

The OLE DB consumer templates define two kinds of accessors: auto and non-auto. They are defined by _ATL_ACCESSOR_INFO:

```
struct _ATL_ACCESSOR_INFO
{
   HACCESSOR    hAccessor;
   bool         bAutoAccessor;
};
```

If the accessor is of the auto type, the consumer will be updated when a row is fetched. If not, the consumer will be updated only when it so requests explicitly. (See Chapter 10 for more details.)

## Multiple Accessors

CAccessor can also support multiple accessor handles. To use multiple accessors, you first need to indicate how many accessors the class supports through the BEGIN_ACCESSOR_MAP macro. You then need to define each accessor starting with the BEGIN_ACCESSOR macro:

```
#define BEGIN_ACCESSOR(num, bAuto)
```

where num represents the accessor index, while bAuto specifies whether the accessor is of the auto type.

For example, the following class contains two accessors: The first binds only the first column and is an auto accessor; the second binds only the second column and is not an auto accessor:

```
class CMyTable
{
public:
// Data Elements
   int m_column1;
   CHAR m_column2 [2048];

// output binding map
BEGIN_ACCESSOR_MAP(CMyTable, 2) //it has two accessors
   BEGIN_ACCESSOR(0, true)
    COLUMN_ENTRY(1, m_column1)
   END_ACCESSOR()
   BEGIN_ACCESSOR(1, false) // this is not an auto accessor
    COLUMN_ENTRY(2, m_ column2)
   END_ACCESSOR()
END_ACCESSOR_MAP()
};
```

## Binding by Reference

Data that has a variable length, such as strings, can be bound two ways: *directly* or *by reference*. When binding the column directly, the data is copied directly into the buffer, as shown in Figure 9-6. When binding a column by reference, the data in the C++ buffer holds a reference to the data, as shown in Figure 9-7 for column A.

Binding by reference can be convenient for variable-length data. Because the C++ class does not have to know the length of the data in advance, there is no risk of truncation. In addition, the buffer has the exact length, thus avoiding overkill memory allocation.

When binding by reference, you can choose who is responsible for freeing the memory. If the provider, the memory is said to be *provider* owned. If the consumer, the memory is said to be *client* owned. Client owned is another way to say *consumer owned*.

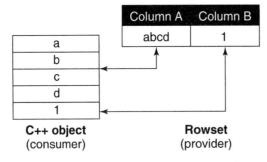

**Figure 9-6** Direct Binding

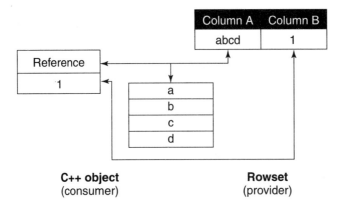

**Figure 9-7** Binding by Reference

## Provider-Owned Memory

When the memory is owned by the provider, the consumer gets a direct reference on it but should not try to free it (see Figure 9-8). This is the provider's responsibility when the row is released.

To use a string by reference owned by the provider, declare your class member, say, char*:

```
char* m_column1;
```

Then bind it with type DBTYPE_STR|DBTYPE_BYREF:

```
COLUMN_ENTRY_TYPE(1, DBTYPE_STR|DBTYPE_BYREF, m_column1)
```

When you bind by reference, the OLE DB consumer templates assume that the memory is provider owned.

If you look at CAccessorBase::Bind, you will see the code that makes it possible:

```
if (wType & DBTYPE_BYREF)
    pBinding->dwMemOwner = DBMEMOWNER_PROVIDEROWNED;
else
    pBinding->dwMemOwner = DBMEMOWNER_CLIENTOWNED;
```

In other words, if the type is by reference, by default the memory is owned by the provider; otherwise, it is owned by the client by default.

There are three drawbacks with provider-owned memory:

- The type of the provider and the type of the consumer must match. Indeed, since there is no copy of memory, no conversion is possible.

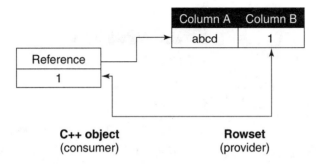

C++ object          Rowset
(consumer)          (provider)

**Figure 9-8** Binding by Reference, Provider Owned

- The provider controls the lifetime of the memory. In other words, you should try to avoid passing the pointer around because it might become invalid.

- Not all providers support provider-owned memory.

If one of these drawbacks is a problem for you, you can use *client-owned memory*.

## Client-Owned Memory

Client-owned memory is allocated by the provider and passed to the consumer; the consumer is then responsible for releasing it. Since the provider uses the COM IMalloc allocator, the client should free the memory with IMalloc::Free when finished. Using free instead of IMalloc::Free is a great way to crash your application. Figure 9-9 summarizes memory allocation with client-owned memory.

This method can be slower because the content of the string is copied from the provider buffer to the intermediate buffer. In addition, it is not supported by the OLE DB consumer templates, which, as we saw previously, assume that all binding by reference is provider owned. The OLE DB extensions do support this method through the CLIENT_OWNED and FREE_MEMORY macros.

First, add CLIENT_OWNED after the column entry column to force a client ownership. Second, add FREE_MEMORY to indicate that FreeRecordMemory should free the memory. Otherwise, you need to manage the memory by hand.

```
    char * m_column1;
    char * m_column2;

BEGIN_COLUMN_MAP(CTable1Accessor4)
    //...
    COLUMN_ENTRY_TYPE (1, DBTYPE_STR|DBTYPE_BYREF, m_column1)
    CLIENT_OWNED
        // Column 1 is not freed by FreeRecordMemory
    COLUMN_ENTRY_TYPE (2, DBTYPE_STR|DBTYPE_BYREF, m_column2)
    CLIENT_OWNED FREE_MEMORY(m_column2)
        // Column 2 is freed by FreeRecordMemory
```

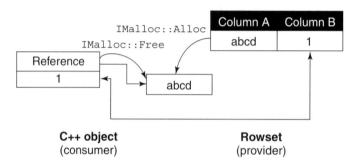

**Figure 9-9** Binding by Reference, Client Owned

As in the provider-owned memory case, you should specify the type directly. Do not attempt to have the compiler deduce this for you. Also, you should call `FreeRecordMemory` after each row movement to free any memory.

## BSTR

Put simply, a BSTR is the standard way to use strings with COM. It is a UNICODE string that you manipulate with specific functions.

The following code shows how to use and bind BSTRs.

```
BSTR m_column2;

BEGIN_COLUMN_MAP(CTable1Accessor5)
   //...
   COLUMN_ENTRY_TYPE(2, DBTYPE_BSTR, m_column2)
END_COLUMN_MAP()
```

You should specify the type explicitly, or else the generated code will fail.

This approach is simple and convenient. However, it locks you in with BSTR, which can be allocated and destroyed only with the BSTR functions. In addition, it forces you to use double-byte characters.

When using BSTR, you should call `FreeRecordMemory` after each row movement to free any memory.

## Binding Method Summary

The pros and cons of each column binding method are as follows:

- Method 1 represents a direct binding.
- Method 2 represents a binding by reference with provider-owned memory.
- Method 3 represents a binding by reference with client-owned memory.
- Method 4 represents a binding with a BSTR.

Table 9-9 summarizes the different methods and their characteristics.

## Parameter Binding

Parameter binding works almost like column binding. The binding declaration starts with `BEGIN_PARAM_MAP(x)` and ends with `END_PARAM_MAP()`, where x is the class itself. The parameters are declared like columns. For example:

```
BEGIN_PARAM_MAP(CTable1Accessor9)
   COLUMN_ENTRY(1, m_column1)
END_PARAM_MAP()
```

**Table 9-9** Binding Methods

| Method | 1 | 2 | 3 | 4 |
|---|---|---|---|---|
| Memory allocated by | Consumer | Provider | Provider | Provider |
| Possible truncation | Yes | No | No | No |
| Data transfer | Slow | Fast | Slow | Slow |
| Memory freed by | Consumer | Provider | Consumer | Consumer |
| Memory automatically freed | Yes, by FreeRecord Memory | Does not apply | Depends on FREE_MEMORY | Yes, by FreeRecord Memory |
| Supported by provider | Yes | Some | Yes | Yes |
| Supported by OLE DB consumer templates | Yes | Yes | No | Yes |
| Single-byte characters allowed | Yes | Yes | Yes | No |

**Table 9-10** Parameter Type Flags

| Symbol | Description |
|---|---|
| DBPARAMIO_NOTPARAM | Accessor is not used for parameters; in most cases, eParamIO is set to this value in row accessors to remind the programmer that it is ignored |
| DBPARAMIO_INPUT | Parameter is an input parameter |
| DBPARAMIO_OUTPUT | Parameter is an output parameter |

In addition, you can specify the parameter type with SET_PARAM_TYPE. Use this macro before the column you declare. The parameter type is one of those in Table 9-10. Note that BEGIN_PARAM_MAP sets eParamIO to DBPARAMIO_INPUT. Therefore, if all your parameters are of the input type, you do not need to use SET_PARAM_TYPE.

## DYNAMIC ACCESSORS

Sometimes, you do not know the columns or the parameters of the rowset at compile time. Therefore, the accessor needs to allocate the consumer buffer dynamically. Accessors that allocate the buffer according to the rowset or parameter are called *dynamic accessors*.

OLE DB templates come with two dynamic accessors: CDynamicAccessor and CDynamicParameterAccessor. The CDynamicAccessor binds columns only, while the CDynamicAccessor binds both columns and parameters. CDynamicParameterAccessor derives from CDynamicAccessor. Figure 9-10 presents the inheritance relationship.

When CDynamicAccessor allocates the buffer dynamically, it first requests the number of columns and the length of each column. For each column, it allocates enough memory for the data part, 4 bytes for the length, and 4 bytes for the status. CDynamicAccessor binds all three parts. Its layout is represented in Figure 9-11. Note that the size of the data part can vary from column to column.

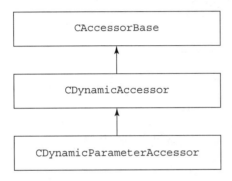

**Figure 9-10** Dynamic Accessor Inheritance

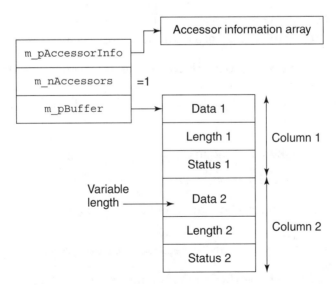

**Figure 9-11** CDynamicAccessor Layout

Although CDynamicAccessor inherits the capabilities for supporting several accessor handles, it uses only one.

## Using Dynamic Accessors

This section explains how to use an instance of CDynamicAccessor on a table with two columns: The first column is of type integer; the second is of type string. The section also explains how to discover the content of this dynamic accessor.

First, we need to open the table:

```
CTable<CDynamicAccessor> table;
hr = table.Open(Session, "Table1");
```

### Number of Columns

The next step is getting the number of columns:

```
ULONG ColumnCount = table.GetColumnCount();
OutputDebugString ("Number of columns:\n");
OutputDebugString (I2T (ColumnCount));
```

If you run the program, you will get the following output:

```
Number of columns:
3
```

Why three, not two, since we have only two columns? In certain cases, the provider adds a column for a bookmark. This is the only column with ordinal zero; all others are greater than or equal to 1. In short, we have two cases:

- The provider added a bookmark column, and the ordinals go from zero to ColumnCount() - 1.
- The provider did not add a bookmark column, and the ordinals go from 1 to ColumnCount().

To determine if there is a bookmark, look at the ordinal of the first column:

```
bool HasBookmark = table.m_pColumnInfo->iOrdinal == 0;
```

You can also attempt to get a bookmark and check if it was successful:

```
CBookmark<> Bookmark;
HasBookmark = SUCCEEDED (table.GetBookmark(&Bookmark));
```

Another method is to check whether the column flag contains DBCOLUMNFLAGS_ ISBOOKMARK, as shown in the next section.

Once you know the number of columns and the presence of a bookmark column, you know the range of column ordinals.

### Types, Names, and Flags

The next step is getting the types of the columns and eventually their names. `CDynamicAccessor` defines three methods:

- `GetColumnType` gets the type of the column either by name or by ordinal.
- `ColumnName` gets the name of the column.
- `GetColumnFlags` gets the flags of the column either by name or by ordinal.

Column flags are a combination of the values in Table 9-11.

**Table 9-11** Column Flags

| Symbol | Value | Description |
|---|---|---|
| DBCOLUMNFLAGS_ISBOOKMARK | 0x1 | Column contains a bookmark |
| DBCOLUMNFLAGS_MAYDEFER | 0x2 | Deferred column; provider is not required to retrieve the data until `GetData` is called for this column |
| DBCOLUMNFLAGS_WRITE | 0x4 | Column is writable |
| DBCOLUMNFLAGS_WRITEUNKNOWN | 0x8 | Provider does not know if the data is writable in this column |
| DBCOLUMNFLAGS_ISFIXEDLENGTH | 0x10 | Column has a fixed length |
| DBCOLUMNFLAGS_ISNULLABLE | 0x20 | NULLs can be inserted in this column |
| DBCOLUMNFLAGS_MAYBENULL | 0x40 | NULLs can be read from this column |
| DBCOLUMNFLAGS_ISLONG | 0x80 | Columns contain very large objects (see Chapter 11) |
| DBCOLUMNFLAGS_ISROWID | 0x100 | Set if column contains a persistent row identifier that cannot be written to and has no meaningful value except to identify the row |
| DBCOLUMNFLAGS_ISROWVER | 0x200 | Set if column contains a timestamp or other versioning mechanism that cannot be written to directly and is automatically updated to a new, increasing value when the row is updated and committed |
| DBCOLUMNFLAGS_CACHEDEFERRED | 0x1000 | Set if, when deferred column is first read, its value is cached by the provider |

When a function returns a boolean, returning `true` means that the function did not encounter any error. It returns `false` if there was an error. For example, the column ordinal might be out of range.

The following example iterates on the columns and gets the type, name, and flags of each one:

```
ULONG MinOrdinal, MaxOrdinal;
if (HasBookmark)
{
   MinOrdinal = 0;
   MaxOrdinal = ColumnCount - 1;
}
else
{
   MinOrdinal = 1;
   MaxOrdinal = ColumnCount;
}
for (ULONG Ordinal = MinOrdinal;Ordinal <= MaxOrdinal; Ordinal++)
{
   DBTYPE Type;
   DBCOLUMNFLAGS Flags;
   table.GetColumnType(Ordinal,&Type);
   table.GetColumnFlags(Ordinal,&Flags);
   LPOLESTR ColumnName = table.GetColumnName(Ordinal);
   OutputDebugString (_T("Column "));
   OutputDebugString (I2T(Ordinal));
   OutputDebugString (_T(" type: "));
   OutputDebugString (I2T(Type));
   OutputDebugString (_T(" flags: "));
   OutputDebugString (H2T(Flags));
   OutputDebugString (_T(" name: "));
   if (ColumnName)
      OutputDebugString (W2T(ColumnName));
   else
      OutputDebugString (_T("no column name"));
   OutputDebugString(_T("\n"));
}
```

The output will be something like

```
Column 0 type: 3 flags: 0x13 name: no column name
Column 1 type: 3 flags: 0x76 name: column1
Column 2 type: 129 flags: 0x66 name: column2 3 is DBTYPE_I4
```

Note that the bookmark column does not have any name and that its flags include `DBCOLUMNFLAGS_ISBOOKMARK`.

## Getting and Setting Data Parts

You can get and set the value in the buffer with the GetValue and SetValue methods, both of which interact with the *buffer*. There is no data exchange between the rowset, or to the data store, at this time.

### Getting a Value

The GetValue method has four forms. The first two use the templates; the first form requires a column ordinal:

```
template <class ctype>
bool GetValue(ULONG nColumn, ctype* pData) const
```

The second form requires a column name:

```
template <class ctype>
bool GetValue(TCHAR *pColumnName, ctype* pData) const
```

The last two forms get the value directly:

```
void* GetValue(ULONG nColumn) const
```

and

```
void* GetValue(TCHAR* pColumnName) const
```

In the first two forms, the OLE DB templates check that the size of the column is the same as the size of the type:

```
ATLASSERT(m_pColumnInfo[nColumn].ulColumnSize == sizeof(ctype));
```

Therefore, they do not work with variable-size columns. For those use the "raw" form with a type cast.

The code shows how to use GetValue in both cases:

```
case DBTYPE_I4:
{
   int Value;
   table.GetValue (Ordinal, &Value);
   OutputDebugString (_T(" Integer value: "));
   OutputDebugString(I2T(Value));
   break;
}
```

```
case DBTYPE_STR:
{
   char * Value;
   Value = (char *)table.GetValue (Ordinal);
   OutputDebugString (_T(" String value: "));
   OutputDebugString(A2T(Value));
   break;
}
```

You get the length with `GetLength`. You get the status with `GetStatus`.

```
ULONG Length;
table.GetLength (Ordinal, &Length);
OutputDebugString(_T(" Length: "));
OutputDebugString(I2T(Length));
ULONG Status;
table.GetStatus(Ordinal, &Status);
OutputDebugString (_T(" Status: "));
OutputDebugString(I2T(Status));
```

### Setting a Value

The `SetValue` method has two forms with templates:

```
template <class ctype>
bool SetValue(ULONG nColumn, const ctype& data)
```

and

```
template <class ctype>
bool SetValue(TCHAR *pColumnName, const ctype& data)
```

These methods are useful when the column has a fixed length. For example, to set the value of the first column to 1, you write

```
table.SetValue(1, 1);
```

However, if the column is of a variable length, you need to copy the content of your value and then set the length. For example:

```
strcpy((char*)table.GetValue(2), "a string");
table.SetLength(2, strlen ("a string"));
```

You set the length with `SetLength` and the status with `SetStatus`.

## Using CDynamicParameterAccessor

`CDynamicParameterAccessor` extends `CDynamicAccessor` by adding features to handle parameters. In fact, handling parameters is very similar to handling column values, so there is no need to repeat all the steps of the previous section.

**Table 9-12** Parameter and Column Methods

| Parameter Method | Column Equivalent |
|---|---|
| GetParamCount | GetColumnCount |
| GetParamName | GetColumnName |
| GetParamType | GetColumnType |
| GetParam | GetValue |
| SetParam | SetParam |

Table 9-12 summarizes the parameter methods and their column method equivalents.

## Extending Dynamic Accessors

If you have a look at `CDynamicParameterAccessor`, you might notice that there is no method to read and write the length and status of the parameters. For that reason, the OLE DB extensions offers `CDynamicParameterAccessorEx`, a new class that implements these features (Figure 9-12). It comes with 12 additional methods.

You can get the length either by name or by ordinal:

```
bool GetParamLength (ULONG nParam, ULONG* pLength) const
bool GetParamLength (TCHAR* pParamName, ULONG* pLength) const
```

`CDynamicParameterAccessorEx`'s methods work like similar OLE DB template accessor methods, returning `true` if they succeed and `false` if they fail (for example, if the parameter ordinal was out of range). If the method succeeds, the length is written in `pLength`.

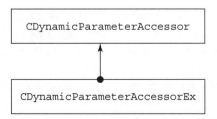

**Figure 9-12** `CDynamicParameterAccessorEx` Inheritance

Similarly, you can write the length either by ordinal or by parameter name:

```
bool SetParamLength(ULONG nParam, ULONG Length)
bool SetParamLength(TCHAR* pParamName, ULONG Length)
```

Two additional methods are used for implementations:

```
void * _GetParamLength(ULONG nParam)const
void* _GetParamLength(TCHAR* pParamName) const
```

There are six methods for reading and writing the status:

```
bool GetParamStatus (ULONG nParam, DBSTATUS* pStatus) const
bool GetParamStatus (TCHAR* pParamName, DBSTATUS* pStatus) const
bool SetParamStatus(ULONG nParam, DBSTATUS  Status)
bool SetParamStatus(TCHAR* pParamName, DBSTATUS Status)
void * _GetParamStatus(ULONG nParam)const
void* _GetParamStatus(TCHAR* pParamName) const
```

Here is an example that demonstrates the use of all of the high-level methods of CDynamicParameterAccessorEx:

```
   // my_accessor  accessor declared as descendent of
CDynamicParameterAccessorEx
   DBSTATUS status;
   ULONG length;
   my_accessor.GetParamLength("paramname", &length);
   my_accessor.GetParamLength(1, &length);
   my_accessor.GetParamStatus("paramname ", &status);
   my_accessor.GetParamStatus(1, &status);
   my_accessor.SetParamLength("paramname ", length);
   my_accessor.SetParamLength(1, length);
   my_accessor.SetParamStatus("paramname ", status);
   my_accessor.SetParamStatus(1, status);
```

# SUMMARY

This chapter introduced accessors, which bind the C++ object with the columns or parameters of a rowset. The OLE DB consumer templates offer a wide range of accessor classes, both static and dynamic. These are useful in exchanging data between rowsets and C++ classes.

The next chapter will explore data exchange between the application and the OLE DB rowset.

# 10 Exchanging Data

The purpose of accessors is to exchange data between the C++ object and the OLE DB rowset object. Exchanging data includes getting it (from the data store to the consumer) and setting it (from the consumer to the data store). Getting data is the easy part. Setting data is a bit more complex because of the possibility that two rowsets will update the same row at the same time.

## GETTING DATA

As we learned in previous chapters, rowset classes have a current row handle. Accessor classes define a list of accessor handles and a buffer. When getting data, we need to specify what row we want (the row handle), how we want to get it (the accessor handle), and where we want to get it (the buffer). CRowset packages this in the GetData method:

```
HRESULT GetData(int nAccessor)
```

where nAccessor represents the index of the accessor handle to use.

For example, to get data using the accessor at index 3, we write

```
MyRowset.GetData(3);
```

GetData simply calls the COM method and passes the current row handle, the accessor handle, and the buffer:

```
HRESULT GetData(int nAccessor)
{
    ATLASSERT(m_spRowset != NULL);
    ATLASSERT(m_pAccessor != NULL);
```

```
ATLASSERT(m_hRow != NULL);
    // Note that we are using the specified buffer if it has
    // been set, otherwise we use the accessor for the data.
return m_spRowset->GetData(m_hRow, m_pAccessor->GetHAccessor
    (nAccessor), m_pAccessor->GetBuffer());
}
```

Although getting data this way is not difficult, CRowset goes a little further by calling the GetData method at each cursor movement. The methods that call GetData are MoveToBookmark, MoveToRatio, MoveNext, MovePrev, and MoveLast. In addition, methods such as MoveFirst that call MoveNext call GetData indirectly.

The bottom line is that the content of the buffer is always synchronized with the current row. However, this creates an issue for columns that are expensive to get. Imagine a table with two columns: The first is an integer while the second contains large strings. If one accessor binds the second column, each cursor movement will be expensive because it will need to transfer a large string. Conversely, if the second column is not bound, it will be impossible to get its value. We need a way to specify that some columns should be transferred at each cursor movement while others should be transferred only on demand: The inexpensive column could be transferred systematically while the more expensive column could be transferred only if the consumer knows that it needs it. This is where *auto accessors* come in.

## Auto Accessors

Chapter 9 briefly described auto accessors. Note that OLE DB does not define this notion, which is present only at the C++ level with the OLE DB consumer templates.

An accessor is *automatic* only if a rowset gets the data for it for each cursor movement. In other words, auto accessors regroup columns that are either cheap to get or always needed. Conversely, non-auto accessors contain columns that are expensive to get and not always needed.

At each cursor movement, the rowset calls another version of GetData:

```
HRESULT GetData();
```

This function does not take any accessor index. GetData gets the data for all automatic accessors essentially by iterating on all accessors. If it finds an auto accessor, it calls GetData(int nAccessor) on it:

```
HRESULT GetData()
{
   HRESULT hr = S_OK;
   ATLASSERT(m_pAccessor != NULL);
   ULONG nAccessors = m_pAccessor->GetNumAccessors();
   for (ULONG i=0; i<nAccessors; i++)
   {
      if (m_pAccessor->IsAutoAccessor(i))
      {
         hr = GetData(i);
         if (FAILED(hr))
            return hr;
      }
   }
   return hr;
}
```

There is no reason to call GetData() explicitly, since the OLE DB consumer templates do this for you. However, you should call GetData() after a cursor movement not implemented by the templates.

GetData(int nAccessor) is useful for getting data for nonauto accessors. Take, for example, the following class:

```
class CMyAccessor
{
public:
   LONG m_Column1;
   LONG m_Column2;
   LONG m_Column3;
   LONG m_Column4;

BEGIN_ACCESSOR_MAP(CdboCustomerAccessor, 4) \
   BEGIN_ACCESSOR(0, true)
      COLUMN_ENTRY(1, m_ Column1)
   END_ACCESSOR()
   BEGIN_ACCESSOR(1, true)
      COLUMN_ENTRY(2, m_ Column2)
   END_ACCESSOR()
   BEGIN_ACCESSOR(2, false)
      COLUMN_ENTRY(3, m_ Column3)
   END_ACCESSOR()
   BEGIN_ACCESSOR(3, false)
      COLUMN_ENTRY(4, m_ Column4)
   END_ACCESSOR()
END_ACCESSOR_MAP()

DEFINE_COMMAND(CMyAccessor, _T(" \
   SELECT  ...the rest as usual"
```

Only `Column1` and `Column2` are part of an auto accessor. `Column3` and `Column4` are part of nonauto accessors.

By default, only `Column1` and `Column2` will be synchronized with the current row. For example, in the following code only those columns are filled in.

```
CCommand<CAccessor<CMyAccessor> > Command;
Command.Open (Session);
Command.MoveNext();
```

When you call `GetData(2)`, `Column3` will be updated with the value in the row:

```
Command.GetData(2); // will update Column3
Command.GetData(3); // will update Column4
```

## GetDataHere

Until now, `GetData` updated data in the current object (or, more precisely, in its buffer). In some cases, it is useful to get data outside the current object. That is, it is necessary to pass a buffer in which the rowset should write the values. `GetDataHere` does this. Though similar to `GetData`, `GetDataHere` has an extra argument for the buffer. Like `GetData`, it comes in two flavors:

- `HRESULT GetDataHere(int nAccessor, void* pBuffer)`
- `HRESULT GetDataHere(void* pBuffer)`

Notice that `GetDataHere(int nAccessor, void* pBuffer)` corresponds to `GetData(int nAccessor)`. In other words, it is equivalent to write

```
MyAccessor.GetData(nAccessor);
```

and

```
MyAccessor.GetDataHere(nAccessor, m_pAccessor->GetBuffer());
```

The same applies for `GetDataHere(void* pBuffer)` and `GetData()`.

`GetDataHere` can be useful when you want to store data outside an instance of `CCommand`. For example, you might have an accessor class that holds class members:

```
class CMyAccessor
{
   LONG m_Column1;
   LONG m_Column2;
```

```
BEGIN_ACCESSOR(CMyAccessor)
   COLUMN_ENTRY(1, m_Column1)
   COLUMN_ENTRY(2, m_Column2)
END_ACCESSOR()
};
```

However, you will need to declare a command to access the data:

```
CCommand<CAccessor<CMyAccessor> > Command;
```

Imagine that you want to store the set of row values in an array. If you declare the array as

```
CCommand <CAccessor<CMyAccessor> > MyArray [12];
```

each item will contain a pointer to the command object that is inherited from CCommandBase, which will lead to inefficiencies. The solution is to declare an array of type

```
CMyAccessor MyArray [12];
```

However, each item in the array now has a type that is not compatible with Command<..>. This means that it is not possible to write something like

```
MyArray[3] = Command; // not possible
```

When you fill up the array, one solution is to copy the data from buffer to buffer:

```
Command.MoveNext();
memcpy(MyArray[3], Command.GetBuffer(), sizeof(CMyAccessor));
```

Another solution is to use GetDataHere:

```
Command.MoveNext();
Command.GetDataHere((void*) MyAccessor [3]);
```

# FROM THE CONSUMER TO THE DATA STORE

Consumers can perform three operations on rows: setting, inserting, and deleting. While it is possible to carry out these operations with commands, OLE DB provides an attractive alternative. The rowset can support the optional interface IRowsetChange, whose methods perform these actions directly. The benefit of this is that there is no need for command text or command parameters. As a result, the code is usually easier to maintain.

`IRowsetChange` has three methods:

- `DeleteRows` deletes one or several rows in the rowset.
- `SetData` changes the content of a row.
- `InsertRow` inserts a row.

```
virtual HRESULT STDMETHODCALLTYPE DeleteRows(
   HCHAPTER hReserved,
   ULONGcRows,
   const HROW __RPC_FAR rghRows[  ],
   DBROWSTATUS __RPC_FAR rgRowStatus[  ]) = 0;

virtual HRESULT STDMETHODCALLTYPE SetData(
   HROW hRow,
   HACCESSOR hAccessor,
   void __RPC_FAR *pData) = 0;

virtual HRESULT STDMETHODCALLTYPE InsertRow(
   HCHAPTER hReserved,
   HACCESSOR hAccessor,
   void __RPC_FAR *pData,
   HROW __RPC_FAR *phRow) = 0;
```

## Deleting a Row

There are three ways to delete a row in a rowset:

- A command
- A command with parameters
- The `Delete` method

Suppose that we have one table that contains one column, "Value," of type `integer`. Also suppose that this table contains two rows with values 1 and 2. This section will demonstrate how to delete the first row.

The first method consists simply of sending an SQL command such as

```
DELETE FROM TABLE_NAME WHERE VALUE  = 1
```

It is very simple and easy to debug. However, it forces the programmer to generate SQL text for each command.

To avoid this use the second method: a command with parameters, in which the first step is to define an accessor class with one parameter binding:

```
class CdboDataExchangeAccessor
{
public:
   LONG m_Value;
```

```
// some code

BEGIN_PARAM_MAP(CdboDataExchangeAccessor)
    COLUMN_ENTRY(1, m_Value)
END_PARAM_MAP()

// some code
};
```

The second step is to execute the command:

```
CCommand<CdboDataExchangeAccessor> Command;
Command.m_Value = 1;
Command.Open("DELETE FROM DataExchange WHERE Value = ?");
```

The benefit of this method is that the same SQL text can be executed several times with different parameters. The less SQL code there is, the easier it is to manage. In addition, this command can be prepared, making it faster than the first method.

It would be great if we could remove SQL altogether. This is where IRowsetChange comes in. CRowset provides the Delete method, which encapsulates IRowsetChange::Delete:

```
HRESULT Delete() const
```

Before using Delete, it is important to make sure that the rowset supports the IRowsetChange interface.

The following code demonstrates how to delete the first row:

```
CDBPropSet    propset(DBPROPSET_ROWSET);
propset.AddProperty(DBPROP_IRowsetChange, true);

CTable <CAccessor <CdboDataExchangeAccessor> > Table;
Table.Open(Session, "DataExchange", &propset);
Table.MoveFirst();
Table.Delete();
```

## Setting Data

Consumers can set data with a command or a method of CRowset. They set the values of a row by calling one of the SetData methods:

```
HRESULT SetData(int nAccessor) const
```

or

```
HRESULT SetData() const
```

The first `SetData` method sets all the values that are defined in the accessor at index nAccessor for the current row. The accessor does not need to bind all the values. If it binds only a subset, the provider will set only those values and the remaining values will stay unchanged.

The second `SetData` sets all values for all accessors (unlike `GetData`, which does so only for auto accessors). If a column is bound in several accessors, `SetData` sets this value several times. Keep this in mind for columns that are expensive to set, such as long text columns or BLOBs.

The following code demonstrates how to set the value of the first row to 3:

```
CDBPropSet   propset(DBPROPSET_ROWSET);
propset.AddProperty(DBPROP_IRowsetChange, true);

CTable <CAccessor <CdboDataExchangeAccessor> > Table;
Table.Open(Session, "DataExchange", &propset);
Table.MoveFirst();
Table.m_Value = 3;
Table.SetData();
```

## Inserting a Row

Consumers insert a row by calling the `Insert` method.

```
HRESULT Insert(int nAccessor = 0, bool bGetHRow = false)
```

As with the `SetData` method, the consumer can specify the accessor to use. By default, `Insert` uses the first accessor (index 0). It is important to choose an accessor that binds enough columns; otherwise, the provider may not be able to decide which value to insert and the insertion will fail.

In addition, the consumer can specify whether to get the inserted row with the bGetHRow parameter. If bGetHRow is false, the current row does not change. Otherwise, it becomes the new row. On the left of Figure 10-1, the rowset inserts a new row without getting it, so the current row does not change. On the right, the rowset inserts a row and gets the new row, so the current row becomes the newly inserted row.

The following code demonstrates how to insert a column with a value set to 4:

```
CDBPropSet   propset(DBPROPSET_ROWSET);
propset.AddProperty(DBPROP_IRowsetChange, true);

CTable <CAccessor <CdboDataExchangeAccessor> > Table;
Table.Open(Session, "DataExchange", &propset);
Table.MoveFirst();
Table.m_Value = 4;
Table.Insert();
```

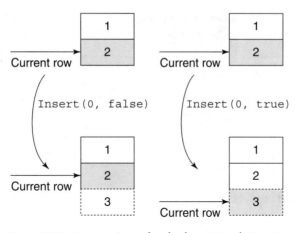

**Figure 10-1**  Inserting a Row with and without Getting the New Row

**Table 10-1**  `IRowsetChange` Methods

| IRowsetChange/CRowset Method | SQL Equivalent |
| --- | --- |
| SetData() | UPDATE |
| Insert() | INSERT |
| Delete() | DELETE |

## Rowset Method versus SQL

In summary, OLE DB offers two ways to set data: through a language such as SQL or through the OLE DB interface methods, both summarized in Table 10-1.

In general, it is easier to use the CRowset methods. Note, however, that they can be slower. When setting or updating data, you usually get it first. This involves two operations: reading and writing. These are not involved in insertion.

## DEFERRED UPDATES

All the changes we have seen so far are immediate: A row insertion, deletion, or change is immediately transmitted to the data store. Some OLE DB providers also offer deferred updates. When in deferred update mode, the consumer does not transmit the changes immediately to the data store, but rather records them in a

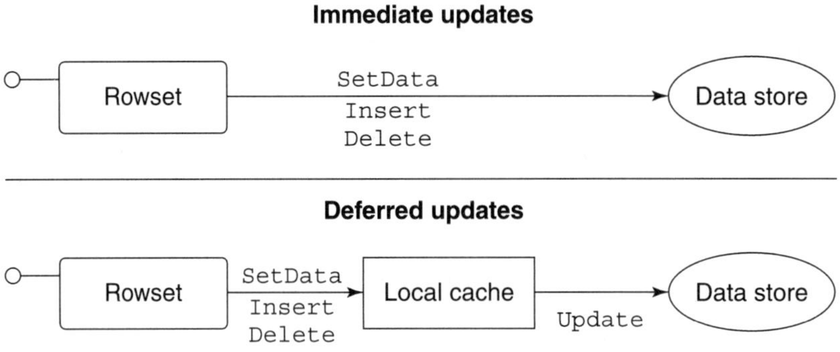

**Immediate updates**

**Deferred updates**

**Figure 10-2** Immediate and Deferred Updates

local cache. When the consumer calls the `Update` method, the changes are transmitted to the data store.

Figure 10-2 shows the difference between immediate and deferred updates.

One of the benefits of deferred updates is their flexibility. The consumer has greater control over what is sent to the data store and when. For example, the consumer can make several changes to one rowset but transmit them only after the last one. In addition, deferred changes can be undone.

Another benefit is performance. Because several changes can be transmitted at once, the provider can group them into one network call. Obviously, such an improvement is more critical when the network is slow, as in Internet scenarios.

The main drawback of deferred updates is their complexity. The programmer needs to explicitly call `Update` when finished. Otherwise, the changes are never transmitted to the data store. In addition, deferred updates can lock rows for a long period of time and therefore should be used with caution.

## Setting Deferred Changes

When a rowset is in deferred mode, it supports the `IRowsetUpdate` interface; a rowset in immediate mode does not. The consumer specifies the update mode with the `DBPROP_IRowsetUpdate` property, which, like any rowset property, is valid for the rowset lifetime. In other words, once you choose an update mode for a rowset, there is no way to change it.

The following example shows how to create one rowset in immediate mode and another in deferred mode:

```
CCommand <CMyAccessor> ImmediateRowset
CDBPropSet Propset (DBPROPSET_ROWSET);
Propset.AddProperty(DBPROP_IRowsetUpdate, false);
ImmediateRowset.Open(Session, sometext, &Propset);
```

```
///
CCommand <CMyAccessor> DeferredRowset;
CDBPropSet Propset (DBPROPSET_ROWSET);
Propset.AddProperty(DBPROP_IRowsetUpdate, true);
DeferredRowset.Open(Session, sometext, &Propset);
```

## Using Deferred Updates

OLE DB does not define any implementation for deferred updates, but the natural implementation is transparent. The following section will explore how deferred updates work.

## Pending Status

The pending status of a row describes the pending changes to it. It has one of the values in Table 10-2.

It is important to remember that the pending status describes only the pending operations, not the transmitted changes. For example, if a row is inserted in a rowset with pending changes, its status will be DBPENDINGSTATUS_NEW. However, once the rowset transmits the changes, the row's status becomes DBPENDINGSTATUS_UNCHANGED.

The pending status grows more complex when there are several consecutive operations for a given row. The simplest way to understand pending status is to go back to the basics: the rowset cache.

Figure 10-3 represents the different configurations of the cache and the corresponding pending status. The "Cache" column represents the value in the cache. If there is no value, the cache holds no changes. The "Data Store" column represents the value in the data store.

**Table 10-2** Pending Status

| Symbol | Description |
| --- | --- |
| DBPENDINGSTATUS_UNCHANGED | No pending change |
| DBPENDINGSTATUS_CHANGED | Values of the row have been changed |
| DBPENDINGSTATUS_DELETED | Row has been deleted |
| DBPENDINGSTATUS_NEW | Row has been inserted |
| DBPENDINGSTATUS_INVALIDROW | Row is invalid |

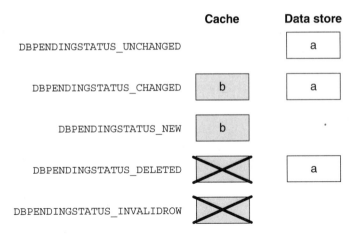

**Figure 10-3** Meanings of the Pending Changes

In the first case in the figure above, the cache does not hold any value, which means that there is no pending change. The pending status is thus DBPENDINGSTATUS_UNCHANGED for one of the following reasons:

- There has been no change for this row.
- The changes have been transmitted to the data store and hence deleted from the cache.
- The changes have been undone.

In the second case, the data store holds the value a and the cache holds the value b. The pending status thus is DBPENDINGSTATUS_CHANGED, which can happen after setting data.

In the third case, the cache has a row that has no equivalent in the data store, so the pending status is DBPENDINGSTATUS_NEW, which obviously occurs after inserting a row. Moreover, the status stays the same even after the values of a newly inserted row change.

In the fourth case, the cache shows that the row should be deleted, indicated by a cross. The data store has a corresponding row, and the pending status is DBPENDINGSTATUS_DELETED. This occurs after deleting a row regardless of whether the values of the row were previously changed.

The last case—DBPENDINGSTATUS_INVALIDROW—represents an example of invalid pending status. If you insert a new row and then delete it, it will be invalid since there is no corresponding row in the data store; transmitting its changes actually does nothing. In addition, a row will become invalid when you delete it and then set its data.

## Pending Rows: Navigating the Cache

A rowset can get the list of rows with a given pending status. This functionality is not part of the OLE DB consumer templates, but it is implemented in CRowsetEx in the OLE DB extensions.

The method is

```
HRESULT GetPendingRows(DBPENDINGSTATUS dwRowStatus,
    ULONG *pcPendingRows, HROW **prgPendingRows,
    DBPENDINGSTATUS **prgPendingStatus)
```

where

- dwRowStatus represents the row status of the requested rows. It can be a combination of DBPENDINGSTATUS_NEW, DBPENDINGSTATUS_CHANGED, and DBPENDINGSTATUS_DELETED.
- pcPendingRows receives the number of rows that have the given status.
- prgPendingRows receives the row handles.
- prgPendingStatus receives the row status.

The last two parameters are allocated by the COM memory allocator and should be freed by it as well.

The following code shows how to get the rows that have been inserted or deleted:

```
// Rowset inherits from CRowsetEx

ULONG cPendingRows;
HROW*              rgPendingRows;
DBPENDINGSTATUS*   rgPendingStatus;
hr = Rowset.GetPendingRows( DBPENDINGSTATUS_NEW |
    DBPENDINGSTATUS_ DELETED, &cPendingRows, &rgPendingRows,
    &rgPendingStatus);
if (FAILED(hr))
    return hr;
// Use rgPendingRows and rgPendingStatus
CoTaskMemFree(rgPendingStatus);
CoTaskMemFree(rgPendingRows);
```

## Transmitting the Changes

The CRowset::Update method transmits the changes from the cache to the data store and wipes out the cache. The name "Update" can be misleading for SQL programmers because it has nothing to do with an SQL UPDATE statement. The equivalent of the UPDATE statement is SetData. Another name for Update could have been TransmitChanges.

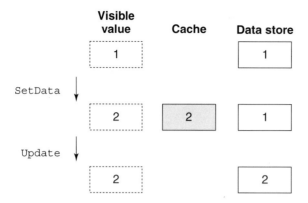

**Figure 10-4** Updating a Row

Figure 10-4 shows an update example. The value in the right column shows the value stored in the data store. Since we are in deferred mode, there is a local cache. The values in gray in the middle column represent the values in the cache. (If the cache did not contain any value, none would be shown). Finally, the visible value represents the value that we get when calling GetData. Simply put, the visible value is the value in the cache, if any, or the value in the data store otherwise. The visible value is not stored anywhere—it does not have any material reality—and is therefore represented with a dotted line.

As the same principle applies for single and multiple columns, we will consider only one column for simplicity. At first, the data store contains the value 1. Since no deferred action has been performed, there is no value in the cache for the row. When the rowset sets the column value to 2, the cache value becomes 2, but the value in the data store is still 1. When the consumer calls Update, the provider transmits the value to the data store and removes the value from the cache.

Consumers transmit changes by calling CRowset::Update():

```
HRESULT Update(ULONG* pcRows = NULL, HROW* phRow = NULL,
    DBROWSTATUS* pStatus = NULL)
{
    ATLASSERT(m_spRowset != NULL);

    CComPtr<IRowsetUpdate> spRowsetUpdate;
    HRESULT hr = m_spRowset->QueryInterface(&spRowsetUpdate);
    if (FAILED(hr))
        return hr;

    HROW*          prgRows;
    DBROWSTATUS*   pRowStatus;
    if (phRow != NULL)
        hr = spRowsetUpdate->Update(NULL, 1, &m_hRow, pcRows,
            &prgRows, &pRowStatus);
```

```
      else
         hr = spRowsetUpdate->Update(NULL, 1, &m_hRow, pcRows,
            NULL, &pRowStatus);
      if (FAILED(hr))
         return hr;

      if (phRow != NULL)
      {
         *phRow = *prgRows;
         CoTaskMemFree(prgRows);
      }
      if (pStatus != NULL)
         *pStatus = *pRowStatus;

      CoTaskMemFree(pRowStatus);
      return hr;
   }
```

Note that Update transmits the changes only for the current row. Indeed, the Update method from the IRowsetUpdate interface updates only a set of rows, not all the rows in the rowset. It is the responsibility of the consumer to pass the correct set. In other words, you should call Update for every row that needs to be transmitted to the data store. In the following example, the programmer calls Update for the second row but not for the first:

```
MyRowset.MoveFirst();
MyRowset.m_Column1 = 1;
MyRowset.SetData();

MyRowset.MoveNext();
MyRowset.m_Column1 = 2;
MyRowset.SetData();
MyRowset.Update();
```

Therefore, the changes for the first row can be lost.

## Updating All Changes

Sometimes it can be tricky to remember which row to update. Of course, it is always possible to call Update before any row movement, but by doing so you lose the inherent benefits of deferred updates. The OLE DB extensions provide an easy way to update all of the rows with pending changes: the UpdateAll method from CRowsetEx. UpdateAll simply passes zero as the number of rows to update, which OLE DB providers interpret as all rows. UpdateAll is defined as

```
HRESULT UpdateAll()
{
   ATLASSERT(m_spRowset != NULL);
   CComPtr<IRowsetUpdate> spRowsetUpdate;
```

```
        HRESULT hr = m_spRowset->QueryInterface(&spRowsetUpdate);
        if (FAILED(hr))
            return hr;
        return spRowsetUpdate->Update(GetHChapter(), 0, NULL, NULL,
            NULL, NULL);
}
```

For example:

```
CRowsetEx MyRowset;
// Perform some actions
MyRowset.UpdateAll(); // Update all the rows
```

## Undoing Changes

One of the benefits of deferred updates is that you can undo the deferred changes in the same way you undo changes in an Office document.

Usually, implementing an Undo is a big job. For OLE DB providers, however, it is simple, consisting of deleting the cache for a given set of rows.

Figure 10-5 represents an example of Undo. When we call SetData with a value of 2, the OLE DB provider looks for a value in the cache. Since there is no value, the provider inserts the new one. The value in the data store remains unchanged because we are in deferred mode. The visible value becomes the value in the cache.

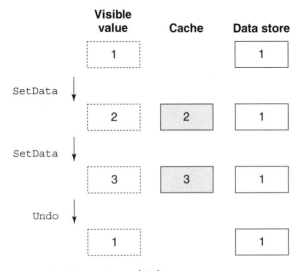

**Figure 10-5** Setting Data and Undoing

When we call `SetData` again with a value of 3, the provider looks for a value in the cache, finds it, and updates it. Again, the value in the data store does not change. The visible value becomes 3.

When we call `Undo`, the OLE DB provider looks for a value in the cache. It finds the value 3 and removes it. As a result, the visible value becomes the value in the data store—1 in this example. Intuitively, `Undo` should go back one step and set the value to 2. However, for simplicity the cache does not keep track of the history of values but knows only about the current value. Another name for `Undo` could be `DeleteTheCacheValue`.

## Undoing All Changes

The `Undo` method undoes changes for the current row only. `CRowsetEx` provides the `UndoAll` method, which is similar to `UpdateAll` in that it performs `Undo` on all the rows.

## Original and Last Visible Data

Imagine the following scenario: You get a row with one column with value 1. In deferred mode, you change the value to 2. At the same time, some other process changes it to 3. Thus, you end up with three values: the original data (the fetched data) holds 1, the new value in the cache holds 2, and the data store visible data holds 3 (Figure 10-6).

When the rowset fetches a row, it gets the corresponding column values. The `GetData` method first looks for a new value in the cache. If there is one, it returns it. Otherwise, it gets the original cache value (fetched) data.

`CRowsetEx` provides two additional methods: `GetOriginalData` and `GetLastVisibleData`. Unlike `GetData`, `GetOriginalData` does not look at the value in the cache but always gets the original data. In other words, its behavior does not depend on the new value in the cache.

`GetLastVisibleData` gets the data from the data store. As Chapter 12 will show, transaction isolation has an effect on the visibility of changes between

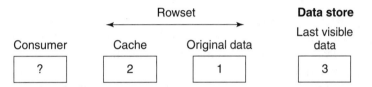

**Figure 10-6** Cache, Original Data, and Last Visible Data

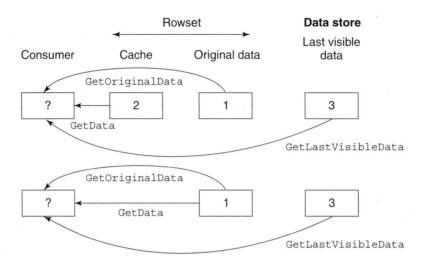

**Figure 10-7** Behavior of `GetData`, `GetOriginalData`, and `GetLastVisibleData`

transactions. `GetLastVisibleData` simply gets the data from the data store according to the isolation level.

Figure 10-7 summarizes the behavior of `GetData`, `GetOriginalData`, and `GetLastVisibleData` with and without data in the cache.

## Deferred Changes and Transactions

This section assumes that you understand transactions. If not, jump to Chapter 12 and come back to this section afterward.

In a sense, deferred changes are comparable to changes that occur in a transaction: Transmitting them is equivalent to committing a transaction, while undoing them is equivalent to aborting it. However, deferred changes do not have the functionality of regular transactions. For example, they are not as robust and they apply to only one rowset at a time. You might say that deferred changes are comparable to a "baby" transaction. The natural question is what happens when you mix the two.

The first point to keep in mind is that deferred changes occur locally inside the rowset object. As a result, transactions are not aware of them. In particular, the issue of visibility of changes between transactions does not arise: Since a transaction is not aware of the changes inside a rowset, these changes cannot be visible to any other transaction.

Figure 10-8 summarizes the relation between the transaction and the deferred changes.

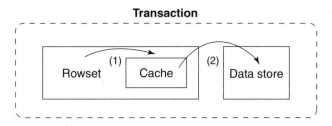

**Figure 10-8** Deferred Changes and Transactions

In addition, when you undo changes, the transaction does not even notice. In other words, the changes will not reach the data store whatever the outcome of the transaction.

The transaction is not aware of the deferred status of a rowset. Therefore, once the deferred changes are transmitted, they flow in the transaction exactly like immediate changes. The transaction has the final word: If it aborts, the changes will be discarded in any case.

In short, deferred changes are comparable to nested transactions. However, there is still the question of what happens to pending changes when a transaction commits or aborts. In this case, the behavior depends on the rowset preservation of the transaction (see Chapter 12). If the transaction does not preserve the rowset, all the pending changes are lost. If the transaction does preserve the rowset, the pending changes are still alive and behave as if there had been no previous transaction.

To sum up, deferred changes do not have all the capabilities of a regular transaction, but they can be a handy and efficient alternative in simple cases.

## NOTIFICATIONS

The rowset object is quite complex. It can fetch rows and make, undo, or update changes. All this is manageable when there is only one local rowset object. However, things change when rowsets are shared. For example, two components A and B might share a rowset object. If A inserts a row in the rowset, how can B know about it and respond? The COM answer to this problem is notification.

A rowset that supports notifications should support the COM interface, `IConnectionPointContainer`, which, as the name suggests, contains a list of connection points. Clients call the `FindConnectionPoint` method to get the connection point they need. A connection point is a COM object that supports the `IConnectionPoint` COM interface. Objects that receive rowset notifications are called *rowset listeners*. A rowset listener passes itself to the connection point object through the `Advise` method. When the component no longer wants

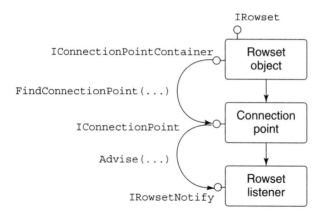

**Figure 10-9** Connection Point Architecture

to be notified of events, it calls Unadvise. In the case of rowsets, objects that want rowset notification need to support the IRowsetNotify interface.

Figure 10-9 summarizes the architecture of connection points for rowsets. As usual, you can use rowset connection points by calling a raw COM interface or via the ATL function. This section assumes that you will be using the ATL function.

To listen to the notification of a rowset, use the AtlAdvise function. In the following sample, the spRowsetListener object requests the notifications of spRowset:

```
CComPtr<IRowset> spRowset;
CComPtr<IRowsetNotify> spRowsetListener;
// create both object
DWORD Cookie;
spRowset.Advise(spNotif, IID_IRowsetNotify,&Cookie);
// equivalent to
AtlAdvise(spRowset, spNotif, IID_IRowsetNotify,&Cookie);
```

Here, Cookie is an integer that uniquely identifies the notification between the rowset and the rowset listener. It is useful when you want to stop receiving the notifications using the AtlUnadvise function:

```
AtlUnadvise(spRowset, IID_IRowsetNotify,Cookie);
```

## Rowset Listeners

Implementing a rowset listener is equivalent to implementing a COM object that supports the IRowsetNotify interface. IRowsetNotify handles all rowset events. Rowsets define many events, which must be categorized as corresponding to a certain domain. OLE DB defines three domains: *rowset*, *row*, and *column*.

- The *rowset domain* includes all events that affect the entire rowset, as, for example, when a client releases a rowset interface.
- The *row domain* comprises all events that correspond to a given row, as, for example, when a row is deleted.
- The *column domain* includes all events related to a given column of a given row, as, for example, when you set the value of a column.

Figure 10-10 summarizes the rowset, row, and column domains.

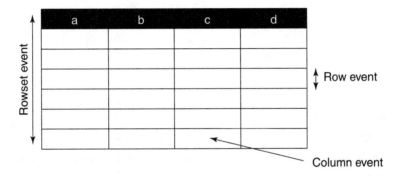

**Figure 10-10** Rowset, Row, and Column Events

`IRowsetNotify` declares one method for each event domain:

- `OnRowsetChange` is called for events for an entire rowset.
- `OnRowChange` is called for events for one or several rows.
- `OnFieldChange` is called for events for one or several fields for a given row ("field" is a synonym for "column").

Each method has at least one event reason and one event phase argument.

## Event Reasons

The event reason is an integer that indicates what happened. It has one of the values in Table 10-3.

**Table 10-3** Notification Reasons

| Symbol | Domain | Typical Rowset Method | Comments |
|---|---|---|---|
| DBREASON_ROWSET_CHANGED | Rowset | | Rowset changed |
| DBREASON_ROWSET_FETCHPOSITIONCHANGE | Rowset | MoveNext | Fetch position changed |
| DBREASON_ROWSET_RELEASE | Rowset | Release | Rowset was released |
| DBREASON_ROWSET_CHANGED | Rowset | | Rowset changed |
| DBREASON_ROWSET_FETCHPOSITIONCHANGE | Rowset | MoveNext | Fetch position changed |
| DBREASON_ROWSET_RELEASE | Rowset | Release | Rowset was released |
| DBREASON_ROW_ACTIVATE | Row | MoveNext | |
| DBREASON_ROW_ASYNCHINSERT | Row | Insert | Row was inserted asynchronously |
| DBREASON_ROW_DELETE | Row | Delete | Row was deleted |
| DBREASON_ROW_FIRSTCHANGE | Row | | |
| DBREASON_ROW_INSERT | Row | Insert | Row was inserted |
| DBREASON_ROW_RELEASE | Row | ReleaseRows | Row was released |
| DBREASON_ROW_RESYNCH | Row | | |
| DBREASON_ROW_UNDOCHANGE | Row | Undo | Row change was undone |
| DBREASON_ROW_UNDODELETE | Row | Undo | Row deletion was undone |
| DBREASON_ROW_UNDOINSERT | Row | Undo | Row insertion was undone |
| DBREASON_ROW_UPDATE | Row | Update | Row was updated |
| DBREASON_ROWPOSITION_CHANGED | Row | | |
| DBREASON_ROWPOSITION_CHAPTERCHANGED | Row | | |
| DBREASON_ROWPOSITION_CLEARED | Row | | |
| DBREASON_COLUMN_RECALCULATED | Column | | |
| DBREASON_COLUMN_SET | Column | SetData | Column value changed |

## Event Phase

For many notification interfaces, a method is called once per event; the notification object is just there to listen. IRowsetNotify is different because it has a say in the event. The rowset listener has the power to cancel the event for certain event reasons. As a result, the rowset object needs to notify several times for each event, each time corresponding to a given event phase.

OLE DB defines five event phases:

- DBEVENTPHASE_OKTODO
- DBEVENTPHASE_ABOUTTODO
- DBEVENTPHASE_SYNCHAFTER
- DBEVENTPHASE_FAILEDTODO
- DBEVENTPHASE_DIDEVENT

When the listeners do not have any influence on the event, the rowset notifies only for the DBEVENTPHASE_DIDEVENT phase. However, things become more complex when listeners have the power to stop the event from happening. The rowset then notifies for four phases, illustrated in Figure 10-11 and described in the following paragraphs.

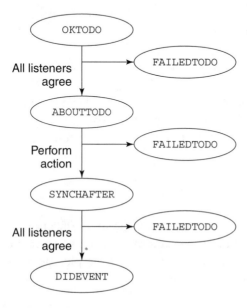

**Figure 10-11** Event Phases

First, the rowset notifies all listeners for DBEVENTPHASE_OKTODO. In this phase, the rowset makes sure that all listeners agree with this event—if one or more return S_FALSE, the event is aborted. All of the listeners that receive DBEVENTPHASE_OKTODO then receive DBEVENTPHASE_FAILEDTODO. If no listener returns S_FALSE, the rowset proceeds to the next phase.

The rowset then notifies all listeners for DBEVENTPHASE_ABOUTTODO. At this stage, all listeners have agreed at DBEVENTPHASE_OKTODO, so there is a high probability that all phases will be accepted. As a result, each listener should perform the preparation at DBEVENTPHASE_ABOUTTODO. As for the previous phase, if one or more listeners return S_FALSE, the event is aborted and the rowset notifies for DBEVENTPHASE_FAILEDTODO. Otherwise, it performs the action.

After performing the action, the rowset notifies for DBEVENTPHASE_ SYNCHAFTER, which means that the action has been performed. If at least one listener returns S_FALSE, the rowset notifies for DBEVENTPHASE_FAILEDTODO. Otherwise, it notifies DBEVENTPHASE_DIDEVENT. This phase means that all listeners have successfully synchronized.

For each phase, the rowset can also indicate that the rowset listener does not have the power to cancel the event. Each method of IRowsetNotify has a boolean parameter called bCantDeny. For example, OnRowsetChange has the following parameters:

```
HRESULT OnRowsetChange (
    IRowset *       pRowset,
    DBREASON        eReason,
    DBEVENTPHASE    ePhase,
    BOOL            fCantDeny);
```

As the name suggests, if bCantDeny is TRUE, the rowset listener cannot cancel the event.

By returning DB_S_UNWANTEDPHASE, the rowset listener indicates that it is not interested in this phase for a given notification reason. Similarly, by returning DB_S_UNWANTEDREASON, it indicates that it is not interested in this reason for all phases.

## Notification Example

The following example shows how to set up a rowset notification. Note that the rowset is created with the DBPROP_IConnectionPointContainer property, which ensures that it supports notifications. In this example, the rowset listener is implemented in a separate server.

```
CCommand<CAccessor<CdboDataExchangeAccessor> > DataExchange;
CDBPropSet PropSet(DBPROPSET_ROWSET);
PropSet.AddProperty(DBPROP_IRowsetChange, true);
PropSet.AddProperty(DBPROP_IConnectionPointContainer, true);
PropSet.AddProperty(DBPROP_UPDATABILITY, DBPROPVAL_UP_CHANGE |
   DBPROPVAL_UP_INSERT | DBPROPVAL_UP_DELETE);
hr = DataExchange.Open(Session, NULL, &PropSet);
if (FAILED(hr))
   return hr;
CComPtr <IRowsetNotify> Notif;
hr = Notif.CoCreateInstance(CLSID_NotifiedObject);
if (FAILED(hr))
   return hr;
DWORD Cookie;
hr = DataExchange.m_spRowset.Advise(Notif, IID_IRowsetNotify,&Cookie);
```

It is interesting to listen to the events once the rowset is open. When the rowset moves to the first row,

```
hr = DataExchange.MoveFirst();
```

it triggers the DBREASON_ROWSET_FETCHPOSITIONCHANGE event for all phases. The listener has the opportunity to cancel the row fetching, but in our example it is passive and agrees to all events. After that the rowset then triggers the DBREASON_ROW_ACTIVATE event at the "did event" phase only: It does not have the opportunity to interfere with this event.

When the rowset sets the column value,

```
DataExchange.m_Value = 123;
hr = DataExchange.SetData();
```

it triggers the DBREASON_COLUMN_SET event for all phases.

When the rowset moves to the next column,

```
hr = DataExchange.MoveNext();
```

it triggers the DBREASON_ROW_RELEASE event for the "did event" phase; the listener cannot interfere with this event.

When the rowset deletes the current row,

```
hr = DataExchange.Delete();
```

it triggers the DBREASON_ROW_DELETE event for all phases. Similarly, when the rowset inserts a row (Insert method), it triggers the DBREASON_ROW_INSERT event.

When you are finished, call the Unadvise function:

```
hr = AtlUnadvise(DataExchange.m_spRowset, IID_IRowsetNotify,Cookie);
```

## SUMMARY

This chapter explained how to get and set data. As in other parts of the OLE DB consumer templates, there are several levels to these functions. At a minimum, you can use `SetData`, `Insert`, and `Delete` in immediate mode, which represent an easy way to set data. At the same time, OLE DB offers many options with deferred updates, which are a bit more difficult but present many benefits. Finally, notifications offer a standard and elegant way to be notified of rowset events.

This chapter concludes the core of the OLE DB consumer templates. The next two chapters will present two advanced techniques: BLOBs and transactions.

# 11 BLOBs

Until now, we used simple types, like integer, real, date, and string. OLE DB also supports another type: *binary large objects*, known as BLOBs. Since providers are not required to support this type, you might check that your provider does before going further.

As the name suggests, BLOBs store a large amount of data. Thus, they are ideal for multimedia types such as bitmaps, sound, video, or large texts. However, precisely because of their large capacity, BLOBs need some special mechanism to store and retrieve data without risking a lack of memory.

This chapter will

- Explain the different kinds of BLOBs.
- Explain the different methods to access BLOBs.
- For each method, explain how to read and write data.

## BLOB TYPES

We can classify BLOBs by their content and access method.

### Content

From the perspective of OLE DB, there are two kinds of BLOB content: *regular BLOBs* and *COM objects*.

A regular BLOB is just a sequence of bytes, which the consumer must interpret. In contrast, COM objects can read and write themselves in a stream or storage and do not need to be interpreted. Note, however, that COM objects are also regular BLOBs, which means that, even if not recommended, it is still possible to read and write them as a sequence of uninterpreted bytes.

Although OLE DB providers can support COM objects as well as regular BLOBs, in practice only a few do so. For this reason, this chapter will concentrate on regular BLOBs.

The `DBPROP_OLEOBJECTS` data source information property specifies whether the data source supports BLOBs or persistent COM objects. It can have a combination of `DBPROPVAL_OO_BLOB` and `DBPROPVAL_OO_IPERSIST`.

## Access Method

The two ways to access BLOBs are in memory and through a storage object. With in-memory access, the entire content of the BLOB is transferred to the consumer at once. With access through a storage object, you can read and write data chunk by chunk. In-memory access is ideal for short BLOBs; storage object access is great for long ones.

## Long and Short BLOBs

OLE DB distinguishes between short and long BLOBs. However, there is no cutoff or formula that says whether short or long BLOBs are contained in a BLOB column. The definition of a short BLOB is just that it can be safely retrieved all at once in memory. Conversely, a long BLOB should not be retrieved in memory but rather through a storage object. This does not mean that a long BLOB can *never* be retrieved in memory, only that there is a risk that reading or writing data this way can produce errors. As a rule, you should retrieve short BLOBs in memory and long ones through a storage interface.

Consumers can determine whether a BLOB column is long or short via the `DBCOLUMNFLAGS_ISLONG` column flag. `CDynamicAccessor` is a convenient class to get column flags. The following example shows how to find out whether a column (the first column in this case) holds long BLOBs:

```
CBLOBTable<CDynamicAccessor> myTable;
HRESULT hr = myTable.Open();
if (FAILED(hr))
   return hr;
DBCOLUMNFLAGS flags;
myTable.GetColumnFlags(1, &flags);
bool is_long = flags & DBCOLUMNFLAGS_ISLONG;
```

**Table 11-1** BLOB Types and Access Methods

|  | Short Fixed-Size | Short Variable-Size | Long |
|---|---|---|---|
| In memory | Preferred | Possible but need to allocate enough memory | Not recommended |
| In memory by reference | Possible but complicated for no reason | Preferred | Not recommended |
| Storage object | Possible but complicated for no reason | Possible but complicated for no reason | Preferred |

## Fixed-Size and Variable-Size BLOBs

Short BLOBs can be divided into two categories: fixed-size and variable-size. OLE DB does not have this notion, but the underlying database usually does.

Short fixed-size BLOBs have a fixed size declared in the database. With SQL Server, for example, binary (n) is a fixed-size BLOB (n is the size of the data). The simplest way to retrieve a short fixed-size BLOB is to allocate a buffer and request that the provider write the BLOB content on it.

Short variable-size BLOBs can be retrieved in one piece, but the size of the data varies from row to row. With SQL Server, for example, varbinary (n) is a short variable-size BLOB. In a varbinary (n) column, all data pieces have length n or less. The simplest way to retrieve a short variable-size BLOB is to ask the provider to allocate the memory buffer and write the BLOB content on it. I refer to this method as "in memory by reference" since the provider supplies a reference to the buffer.

From the OLE DB perspective, there is no way to tell if a short BLOB column contains variable-size data. The consumer can retrieve the name of the column type and deduce it from there.

Table 11-1 summarizes the different of BLOB columns and access methods.

## BLOBS AS IN-MEMORY DATA

When using in-memory data, the consumer allocates a piece of memory and passes it to the provider. The provider then writes the BLOB data in it. This method is very straightforward to use and debug. However, the data might be truncated if the consumer allocates memory that is too small. For this reason, in-memory data is ideally suited for fixed-size BLOB columns since the programmer can allocate a buffer that is exactly their size. This method is also very efficient because there is no repetitive memory allocation on the consumer's part.

The following example shows an accessor class with a fixed-length column binding.

```
class CBLOBAccessorFixedLength
{
public:
   BYTE m_Column1 [50];

BEGIN_COLUMN_MAP(CBLOBAccessorFixedLength)
   COLUMN_ENTRY(1, m_Column1)
END_COLUMN_MAP()

DEFINE_COMMAND(CBLOBAccessorFixedLength, _T(" \
   SELECT \
   Column1  \
   FROM TABLE1"))
};
```

## BLOBs AS IN-MEMORY DATA BY REFERENCE

When using in-memory data by reference, the provider, not the consumer, allocates a piece of memory and writes the BLOB data in it. The consumer gets a reference to this buffer and can choose whether the memory is owned by itself or the provider (the default). For more information about memory ownership and management, refer to chapter 9. This method works well for short variable-size BLOB columns since there is no risk of truncation. It can be less efficient than in-memory data when the consumer owns the memory, because the memory needs to be allocated and freed for each row.

The following example shows an accessor class with variable-length BLOB binding.

```
class CBLOBAccessorVariableLength
{
public:
   BYTE* m_Column1;
   ULONG m_Column1Length;

BEGIN_COLUMN_MAP(CBLOBAccessorVariableLength)
   COLUMN_ENTRY_TYPE_LENGTH(1, DBTYPE_BYTES | DBTYPE_BYREF,
      m_Column1, m_Column1Length)
END_COLUMN_MAP()
```

```
DEFINE_COMMAND(CBLOBAccessorVariableLength, _T(" \
    SELECT \
        Column1  \
        FROM TABLE1"))
};
```

# BLOB AS STORAGE OBJECT

A storage object is a COM object used to store and retrieve BLOB data. It has methods to read and write small amounts of memory. As illustrated in Figure 11-1, the provider creates an instance of a storage object and passes it to the consumer. The consumer is then responsible for reading the BLOB piece by piece. The benefit of this method is that large objects can be read in small chunks. For example, if the BLOB column contains a large video, the consumer can retrieve small bits of the video as the user watches it. This method can also be used for short BLOBs, but the complexity of storage objects is probably unnecessary in this case.

Note that the storage object is not stored in the data source. It is used for accessing the BLOB data in small chunks.

## Storage Interfaces

A storage object supports at least one of the four storage interfaces:

- ISequentialStream
- IStream
- IStorage
- ILockBytes

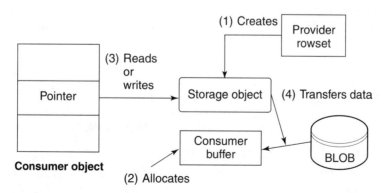

**Figure 11-1** Storage Object Architecture

The data source information property DBPROP_STRUCTUREDSTORAGE indicates which storage interface is supported. Its value is a combination of those in Table 11-2. ISequentialStream is the simplest interface, having only the Read and Write methods:

```
HRESULT Read(
    void * pv, //Pointer to buffer into which the stream is read
    ULONG cb,  //Specifies the number of bytes to read
    ULONG * pcbRead
       //Pointer to location that contains actual
       // number of bytes read
);
HRESULT Write(
    void const* pv,
       //Address of buffer from which stream is written
    ULONG cb,       //Specifies the number of bytes to write
    ULONG * pcbWritten
       //Specifies the actual number of bytes written
);
```

Objects that implement ISequentialStream should keep track of the current position, which at creation time is at the beginning of the BLOB. Both Read and Write increment the current position of the amount of bytes processed. Figure 11-2 shows an example where the consumer calls Read two times. The first time, it requests 3 bytes and therefore moves the current position 3 bytes forward. It then calls Read again with 4 bytes.

ISequentialStream is very primitive. For example, there is no way to go backward. On the positive side, this translates into an easy implementation for the provider. Often, ISequentialStream is the only interface the provider supports. For this reason, it is the focus of the rest of this chapter.

The IStream interface is a descendant of ISequentialStream. In addition to the Read and Write methods, it contains methods to seek a given position, copy memory, and clone itself. Unlike ISequentialStream, IStream allows the client to go backward when reading or writing data. Its methods are close to the file API functions, which makes it perfect for accessing files.

**Table 11-2** DBPROPSTRUCTUREDSTORAGE Property Values

| Symbol | Description |
| --- | --- |
| DBPROPVAL_SS_ISEQUENTIALSTREAM | ISequentialStream is supported |
| DBPROPVAL_SS_ISTREAM | IStream is supported |
| DBPROPVAL_SS_ISTORAGE | IStorage is supported |
| DBPROPVAL_SS_ILOCKBYTES | ILockBytes interface is supported |

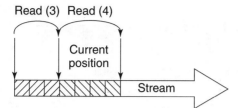

**Figure 11-2** Reading a Sequential Stream

IStorage represents a collection of streams and storage. Together, IStream and IStorage represent the equivalent of a file system.

ILockBytes represents an interface to an array of bytes in memory, on disk, or on some other device such as a database BLOB.

ISequentialStream is the preferred interface and so will be used in the following example. Examples using a different storage interface would be very similar.

## Retrieving BLOB Data with a Storage Object

Accessing a BLOB requires two steps:

**1.** Declaring an accessor class binding a storage object
**2.** Creating an instance, getting the stream, and reading the data

The most natural way to define the accessor is via the OLE DB consumer template macros, the most basic being BLOB_ENTRY, defined as

```
#define BLOB_ENTRY(nOrdinal, IID, flags, data) \ ...
```

where

- nOrdinal represents the column ordinal in the rowset.
- data is the class member that holds the reference on the storage object.
- IID is the interface identifier (IID) of the object storage, for example IID_ISequentialStream.
- flags represents the access mode of the storage object.

The storage mode can have many different values, the most common of which are listed in Table 11-3.

The OLE DB consumer templates also define BLOB_ENTRY_STATUS, similar to BLOB_ENTRY, which binds the column status as well.

```
#define BLOB_ENTRY_STATUS(nOrdinal, IID, flags, data, status)
```

**Table 11-3** Storage Medium Flags

| Symbol | Description |
|--------|-------------|
| STGM_READ | Only read operations are possible |
| STGM_WRITE | Only write operations are possible |
| STGM_READWRITE | Both read and write operations are possible |

where status is the class member that holds the status of the column.

As shown in the following example, the class binds one BLOB through the ISequentialStream interface:

```
class CBLOBAccessorSequentialStreamRead
{
public:
   ISequentialStream* m_Column1;

BEGIN_COLUMN_MAP(CBLOBAccessorSequentialStreamRead)
   BLOB_ENTRY(1, IID_ISequentialStream, STGM_READ, m_Column1)
END_COLUMN_MAP()

DEFINE_COMMAND(CBLOBAccessorSequentialStreamRead, _T(" \
   SELECT \
      Column1  \
      FROM TABLE1"))

   void ClearRecord()
   {
      memset(this, 0, sizeof(*this));
   }
};
```

Note that we specify STGM_READ as the mode since we only need to read for now.

At first, the following line might be surprising:

```
   ISequentialStream* m_Column1;
```

Indeed, the first chapter explained the benefits of COM pointers (class CComPtr) for automatic reference counting. However, there is no need to use CComPtr in this context, as FreeRecordMemory will decrement the reference count of the COM object and ClearRecord will initialize m_Column1 to NULL.

Once the storage object binding is defined, you can use it as follows:

```
HRESULT ReadWithSequentialStream()
{
    CBLOBTable<CBLOBAccessorSequentialStreamRead> myTable;
    HRESULT hr = myTable.Open();
    if (FAILED(hr))
        return hr;
    hr = myTable.MoveFirst();
    if (hr == S_OK)
    {
        CComPtr<ISequentialStream> myStream;
        myStream = myTable.m_Column1;
        BYTE bytes [50];
        ULONG ActualLength = sizeof(bytes);
        while(ActualLength == sizeof(bytes) || hr == S_OK)
        {
            hr = myStream->Read(bytes,sizeof(bytes),&ActualLength);
            // do something with bytes
        }
        myTable.FreeRecordMemory();
    }
    return S_OK;
}
```

There are a few points to underline in this code sample:

- bytes represents an array that receives the bytes read from the sequential stream. Obviously, this array needs to be allocated prior to calling ISequentialStream::Read.

- When ISequentialStream reaches the end of the stream it should perform two actions. First, it should set the length of the actual bytes read (ActualLength in the code); this value will be less than the requested number of bytes. Second, it should return a success code: S_FALSE. Some providers fail to do one of these actions, so check both hr and ActualLength.

- Once you are finished with the row, you *must* call FreeRecordMemory. Otherwise, the storage object will stay alive and consume unnecessary memory.

- This example uses a CComPtr<ISequentialStream> variable. It would be possible (and slightly faster) to use a variable of type ISequentialStream*.

One of the deficiencies of this approach is that we do not know the *length* of the data held by the storage object before reading the full data. It can be tedious to check for the length after each call to ISequential::Read. Besides, scenarios where the user processes storage objects only for certain lengths are not possible. Surprisingly, the OLE DB consumer templates do not provide macros that bind the length of the data held by a storage object, although they are fairly easy to implement.

Both COLUMN_ENTRY and COLUMN_ENTRY_STATUS are based on the _BLOB_ENTRY_CODE macro defined as

```
#define _BLOB_ENTRY_CODE(nOrdinal, IID, flags, dataOffset,
    statusOffset) \
  if (pBuffer != NULL) \
  { \
     CAccessorBase::FreeType(DBTYPE_IUNKNOWN, pBuffer + \
        dataOffset); \
  } \
  else if (pBinding != NULL) \
  { \
     DBOBJECT* pObject = NULL; \
     ATLTRY(pObject = new DBOBJECT); \
     if (pObject == NULL) \
        return E_OUTOFMEMORY; \
     pObject->dwFlags = flags; \
     pObject->iid     = IID; \
     CAccessorBase::Bind(pBinding, nOrdinal, DBTYPE_IUNKNOWN,
        sizeof(IUnknown*), 0, 0, eParamIO, \
        dataOffset, 0, statusOffset, pObject); \
     pBinding++; \
  } \
  nColumns++;
```

Like other column binding macros, _BLOB_ENTRY_CODE deals with two issues: binding the class member and freeing the data. The first lines are used to release the storage object when not needed. The rest of the lines just call CAccessorBase::Bind with the right parameters. Since the length offset is always zero (the ninth parameter of Bind()), _BLOB_ENTRY_CODE never binds the length of the data held by the storage object.

The OLE DB extensions provide the _BLOB_ENTRY_CODE_EX macro, which is very similar to _BLOB_ENTRY_CODE but with length binding. It is defined as follows:

```
#define _BLOB_ENTRY_CODE_EX(nOrdinal, IID, flags, dataOffset,
lengthOffset, statusOffset) \
   if (pBuffer != NULL) \
   { \
      CAccessorBase::FreeType(DBTYPE_IUNKNOWN, pBuffer + \
         dataOffset); \
   } \
   else if (pBinding != NULL) \
   { \
      DBOBJECT* pObject = NULL; \
      ATLTRY(pObject = new DBOBJECT); \
```

```
    if (pObject == NULL) \
        return E_OUTOFMEMORY; \
    pObject->dwFlags = flags; \
    pObject->iid = IID; \
    CAccessorBase::Bind(pBinding, nOrdinal, DBTYPE_IUNKNOWN,
        sizeof (IUnknown*), 0, 0, eParamIO, \
        dataOffset, lengthOffset, statusOffset, pObject); \
    pBinding++; \
} \
nColumns++;
```

From there, it is possible to define BLOB macros with length:

```
#define BLOB_ENTRY_LENGTH(nOrdinal, IID, flags, data, length) \
_BLOB_ENTRY_CODE_EX(nOrdinal, IID, flags, offsetbuf(data), \
    offsetbuf (length), 0);
```

and

```
#define BLOB_ENTRY_LENGTH_STATUS(nOrdinal, IID, flags, data, \
    length, status) \
    _BLOB_ENTRY_CODE_EX(nOrdinal, IID, flags, offsetbuf(data), \
    offsetbuf (length), offsetbuf (status));
```

The names of these macros are self-explanatory.

The following code sample shows a BLOB binding with length.

```
class CBLOBAccessorSequentialStreamReadWithLength
{
public:
    ISequentialStream* m_Column1;
    ULONG m_Column1Length;

BEGIN_COLUMN_MAP(CBLOBAccessorSequentialStreamReadWithLength)
    BLOB_ENTRY_LENGTH(1, IID_ISequentialStream, STGM_READ,
        m_Column1, m_Column1Length)
END_COLUMN_MAP()

DEFINE_COMMAND(CBLOBAccessorSequentialStreamReadWithLength,
    _T(" \
    SELECT \
    Column1 \
    FROM TABLE1"))

};
```

Calling MoveNext sets m_Column1Length to the length of the data held by the storage object. Some providers might mistakenly set m_Column1Length to 4, which is the length of the storage object pointer, not the length of the data. However, passing the length of the stored data is the correct behavior.

## Storing BLOB Data with a Storage Object

In theory, there are two ways to store a BLOB with storage objects. In the first method, the provider provides a storage object, on which the consumer writes directly. In the second method, the consumer creates a new storage object and passes it to the provider. The provider then reads the data contained in the storage object and stores it in the data store.

OLE DB providers are not required to support both methods and usually support only one. Since you might not have the choice when storing your BLOBs, it is important that you understand both methods.

## Storing BLOBs by Writing on a Storage Object

This technique consists of four steps:

1. The consumer binds a storage object with write access.
2. When the rowset fetches a given row, the provider creates the storage object and passes it to the consumer.
3. The consumer calls the `Write` method on the storage object.
4. The storage object transmits the write to the data store.

The benefit of this method is that it is very simple to use. The following code sample shows how.

```
class CBLOBAccessorSequentialStreamWrite
{
public:
    ISequentialStream* m_Column1;

BEGIN_COLUMN_MAP(CBLOBAccessorSequentialStreamWrite)
    BLOB_ENTRY(1, IID_ISequentialStream, STGM_WRITE, m_Column1)
END_COLUMN_MAP()

DEFINE_COMMAND(CBLOBAccessorSequentialStreamWrite, _T(" \
    SELECT \
        Column1  \
        FROM TABLE1"))

};
```

Once you have defined the binding class, you just have to write on the storage object:

```
HRESULT WriteWithSequentialStream()
{
    CBLOBTable<CBLOBAccessorSequentialStreamWrite> myTable;
    HRESULT hr = myTable.Open();
    if (FAILED(hr))
        return hr;
```

```
    hr = myTable.MoveFirst();
    if (hr == S_OK)
    {
        CComPtr<ISequentialStream> myStream;
        myStream = myTable.m_Column1;
        BYTE bytes [50];
        // initialize bytes with the appropriate data
        ULONG ActualLength = sizeof(bytes);
        myStream->Write(bytes, sizeof(bytes), &ActualLength);
        myTable.FreeRecordMemory();
    }
    return S_OK;
}
```

## Storing BLOBs with a Consumer-Provided Storage Object

This method is a little bit more complex, but it might be the only one available. The big difference with it is that the consumer provides the storage object, which in some cases means that the consumer needs to implement it as well.

Here are the necessary steps:

1. The consumer defines an accessor class with a storage object binding. The access mode can be read only.
2. The consumer creates a storage object.
3. The consumer calls a method such as `SetData` or `Insert`.
4. The provider then reads the content of the storage object and inserts the BLOB data in the database.

Figure 11-3 illustrates this procedure.

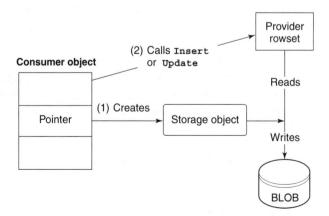

**Figure 11-3** Storing a BLOB with a Consumer-Provided Storage Object

## BLOB Properties

In a perfect world, all providers would be able to do anything. In the real world, some providers have limitations.

One of these limitations is the number of storage objects per rowset a provider supports, specified by the DBPROP_MULTIPLESTORAGEOBJECTS property. If this property is true, you do not have to worry about the number of storage objects you have. Unfortunately, however, many providers do not support several storage objects simultaneously, in which case you must process the rows one by one and release each storage object before processing the next row. In particular, this means that snapshots are not possible. The problem becomes even trickier when a table contains more than one BLOB column. If you create an accessor that binds more that one BLOB column, GetData will fail.

Another limitation is blocking storage objects. A storage object is blocking if it prevents other rowset operations during its lifetime. For example, you might have to release the storage object before moving to the next row. The DBPROP_MULTIPLESTORAGEOBJECTS data source information property specifies whether the storage objects of a given provider are blocking.

## Handling Several BLOBs

If property DBPROP_MULTIPLESTORAGEOBJECTS is false, you should not attempt to get several storage objects at the same time. This affects how you handle rows and columns.

First, if a rowset has a BLOB column that you open with a storage object, you should not keep two rows alive at the same time. Indeed, the first row you get will create and keep a reference on a first storage object, making it impossible for the second row you get to create its storage object. Use CRowset because it holds only one row at a time. CArrayRowset, on the other hand, is designed to get several rows at once and should be avoided in this case. If you really need to hold several rows at the same time, you should switch to in-memory data binding.

Another problem occurs when a rowset contains several BLOB columns. If you bind two or more storage objects, the provider will not get them. The first workaround is to declare some in-memory data bindings, leaving at most one storage object binding. For example, an accessor class with several storage objects such as this one:

```
class CMultipleBLOBAccessorSequentialStreamRead
{
public:
    ISequentialStream* m_Column1;
    ISequentialStream* m_Column2;
```

```
BEGIN_COLUMN_MAP(CMultipleBLOBAccessorSequentialStreamRead)
   BLOB_ENTRY(1, IID_ISequentialStream, STGM_READ, m_Column1)
   BLOB_ENTRY(2, IID_ISequentialStream, STGM_READ, m_Column2)
END_COLUMN_MAP()

///...
};
```

could be transformed into something like

```
class CMultipleBLOBAccessorSequentialStreamRead1
{
public:
   ISequentialStream* m_Column1;
   BYTE m_Column2 [50];

BEGIN_COLUMN_MAP(CMultipleBLOBAccessorSequentialStreamRead1)
   BLOB_ENTRY(1, IID_ISequentialStream, STGM_READ, m_Column1)
   COLUMN_ENTRY(2, m_Column2)
END_COLUMN_MAP()

//...
};
```

If one of the BLOB columns tends to contain more data than the others, you should select it for the storage object column. This assumes that all columns except one can be retrieved in memory. If this is not ensured, you can use a second workaround.

Chapter 9, on accessors, presented a way to define several accessors in the same class. While this is not very useful for simple types, it can be beneficial for handling several BLOBs. The idea is to declare several accessors with at most one storage object for each. For example, the previous class could become something like

```
class CMultipleBLOBAccessorSequentialStreamRead2
{
public:
   ISequentialStream* m_Column1;
   ISequentialStream* m_Column2;

BEGIN_ACCESSOR_MAP(CMultipleBLOBAccessorSequentialStreamRead2,2)
   BEGIN_ACCESSOR(0, false)
      BLOB_ENTRY(1, IID_ISequentialStream, STGM_READ, m_Column1)
   END_ACCESSOR()
   BEGIN_ACCESSOR(1, false)
      BLOB_ENTRY(2, IID_ISequentialStream, STGM_READ, m_Column2)
   END_ACCESSOR()
END_ACCESSOR_MAP()
```

```
DEFINE_COMMAND(CMultipleBLOBAccessorSequentialStreamRead2, _T(" \
    SELECT \
        Column1,  \
        Column2  \
        FROM TABLE1"))

};
```

As a reminder, the second parameter of `BEGIN_ACCESSOR_MAP` is the number of accessors—two in this case. The second parameter of `BEGIN_ACCESSOR` specifies whether this is an automatic accessor—false in this case. When you call one of the cursor movement methods on the rowset, only the data for the automatic accessor is retrieved. At most one automatic accessor should bind a storage object.

When reading data from the data store, you need to explicitly call `GetData` for the specified accessor and call `FreeRecordMemory` before another `GetData` call.

The following example shows how to use a class with multiple accessors. First, open the table and get one row. Then, call `GetData (0)` to get column 1 and process the stream. Once finished with the first column, call `FreeRecordMemory` *and* release any reference on the stream. The same sequence applies for the second column.

```
HRESULT ReadMultipleWithSequentialStream()
{
    CBLOBTable<CMultipleBLOBAccessorSequentialStreamRead>
        myTable;
    HRESULT hr = myTable.Open();
    if (FAILED(hr))
        return hr;
    hr = myTable.MoveFirst();
    if (hr == S_OK)
    {
        myTable.GetData(0);
        CComPtr<ISequentialStream> myStream;
        myStream = myTable.m_Column1;
        BYTE bytes [50];
        ULONG ActualLength = sizeof(bytes);
        while(ActualLength == sizeof(bytes) || hr == S_OK)
        {
            hr = myStream->Read(bytes,sizeof(bytes),&ActualLength);
            // do something with bytes
        }
        myTable.FreeRecordMemory();
        myStream = NULL;
        myTable.GetData(1);
        myStream = myTable.m_Column2;
        while(ActualLength == sizeof(bytes) || hr == S_OK)
        {
```

```
        hr = myStream->Read(bytes,sizeof(bytes),&ActualLength);
        // do something with bytes
    }
    myTable.FreeRecordMemory();
  }
  return S_OK;
}
```

As a note, dynamic accessors do not support multiple accessors. Consequently, CDynamicAccessor will fail to get multiple storage objects on a data source that does not support them.

## Converting Interfaces, Memory, and Files

By now, you should understand all the benefits of storage objects. There is one downside, however: You will probably not want to manipulate ISequential Stream for long. Usually, the consumer uses memory, files, and other interfaces to handle BLOB data. This section will explain how to convert these entities to and from ISequentialStream.

### IStream

Since IStream inherits from ISequentialStream, an IStream pointer can safely be converted to an ISequentialStream pointer. You can, for example, write

```
IStream * MyStream;
//Get MyStream
CComPtr<ISequentialStream> MySequentialStream = MyStream;
```

The reverse, assigning an IStream pointer to an ISequentialStream pointer, is not possible. However, you can always read the entire ISequential Stream into memory and create an IStream on the memory.

The Windows API provides a very convenient function that creates a stream on global memory:

```
WINOLEAPI CreateStreamOnHGlobal(
   HGLOBAL hGlobal,          //Memory handle for the stream object
   BOOL fDeleteOnRelease,    //Whether to free memory when the
                             // object is released
   LPSTREAM * ppstm          //Address of output variable that
                             // receives the IStream interface pointer
);
```

For example, if you want to insert a piece of memory in a BLOB column through a storage object, you can use the following method:

1. Allocate some global memory (call GlobalAlloc).
2. Write on the memory (call GlobalLock, memcpy, and GlobalUnLock).

3. Create a stream on the global memory (call `CreateStreamOnHGlobal`).

4. Insert or update a row as usual.

The following example illustrates this method:

```
HRESULT WriteInMemory()
{
    CBLOBTable<CBLOBAccessorSequentialStreamReadWithLength>
        myTable;
    HRESULT hr = myTable.Open();
    if (FAILED(hr))
        return hr;
    byte memory [123];
    HGLOBAL GlobalMemoryHandle = GlobalAlloc(GMEM_FIXED,
        sizeof(memory));
    void * GlobalMemoryPointer = GlobalLock(GlobalMemoryHandle);
    memcpy(GlobalMemoryPointer, memory, sizeof(memory));
    GlobalUnlock(GlobalMemoryHandle);
    IStream * Stream= NULL;
    hr = CreateStreamOnHGlobal(GlobalMemoryHandle, TRUE,&Stream);
    if (FAILED(hr))
        return hr;
    myTable.m_Column1 = Stream;
    myTable.m_Column1Length = sizeof(memory);
    hr = myTable.Insert();
    myTable.FreeRecordMemory();
    return S_OK;
}
```

The Windows API also provides the inverse function:

```
WINOLEAPI GetHGlobalFromStream(
  IStream * pstm,         //Points to the stream object
  HGLOBAL * phglobal     //Points to the current memory handle
                         // for the specified stream
```

## ILockBytes

In the same way it is possible to convert from global memory to `IStream`, the Windows API provides two functions for converting an `ILockBytes` pointer to and from a global memory handle:

```
WINOLEAPI CreateILockBytesOnHGlobal(
  HGLOBAL hGlobal,   //Memory handle for the byte array object
  BOOL fDeleteOnRelease,   //Whether to free memory when the
                           // object is released
  ILockBytes ** ppLkbyt
  //Address of output variable that
  // receives the ILockBytes interface pointer
);
```

and

```
WINOLEAPI GetHGlobalFromILockBytes(
  ILockBytes * pLkbyt,    //Points to the byte array object
  HGLOBAL * phglobal      //Points to the current memory
                          // handle for the specified byte array
);
```

As a result, it is possible to convert an `ILockBytes` interface to an `IStream` interface by going through a global memory handle. Obviously, you should not use this method for BLOBs that do not fit into global memory.

## IStorage

`IStorage` is the most complex and powerful interface and thus the most difficult. However, there are two functions to get an `IStorage` pointer. One is from an `ILockBytes` pointer:

```
WINOLEAPI StgOpenStorageOnILockBytes(
  ILockBytes * plkbyt,
      //Points to the ILockBytes
      // interface on the underlying byte array
  IStorage * pStgPriority,
      //Points to a previous opening
      // of a root storage object
  DWORD grfMode,
      //Specifies the access mode for the object
  SNB snbExclude,
      //Points to an SNB structure
      // specifying elements to be excluded
  DWORD reserved,            //Reserved, must be zero
  IStorage ** ppstgOpen
      //Points to location for
      // returning the storage object
);
```

For example, the following code gets an `IStorage` interface pointer:

```
ILockBytes * LockBytes;
// get LockBytes
IStorage* Storage;
StgOpenStorageOnILockBytes(LockBytes, NULL, mode, NULL, 0, &Storage);
```

The other is from a file:

```
HRESULT StgOpenStorageEx(
    const WCHAR * pwcsName,
        //Points to the path of the
        // file containing storage object
    DWORD grfMode,
        //Specifies the access mode for the object
    STGFMT stgfmt,
        //Specifies the storage file format
```

```
    DWORD grfAttrs,                  //Reserved; must be zero
    STGOPTIONS ** ppStgOptions,
        //Address of STGOPTIONS pointer
    void * reserved2,                //Reserved; must be zero
    REFIID riid,
        //Specifies the GUID of the interface pointer
    void ** ppObjectOpen
        //Address of an interface pointer
);
```

For example, the following code shows how to get an `IStorage` pointer on the data in a filename:

```
WCHAR * filename = L"c:\whatever";
IStorage* Storage;
StgOpenStorageEx (filename, STGM_READ, STGFMT_STORAGE, 0, NULL,
    0, IID_IStorage, &Storage);
```

## ACCESSING PERSISTENT COM OBJECTS

Until now, we worked with the most basic form of BLOBs, as a plain sequence of bytes. As this chapter first explained, OLE DB also defines a way for COM objects to read and write themselves in a BLOB, thereby releasing the consumer from having to interpret the BLOB content. These persistent COM objects support one of the following interfaces:

- `IPersistStorage`
- `IPersistStream`
- `IPersistStreamInit`

A COM object that supports `IPersistStream` or `IPersistStreamInit` can store and retrieve itself to and from an `IStream` pointer. A COM object that supports `IPersistStorage` can store and retrieve itself to and from an `IStorage` pointer.

Once you understand how to handle storage objects, you will see that handling persistent COM objects is very similar. In fact, it is even easier since the provider does the all the read operations.

To retrieve a persistent COM object, follow these simple steps:

1. Define an accessor class that binds the persistent COM object.
2. Open the rowset and navigate the rows as usual.

For example, the following code binds a persistent COM object with column 1:

```
class CBLOBAccessorIPersistStreamRead
{
public:
   IPersistStream* m_Column1;
BEGIN_COLUMN_MAP(CBLOBAccessorIPersistStreamRead)
   BLOB_ENTRY(1, IID_IPersistStream, STGM_READ, m_Column1)
END_COLUMN_MAP()

DEFINE_COMMAND(CBLOBAccessorIPersistStreamRead, _T(" \
   SELECT \
      Column1  \
      FROM TABLE1"))
};
```

After you call a method such as MoveFirst or MoveNext, m_Column1 will point
to a persistent COM object.

## SUMMARY

BLOBs offer many ways to read and write data. This chapter explored their benefits and drawbacks. Implementing efficient BLOB support is not an easy task,
and you will probably encounter the provider's limits very quickly. In the end,
the best solution is to try out the different methods and see which one best fits
your needs.

# 12 Transactions

Updating data includes inserting, deleting, and updating rows in rowsets. A client program usually consists of several update operations, which until now we performed one by one. In the real world, however, a program usually consists of several actions that need to be coordinated. A transaction is a powerful tool for doing this.

This chapter will

- Explain why transactions can be crucial.
- Explain the characteristics of a transaction.
- Present the different transactions: simple nested, and distributed.
- Explain how to integrate OLE DB with Microsoft Transaction Server (or COM+) components.

## THE NEED FOR TRANSACTIONS

It can be helpful to understand why transactions are essential to applications. You probably have an online bank account, so let's take an online banking application as an example. Here is our scenario:

The user has a checking account and a savings account and can transfer money from one to another. He wants to earn more interest on his money and therefore wants to transfer, say, $100 from the checking account to the savings account. On the application side, the operation consists of two actions (illustrated in Figure 12-1):

- Removing $100 from the checking account
- Adding $100 to the savings account

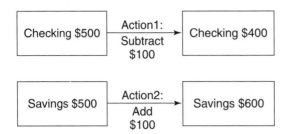

**Figure 12-1** The Two Actions in the Banking Scenario

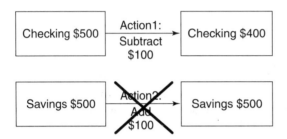

**Figure 12-2** Failure of an Action in the Banking Scenario

That is all there is in theory. In practice, however, one of the actions can fail for one of the following reasons:

- *Hardware failure.* For example, a disk can have a problem or the computer can be turned off.
- *Operating system failure.* For example, the disk can be full or the operating system can be out of memory.
- *Database failure.* One of your actions can violate the integrity of the database.
- *Business application failure,* that is, an error programmed by the programmer. For example, you can set a limit on the amount of money that can be transferred or check for other permissions.

The happy case, of course, is when the deposit in the savings account succeeds while the withdrawal from the checking account fails, although it is unlikely that that will satisfy the bank. The other case is when the deposit fails and the withdrawal succeeds. Figure 12-2 illustrates what happens in this case. Though easy to comprehend, this problem is very difficult to solve.

Of course, it is easy to deal with a failure in the first operation. The code would look like this:

```
HRESULT PerformTwoOperations()
{
    HRESULT hr = PerformFirstOperation();
    if (FAILED(hr))
        return hr;
    hr = PerformSecondOperation();
    return hr;
}
```

To deal with a failure in the second operation, a naïve approach would be to write Undo actions:

```
HRESULT PerformTwoOperations()
{
    HRESULT hr = PerformFirstOperation();
    if (FAILED(hr))
        return hr;
    hr = PerformSecondOperation();
    if (FAILED(hr))
        UndoFirstOperation();
    Return hr;
}
```

There are two problems with this:

- It requires the programmer to provide an Undo function.
- It does not really solve the problem because `UndoFirstOperation` can fail, leaving intact the changes performed by the first operation.

## THE TRANSACTION APPROACH

A *transaction* is composed of a series of actions that either succeed as a whole or fail as a whole. From a programmer's point of view, using a transaction consists of three steps:

1. Start a transaction
2. Perform actions
3. Terminate the transaction

There are two ways to end a transaction: *commit* and *abort*. If the transaction is committed, all actions will be committed to the database. If the transaction is

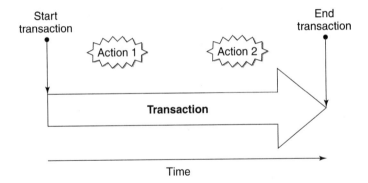

**Figure 12-3** Lifetime of a Transaction

aborted, all actions are automatically undone. Aborting a transaction is sometimes called *rollback*.

Figure 12-3 summarizes the life of a transaction.

The beauty of transactions is that they are very hard to implement for the database provider but very easy to use for the programmer. In other words, they make writing elaborate business applications simple.

The pseudo-code for performing two actions looks like this:

```
HRESULT PerformTwoOperations()
{
    HRESULT hr = StartTransaction();
    if (FAILED(hr))
        return hr;
    hr = PerformFirstOperation();
    if (FAILED(hr))
    {
        Abort();
        return hr;
    }
    hr = PerformSecondOperation();
    if (FAILED(hr))
    {
        Abort();
        return hr;
    }
    return Commit()
}
```

## TRANSACTION PROPERTIES

The purpose of transactions is to maintain the consistency of a given system. They have four properties: atomicity, consistency, isolation, and durability, together known as the acronym *ACID*.

- *Atomicity*. Either all of the actions succeed or none of them do. If one action fails, all the work done by the others is undone.

- *Consistency*. If the system is in a consistent state before the transaction, it will be in a consistent state after the transaction. This is true both if the transaction fails and if the transaction succeeds.

- *Isolation*. A transaction does not see the changes made by other transactions. If two run at the same time, each one will think it is the only one running.

- *Durability*. Once the transaction is finished, the changes are durable. In other words, they will not be lost if the system crashes.

To understand ACID properties, let's see what happens when one property is not verified.

## Atomicity

Atomicity is at the heart of transactions—without it, it would be possible for one action to succeed while another fails.

## Consistency

Consistency is an abstract property that relates to the definition of consistency for your system and derives from the other properties of a transaction. Indeed, if a set of actions preserves the consistency of the system, the system will go into a different consistent state if the transaction is committed. If the transaction is aborted, the system will stay in the same consistent state.

## Isolation

If a transaction were not isolated, it would be possible to see changes made by another transaction, which could lead to inconsistencies. The section on isolation levels will explain this in more detail.

## Durability

If a transaction were not durable, the changes made by it could be lost even after it is completed. For example, if the data store kept the changes only in memory after a commit, these changes would not survive a power failure. Simply put, durability means that the committed changes are stored on disk.

## USING TRANSACTIONS

Up until now, we created session objects without doing anything with them. The real usefulness of class `CSession` is its set of transaction methods: `StartTransaction`, `Commit`, and `Abort`, whose meanings are self-explanatory.

The signature of these methods is

```
HRESULT StartTransaction(ISOLEVEL isoLevel =
   ISOLATIONLEVEL_READCOMMITTED, ULONG isoFlags = 0,
   ITransactionOptions* pOtherOptions = NULL, ULONG*
   pulTransactionLevel = NULL)
HRESULT Abort(BOID* pboidReason = NULL, BOOL bRetaining = FALSE,
   BOOL bAsync = FALSE)
HRESULT Commit(BOOL bRetaining = FALSE, DWORD grfTC =
   XACTTC_SYNC, DWORD grfRM = 0)
```

### Simple Transaction

A single transaction in a session is referred to as a *simple* transaction. A typical use of a simple transaction looks like this:

```
CSession MySession
MySession.Open(...)
MySession.StartTransaction();
CCommand<..> MyCommand;
MyCommand.Open(MySession);
HRESULT hr =..// performs actions
if (FAILED(hr))
   MySession.Abort();
else
   MySession.Commit();
```

### Transaction Retention

Transaction retention indicates whether to start a new transaction after the current one terminates. You can specify retention with the `fRetaining` flag parameter in `Abort` or `Commit`. If `FALSE`, there is no retention; the transaction is terminated and no new one is created. If `TRUE`, a new transaction is restarted just after the current one terminates. This applies to both `Commit` and `Abort`.

There are three benefits to transaction retention:

- It saves you a call to `StartTransaction`.
- It allows the OLE DB provider to perform some optimizations. For example, the provider can keep the locks alive between the old transaction and the new one.

- It allows the OLE DB provider to keep the state of some objects across transactions. For example, if you prepare a command, its state will be kept across transactions.

This code illustrates a transaction with no retention:

```
HRESULT hr = S_OK;
CSession Session;
Session.Open(aDataSource);
Session.StartTransaction();
CCommand<..>MyCommand;
MyCommand.Execute ...;
///
Session.Abort();
// or Session.Commit();
// At this point, the transaction is terminated.
// It is not possible to abort or commit the transaction again
//The following is invalid.

hr = Session.Abort();
// At this point, hr = XACT_E_NOTRANSACTION
```

This one illustrates a transaction with retention:

```
HRESULT hr = S_OK;
CSession Session;
Session.Open(adataSource);
Session.StartTransaction();
// perform actions

Session.Abort(NULL, TRUE);
// The transaction was aborted but a new one was started
//perform other actions
Session.Commit(TRUE);
// The transaction was committed; a new transaction was started
//..perform other actions
Session.Commit(FALSE);
//The transaction was committed;no other transaction was started

hr = Session.Commit(FALSE);
// The last call was invalid because there was no pending
// transaction. At this point, hr = XACT_E_NOTRANSACTION
```

## Rowset Preservation

Rowset preservation determines the behavior of rowsets created during a transaction after the transaction terminates. A preserved rowset will stay fully functional after termination. A nonpreserved rowset will only support the IUnknown interface. If you keep a pointer to other references, it will support only incrementing and decrementing reference counts on accessor and row handles. All other methods will return the error E_UNEXPECTED.

Figure 12-4 illustrates rowset preservation, indicated by the area in gray.

### Setting Preservation Properties

OLE DB provides two rowset properties related to rowset preservation, which can be set independently. They are listed in Table 12-1. The following code sets the preserve on abort to `true` and the preserve on commit to `false`.

```
CDBPropSet propset(DBPROPSET_ROWSET);
propset.AddProperty(DBPROP_ABORTPRESERVE, true);
propset.AddProperty(DBPROP_COMMITPRESERVE,false);
m_Rowset.Open(m_Session, NULL, &propset);
```

Note that the preservation behavior is set at the rowset level, not at the transaction level. Thus, it is possible to have a transaction that preserves certain rowsets

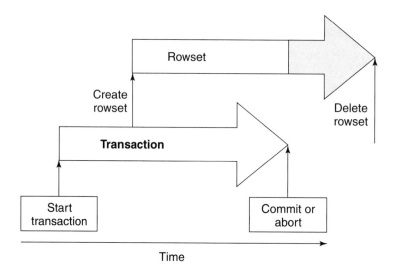

**Figure 12-4** Rowset Preservation

**Table 12-1** Rowset Preservation Properties

| Property | Type | Description |
| --- | --- | --- |
| DBPROP_ABORTPRESERVE | Boolean | Specifies whether rowsets should be preserved after an abort |
| DBPROP_COMMITPRESERVE | Boolean | Specifies whether rowsets should be preserved after a commit |

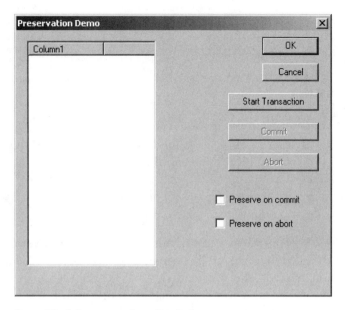

**Figure 12-5** Preservation Demo Main Dialog

and not others. If the preservation properties are not set explicitly, they will default to a value that is provider specific.

### Preservation Demo

This book has a companion online "preservation" project that demonstrates rowset preservation on abort and commit.

First, start a transaction without checking "Preserve on commit." This updates the list view with the content of the preservation table. Then click the "Commit" button. Since the rowset is not preserved, it will not be able to update the list view correctly and so the list view will be empty, as shown in Figure 12-5.

To see preservation in action, click the "Preserve on commit" button. Then start a transaction and commit. After the transaction is committed, the list view will be correctly updated with the content of the table.

Preservation on abort works the same way.

## ISOLATION LEVELS

We saw that transactions have four properties: atomicity, consistency, isolation, and durability. However, a transaction is isolated to a certain degree. The transaction isolation level is a measure of the extent to which changes made outside a transaction are visible to it.

OLE DB supports four isolation levels:

- Read uncommitted (also called browse)
- Read committed (also called cursor stability)
- Repeatable read
- Serializable (also called isolated)

A transaction with a *serializable* isolation level is more isolated than one with a *repeatable read* isolation level, and so forth.

Before we dive into the isolation levels, let's review what can occur between two transactions, known as the *isolation phenomena*. These are dirty reads, non-repeatable reads, and phantoms.

- A *dirty read* occurs when a transaction can read data not yet committed by another transaction. For example, suppose that transaction A changes a row. Transaction B reads the changed row before transaction A commits the change. If transaction A aborts the change, transaction B will have read data that is considered never to have existed.

- A *nonrepeatable read* occurs when a transaction reads the same row twice but gets different data each time. For example, suppose that transaction A reads a row. Transaction B changes or deletes that row and commits this change or deletion. If transaction A attempts to read the row again, it will retrieve different row values or discover that the row has been deleted.

- A *phantom* occurs when a row a matches the search criteria but is not initially seen. For example, suppose that transaction A reads a set of rows that satisfy some search criteria. Transaction B inserts a new row that matches those criteria. If transaction A executes the command that read the rows, it gets a different set of rows.

OLE DB defines the following isolation levels by the absence or presence of any of these phenomena.

- When using a *read uncommitted* transaction, you can see uncommitted changes made by other transactions. At this level, dirty reads, nonrepeatable reads, and phantoms are possible.

- When using a *read committed* transaction, you cannot see changes made by other transactions until those transactions are committed. At this level, dirty reads are not possible but nonrepeatable reads and phantoms are.

- When using a *repeatable read* transaction, you do not see any changes made by other transactions in rows already read. At this level of isolation, dirty reads and nonrepeatable reads are not possible but phantoms are.

- A transaction operating at the *serializable* (or *isolated*) isolation level guarantees that all concurrent transactions interact only in ways that produce the same effect as if they were entirely executed one after the other. At this level, dirty reads, nonrepeatable reads, and phantoms are not possible.

Table 12-2 sums up the isolation levels and the possibility of isolation phenomena.

**Table 12-2** Isolation Levels and Isolation Phenomena

| Isolation Level | Dirty Read | Nonrepeatable Read | Phantom |
|---|---|---|---|
| Read uncommitted | Yes | Yes | Yes |
| Read committed | No | Yes | Yes |
| Repeatable read | No | No | Yes |
| Serializable | No | No | No |

## Transaction Isolation Demo

At first, transaction isolation levels can be difficult to grasp. However, it is crucial that you understand them before using transactions. One way to do this is to interact with them. This book comes with two online sample programs, *A* and *B*, which are meant to run together. They demonstrate the different levels of isolation and the locking mechanisms.

### Program A

The A program makes changes in a database; it consists of one dialog, illustrated in Figure 12-6. When the dialog starts, it automatically creates a new session, which

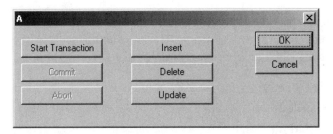

**Figure 12-6** Main Dialog of Program A

**Table 12-3** Transaction Buttons

| Button | Description |
|--------|-------------|
| Start transaction | Starts a transaction in the current session |
| Commit | Commits the current transaction, if any |
| Abort | Aborts the current transaction, if any |

**Table 12-4** Data Update Buttons

| Button | Description |
|--------|-------------|
| Insert | Inserts a new row with value 0 in the table |
| Delete | Deletes the last row in the table |
| Update | Increments the value of the last row by 1 |

will live for the whole life of the dialog. The A dialog controls transactions and updates data using the buttons described in Table 12-3.

We will call "transaction A" the transaction started by the A program.

Three other buttons, described in Table 12-4, change the content of a table named "transac," which is made up of only one column of type `integer`. The insert, delete, and update operations are executed on the current session. If there is a transaction in the current session, the operations will be in it. If not, they will be executed outside of a transaction.

## Program B

The B program is a simple program that reads the changes made by A. it has one dialog and displays the content of the transac table. Figure 12-7 shows its main dialog. When the dialog is started, a session is created that will live for the dialog's lifetime.

The user can start a transaction, commit it, or abort it with the "Start transaction," "Commit," and "Abort" buttons. The transaction will be started with the transaction level specified by the four radio buttons:

- READUNCOMMITTED
- READCOMMITTED
- REPEATABLEREAD
- SERIALIZABLE

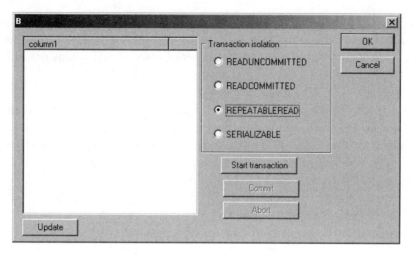

**Figure 12-7** B Main Dialog

A list view displays the content of the transac table. It is not updated automatically. Instead, the user must push the "Update" button. If there is a current transaction, the update operation will take place within it with the transaction isolation level. If not, the update operation will execute outside.

## Read Uncommitted Transactions

A dirty read occurs when a transaction can see new rows inserted by another transaction before they are committed or aborted. To experience a dirty read, follow these steps:

1. Open the A and B programs.
2. Select READUNCOMMITTED in B and then start a transaction.
3. Update the B list view by clicking on the "Update" button. At this point, you see the transac table.
4. Start a transaction in the A program.
5. Insert a row in the A table by clicking on the "Insert" button. At this point, a row has been inserted in the transac table but has not been committed or aborted.
6. Update the B list view by clicking on the "Update" button. The list view now has one more item. This means that the transaction in B can see the row that has been inserted by the transaction in A, although this row has not been committed or aborted.

7. Abort the transaction in A by clicking on the "Abort" button.

8. Update the B list view by clicking on the "Update" button. The list view is updated with the original number of rows, which means that the transaction in B does not see the row anymore.

When a dirty read occurs, a transaction sees the changes made by another transaction "live." Obviously, this is a problem if the transaction in A is aborted, since the transaction in B will have read rows that are not supposed to have existed. It can also be a problem if the transaction is eventually committed. To experience this, follow these steps:

1. Open the A and B programs.

2. Select READUNCOMMITTED in B and then start a transaction.

3. Update the B list view by clicking on the "Update" button. At this point, you see the transac table.

4. Start a transaction in the A program.

5. Insert a row in the transac table by clicking on the "Insert" button. At this point, a row has been inserted in the transac table but has not been committed or aborted

6. Update the B list view by clicking on the "Update" button. The list view now has one more item.

7. Insert another row by clicking on the "Insert" button. At this point, two rows have been inserted in the transac table but not yet committed.

8. Update the B list view by clicking on the "Update" button. The list view now has two items.

9. Commit the transaction in the A program by clicking on the "Commit" button.

If the transaction was truly isolated, the transaction in B would see either zero or two rows. However, it can see partial changes. This fact can lead to an inconsistency, thus violating the consistency property. This example is trivial because we have only one table with one column. However, imagine one order table and one product table, the order table having a product ID column. Imagine also that a first transaction inserts a new order for a new product *and then* inserts a new product in the product table. With dirty read, another transaction can see the order for the new product before the product is inserted. Even if the first transaction is committed, this can lead to an inconsistency in the second transaction. In the previous examples, we inserted rows. The same mechanism applies to a row deletion or a row update.

## Read Committed Transactions

With a read committed transaction, dirty reads are not possible. To experience this, follow these steps:

1. Open the A and B programs.
2. Select READCOMMITTED in B and then start a transaction.
3. Update the B list view by clicking on the "Update" button. At this point, you see the transac table with no row in it.
4. Start a transaction in the A program.
5. Insert a row in the transac table by clicking on the "Insert" button. At this point, this row has not been committed or aborted.
6. Click on the "Update" button. At this point, B is frozen. Indeed, since B is in the read committed isolation level, it cannot read the newly inserted row and is waiting for transaction A to either abort or commit.
7. Commit transaction A by clicking on the "Commit" button. Just after transaction A is committed, program B stops waiting and displays the table in the list view. Alternatively, A can be aborted, which also unfreezes B.

This example uses row insertion. The same would apply to a row deletion or a row update.

If dirty reads are not possible in a read committed transaction, nonrepeatable reads can occur. To experience this, follow these steps:

1. Start the A and B applications.
2. Select READCOMMITTED in B and start a transaction.
3. Insert a row in A, either outside or inside a transaction. If it is inside, make sure you commit the transaction.
4. Update the list view in B by clicking the "Update" button. At this point, the list view shows only one row with column1 = 0.
5. Start a transaction in A. Increment the value of the row by clicking on the "Update" button. Then commit transaction A.
6. Update the list view by clicking on the "Update" button. At this point, the list view shows only one row with column1 = 1.
7. Start a transaction in A, delete a row by clicking on the "Delete" button, and then commit the transaction.
8. Update the list view. At this point, the view shows no row.

During this example, the B transaction read the same row three times. The first time, the row had a value of zero. The second time, the row had a value of 1.

The third time, the row disappeared. This illustrates a nonrepeatable read phenomenon.

## Repeatable Read Transactions

As the name suggests, nonrepeatable reads are not possible with repeatable read transactions. To experience this, follow these steps:

1. Start the A and B applications.
2. Select REPEATABLEREAD in B and start a transaction.
3. Update the content of the list view. At this point, there is no row in the table.
4. Start a transaction in A, insert a row, and commit the changes.
5. Update the content of the list view in B. At this point, there is one row in the table.
6. Start a transaction in A; change the content of the row by clicking on the "Update" button. At this point, A is frozen because it is waiting for B to terminate the transaction.
7. Commit the transaction in B. This should unfreeze application A, which you can then commit.

This example uses a row update. The same behavior occurs with a row deletion. Note that there is no lock with a row insertion. An inserted row cannot be locked by B since it is new. This means that a repeatable read transaction can obtain different results when performing the same query twice, which is known as a phantom.

To experience this, follow these steps:

1. Start applications A and B.
2. Start a repeatable read transaction in B, but do not update the list view.
3. Start a transaction in A. Then insert, update, and delete columns at will and commit the transaction. At this point, there should be no lock.
4. Update the list view in B. At this point, all rows in the table are locked by the B transaction.
5. Start a transaction in A; insert a row. There is no lock on this row at this point because the row is new.
6. Commit the transaction in A. Restart a transaction in A. Change the content on the last row and commit the transaction. Again, there is no lock because B did not read the last row.

7. Start a transaction in A. Delete the last row and commit the transaction. Again, there is no lock because B did not read the row that was just removed.

8. At this point, all the remaining rows have been read by B. Therefore, they have a lock. Start a transaction in A and delete a row. This will freeze A. To unfreeze A, commit the transaction in B. You can then commit the A transaction.

## Serializable Transactions

With serializable transactions, phantoms, nonrepeatable reads, and dirty reads are not possible. From a serializable transaction, you cannot see any effect of other transactions.

To experience this, follow these steps:

1. Start applications A and B.

2. Start a serializable transaction in B, but do not update the list view.

3. Start a transaction in A. Then insert, update, and delete columns at will and commit the transaction.

4. Update the list view in B. In A, try to insert, update, or delete a row. You will not see any change in B. When A is frozen, you will need to commit B to un-freeze it.

## Isolation Levels and Locks

OLE DB defines a standard for transaction isolation levels. However, true to the spirit of COM, it leaves the implementation to the provider. This section is based on the behavior of SQL Server. There is no guarantee that other providers will act the same way.

SQL Server ensures isolation by locking rows. The more isolation you have, the more locks you will get. When a row is changed, SQL Server can mark it as locked. It removes the lock when the transaction is either committed or aborted.

- At the read uncommitted level, SQL Server does not introduce any additional lock, nor does it wait for one.

- At the read committed level, SQL Server does not introduce any lock but waits for locks to be released before reading data.

- At the repeatable read level, SQL Server adds a lock for all the rows it reads. Once a repeatable read transaction reads rows, no other transaction will be able to change them until the transaction releases the locks.

- At the serializable level, SQL Server locks all rows that meet the criteria of any of the SELECT type statements on the save side.

**Table 12-5**  Isolation Levels and Locking

| Transaction Isolation Level | Wait for Other Transaction Lock | Locks Read Rows | Locks Read Rows and Criteria |
|---|---|---|---|
| Read uncommitted | No | No | No |
| Read committed | Yes | No | No |
| Repeatable read | Yes | Yes | No |
| Serializable | Yes | Yes | Yes |

Table 12-5 summarizes the transaction levels and the associated locks under SQL Server.

### Choosing an Isolation Level

Contrary to what instinct might tell you, isolation is not always a good thing. There is a trade-off between isolation and performance/locking. The more isolation you have, the more locking you get. Obviously, isolation is a good thing, whereas locking and loss of performance are bad.

There is no perfect formula for choosing the right isolation level. This is why OLE DB offers a choice between isolation levels. If you do not mind reading uncommitted data, you can choose a read uncommitted transaction. On the other hand, if you absolutely need the highest level of isolation, you can choose the serializable level, but you will have to be careful with locks. By default, the OLE DB consumer templates select the read committed level as a compromise between isolation and lock level.

### Supported Isolation Levels

The OLE DB providers are not required to support all isolation levels. They can support only a few of them if they choose.

The DBPROP_SUPPORTEDTXNISOLEVELS data source information property specifies which isolation levels are supported. Naturally, it is read only. Its only value is a 4-byte integer that is an "or" combination of the values in Table 12-6. Note that

- DBPROPVAL_TI_BROWSE is synonymous with DBPROPVAL_TI_READ UNCOMMITTED.

- DBPROPVAL_TI_CURSORSTABILITY is synonymous with DBPROPVAL_ TI_READCOMMITTED.

- DBPROPVAL_TI_ISOLATED is synonymous with DBPROPVAL_TI_ SERIALIZABLE.

**Table 12-6** Supported Transaction Level Property Values

| Property Symbol | Value | Meaning |
|---|---|---|
| DBPROPVAL_TI_READUNCOMMITTED | 0x00000100L | ISOLATIONLEVEL_READ UNCOMMITTED is supported |
| DBPROPVAL_TI_READCOMMITTED | 0x00001000L | ISOLATIONLEVEL_READ COMMITTED is supported |
| DBPROPVAL_TI_REPEATABLEREAD | 0x00010000L | ISOLATIONLEVEL_REPEATABLE READ is supported |
| DBPROPVAL_TI_SERIALIZABLE | 0x00100000L | ISOLATIONLEVEL_SERIALIZABLE is supported |

The following sample demonstrates how to get the supported isolation levels:

```
CDataSource DataSource;
HRESULT hr = DataSource.OpenFromFileName(L"Transac.udl");
CComVariant Variant;
DataSource.GetProperty(DBPROPSET_DATASOURCEINFO,
DBPROP_SUPPORTEDTXNISOLEVELS, &Variant);
```

For SQL Server, the value of the property is 0x00111100. Therefore, SQL Server supports four isolation levels.

## Sessions with No Transactions

When a session does not have an active transaction, each action is committed after it is completed. In other words, writing

```
CSession Session;
Session.Open(..);
PerformAction1(Session);
PerformAction2(Session);
PerformAction3(Session);
Session.Close();
```

is equivalent to writing

```
CSession Session;
Session.Open(..);
Session.StartTransaction(IsolationLevel);
PerformAction1(Session);
Session.Commit();
Session.StartTransaction(IsolationLevel);
```

**Table 12-7** Auto Commit Levels

| Property Value | Isolation Level |
|---|---|
| DBPROPVAL_TI_READUNCOMMITTED | ISOLATIONLEVEL_READUNCOMMITTED |
| DBPROPVAL_TI_READCOMMITTED | ISOLATIONLEVEL_READCOMMITTED |
| DBPROPVAL_TI_REPEATABLEREAD | ISOLATIONLEVEL_REPEATABLEREAD |
| DBPROPVAL_TI_SERIALIZABLE | ISOLATIONLEVEL_SERIALIZABLE |

```
PerformAction2(Session);
Session.Commit();
Session.StartTransaction(IsolationLevel);
PerformAction3(Session);
Session.Commit();
Session.Close();
```

This behavior is called *auto commit*, for which the DBPROP_SESS_AUTO
COMMITISOLEVELS session property defines the isolation level (Table 12-7).

The following sample gets the default auto commit isolation level, sets it to a
different value, and gets it again:

```
CDataSource DataSource;
HRESULT hr = DataSource.OpenFromFileName(L"Transac.udl");
CSessionEx Session;
hr = Session.Open(DataSource);
CComVariant Variant;
Session.GetProperty(DBPROPSET_SESSION,
    DBPROP_SESS_AUTOCOMMITISOLEVELS, &Variant);
Session.SetProperty(DBPROPSET_SESSION,
    DBPROP_SESS_AUTOCOMMITISOLEVELS, DBPROPVAL_TI_ISOLATED);
Session.GetProperty(DBPROPSET_SESSION,
    DBPROP_SESS_AUTOCOMMITISOLEVELS, &Variant);
```

By default, SQL Server uses ISOLATIONLEVEL_READCOMMITTED as the *auto
commit* isolation level.

## ASYNCHRONOUS TRANSACTIONS

A transaction that contains many actions might take a long time to abort or to
commit. If you want to avoid a long wait, you can perform the Abort or Commit
asynchronously.

To abort a transaction asynchronously, pass TRUE as the bAsync parameter.
For example, you might write

```
CSession MySession;
// perform actions
MySession.Abort (NULL, FALSE, TRUE);
```

To commit a transaction asynchronously, pass XACTTC_ASYNC_PHASEONE as the grfTC parameter. For example, you might write

```
CSession MySession;
// perform actions
MySession.Commit(FALSE, XACTTC_ASYNC_PHASEONE);
```

When the transaction is terminated (committed or aborted) synchronously, you can learn the outcome with the HRESULT returned by the method. This will not work when the transaction is committed or aborted asynchronously.

The solution is to be notified when the transaction actually terminates. OLE DB uses the ITransactionOutcomeEvents interface for notification, which has four methods, described in Table 12-8.

The signature of the methods is the following:

```
virtual HRESULT STDMETHODCALLTYPE Committed(BOOL fRetaining,
    XACTUOW *pNewUOW, HRESULT hr) = 0;

virtual HRESULT STDMETHODCALLTYPE Aborted(BOID *pboidReason,
    BOOL fRetaining, XACTUOW *pNewUOW, HRESULT hr) = 0;

virtual HRESULT STDMETHODCALLTYPE HeuristicDecision(
    DWORD dwDecision, BOID *pboidReason, HRESULT hr) = 0;

virtual HRESULT STDMETHODCALLTYPE Indoubt( void) = 0;
```

The Microsoft transaction server DSK contains more information on these methods.

The OLE DB extensions come with ITransactionOutcomeEventsImpl, a default implementation of ITransactionOutcomeEvents that simply returns E_NOTIMPL (not implemented) for each method.

**Table 12-8** ITransactionOutcomeEvents Methods

| Method | Description |
| --- | --- |
| Committed | Called when the transaction is committed |
| Aborted | Called when the transaction is aborted |
| Heuristic decision | Called when one of the participants makes a heuristic decision about the outcome of the transaction |
| In doubt | Called when the transaction is in doubt |

## Using Transaction Outcome

Using transaction outcome is similar to using a rowset listener (see Chapter 10). The first step is to implement the transaction outcome component. The second step is to request notification from the session.

### Defining Your Transaction Outcome Events COM Class

This class needs to support the ITransactionOutcomeEvents interface. The following code is an example. When the transaction is committed, a message box appears. For the other events, it performs the default behavior.

```
class CMyNotif: public CComObjectRoot,
        public ITransactionOutcomeEventsImpl
{
BEGIN_COM_MAP(CMyNotif)
   COM_INTERFACE_ENTRY(ITransactionOutcomeEvents)
END_COM_MAP()
   STDMETHOD(Committed)(
      BOOL fRetaining,
      XACTUOW *pNewUOW,
      HRESULT hr)
   {
      MessageBox (NULL, "The transaction was committed", NULL,
         NULL);
      return S_OK;
   };
};
```

## Getting Events from the Transaction

The AtlAdvise method helps you add a notification to a transaction. For example:

```
CComObject<CMyNotif> * MyNotification =
   new CComObject<CMyNotif>;
DWORD dwCookie;
hr = AtlAdvise(Transaction, MyNotification,
   IID_ITransactionOutcomeEvents, &dwCookie);
```

Note that dwCookie can be used to end the connection point. For example:

```
hr = AtlUnadvise(Transaction, IID_ITransactionOutcomeEvents,
   dwCookie);
```

Note also that SQL Server does not support connection points for its transactions. However, the Distributed Transaction Coordinator (DTC) does (see more details later).

# NESTED TRANSACTIONS

A nested transaction is one inside another. Figure 12-8 illustrates three such transactions. The changes made inside the nested transaction are visible only to the transaction or any transaction above it. It is possible to create a transaction inside another nested transaction. The nesting level represents the number of transactions from the root transaction to the current transaction. The root transaction has a nesting level of 1.

Providers can choose to support nested transactions or not and can choose the maximum nesting level. Note that SQL Server does not support nested transactions.

## Using Nested Transactions

If the session does not have an active transaction, `StartTransaction` will start a root transaction. If the session already has a transaction, `StartTransaction` will start a nested transaction at the transaction at the highest nesting level.

The following code shows how to create three transactions nested within each other. The transactions at levels 1 and 3 are committed while the one at level 2 is aborted.

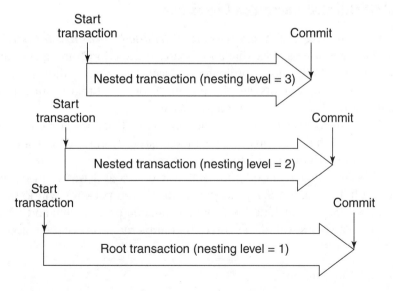

**Figure 12-8** Nested Transactions

```
CSession MySession;
// Start the root transaction, nesting level = 1
MySession.StartTransaction();
// Perform operations in the root transaction
// Start the first nested transaction, nesting level = 2
MySession.StartTransaction();
// Perform operations in the first nested transaction
// Start the second nested transaction, nesting level = 3
MySession.StartTransaction();
// Perform operations in the second nested transaction
// Commit the change in the second transaction
MySession.Commit();
// Abort the changes in the first nested transaction; therefore
// the changes made in the second nested transaction will be
// aborted as well
MySession.Abort();
// Commit the root transaction. Only the changes made outside
// the first nested transaction will be committed
MySession.Commit();
```

# DISTRIBUTED TRANSACTIONS

The previous section presented transactions that occur on one data source. However, one of the ideas behind OLE DB is that the data might stretch across several data sources. In this case, a single transaction that stretches across several data sources is required.

## Microsoft Distributed Transaction Coordinator

As the name suggests, the *Microsoft Distributed Transaction Coordinator* (MS DTC) is a Windows service that coordinates transactions running on different data sources. MS DTC can coordinate transactions even if they are on different machines. It implements a 2-phase commit protocol that ensures that either all transactions abort or all transactions commit.

When using a distributed transaction, the DTC service needs to be running on the client machine and on each machine hosting a data source. Figure 12-9 shows an example with one client and two data sources.

DTC was first released with SQL Server 6.5 and was then integrated with Microsoft Transaction Server as part of an option pack for Windows NT 4.0 and Windows 95. Now included with Windows 2000 professional and Windows 2000 server, it can work with data sources that implement one of the following transaction protocols:

- OLE Transactions
- X/Open XA
- LU 6.2 Sync Level 2

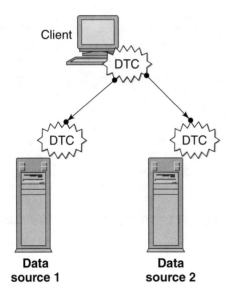

**Figure 12-9** DTC Architecture

DTC must be installed and running. The "Services" control panel applet helps you with this.

Under Windows NT 4.0, Windows 95, and Windows 98, open the control panel and select the "Services" icon. Under Windows 2000, open the "Component Services" administrative tool. Figure 12-10 shows this tool.

## Using MS DTC

The OLE DB extensions come with two classes useful for distributed transactions: CTransactionManager and CSessionEx. CTransactionManager manages distributed transactions; CSessionEx extends the functionalities of CSession.

To use the transaction manager, call the CTransactionManager::Open method:

```
HRESULT Open(char * pszHost = NULL, char * pszTmName = NULL)
```

If you pass the default parameters (NULL and NULL), the default transaction manager on the machine where the component is running will be open. If the Distributed Transaction Coordinator is not started, Open will return XACT_E_TMNOTAVAILABLE (= 0x8004d01b). Once the DTC is open, you can start a distributed transaction with the BeginTransaction method:

```
CComPtr<ITransaction> Transaction;
TransactionManager.BeginTransaction(&Transaction);
```

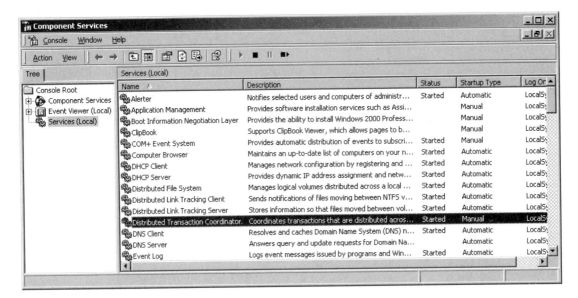

**Figure 12-10** Component Services Management Console

Here is the complete code for `CTransactionManager`:

```
class CTransactionManager
{
public:
   HRESULT Open(char * pszHost = NULL, char * pszTmName = NULL)
   {
      return DtcGetTransactionManager (pszHost, pszTmName,
         IID_ITransactionDispenser, 0, 0, NULL, reinterpret_cast
         <void**> (&m_spTransactionDispenser));
   }
   HRESULT BeginTransaction(ITransaction ** ppTransaction,
      IUnknown * punkOuter = NULL,
      ISOLEVEL isoLevel = ISOLATIONLEVEL_READCOMMITTED,
      ULONG isoFlags = 0,
      ITransactionOptions * pOptions = NULL)
   {
      ATLASSERT(m_spTransactionDispenser  != NULL);
      return m_spTransactionDispenser ->BeginTransaction(
         punkOuter, isoLevel, isoFlags, pOptions,ppTransaction);
   }

   CComPtr <ITransactionDispenser > m_spTransactionDispenser ;
};
```

`CSessionEx` is a descendant of `CSession` with all its transaction features plus the ability to join a distributed transaction. The `CSessionEx::JoinTransaction` code looks like this:

```
HRESULT JoinTransaction(IUnknown* Transaction, ISOLEVEL isoLevel
    = ISOLATIONLEVEL_READCOMMITTED, ULONG isoFlags = 0,
    ITransactionOptions * Options = NULL)
{
    ATLASSERT(m_spOpenRowset != NULL);
    CComPtr<ITransactionJoin> spTransactionJoin;
    HRESULT hr = m_spOpenRowset->QueryInterface(
        &spTransactionJoin);
    if (FAILED(hr))
        return hr;
    return spTransactionJoin->JoinTransaction(Transaction,
        isoLevel, isoFlags, Options);
}
```

In the following code, a distributed transaction is created, which two different sessions then join. One operation is performed in each session. The distributed transaction is then committed.

```
CDataSource DataSource1;
HRESULT hr = DataSource1.OpenFromFileName(L"transaction1.udl");
CSessionEx Session1;
hr = Session1.Open(DataSource1);
CDataSource DataSource2;
hr = DataSource2.OpenFromFileName(L"transaction2.udl");
CSessionEx Session2;
hr = Session2.Open(DataSource2);
CTransactionManager TransactionManager;
TransactionManager.Open();
CComPtr <ITransaction> Transaction;
hr = TransactionManager.BeginTransaction(&Transaction);
hr = Session1.JoinTransaction(Transaction);
hr = Session2.JoinTransaction(Transaction);
// Perform some actions on both Session1 and Session2
hr = Transaction->Commit(FALSE, XACTTC_SYNC_PHASEONE, 0);
```

Do not attempt to commit or abort the individual transactions that join the distributed transaction. The transaction manager takes care of that.

## TRANSACTIONS AND COMPONENTS

At this point, you probably understand the benefits of transactions, but there is something missing. In the COM approach, the goal is component reuse. How can we mix transactions with components?

So far, we have been in control of the transactions we use: The components we write start a transaction and commit or abort it. However, since this goes against the idea of reusability, our components need to be part of a transaction they did not start. One way to understand this better is to look at component granularity.

## Component Granularity

The number of tasks a component performs determines its *granularity*. A *fine-grained* component performs one or just a few tasks, while *a coarse-grained* component performs many tasks.

If we use the analogy of constructing a building, we can think of fine-grained components as bricks and coarse-grained components as entire walls. Intuitively, we know that bricks are more reusable than walls. However, an entire wall might be more convenient to reuse if it fits your exact needs, even though bricks are easier to repair because they are smaller.

Ideally, a system is composed of both fine-grained and coarse-grained components. Coarse-grained components use the fine-grained components for their implementation, as shown in Figure 12-11. Such an approach breaks the complexity and the manageability of components:

- The coarse-grained components are less complex because they do not implement the basic actions themselves.

- The system is easier to manage because it is broken down. For example, if there is a bug fix or an improvement in a fined-grained component, the coarse-gained components take advantage of it automatically.

The code for coarse-grained components looks like this:

```
HRESULT PerformCoarseGrainedAction()
{
    CComPtr<IFinedGrainedComponent1> Component1;
    CComPtr<IFinedGrainedComponent2> Component2;
    Component1.CoCreateInstance(..);
    Component2.CoCreateInstance(..);
    Component1.PerformFinedGrainedAction1();
    Component2.PerformFinedGrainedAction2();
    return S_OK;
}
```

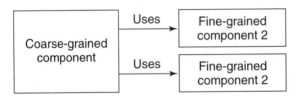

**Figure 12-11** Coarse-Grained and Fine-Grained Components

Each fined-grained component looks like this:

```
HRESULT PerformFinedGrainedActioni()
{
    UpdateTablei();
}
```

In this scenario, where should a transaction start and finish? Clearly, if it starts and ends in a fined-gained component, it will not be possible to coordinate the outcome of the different fine-grained actions. For that reason, the transaction should start and end in the coarse-grained component. At this point, the code looks like this:

```
HRESULT PerformCoarseGrainedAction()
{
    CComPtr<IFinedGrainedComponent1> Component1;
    CComPtr<IFinedGrainedComponent2> Component2;
    CComPtr<ITransaction> Transaction;
    //get Transaction
    Component1.CoCreateInstance(..);
    Component2.CoCreateInstance(..);
    HRESULT hr;
    hr = Component1.PerformFinedGrainedAction1(Transaction, other
        parameters);
    if(FAILED(hr))
    {
        Transaction->Abort(..);
        return hr;
    }
    hr = Component2.PerformFinedGrainedAction1(Transaction, other
        parameters);
    {
        Transaction->Abort(..);
        return hr;
    }
    Transaction->Commit(..);
    return S_OK;
}
```

and each fine-grained component looks like

```
HRESULT PerformFineGrainedActioni(ITransaction* Transaction,...)
{
    CSessionEx MySession;
    //Get my session
    MySession.JoinTransaction(Transaction);
    // Perform action on MySession
}
```

The drawback to this approach is that every method ends up having a transaction as a parameter, which clearly can become a heavy burden.

## Microsoft Transaction Server and COM+ Components

Microsoft Transaction Server (MTS) introduced the idea that a COM instance can be associated with a *context*. A context is a COM object that maintains information about the environment of the COM instance, including a transaction, if any. As a result, there is no need for a transaction parameter for each method; the context holds the transactions, and MTS is responsible for coordinating the two. With Windows 2000 and COM+, this idea is expanded to many other areas such as concurrency. Except for small programming details, however, the idea stays the same concerning transactions.

This section is a brief introduction to Microsoft Transaction Server/COM+. It will not cover all aspects of MTS but only those needed for OLE DB.

### Object Context

The GetObjectContext gives you access to the object context.

```
HRESULT GetObjectContext (IObjectContext** ppInstanceContext);
```

For example, the following code shows how to get the object context:

```
CComPtr<IObjectContext> spObjectContext;
GetObjectContext(&spObjectContext);
```

GetObjectContext can be confusing at first because it does not have the current object as an argument. In other words, you have to ask which object context it returns. The answer is the object context of the calling object. MTS/COM+ takes care of tracking which object is calling GetObjectContext in the runtime.

If a COM object is not an MTS object, its object context is NULL.

Unlike the traditional approach where one object controls the transaction, each MTS object has partial control over the transaction through its context. The object context supports the IObjectContext interface, whose methods are listed in Table 12-9.

The object context indicates whether the transaction can be committed. However, this is only an indication. For example, calling SetComplete signifies that the current object agrees with a transaction Commit. If another object disagrees, the transaction will be aborted anyway.

Table 12-10 summarizes the methods of the object context.

**Table 12-9** `IObjectContext` Methods

| Method | Description |
|---|---|
| SetComplete | Indicates that the object has successfully completed its task |
| SetAbort | Indicates that an unrecoverable error occurred and that all the work should be aborted |
| EnableCommit | Indicates that the work performed by the object is in a state that could be committed; however, the object is not finished with its task |
| DisableCommit | Indicates that the work performed by the object cannot be committed now; however, the object is not finished with its task |

**Table 12-10** `IObjectContext` Methods and Transactions

| Method | Can the Transaction Be Committed? | Is the Work Completed? |
|---|---|---|
| SetComplete | Yes | Yes |
| SetAbort | Never | Yes but it failed |
| EnableCommit | Yes | No |
| DisableCommit | Not yet | No |

## Transaction Attributes

Each MTS/COM+ component can have an attribute that specifies the behavior of its transaction. This attribute is specified at the COM class level, so all instances of a given class will have the same one. In addition, this attribute cannot change during the life of an object.

When object A creates object B, the object context of B might use the same transaction as that in the object context of A. The transaction attribute of B specifies how the object context of A and B relate to each other. In this example, A is a *client* of B.

The transaction attribute can have one of the following values:

• *Requires a transaction* indicates that the object must always run in a context with a transaction. When created, it checks if the client is running in a context with a transaction. If so, the object will run in this context. If not, MTS creates a new transaction for it.

- *Requires a new transaction* indicates that the object must always run in its own transaction. When the object is created, MTS always creates a new transaction for it.

- *Supports transactions* indicates that the object can run with a transaction but this is not required. When a new object is created, the context inherits the transaction from the client's context. If the client already uses a transaction, the new object runs within it. If the client runs with no transaction, the new object does not use any transaction, either.

- *Does not support transactions* indicates that the object will never run within a transaction. When created, its context is created without a transaction.

There are three types of MTS object creation:

- The MTS object can be a *root object*. In this case, its client is not an MTS object, so no object context attribute can be inherited.

- The MTS object can be created by another MTS object with no transaction. From a transaction point of view, this case is similar to the first one.

- The MTS object can be created by another MTS object that runs within a transactional context.

Table 12-11 summarizes the transaction attributes in the different creation types. It is important to clarify three points:

- With "requires a new transaction," the new transaction is not nested but independent. Therefore, it can be successfully committed while the client transaction aborts. Conversely it can be aborted while the client transaction successfully commits.

- With "Does not support transaction," the new object creation will not fail if the client has a transaction but will simply ignore the transaction. In other words, the transaction attribute could be called "Does not use transaction."

- The MTS component can use nontransacted resources or transacted resources outside of the MTS transaction. In this case, the transaction attributes do not apply; for example, the MTS component can perform file operations. Since the file system does not support transactions, the file operations cannot be aborted. Likewise, the MTS component can open an OLE DB data source but not enlist the transaction. In this case, the outcome of the transaction is totally disconnected from the object's transaction.

**Table 12-11** Transaction Attributes and Transactions

| Transaction Attribute | Requires a Transaction | Requires a New Transaction | Supports a Transaction | Does Not Support a Transaction |
|---|---|---|---|---|
| Root object | New transaction | New transaction | No transaction | No transaction |
| Nonroot object; client does not have a transaction | New transaction | New transaction | No transaction | No transaction |
| Nonroot object; client has a transaction | Inherited transaction | New transaction | Inherited transaction | No transaction |

## Transaction Enlistment

The last service component is *transaction enlistment*. When you open a data source with transaction enlistment, you indicate that each session should attempt to join the transaction of the instance that created the session. If the component that created the session does not have a transaction, transaction enlistment does not have any effect. Otherwise, the session creates a transaction and joins the object's transaction. As a result, you should not commit or abort the session's transaction but instead act on the object's transaction with functions such as `SetComplete` and `SetAbort`.

Transaction enlistments use the following elements:

- A *resource manager*, which manages durable data. SQL Server and Oracle are examples of resource managers.

- A *resource dispenser* manages *connections* to resource managers. The connections themselves are not durable; they do not survive the shutdown of the resource dispenser.

- The *dispenser manager* manages the different resource dispensers.

- MTS/COM+ uses MS DTC as a *transaction coordinator*.

Figure 12-12 on the next page shows the different elements that play a role in transaction enlistment.

The MTS/COM+ runtime intercepts the creation of the transactional instance, and transmits the transaction attribute according to the rules described above.

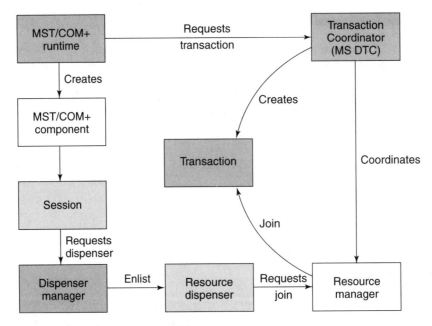

**Figure 12-12** Transaction Enlistment Architecture

When the transactional component opens an OLE DB session, this session requests a resource dispenser from the dispenser manager. The resource dispenser then asks the resource manager to join the transaction of the component. From there, all actions performed through the session will be part of the object's transaction.

Using transaction enlistment is not a challenge for the programmer. The main point is to enable it:

```
{
    CDataSource db;
    CDBPropSet dbinit(DBPROPSET_DBINIT);

    dbinit.AddProperty(DBPROP_AUTH_INTEGRATED, OLESTR("SSPI"));
    dbinit.AddProperty(DBPROP_INIT_CATALOG, OLESTR(database));
    dbinit.AddProperty(DBPROP_INIT_DATASOURCE, OLESTR(servername));
    dbinit.AddProperty(DBPROP_INIT_OLEDBSERVICES,
    DBPROPVAL_OS_RESOURCEPOOLING | DBPROPVAL_OS_TXNENLISTMENT);
    db.OpenWithServiceComponents(_T("SQLOLEDB.1"), &dbinit);

    CSession Session;
    Session.Open(db)
    // Perform actions of Session
}
```

You can also choose to work outside the object's transaction by opening the data source without transaction enlistment, as follows:

```
{
    CDataSource db;
    CDBPropSet dbinit(DBPROPSET_DBINIT);

    dbinit.AddProperty(DBPROP_AUTH_INTEGRATED, OLESTR("SSPI"));
    dbinit.AddProperty(DBPROP_INIT_CATALOG, OLESTR(database));
    dbinit.AddProperty(DBPROP_INIT_DATASOURCE, OLESTR(servername));
    dbinit.AddProperty(DBPROP_INIT_OLEDBSERVICES, 0);
    db.Open (_T("SQLOLEDB.1"), &dbinit);

    CSession Session;
    Session.Open(db)
    Session.StartTransaction();
    // Perform actions of Session
    // abort or commit the transaction
}
```

## SUMMARY

This chapter covered simple, nested, and distributed transactions, transaction isolation, and the Microsoft Transaction Server and COM+ transactional components.

Microsoft Transaction Server and COM+ are the cornerstones for building components. At first, transactions might not seem natural. However, once you use them, you will wonder how you ever lived without them.

# 13 Indexes, Chapters, and Views

This chapter presents four advanced concepts: *indexes*, *OLE DB chapters*, *hierarchical rowsets*, and *views*. Indexes represent an encapsulation of database indexes and are not related to the other concepts. They are here simply because they do not warrant a chapter of their own. OLE DB chapters provide a convenient and efficient way to specify a group of rows in a rowset. The chapters have two applications: hierarchical rowsets and views.

The OLE DB consumer templates do not cover these concepts. Thus, you have two options: Use the raw OLE DB interfaces directly or use the OLE DB extensions provided with this book. This chapter assumes that you will use the latter option. However, it is relatively easy to unfold the raw code from the OLE DB extensions.

## INDEXES

The basic idea behind tabular databases is that the data is in a series of tables, from which it can be efficiently extracted. For example, when you execute a query such as

```
SELECT * FROM mytable WHERE column1 = 3
```

the response time should not be proportional to the number of rows in `mytable`. This is where indexes come in.

An index is an ordered, balanced tree for one or more columns: Given a value, the index can get you quickly to the rows that match it. The database engine finds the appropriate indexes and uses them to optimize the query execution. This is one of the features of a good query processor.

Typically, you do not have to worry about indexes when accessing data, since the database engine takes care of that. In fact, the database engine will usually do a better job. In addition, using indexes explicitly increases the coupling between your program and the underlying data store.

Still, there are cases when you might want to access indexes directly. For example, indexes can be useful for optimizing queries on multiple databases. They also give you more functionality than regular commands. Finally, some providers support indexes as the only efficient way to access data.

OLE DB defines two kinds of indexes: *integrated* and *separate*. An integrated index is part of the table it indexes. In this case, consumers can open a rowset that contains both the index and the table content. A separate index is not part of the any table, but only references rows of another table. In practice, providers tend not to support indexes. However, the Jet Provider 4.0 on Access 2000 databases supports integrated indexes, which will be the focus of this section.

## Index Type

Indexes have their own OLE DB type, which is very close to the rowset type. After all, a database index is somewhat related to a database table, so it is not surprising that OLE DB indexes and OLE DB rowsets support many common interfaces. More precisely, OLE DB indexes support many of the rowset interfaces, such as `IRowset` and `IAccessor` or `IRowsetLocate`. In addition, they support `IRowsetIndex`, which allows seek and range operations. Figure 13-1 shows the interfaces supported by indexes. Those that are mandatory are in bold while optional interfaces are not.

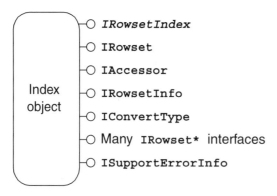

**Figure 13-1** Index Interfaces

## Using Indexes

Class `CIndex` encapsulates an integrated index. It is very similar to `CTable` and is used in a very similar way, although it has a few more features.

`CIndex` is declared as

```
template <class TAccessor , class TRowset = CRowset>
class CIndex :
    public CAccessorRowset<TAccessor, TRowset>
```

Like `CTable`, `CIndex` needs an accessor and a rowset class. Internally it keeps a pointer to the `IRowsetIndex` interface of the OLE DB index. The `TRowset` class should be `CRowset` or any other rowset class that holds an `m_spRowset` pointer to the OLE DB rowset. Like `CTable`, `CIndex` sets this class member. Figure 13-2 shows the layout of the class members.

While the rowset is similar to the one you use with a table, the accessor has a restriction. Accessors are used to get column values and transmit a criterion. It is recommended that you bind the accessor entries in the order they appear in the index and start with the index column. Consider the example of a table with `column1`, `column2`, and `column3`. Suppose that the index uses `column2` and `column3` in this order so that it would be proper to bind

```
BEGIN_COLUMN_MAP(CTableAccessor)
    COLUMN_ENTRY(1, m_Column2)
    COLUMN_ENTRY(2, m_Column3)
    COLUMN_ENTRY(3, m_Column1)
END_COLUMN_MAP()
```

or

```
BEGIN_COLUMN_MAP(CTableAccessor)
    COLUMN_ENTRY(1, m_Column2)
    COLUMN_ENTRY(2, m_Column1)
END_COLUMN_MAP()
```

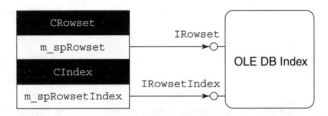

**Figure 13-2** Layout of `CIndex` and `CRowset` Class Members

However, the following binding would not be proper because it does not start with a column that is part of the index.

```
BEGIN_COLUMN_MAP(CTableAccessor)
    COLUMN_ENTRY(1, m_Column1)
    COLUMN_ENTRY(2, m_Column2)
    COLUMN_ENTRY(3, m_Column3)
END_COLUMN_MAP()
```

The following binding also would not be proper because the columns do not appear in the order defined in the index:

```
BEGIN_COLUMN_MAP(CTableAccessor)
    COLUMN_ENTRY(1, m_Column3)
    COLUMN_ENTRY(2, m_Column2)
    COLUMN_ENTRY(3, m_Column1)
END_COLUMN_MAP()
```

## Opening an Index

Opening an index is similar to opening a table except that you pass an index name and a table name. `Cindex::Open` is declared as

```
HRESULT Open(const CSession& session, LPCTSTR szIndexName,
    LPCTSTR szTableName, DBPROPSET* pPropSet = NULL)
```

where

- `session` represents the session on which to open the index.
- `szIndexName` and `szTableName` represent the index name and table name, respectively. If the index name uniquely identifies the index, you can pass `NULL` as the table name. Otherwise, the table name is required.
- `pPropSet` represents an optional property set.

The following code shows how to open the index `PrimaryKey` on the table `Table1`.

```
CIndex <CAccessor<CTable1Accessor> > index;
hr = index.Open (mysession, "PrimaryKey", "Table1");
```

Internally, `Open` calls the `IOpenRowset::OpenRowset` function to retrieve the `IRowsetIndex` interface pointer. If successful, it gets additional interfaces and binds columns:

```
hr = session.m_spOpenRowset->OpenRowset(NULL, TableID, &IndexID,
    __uuidof(m_spRowsetIndex), (pPropSet) ? 1 : 0, pPropSet,
    (IUnknown**)&m_spRowsetIndex);
if (SUCCEEDED(hr))
{
    SetupOptionalRowsetInterfaces();

    // If we have output columns then bind
    if (_OutputColumnsClass::HasOutputColumns())
        hr = Bind();
}
```

SetupOptionalRowsetInterfaces requests an interface for the rowset (GetInterfacePtr is inherited from TRowset) and then forwards the call to TRowset:

```
void SetupOptionalRowsetInterfaces()
    {
        if (m_spRowsetIndex != NULL)
            m_spRowsetIndex.p->QueryInterface (GetIID(),
                GetInterfacePtr());
        TRowset::SetupOptionalRowsetInterfaces();
    }
```

Once the index is open, you can navigate it the same way you navigate a table, using rowset methods such as MoveFirst and MoveNext. You can also perform two index-specific actions: seeking a specific row and restricting the index range. These are explained in the following sections.

## Seeking a Row

An index can get to, or *seek*, a row whose columns match a particular value as long as the column is part of the index. The Seek method changes the current row and the rowset cursor, which makes it equivalent to methods such as MoveNext. To seek a row, set the column with the values you want to match and call Seek with the number of significant columns.

The Seek method has additional parameters:

```
HRESULT Seek (ULONG cKeyValues, DBSEEK dwSeekOptions =
    DBSEEK_FIRSTEQ, int nAccessor = 0)
```

dwSeekOptions represents the seek option and can be one of the values in Table 13-1 on the next page. Usually, you want to get the first row that matches the criterion. Therefore, DBSEEK_FIRSTEQ is the default.

nAccessor represents the index of the accessor on which to perform the comparison. In other words, Seek considers the cKeyValues first values in this accessor. It is zero by default.

**Table 13-1** Seek Options

| Symbol | Description |
|---|---|
| DBSEEK_FIRSTEQ | Seek the first keys that match the values |
| DBSEEK_LASTEQ | Seek the last keys that match the values |
| DBSEEK_AFTEREQ | Seek the first keys that are after or equal to the values in the order defined by the index |
| DBSEEK_AFTER | Seek the first keys that are strictly after the values in the order defined by the index |
| DBSEEK_BEFOREEQ | Seek the last keys that are before or equal to the values in the order defined by the index |
| DBSEEK_BEFORE | Seek the last keys that are strictly before the values in the order defined by the index |

Internally, Seek calls IRowsetIndex::Seek, passing the accessor handle and accessor buffer to specify the criterion. This operation is somewhat similar to using command parameters. The code is equivalent to

```
HRESULT hr =  m_spRowsetIndex->Seek(m_pAccessor->GetHAccessor
   (nAccessor), cKeyValues, m_pAccessor->GetBuffer(),
   dwSeekOptions);
if (FAILED (hr))
   return hr;
return GetData();
```

For example, if the first index column is ID and you want to get the value 3, you write

```
index.m_ID = 3;
hr = index.Seek (1);
```

If the second index column is ID2 and you want to get to the first row that matches ID = 3 and ID2 = 5, you write

```
index.m_ID = 3;
index.m_ID2 = 5;
hr = index.Seek (2);
```

If you want to get to the last row that matches ID = 3 and ID2 = 5, you write

```
index.m_ID = 3;
index.m_ID2 = 5;
hr = index.Seek (2, DBSEEK_LASTEQ);
```

After seeking a row, you can call `MoveNext` and eventually reach a row that does not match the criterion. In this respect, `Seek` offers some functionality that is not matched by traditional commands.

## Restricting the Index Range

In some cases, indexes have unique values: Only one row can match a given criterion. In this case, `Seek` is appropriate. In other cases, indexes do not have unique values: Several rows can match a given criterion. In this case, `Seek` is less appropriate because it gets only one row rather than a set of rows.

As the previous section showed, there is no warning when `MoveNext` reaches a row that does not meet the criterion anymore. Fortunately, however, indexes can also handle ranges. Each index contains a current range, which is the entire index when the index is created. The current range cannot be accessed explicitly. However, it modifies the behavior of the index's cursor movements, so that, for example, `MoveFirst` moves to the first row in the range while `MoveNext` moves to the next row. The left part of Figure 13-3 shows an index with a full range, in which the behavior of `MoveFirst` and `MoveNext` is not altered. The right part of the figure shows the same index after setting the current range with rows of value 2 and 3 (the rows in the current range are in gray). Here the behavior of `MoveFirst` and `MoveNext` is altered so that only the rows in the current range are traversed.

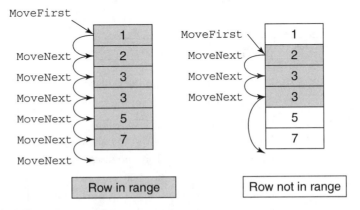

**Figure 13-3** Changing the Current Range of an Index

The `SetRange` method specifies the current range with a starting and an ending criterion:

```
HRESULT SetRange (
    ULONG       cStartKeyColumns,
    void *      pStartData,
    ULONG       cEndKeyColumns,
    void *      pEndData,
    DBRANGE     dwRangeOptions = DBRANGE_INCLUSIVESTART |
        DBRANGE_INCLUSIVEEND,
    int nAccessor = 0)
```

In the code, `SetRange` is a straight encapsulation of `IRowsetIndex::SetRange`. `pStartData` is an array of data that specifies the beginning of the range, and `cStartKeyColumns` is the number of items in `pStartData`. The same applies for the end of the range with the two arguments, `=cEndKeyColumns` and `pEndData`.

`dwRangeOptions` is the range option. It is a combination of the values in Table 13-2. This sample shows how to set a range of values between 2 and 4:

```
int   start [] = {2};
int   end [] = {4};
hr = index.SetRange(1, start, 1, end);
hr = index.MoveFirst();
while (hr = S_OK)
{
    hr = index.MoveNext();
}
```

You can get a full range by passing an empty criterion, as here:

```
hr = index.SetRange(0, NULL, 0, NULL);
```

**Table 13-2** Range Flags

| Symbol | Description |
| --- | --- |
| DBRANGE_INCLUSIVESTART | Include the start value in the range |
| DBRANGE_INCLUSIVEEND | Exclude the end value from the range |
| DBRANGE_EXCLUSIVESTART | Include the start value in the range |
| DBRANGE_EXCLUSIVEEND | Exclude the end value from the range |
| DBRANGE_EXCLUDENULLS | Exclude NULL values from the range |
| DBRANGE_PREFIX | Range includes all values that start with `pStartData`. This is mainly useful for strings; `pEndData` is ignored |
| DBRANGE_MATCH | Range includes all values that match `pStartData`; `pEndData` is ignored |

## CHAPTERS

Chapter 8 presented rowset bookmarks, which identify a row and enable you to go back to it quickly. Whereas a bookmark represents one row, a *chapter* represents a set of rows. Thus, for example, Figure 13-4 represents a rowset with a bookmark on the second row and a chapter on rows 3, 4, and 5. Like bookmarks, chapters are opaque values. The figure describes only the concept of chapter. There is no guarantee that the actual implementation will use some kind of array.

A book analogy works fine with the bookmark, but it does not work with the chapter for two reasons. First, the rows contained in a chapter do not need to be consecutive, as illustrated in Figure 13-5. In other words, an OLE DB chapter is more than a range of rows. Second, the rows in a chapter do not need to reflect the order in the rowset. In other words, a chapter keeps track of the order in which the rows should appear. Figure 13-6 shows a chapter on non-ordered rows.

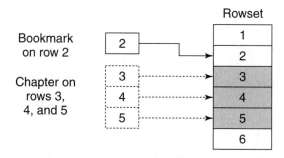

**Figure 13-4** Rowset, Bookmark, and Chapter

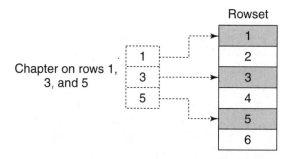

**Figure 13-5** Rows in the Chapter Do Not Need to Be Consecutive

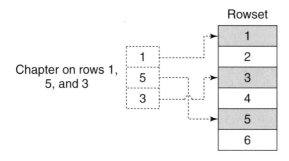

**Figure 13-6** Chapter on Nonordered Rows

Chapters are used primarily for filtering and sorting. Since a chapter can contain any subset of rows, it is ideal for identifying the result of filtering. Also, since it contains the order of the rows, it is good for storing the result of a sort. A chapter can contain the result of a combined sorting/filtering operation.

## Using a Chapter

Like rows, a chapter is not represented by a COM object but rather by a handle:

```
typedef ULONG HCHAPTER;
```

The reason is that a chapter cannot live without an underlying rowset. Also, a handle is more efficient.

Chapter handles belong to a given rowset; a rowset should use only the chapter handles that belong to it. Chapters are opaque values; you should not try to interpret them.

OLE DB defines a special, NULL chapter:

```
#define DB_NULL_HCHAPTER 0x00
```

One way to understand the NULL chapter is to consider that the underlying object will ignore the chapter. Another way is to consider the Null chapter as containing all the rows in the same order as in the rowset.

At the OLE DB level, many functions accept a chapter handle as a parameter. However, the OLE DB consumer templates do not take advantage of this parameter and pass DB_NULL_HCHAPTER. The following methods of CRowset pass DB_NULL_HCHAPTER to the OLE DB function:

- GetRowCount
- Compare
- MoveNext
- MoveFirst
- MoveLast
- MoveToBookmark
- Insert
- Delete
- GetRowStatus
- MoveToRatio
- Undo
- Update
- RefreshVisibleData
- GetApproximatePosition

As an example, let us examine the code for CRowset::MoveFirst:

```
HRESULT MoveFirst()
{
    HRESULT hr;

    // Check the data was opened successfully and the accessor
    // has been set.
    ATLASSERT(m_spRowset != NULL);
    ATLASSERT(m_pAccessor != NULL);

    // Release a row if one is already around
    ReleaseRows();

    hr = m_spRowset->RestartPosition(NULL);
    if (FAILED(hr))
        return hr;

    // Get the data
    return MoveNext();
}
```

m_spRowset->RestartPosition positions the cursor at the beginning of the rows in the chapter parameter. The OLE DB consumer templates pass NULL (i.e., DB_NULL_HCHAPTER) as a parameter. Therefore, MoveFirst moves to the beginning of the entire rowset.

## CRowsetEx

CRowsetEx is an extended version of CRowset that supports chapters. It has one template parameter that defines the level of chapter support.

```
template<class ChapterClass>
class CRowsetEx: public CRowset, public ChapterClass
```

ChapterClass can be any class that has at least the following method:

```
HCHAPTER GetHChapter() const
```

Figure 13-7 represents the inheritance of CRowsetEx.

The implementation of CRowsetEx is somewhat similar to that of CRowset. However, instead of passing NULL to the OLE DB functions, it passes the result of GetHChapter. For example, MoveFirst passes GetHChapter() as a parameter for RestartPosition:

```
HRESULT MoveFirst()
{
    HRESULT hr;

    // Check the data was opened successfully and the accessor
    // has been set.
    ATLASSERT(m_spRowset != NULL);
    ATLASSERT(m_pAccessor != NULL);

    // Release a row if one is already around
    ReleaseRows();
    hr = m_spRowset->RestartPosition(GetHChapter());
    if (FAILED(hr))
        return hr;

    // Get the data
    return MoveNext();
}
```

As a result, CRowsetEx::MoveFirst moves the cursor to the beginning of the chapter, which is not necessarily the beginning of the rowset.

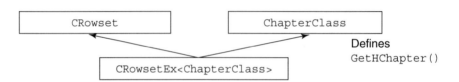

**Figure 13-7** CRowsetEx Inheritance

CNoChapter is the most trivial chapter support class: The GetHChapter method always returns DB_NULL_HCHAPTER:

```
class CNoChapter
{
public:
   HCHAPTER GetHChapter() const
   {
      return DB_NULL_HCHAPTER;
   }
};
```

Using CNoChapter does not represent any overhead since it does not define any new class member. CRowsetEx<CNoChapter> is equivalent to CRowset.

Class CHasChapter is a more interesting chapter support class. It has a class member that represents the current chapter.

```
class CHasChapter
{
public:
   CHasChapter()
   {
      m_hChapter = DB_NULL_HCHAPTER;
   }
   HRESULT SetChapter(HCHAPTER Chapter, IRowset* Rowset)
// more code
   HRESULT ReleaseChapter(IRowset* Rowset)
// more code

   HCHAPTER GetHChapter() const
   {
      return m_hChapter;
   }

      void Close()
// more code
   HCHAPTER m_hChapter;
};
```

Figure 13-8 represents the inheritance of CRowsetEx<CHasChapter>.

The methods of CRowsetEx<CHasChapter> will take into account the selected chapter. MoveFirst moves the cursor to the first row of the chapter. MoveNext moves to the next row according to the row order defined by the chapter.

Chapters have two applications: They help navigate relations between hierarchical rowsets, and they offer support for filtering and sorting with views. The next two sections delve into these applications.

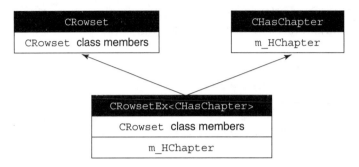

**Figure 13-8** `CRowsetEx<CHasChapter>` Inheritance

## HIERARCHICAL ROWSETS

A relational database contains a series of tables. Usually, you use relations between these tables. That is, two rows in two tables are in relation if the values of the two columns are the same. You can define one-to-one, one-to-many, and many-to-many relationships, but OLE DB is indifferent to the relationship type.

### Example

In the following sections, we will use a typical example: a simplified customer, order, and product schema. The customer table contains two columns: `Name` represents the name of the customer, and `Id` is the customer's unique identifier. (In a typical, real database, the customer table would have additional information such as address, email, or phone number.) The order table contains three columns: `Id` uniquely identifies the order; `CustomerId` identifies the customer who placed the order, and `Date` represents the date of the order. Each order contains a collection of items, summarized in the `OrderItems` table. As expected, the `OrderId` column identifies the order the item belongs to, while the `ProductId` column identifies the product the item corresponds to. The product table contains two columns: `Id` identifies the product and `Description` briefly describes the product. Figure 13-9 is a graphical representation of this schema in the SQL Server diagram editor.

The following sections explain how to traverse the database starting with the customer table. We will focus on the orders of each customer, the products in each order, and the quantity ordered.

These issues are well represented by a hierarchical structure such as the one in Figure 13-10. The next sections explain the methods to navigate this tree structure.

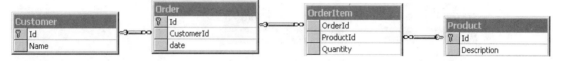

**Figure 13-9** Schema Representation of the Example

| | customerid | name | Customerid | orderid | date | OrderId | ProductId | Quantity | description | productid |
|---|---|---|---|---|---|---|---|---|---|---|
| | customerid | name | Customerid | orderid | date | OrderId | ProductId | Quantity | description | productid |
| ⊟ | | | ⊟ | | | 1 | 1 | 1 | Apple | 1 |
| | | | | 1 | 1 2000-11-12 | 1 | 2 | 1 | Bannana | 2 |
| | 1 | Albert | ⊟ | | | 3 | 2 | 2 | Bannana | 2 |
| | | | 1 | 3 | 2000-12-12 | 3 | 3 | 1 | Carrot | 3 |
| | customerid | name | Customerid | orderid | date | OrderId | ProductId | Quantity | description | productid |
| ⊟ | | | ⊟ | | | 2 | 1 | 1 | Apple | 1 |
| | | | 2 | 2 | 2000-11-12 | 2 | 3 | 1 | Carrot | 3 |
| | 2 | Bob | ⊟ | | | 4 | 3 | 1 | Carrot | 3 |
| | | | 2 | 4 | 2000-12-12 | 4 | 1 | 3 | Apple | 1 |

**Figure 13-10** Graphical Representation of the Hierarchy

## Traditional Approach

In the traditional approach, there are no chapters. Instead, the idea is to open a rowset for each child row, as illustrated in Figure 13-11. In the figure, the lines between the rowsets are dotted and represent abstract links. The programmer is responsible for knowing which rowset corresponds to which row.

The following code demonstrates how to traverse the customer and order tables:

```
CCommand<CAccessor<CdboCustomersAccessor2>, CRowset> Customers;
hr = Customers.Open (Session);
if (FAILED(hr))
    return hr;
hr = Customers.MoveFirst();
while (hr == S_OK)
{
    {
        CCommand<CAccessor<CdboOrdersAccessor2>, CRowset> Orders;
        Orders.m_CustomerId = Customers.m_Id;
        Orders.Open(Session);
        HRESULT hr2 = Orders.MoveFirst();
        while (hr2 = S_OK)
        {
            // Do something with the order.
            hr2 = Orders.MoveNext();
        }
    }
    hr = Customers.MoveNext();
}
```

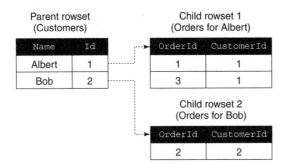

**Figure 13-11** Parent/Child Rowset without Chapter

This code assumes that the command text associated with the order accessor is the following:

```
DEFINE_COMMAND(CdboOrdersAccessor2, _T(" \
    SELECT \
        Id, \
        CustomerId, \
        date   \
        FROM dbo.Orders WHERE CustomerId = ?"))
```

While this method is acceptable, it can be improved. Its main drawback is that you end up with as many order rowsets as there are customers, which not only is complex to manage but can also lead to inefficiencies.

## Chapter Approach

When you use chapters, you do not need to create one rowset per parent row. Instead, the parent rowset has one child rowset, which contains all the rows of the underlying table. However, each row in the parent rowset contains a chapter column that holds a chapter handle to the subset of child rows that correspond to the parent row. Figure 13-12 shows the customer/order example. Note that there is only one order rowset, which stays open during the lifetime of the customer (parent) rowset. The dotted components are not accessible by the programmer; they are represented only to help explain the structure.

## Data Shaping Service

Many providers do not support hierarchical rowsets natively. However, this is of little importance because OLE DB comes with a service that simplifies their construction, the *data shaping service*. As Chapter 2 explained, the data shaping

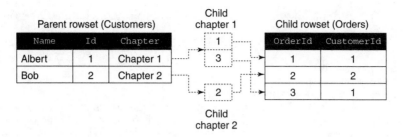

**Figure 13-12** Parent and Child with Chapter

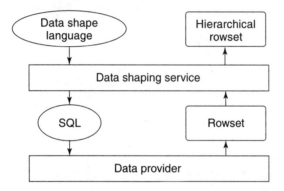

**Figure 13-13** Data Shaping Service Architecture

service is not a data provider by itself. Instead, it transforms queries and relies on another provider to store and manage the actual data. The data shaping service translates its own language (*data shape language*) into a series of SQL queries and sends them to the data provider. Then it uses the rowset returned by the data provider to build a hierarchical rowset. Figure 13-13 illustrates this architecture.

Describing the data shape language is out of the scope of this book. However, the Microsoft documentation defines it well, so please refer to it for more information.

Opening a data source with the data shaping service is similar to opening it on a regular provider. If you open the data source with a CLSID and a set of properties, use the data shape provider—CLSID_DataShapeProvider—which is defined in MSDShape.h. One important property is DBPROP_MSDS_DBINIT_DATAPROVIDER, part of the DBPROPSET_MSDSDBINIT property set, which represents the underlying provider's ProgID.

For example, if you write the following to open a data source on the underlying provider:

```
CdataSourcedb;
CDBPropSet dbinit;
dbinit.SetGUID(DBPROPSET_DBINIT);
dbinit.AddProperty(DBPROP_INIT_DATASOURCE, OLESTR("server name"));
dbinit.AddProperty(DBPROP_AUTH_INTEGRATED, OLESTR("SSPI"));
dbinit.AddProperty(DBPROP_INIT_CATALOG, OLESTR("database name"));
hr = db.Open(_T("SQLOLEDB"), &dbinit);
```

the corresponding code to get the data shape provider with the same underlying provider is

```
CDataSource db;
CDBPropSet dbinit[2];
dbinit[0].SetGUID(DBPROPSET_DBINIT);
dbinit[0].AddProperty(DBPROP_INIT_DATASOURCE, OLESTR("server name"));
dbinit[0].AddProperty(DBPROP_AUTH_INTEGRATED, OLESTR("SSPI"));
dbinit[0].AddProperty(DBPROP_INIT_CATALOG, OLESTR("database name"));
dbinit[1].SetGUID(DBPROPSET_MSDSDBINIT);
dbinit[1].AddProperty(DBPROP_MSDS_DBINIT_DATAPROVIDER,
OLESTR("SQLOLEDB"));

hr = db.Open(CLSID_DataShapeProvider, dbinit, 2);
```

## Navigating Hierarchical Rowsets

When navigating hierarchical rowsets, you deal with a parent rowset and a child rowset. The parent rowset can be of any type; however, the child rowset can open itself from the parent rowset only. Class CChildRowset implements support for child rowsets. It is declared as

```
template <class TAccessor, ULONG Ordinal = 0, class TRowset =
  CChapteredRowset >
class CChildRowset: public CAccessorRowset<TAccessor, TRowset>
```

CChildRowset is very similar to CTable. One notable difference is the Ordinal template parameter, which represents the column ordinal in the rowset of the chapter column that corresponds to the child rowset. It is possible to leave it at zero and specify it dynamically.

You open the child with the Open method. It accepts two parameters: the parent IRowset interface pointer and the ordinal. If you do not specify the ordinal, it will default to the ordinal in the template parameter. Open is defined as

```
HRESULT Open(IRowset* Parent, ULONG iOrdinal = Ordinal)
{
    ATLASSERT(Parent != NULL);
    CComPtr<IRowsetInfo> RowsetInfo;
    HRESULT hr = Parent->QueryInterface(&RowsetInfo);
    if (FAILED(hr))
        return hr;
    hr = RowsetInfo->GetReferencedRowset(iOrdinal,GetIID(),
        reinterpret_cast<IUnknown**> (GetInterfacePtr()));
    if (FAILED(hr))
        return hr;
    SetupOptionalRowsetInterfaces();
    if (_OutputColumnsClass::HasOutputColumns())
        hr = Bind();
    return hr;
}
```

Figure 13-14 illustrates how Open gets the interface pointer to the child rowset. The following example shows two equivalent ways to open a child rowset:

```
CTable<CParentAccessor> ParentRowset;
CChildRowset<CChildAccessor, 3> ChildRowset1;
ChildRowset1.Open(ParentRowset.m_spRowset);
// or
CChildRowset<CChildAccessor> ChildRowset2;
ChildRowset2.Open(ParentRowset.m_spRowset, 3);
```

There are two approaches for navigating hierarchical rowsets. The first is to have two separate instances for the parent and the child rowset. The second is to make the child rowset part of the parent rowset.

### Separate Parent and Child

With one instance for the parent and one for the child, a difficulty is that the parent gets the chapter handle even though the child needs it. As a result, you need

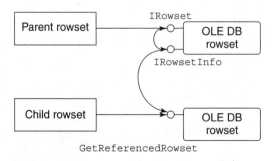

**Figure 13-14** Getting the Child Rowset

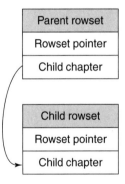

**Figure 13-15** Architecture—Separate Parent and Child

to copy the chapter handle from the parent to the child at each cursor movement. Figure 13-15 illustrates the object layout.

In this approach, the parent and the child rowsets are independent. The parent simply binds the child chapter, which the child rowset is responsible for updating.

The benefit of this approach is that it is very readable. For example, the accessor for the orders class can be

```
class CdboOrdersAccessor
{
public:
    LONG m_Id;
    LONG m_CustomerId;
    DBTIMESTAMP m_date;
    HCHAPTER m_OrderItemChapter;

BEGIN_COLUMN_MAP(CdboOrdersAccessor)
    COLUMN_ENTRY(1, m_Id)
    COLUMN_ENTRY(2, m_CustomerId)
    COLUMN_ENTRY(3, m_date)
    COLUMN_ENTRY_TYPE(4, DBTYPE_HCHAPTER, m_OrderItemChapter)
END_COLUMN_MAP()
```

Note that since HCHAPTER is actually ULONG, it is necessary to explicitly specify the OLE DB type DBTYPE_HCHAPTER.

Given an instance of order, the following example traverses the corresponding items:

```
CChildRowset<CAccessor<CdboOrderItemsAccessor> > OrderItems;
OrderItems.Open (Customers.m_Orders.GetInterface(), 4);
OrderItems.SetChapter(Customers.m_Orders.m_OrderItemChapter);
HRESULT hr3 = OrderItems.MoveFirst();
while (hr3 == S_OK)
{
    // Do something with OrdersItems
    hr3 = OrderItems.MoveNext();
}
```

## The Child as Part of the Parent

With the child rowset as a class member of the parent rowset, the parent rowset can bind the chapter of the child rowset in its own binding. As a result, there is no need to copy the chapter handle at each cursor movement. Figure 13-16 shows the object layout with this method.

You use CChildRowset in conjunction with the CHILD_ROWSET_ENTRY macro, which binds the chapter of the child rowset in the parent class. When the row position of the parent changes, the chapter of the child is automatically updated. You use CHILD_ROWSET_ENTRY simply by passing the variable.

Internally, CHILD_ROWSET_ENTRY gets the chapter ordinal from the variable and binds its chapter. It is defined as

```
#define CHILD_ROWSET_ENTRY(variable) \
    COLUMN_ENTRY_TYPE(_GetChapterOrdinal(((_classtype*)0)->
        ##variable##), DBTYPE_CHAPTER, variable##.m_hChapter)
```

For example, the accessor class for customers is

```
class CdboCustomersAccessor
{
public:
    LONG m_Id;
    TCHAR m_Name[11];
    CChildRowset<CAccessor<CdboOrdersAccessor>, 3> m_Orders;

BEGIN_COLUMN_MAP(CdboCustomersAccessor)
    COLUMN_ENTRY(1, m_Id)
    COLUMN_ENTRY(2, m_Name)
    CHILD_ROWSET_ENTRY(m_Orders)
END_COLUMN_MAP()
```

The following code shows how to traverse the customers and orders:

```
CCommand<CAccessor<CdboCustomersAccessor>, CRowset> Customers;
hr = Customers.Open (Session, CommandText);
if (FAILED(hr))
    return hr;
hr = Customers.m_Orders.Open(Customers.GetInterface());
hr = Customers.MoveFirst();
while (hr == S_OK)
{
    HRESULT hr2 = Customers.m_Orders.MoveFirst();
    while (hr2 == S_OK)
    {
        // Do something with the order
        hr2 = Customers.m_Orders.MoveNext();
    }
    hr = Customers.MoveNext();
}
Customers.m_Orders.Close();
Customers.Close();
```

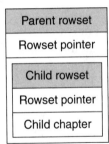

**Figure 13-16** Architecture—Child Rowset as Part of the Parent Rowset

Finally, this example combines the different methods to traverse the whole `Customers`, `Orders`, `OrderItems`, and `Product` hierarchy:

```
CCommand<CAccessor<CdboCustomersAccessor>, CRowset> Customers;
hr = Customers.Open (Session, CommandText);
if (FAILED(hr))
    return hr;
hr = Customers.m_Orders.Open(Customers.GetInterface());
hr = Customers.MoveFirst();
while (hr == S_OK)
{
    OutputDebugString(_T("————\n"));
    OutputDebugString(Customers.m_Name);
    OutputDebugString(_T(" has "));
    ULONG RowCount;
    Customers.m_Orders.GetRowCount(RowCount);
    OutputDebugString(I2T(RowCount));
    OutputDebugString(_T(" orders:\n"));
    HRESULT hr2 = Customers.m_Orders.MoveFirst();
    while (hr2 == S_OK)
    {
        CChildRowset<CAccessor<CdboOrderItemsAccessor> >
            OrderItems;
        OrderItems.Open (Customers.m_Orders.GetInterface(), 4);
        OrderItems.SetChapter(
            Customers.m_Orders.m_OrderItemChapter);
        HRESULT hr3 = OrderItems.MoveFirst();
        OutputDebugString(_T("order "));
        OutputDebugString(I2T(OrderItems.m_OrderId));
        OutputDebugString(_T("\n"));
        while (hr3 == S_OK)
        {
            OutputDebugString(I2T(OrderItems.m_Quantity));
            CChildRowset<CAccessor<CdboProductsAccessor> >Products;
            Products.Open (OrderItems.GetInterface(), 4);
            Products.SetChapter(OrderItems.m_ProductChapter);
```

```
        HRESULT hr4 = Products.MoveFirst();
        OutputDebugString(_T(Products.m_Description));
        OutputDebugString(_T("\n"));
        hr3 = OrderItems.MoveNext();
      }
      hr2 = Customers.m_Orders.MoveNext();
    }
  hr = Customers.MoveNext();
}
Customers.m_Orders.Close();
Customers.Close();
```

## VIEWS

Languages such as SQL are very powerful, allowing complex operations such as joins from several tables. However, SQL is often used for much simpler queries, such as those on only one table that perform a combination of filtering and sorting. In effect, such queries take a table and produce a resulting rowset. The question is, how can we use this rowset and query it again? The answer is *views*.

As the name suggests, OLE DB views are objects that are applied on rowsets for "viewing" them through a combination of filtering and sorting. In this respect, OLE DB views are to rowsets what database views are to database tables. Figure 13-17 shows the whole architecture: The database query filters all the items with values less than or equal to 3 and produces the corresponding rowset, on which a view is applied. In this example, the view filters out the items greater than 2 and reorders the rows by decreasing value.

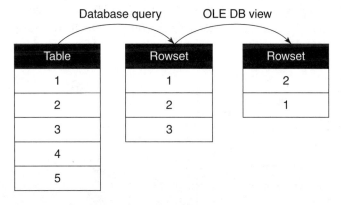

**Figure 13-17** Tables, Rowsets, and Views

## When to Use Views

Views can be useful for performing operations on already open rowsets, particularly when you do not have control over the source of a rowset. Also, because some providers do not support commands with rich languages such as SQL, views can perform some sorting and filtering operations equivalent to basic SQL commands. They can also be useful when you want to avoid a language such as SQL.

The client cursor service that comes with OLE DB supports views. As a result, providers do not have to implement views natively: When a consumer needs view support, it only needs to open the data source with the client cursor service and request the right interface.

The following sections will explain this in more detail. The bottom line for now is that you can use views against *any* OLE DB tabular provider. The drawback is that in order to perform its operations, a view is likely to load the entire rowset on the client.

## Opening a View

In theory, there are two ways to open a view. The first is to open it directly against the database table. The second is to open it on an already open rowset. Figure 13-18 illustrates the two methods. In fact, it is always possible to simulate the first method by first opening a rowset on the entire table and then opening a view on it. However, OLE DB providers tend not to support opening a view against a table. As a result, this chapter will concentrate on the second method.

## View Type

Like indexes, OLE DB views have their own type. This type includes four new interfaces: IViewSort, which defines sorting operations; IViewFilter, which supports filtering operations; IViewChapter, which gives access to the chapter that defines the view; and IViewRowset, which is usually not supported and not used by the OLE DB extensions. Figure 13-19 summarizes the different interfaces of the OLE DB view type.

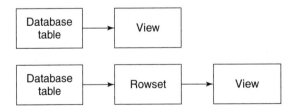

**Figure 13-18** Two Methods for Opening a View

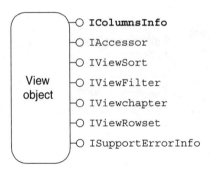

**Figure 13-19** View Interfaces

Class `CView` encapsulates the OLE DB view type. To open a view, you simply pass a rowset object. However, this rowset must support views. In COM parlance, it needs to support the `IRowsetView` interface. Obtaining a rowset that supports views is not always straightforward.

First, in many cases the OLE DB provider does not support views natively. Therefore, you must load the client cursor service component when creating the data source. For example, you might write something like

```
CDataSource db;
CDBPropSet   dbinit(DBPROPSET_DBINIT);

dbinit.AddProperty(DBPROP_INIT_OLEDBSERVICES,
    (long)DBPROPVAL_OS_ENABLEALL);
// more properties
hr = db.OpenWithServiceComponents(_T("SQLOLEDB.1"), &dbinit);
if (FAILED(hr))
    return hr;
CSession Session;
hr = Session.Open(db);
if (FAILED(hr))
    return hr;
```

Second, the rowset properties need to specify `IRowsetView` support. The corresponding property is `DBPROP_IRowsetView`. This might seem enough, but some providers also require that you explicitly specify that the cursor be on the client side with the `DBPROP_CLIENTCURSOR` property.

For example, you might write something like

```
CDBPropSet PropSet(DBPROPSET_ROWSET);
PropSet.AddProperty (DBPROP_IRowsetView, true);
PropSet.AddProperty (DBPROP_CLIENTCURSOR, true);

CCommand<CAccessor<CdboOrdersAccessor>, CChapteredRowset > Orders;
hr = Orders.Open(Session, NULL, &PropSet);
```

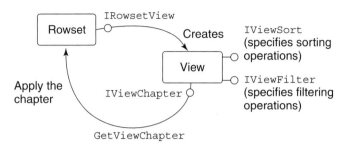

**Figure 13-20** View Interfaces

Once the rowset is successfully open, you can open the view on the rowset:

```
CView View;
hr = View.Open(Orders);
```

At this stage, the view is canonical. In other words, it does not contain any transformation. However, you can now specify sorting and filtering operations on it. Figure 13-20 summarizes the different interfaces and corresponding operations.

## Sorting a View

The `SetSortOrder` method is a straight encapsulation of `IViewSort::Set SortOrder`. It specifies the sort order given a set of columns and their sort order:

```
HRESULT SetSortOrder(LONG cValues,
    ULONG rgColumns[  ],
    DBSORT rgOrders[  ])
```

where

- `cValues` is the number of columns to sort.
- `rgColumns` is an array containing the ordinals of the `cValues` columns to sort.
- `rgOrders` is an array containing the `cValues` sort orders. The sort order can be either `DBSORT_DESCENDING` (sort in descending order) or `DBSORT_ ASCENDING` (sort in ascending order).

The following example shows how to sort with the first column descending and then the second column ascending:

```
ULONG rgColumns [] = {1, 2};
DBSORT rgOrders [] = {DBSORT_DESCENDING, DBSORT_ASCENDING};
hr = View.SetSortOrder(2, rgColumns, rgOrders);
```

In many cases, you want to sort on only one column. `SetSortOrder` has another version for this case:

```
HRESULT SetSortOrder(ULONG Column, DBSORT Order)
```

The following example shows how to sort on the first column:

```
hr = View.SetSortOrder(1, DBSORT_DESCENDING);
```

It is also possible to get the sort order with the `GetSortOrder` method.

## Filtering a View

While sorting a view is relatively simple, filtering one is more complex because it allows many `"OR"` and `"AND"` combinations. For example, it is possible to filter the values that verify a criterion such as

```
Column1 > 3 and column2 < 4 or column1 < 2
```

`CView` has two `SetFilter` methods. The first method is a straight encapsulation of `IViewFilter::SetFilter`:

```
HRESULT SetFilter(HACCESSOR hAccessor, ULONG cRows, DBCOMPAREOP
    CompareOps[ ], void  *pCriteriaData)
```

Because this method is somewhat complex and because the OLE DB extensions do not add anything, it is best that you go to the Microsoft documentation for more details.

In many cases, you only need to filter on a single column. This is where the second `SetFilter` method comes in:

```
template <class VALUE>
HRESULT SetFilter(VALUE v, ULONG iOrdinal, DBCOMPAREOP CompareOp =
    DBCOMPAREOPS_EQ)
```

where

- v represents the value of the filter condition.
- iOrdinal is the ordinal of the column where the condition applies.
- CompareOp is the comparison operator.

For example, to filter all the values that verify `Column2 = 1`, you write

```
CView View;
// Open the view
hr = View.SetFilter(1, 2);
```

## View Chapters

Once the view is set up, the next step is to get the result. It is important to understand that the view object is not a rowset and does not hold any data. Rather, it works in partnership with a rowset to produce the result. As you might have guessed, the view object holds a chapter, which is the binary equivalent of the sorting and filtering operation of the view. A good candidate for applying the chapter is the rowset that created the view. Figure 13-21 summarizes the relationship between the rowset, the view, and the chapter.

Note that, in the end, both the view and the rowset keep a reference on the chapter. The following example shows how to do it in code:

```
CCommand<CAccessor<CdboOrdersAccessor>,CChapteredRowset> Orders;
hr = Orders.Open(Session, NULL, &PropSet);
CView View;
hr = View.Open(Orders);
//Apply filter and order on the view
hr = View.SetViewChapter();
Orders.SetChapter(View.GetHChapter());
```

The `SetViewChapter` method of `CView` gets the chapter and sets the `m_HChapter` CView class member. By calling `SetChapter` on the rowset, you set the chapter of the rowset to the chapter of the view.

## Stacking Views

The previous sections explained how to use views on rowsets. It is also possible to create views on views. For example, a first view might perform some filtering operation while a second might perform some ordering operation on the result of the first view. This can be achieved in a single view, but doing it in several views and

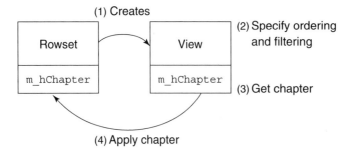

**Figure 13-21**   Rowset, View, and Chapter

stacking them has several benefits. First, it gives greater programming flexibility. Second, it enables scenarios where views can be stacked without knowing any details about each other.

The simple trick is that the `SetViewChapter` method accepts a chapter argument:

```
HRESULT SetViewChapter(HCHAPTER hSource = DB_NULL_HCHAPTER)
```

where hSource represents the chapter to stack on.

As a result, you can stack one view on another simply by passing the chapter of the first to the second view. The following code shows how to create a first view (`View1`) and stack a second view (`View2`).

```
CCommand<CAccessor<CdboOrdersAccessor>,CChapteredRowset> Orders;
hr = Orders.Open(Session, NULL, &PropSet);
CView View1;
hr = View1.Open(Orders);
//Apply filter and order on the view
hr = View1.SetViewChapter();
CView View2;
hr = View2.Open(Orders);
//Apply filter and order on the view
hr = View2.SetViewChapter(View1.GetHChapter());
Orders.SetChapter(View2.GetHChapter());
```

At the end of this sample, the rowset will contain a chapter that contains the view operations of both `View1` and `View2`.

Note that this stacking operation is not limited to chapters created by views. It can be applied to any chapter as long as the chapter corresponds to the right rowset.

## SUMMARY

Indexes can provide low-level, high-performance access to the data store. You should use indexes only when commands are not available or are not doing the job.

Chapters are a powerful concept with two applications: hierarchical rowsets and views. Using chapters should change the way you access, cache, and navigate relational data.

# 14 Schema, Definitions, and Synchronization

In the previous chapters, which explained navigating, getting, and setting data, there was the implicit assumption that the consumer already knew the layout of the underlying data store. For example, the consumer had to know what table was in the data store and, most of the time, assumed it knew the columns of the table. This assumption is valid in many cases, but there are instances when the consumer wants to know and manipulate the *meta-information*, or *schema*, of a data store.

This chapter comprises three parts. The first part explains how to query and traverse the schema of a data store. The second part describes how to modify the schema. Finally, the third part suggests a few methods to keep the consumer code and the schema synchronized.

## QUERYING AND NAVIGATING THE SCHEMA

The OLE DB consumer templates comprise two include files: `atldbcli.h`, which contains all the OLE DB consumer templates code we have been using; and `atldbsch.h`, which includes all the schema classes. While `atldbsch.h` depends on `atldbcli.h`, it is possible to use `atldbcli.h` alone. Because `atldbsch.h` contains all the schema classes, it is necessary to explicitly include it when using them.

The schema information is very similar to other kinds of information. In fact, many data stores store the schema information in a set of tables. For example, SQL Server has a table that contains the list of all the tables and another that contains the list of all the columns. Many data stores give access to these tables, and it is possible to get schema information this way. However, there is no standard way to query these tables; the code you write for a particular data store will not necessarily work with another data store. However, OLE DB introduces a standard for accessing schema information. Although it does not offer all the flexibility offered by the system tables, it provides most of the useful functionality.

## Restrictions

In most cases, consumers need to perform very simple schema queries. For example, you might need the list of the columns of a particular table. The corresponding query would be equivalent to

```
SELECT * FROM columns where table_name = a_name
```

In this case, a_name is a called a *restriction* because it restricts the columns to the one needed by the user, who usually does not need to perform more complex queries containing AND or OR operators. The OLE DB schema rowsets support only the simple cases. Because the queries are very simple, there is no need of a command language. Instead, it is possible to use an OLE DB API function such as

```
// (pseudo code)
Rowset = GetRowset(ColumnsGUID, "a_name");
```

The OLE DB schema mechanism goes a little further by allowing several restrictions of different types:

```
CComVariant * Restrictions = {Restriction1, Restriction2};
Rowset = GetRowset(DBSCHEMA_COLUMNS, Restrictions, RestrictionCount);
```

In this pseudo-code example, Restrictions contains an array of variants, each containing the value of a restriction.

Figure 14-1 illustrates the restrictions and schema rowsets. It is equivalent to an SQL query like

```
SELECT Column1, Column2, Column3 from xx where Column1 = Restriction1
AND Column2 = Restriction2 AND Column3 = Restriction3
```

If you pass a NULL restriction, OLE DB will ignore it and pass all the values. In general, the restrictions are the first columns of the corresponding schema rowset.

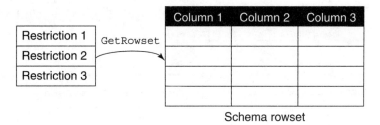

**Figure 14-1** Restrictions and Schema Rowsets

## CRestrictions

Class CRestrictions is a generic class that implements the code common to all schema rowset classes:

```
template <class T, short nRestrictions, const GUID* pguid>
class CRestrictions : public CSchemaRowset<T, nRestrictions>
```

where

- T represents the accessor class to use.

- nRestriction represents the maximum number of restrictions.

- pguid is a GUID that identifies the schema rowset. OLE DB defines a set of standard GUIDs, but providers can define their own. (This chapter will focus only on the OLE–DB-defined schema rowsets.)

The Open method CRestrictions is defined as follows:

```
HRESULT Open(const CSession& session, LPCTSTR lpszParam1 = NULL,
    LPCTSTR lpszParam2 = NULL, LPCTSTR lpszParam3 = NULL,
    LPCTSTR lpszParam4 = NULL, LPCTSTR lpszParam5 = NULL,
    LPCTSTR lpszParam6 = NULL, LPCTSTR lpszParam7 = NULL)
```

where lpszParam$i$ is the $i$th restriction. In almost all cases, restrictions are of type string and CRestrictions covers only this case. CRestrictions has up to seven restrictions, but only the first nRestriction restrictions will be taken into account; all those remaining will be ignored.

All the schema rowset classes inherit from CRestrictions. The following sections will explore them. Figure 14-2 shows the inheritance hierarchy of CRestrictions. Each class plays a different role:

- _CStoreRestrictions keeps a reference on the array of $n$ restrictions and can get a schema rowset. As the underscore at the beginning of the

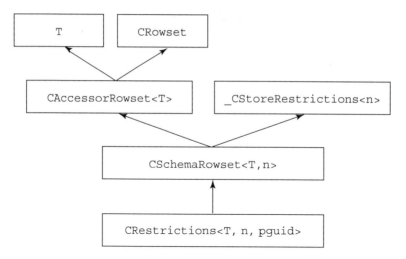

**Figure 14-2** `CRestrictions` Inheritance

name suggests, this is an implementation class; the consumer is not supposed to use it directly.

- `CSchemaRowset` binds the features of `CAccessorRowset` and `_CStore Restrictions`. In particular, it calls the `Bind` method after getting the rowset from `_CStoreRestrictions`.

- `CRestrictions` adds an `Open ()` method to `CSchemaRowset`.

This class hierarchy could be smaller, given the relative simplicity of schema rowsets. In particular, `CSchemaRowset` could have been merged with `CRestrictions`.

## THE CATALOG/SCHEMA MODEL

OLE DB assumes that the underlying data store conforms to the *schema/catalog* model as defined by the ANSI SQL.

A *schema* is a collection of database objects owned by a particular user. A simpler way to say this is that a schema is an *owner*. With SQL Server, for example, "dbo" is a typical schema name.

A *catalog* is a collection of related schemas. Simply put, "catalog" is another name for a database. Note, for example, that the data source initialization property identifier for a database is `DBPROP_INIT_CATALOG`.

For providers such as Microsoft Access that do not support schemas or catalogs, these two columns will be `NULL`. Catalog and schema restrictions are ignored.

## Catalogs

The first step is usually to enumerate the catalogs. Class `CCatalogs` serves this purpose. It has two class members:

- `m_szName`, the name of the catalog
- `m_szDescription`, a description of the catalog

The following example shows how to traverse the list of catalogs:

```
CCatalogs Catalogs;
hr = Catalogs.Open (Session);
hr = Catalogs.MoveFirst();
while (hr == S_OK)
{
    hr = Catalogs.MoveNext();
}
```

`CCatalogs` has only one restriction column: the name of the catalog. For example, to get the description of a given catalog, write

```
CCatalogs Catalogs;
hr = Catalogs.Open (Session, CatalogName);
hr = Catalogs.MoveFirst();
// the description is Catalogs.m_szDescription
while (hr == S_OK)
{
    hr = Catalogs.MoveNext();
}
```

## Tables

Class `CTables` enumerates the tables of a data server. It has the following class members:

- `m_szCatalog`, the name of the catalog of the table
- `m_szSchema`, the name of the schema of the table
- `m_szName`, the name of the table
- `m_szType`, the textual representation of the type of the table, such as `"TABLE"` or `"SYSTEM"` table

These four class members are also the four restrictions of the table schema rowset. In addition, `CTable` has the following class members:

- `m_guidTable`, the GUID of the table
- `m_szDescription`, the description of the table

For example, to get all the tables of a given catalog, write

```
CTables Tables;
hr = Tables.Open (Session, CatalogName);
hr = Tables.MoveFirst();  // the rest as usual
```

To get the type and description of a table, write

```
CTables Tables;
hr = Tables.Open (Session, CatalogName, SchemaName, TableName);
hr = Tables.MoveFirst();  // the rest as usual
```

To get all the system tables of a server, write

```
CTables Tables;
hr = Tables.Open (Session, NULL, NULL, NULL, "SYSTEM TABLE");
hr = Tables.MoveFirst();  // the rest as usual
```

## Columns

Class CColumns implements the column schema rowset. It follows the catalog/schema model and therefore starts with the catalog name and schema name class members and restrictions. The following class members and restrictions are the table name and the column name.

For example, to get all the columns of a given table, write

```
CColumns Columns;
hr = Columns.Open (Session, CatalogName, SchemaName, TableName);
hr = Columns.MoveFirst();
while (hr == S_OK)
{
    hr = Columns.MoveNext ();
}
```

To get all the attributes of a given column, write

```
CColumns Columns;
hr = Columns.Open (Session, CatalogName, SchemaName, TableName,
    ColumnName);
hr = Columns.MoveFirst();
```

CColumns has additional class members:

- m_guidColumn and m_nColumnPropID, the column GUID and the column property id, if they apply. Since most providers identify the column by name, these two class members are often blank.

- m_nOrdinalPosition, the ordinal of the column in the table (1 for the first column, 2 for the second column, etc.).
- m_nDataType, the OLE DB type of the column (for example, DBTYPE_I4).

## Views

The view schema information summarizes the views of the data store. These views are not OLE DB views; they reside on the server, not the client. In Microsoft Access, views are called "queries"; in other databases such as SQL Server, "view" is the official name.

Views follow the catalog and schema model. As a result, the first two class members/restrictions represent the catalog and schema.

The next class member/restriction is the view name (m_szTableName). m_szDefinition is the textual definition of the view. For an SQL data store, it is simply the SQL statement that generates the current view.

The following example shows how to get all the views of a catalog/schema:

```
CViews Views;
hr = Views.Open(Session, CatalogName, SchemaName);
hr = Views.MoveFirst();
while (hr == S_OK)
{
    hr = Views.MoveNext();
}
```

The following code shows how to get the definition of a view:

```
CViews Views;
hr = Views.Open(Session, CatalogName, SchemaName, ViewName);
hr = Views.MoveFirst();
// definition is Views.m_szDefinition.
```

## Procedures

The procedure schema information covers the stored procedures, their columns, and parameters.

Procedures are very similar to views. They have only one additional class member, m_nType, which is the type of procedure and one of the values in Table 14-1. The following code enumerates the stored procedures of a catalog:

```
CProcedures Procedures;
hr = Procedures.Open(Session, CatalogName);
hr = Procedures.MoveFirst();
while (hr == S_OK)
{
    hr = Procedures.MoveNext();
}
```

**Table 14-1** Procedure Values

| Symbol | Description |
|--------|-------------|
| DB_PT_UNKNOWN | Unknown type |
| DB_PT_PROCEDURE | Procedure does not return any value |
| DB_PT_FUNCTION | A function; returns a value |

Procedure columns have the same relationship to procedures that columns have to tables. In fact, the class members of CProcedureColumns are virtually identical to those of CColumns.

You can query the parameters of a stored procedure with class CProcedure Parameters. In addition to the usual catalog and schema class members/ restrictions, CProcedureParameters has the following:

- m_szName: the name of the procedure that contains the current parameter
- m_szParameterName: the name of the parameter itself

The following example enumerates the parameters of a procedure:

```
CProcedureParameters ProcedureParameters;
hr = ProcedureParameters.Open(Session, CatalogName, SchemaName,
    ProcedureName);
hr = ProcedureParameters.MoveFirst();
while (hr == S_OK)
{
    hr = ProcedureParameters.MoveNext();
}
```

## Indexes

Class CIndexes enumerates the indexes, each of which corresponds to a table. OLE DB does not assume that the table is in the same schema or catalog. As a result, CIndexes contains schema and catalog information for both the table and the index (m_szTableCatalog, m_szTableSchema and m_szIndexCatalog, m_szIndexSchema).

m_szTableName represents the name of the table to which the index applies, while m_szIndexName represents the name of the index itself.

Indexes apply to one or more columns. If the index applies to only one column, the CIndexes rowset will have only one row for it. If the index applies to several columns, CIndexes will have one row per column. Each column is identified by m_szColumnName, m_guidColumn, and m_nColumnPropID, as in class CColumns.

The following code shows how to enumerate the indexes of a table:

```
CIndexes Indexes;
Indexes.Open(Session, CatalogName, SchemaName, TableName);
hr = Indexes.MoveFirst();
while (hr == S_OK)
{
    hr = Indexes.MoveNext();
}
```

CIndexes provides some additional information. The names of the class members explain their meaning. For example, m_bPrimaryKey indicates whether the index is a primary key; m_bUnique indicates whether the index contains only unique values; and m_bClustered indicates whether the index is clustered.

## Keys

A data store can contain primary and foreign keys. CPrimaryKeys enumerates the primary keys with the catalog, schema, and table name restrictions. There is only one primary key per table, but it can contain several columns. In this case, the CPrimaryKeys rowset contains one row per column.

For example:

```
CPrimaryKeys PrimaryKeys;
PrimaryKeys.Open(Session, CatalogName, SchemaName, TableName);
hr = PrimaryKeys.MoveFirst();
while (hr == S_OK)
{
    hr = PrimaryKeys.MoveNext();
    // the column name is PrimaryKeys.m_szColumnName;
}
```

In addition, CPrimaryKeys also contains the usual class member to identify the column, as well as the m_nOrdinal class member, which is the ordinal of the column in the key, not that of the column itself.

Class CForeignKeys enumerates the foreign keys. Since a foreign key is always related to a primary key, CForeignKeys contains the class members of CPrimaryKeys (class members containing "PK" such as m_szPKTableName). It also contains information about the foreign key itself (class members containing "FK" such as m_szFKTableName). Figure 14-3 shows an example of three tables with two foreign keys.

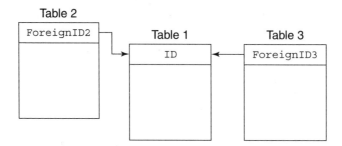

**Figure 14-3** Foreign Keys

**Table 14-2** Foreign Keys

| m_szPKTableName | m_szPKColumnName | m_szFKTableName | m_szFKColumnName |
|---|---|---|---|
| Table1 | ID | Table2 | ForeignID2 |
| Table1 | ID | Table3 | ForeignID3 |

You query the foreign keys on `Table1`:

```
CForeignKeys ForeignKeys;
ForeignKeys.Open(Session, CatalogName, SchemaName, _T("Table1"));
hr = ForeignKeys.MoveFirst();
while (hr == S_OK)
{
    hr = ForeignKeys.MoveNext();
}
```

In this example, `ForeignKeys` contains the rows listed in Table 14-2.

## Privileges

Some data stores define a set of privileges for tables and columns. A privilege specifies whether a user (the *grantee*) can perform a given operation on a given object (table or column). The user who grants the privilege is called the *grantor*. The OLE DB consumer templates provide two classes: `CTablePrivileges` for table privileges and `CColumnPrivileges` for column privileges. Each has the name of the grantor (`m_szGrantor`) and the name of the grantee (`m_szGrantee`) as well as the catalog and schema information.

- `m_szType` or `m_szPrivilegeType` is a textual representation of a type of privilege. Usually, it is INSERT, DELETE, UPDATE, SELECT, or REFERENCES.

- `m_bIsGrantable` specifies whether the grantee can transmit the privilege to other users. If false, the grantor gives the privilege to the grantee, but the grantee cannot transmit this privilege to anybody else. If true, the grantee has the privilege and can transmit it to anybody.

`CTablePrivileges` combines the privilege information with the table information. For example, to know the privilege of a table, you write

```
CTablePrivilegeInfo TablePrivilegeInfo;
TablePrivilege.Open(Session, GrantorName, GranteeName,
    CatalogName, SchemaName, TableName);
hr = TablePrivilege.MoveFirst();
while (hr == S_OK)
{
    hr = TablePrivilege.MoveNext();
}
```

`CColumnPrivileges` combines the privilege information with the column information. For example, to determine the privilege of a column, you write

```
CColumnPrivileges ColumnPrivileges;
ColumnPrivileges.Open(Session, GrantorName, GranteeName,
    CatalogName, SchemaName, TableName, ColumnName);
hr = ColumnPrivilege.MoveFirst();
while (hr == S_OK)
{
    hr = ColumnPrivilege.MoveNext();
}
```

## Provider Types

OLE DB defines a set of types, each represented by an integer constant. For example, `DBTYPE_I4` represents a 4-byte signed integer. The provider type schema rowset gives the relationship between OLE DB and provider types, which are identified by a name. For example, the provider type name of an integer might be `int`.

`CProviderTypes` is the schema rowset class for traversing the provider type information. It has two restrictions: the OLE DB type and an indicator for a best match. `CProviderTypes` is somewhat misleading because the restrictions are not the first two class members, nor are they of type `string`. As a result, `CProviderTypes` is fine as long as you do not use any restriction. It is useless otherwise.

The OLE DB extensions class CProviderTypesEx fills this hole. It is defined as follows:

```
class CProviderTypesEx: public CProviderTypes
{
public:
    HRESULT Open(const CSession& session, DBTYPE Type,
    bool bMatch = true)
    {
        USES_CONVERSION;
        CComVariant* pVariant;

        if (m_pvarRestrictions == NULL)
            return E_OUTOFMEMORY;

        *m_pvarRestrictions = Type;
        pVariant = m_pvarRestrictions + 1;
        *pVariant = match;

        return CSchemaRowset<CAccessor<CProviderTypeInfo>,
            2>::Open(session, DBSCHEMA_PROVIDER_TYPES);
    }
};
```

In the Open method, Type represents the OLE DB type while bMatch specifies whether to restrict only the best match. For example, to get the data store type corresponding to a signed integer, write

```
CProviderTypesEx ProviderTypes;
ProviderTypes.Open(Session, DBTYPE_I4, true);
hr = ProviderTypes.MoveFirst();
// data store type name is ProviderTypes.m_szTypeName
```

To get all the data store types for string, including the ones that are not the best match, write

```
CProviderTypesEx ProviderTypes;
ProviderTypes.Open(Session, DBTYPE_STR, false);
hr = ProviderTypes.MoveFirst();
while (hr == S_OK)
{
    // data store type name is ProviderTypes.m_szTypeName
    hr = ProviderTypes.MoveNext();
}
```

CProviderTypes also provides some additional information such as whether the type is nullable and/or long (in the sense of BLOB) and the prefix and suffix for literals. The names of the attributes are self-explanatory.

## MODIFYING THE SCHEMA

OLE DB provides two ways to modify the schema information. First, you can execute a command with some kind of data definition language (DDL). In SQL, such a command could have the following text:

```
CREATE TABLE TableName( Column1 int)
```

Alternatively, you can use specialized OLE DB interfaces. These are not supported by the OLE DB consumer templates, but you can use them either directly or through the OLE DB extensions.

A data definition language is easy to program and read. Moreover, it enables you to use the same language in your code and external tools. On the other hand, the C++ compiler cannot check any validity for the DDL. If there is a syntax error, there is no way to find out other than to try the compiled code.

When using OLE DB interfaces, there is only one language and therefore no space for a syntax error. On the other hand, the OLE DB interfaces are slightly more complex to use. Even so, they are useful when the underlying data store does not support any data definition language.

DDLs are out of the scope of this book. As a note, however, you should execute a DDL command like any other command with no result (see Chapter 7). This section concentrates on the OLE DB extensions.

The OLE DB extensions provide two classes:

- `CTableDefinition` creates, deletes, and modifies tables and columns.
- `CIndexDefinition` creates and deletes indexes on already existing tables.

### Using CTableDefinition

Like many OLE DB consumer template objects, `CTableDefinition` first needs to be opened against a session. Then it defines operations at the table and at the column levels.

#### Table Operations

The `CreateTable` method creates a table with a name, a set of columns, and eventually a set of properties:

```
HRESULT CreateTable(LPCTSTR szTableName, DBCOLUMNDESC*
   rgColumnDesc = NULL, ULONG cColumnDesc = 0,
   DBPROPSET *pPropSet = NULL, ULONG cPropertySets = 0,
   DBID** out = NULL)
```

`szTableName` represents the name of the table to create. `rgColumnDesc` is an array of `DBCOLUMNDESC`, each describing a column to add, and `cColumnDesc` is the number of columns of the new table. The columns will be ordered as they appear in `rgColumnDesc`.

The `DBCOLUMNDESC` structure is defined as

```
typedef struct  tagDBCOLUMNDESC
    {
    LPOLESTR pwszTypeName;
    ITypeInfo __RPC_FAR *pTypeInfo;
    /* [size_is] */ DBPROPSET __RPC_FAR *rgPropertySets;
    CLSID __RPC_FAR *pclsid;
    ULONG cPropertySets;
    ULONG ulColumnSize;
    DBID dbcid;
    DBTYPE wType;
    BYTE bPrecision;
    BYTE bScale;
    }   DBCOLUMNDESC;
```

where

- `dbcid` contains the name of the column.
- The type is defined by `wType` (OLE DB type) and `pwszTypeName` (data store type name). If `pwszTypeName` is NULL, the data store will choose an appropriate type name.
- `bPrecision`, `bScale`, and `ulColumnSize` represent the precision, scale, and size of the column, if applicable.
- Each column can also have a set of properties. `rgPropertySets` represents an array of property sets and `cPropertySets` represents the number of items in `rgPropertySets`. OLE DB defines the standard properties listed in Table 14-3.

**Table 14-3** Column Properties

| Symbol | Description |
|---|---|
| DBPROP_COL_AUTOINCREMENT | Column automatically increments values |
| DBPROP_COL_DEFAULT | Default value; must be compatible with the type of the column |
| DBPROP_COL_DESCRIPTION | Textual description of the column |
| DBPROP_COL_FIXEDLENGTH | Column is fixed length |
| DBPROP_COL_NULLABLE | Column is nullable |
| DBPROP_COL_PRIMARYKEY | Column is a primary key |
| DBPROP_COL_UNIQUE | Column restricts only unique values |
| DBPROP_COL_ISLONG | Column contains a long type (see Chapter 11 on BLOBs) |

The following example shows how to create a table with two columns. One is a primary key and the other is not nullable:

```
CTableDefinition TableDefinition;
hr = TableDefinition.Open(Session);
hr = TableDefinition.DropTable("TableName");
CDBColumnDesc Columns[2];
Columns[0].SetName("Column1");
Columns[0].wType = DBTYPE_I4;
CDBPropSet Column1Properties (DBPROPSET_COLUMN);
Column1Properties.AddProperty(DBPROP_COL_PRIMARYKEY, true);
Columns[0].rgPropertySets = &Column1Properties;
Columns[0].cPropertySets = 1;
Columns[1].SetName("Column2");
Columns[1].wType = DBTYPE_STR;
Columns[1].ulColumnSize = 10;
CDBPropSet Column2Properties (DBPROPSET_COLUMN);
Column1Properties.AddProperty(DBPROP_COL_NULLABLE, false);
Columns[1].rgPropertySets = &Column1Properties;
Columns[1].cPropertySets = 1;
hr = TableDefinition.CreateTable("TableName", Columns, 2);
```

Deleting a table is simpler since there is no column involved. The following code shows how to delete a table named `TableName`:

```
CSession Session;
// Open the session
CTableDefinition TableDefinition;
TableDefinition.Open(Session);
TableDefinition.DropTable(TableName);
```

It is also possible to rename a table once it is created. This is faster and more convenient than deleting and recreating it. The following code shows how to rename a table called `oldname` as `newname`:

```
CTableDefinition TableDefinition;
TableDefinition.Open(Session);
TableDefinition. AlterTable(_T("oldname"), _T("newname"));
```

## Column Operations

After a table is created, it is still possible to add, delete, and modify columns. The `AddColumn` method of `CTableDefinition` adds one column:

```
HRESULT AddColumn(LPCTSTR szTableName,
    DBCOLUMNDESC* pColumnDesc, DBID** idColumn = NULL)
```

where

- `szTableName` represents the table name.
- `pColumnDesc` represents the description of the column to add.

You can use an instance of `CDBColumnDesc` for `pColumnDesc`. The following example demonstrates how use the `AddColumn` method:

```
CTableDefinition TableDefinition;
CDBColumnDesc ColumnDesc;
ColumnDesc.SetName(ColumnName1);
ColumnDesc.wType = DBTYPE_I4;
TableDefinition.AddColumn(TableName, &ColumnDesc);
```

The column description behaves like the `CreateTable` method. For example, you can specify the data store type or a set of properties as in the following code sample:

```
CTableDefinition TableDefinition;
CDBColumnDesc ColumnDesc;
ColumnDesc.SetName(ColumnName1);
ColumnDesc.wType = DBTYPE_STR;
ColumnDesc.pwszTypeName = T2W(_T("varchar"));
CDBPropSet PropSet(DBPROPSET_COLUMN);
PropSet.AddProperty(DBPROP_COL_NULLABLE, true);
TableDefinition.AddColumn(TableName, &ColumnDesc);
```

Deleting a column is easier than adding one because there is no property involved. The following example shows how to delete a column from a table:

```
CTableDefinition TableDefinition;
TableDefinition.Open(Session);
TableDefinition. DropColumn(TableName, ColumnName);
```

Finally, it is possible to rename a column or change its properties with the `AlterColumn` method:

```
HRESULT AlterColumn(LPCTSTR szTableName, LPCTSTR szColumnName,
DBCOLUMNDESCFLAGS   ColumnDescFlags, DBCOLUMNDESC* pColumnDesc)
```

where `szTableName` and `szColumnName` represent the table name and column name of the column to change; `pColumnDesc` contains the new column name or the new column properties; and `ColumnDescFlags` is a flag that specifies which field is valid in `pColumnDesc`.

## Using CIndexDefinition

Class `CIndexDefinition` is somewhat similar to `CTableDefinition`: Before using it, you need to open it against a session. Once the index definition is open, you can create and delete indexes.

To create an index, you must specify a table name and a list of column names. Obviously, the table needs to be created before creating the index. The following example creates an index on two rows:

```
CIndexDefinition IndexDefinition;
IndexDefinition.Open(Session);
TCHAR ColumnNames [] = {_T("Column1"), _T("Column1")};
IndexDefinition.CreateIndex(TableName, IndexName, ColumnNames,
    2);
```

Optionally, you can specify the index order for each column. By default, the index is created with each column order increasing. However, it is possible to override this default, as, for example, in the following code, which creates an index on column1 with values increasing and column2 with values decreasing:

```
CIndexDefinition IndexDefinition;
IndexDefinition.Open(Session);
TCHAR ColumnNames [] = {_T("Column1"), _T("Column1")};
DBINDEX_COL_ORDER ColumnOrders [] = {DBINDEX_COL_ORDER_ASC ,
    DBINDEX_COL_ORDER_DESC};
IndexDefinition.CreateIndex(TableName, IndexName, ColumnNames,
    2, ColumnOrder);
```

Finally, the index can be created with a set of properties. Table 14-4 summarizes the index properties defined by OLE DB.

**Table 14-4** Index Properties

| Symbol | Description |
| --- | --- |
| DBPROP_INDEX_AUTOUPDATE | Index updates itself automatically |
| DBPROP_INDEX_CLUSTERED | Index is clustered |
| DBPROP_INDEX_FILLFACTOR | Fill-factor |
| DBPROP_INDEX_INITIALSIZE | Initial size of the index |
| DBPROP_INDEX_NULLCOLLATION | Indicates how NULLs are collated |
| DBPROP_INDEX_NULLS | Indicates whether NULLs are allowed |
| DBPROP_INDEX_PRIMARYKEY | Index is also a primary key |
| DBPROP_INDEX_SORTBOOKMARKS | Indicates how repeated keys are handled |
| DBPROP_INDEX_TYPE | Index type |
| DBPROP_INDEX_UNIQUE | Index contains only unique values |

The following code shows how to create a clustered index:

```
CIndexDefinition IndexDefinition;
IndexDefinition.Open(Session);
CDBPropSet IndexPropSet(DBPROPSET_INDEX);
IndexPropSet.AddProperty(DBPROP_INDEX_CLUSTERED, true);
TCHAR ColumnNames [] = {_T("Column1"), _T("Column1")};
IndexDefinition.CreateIndex(TableName, IndexName, ColumnNames,
    2, NULL, &IndexPropSet);
```

Deleting an index is easier than creating it, requiring only that the table name and index name be specified. The following example shows how:

```
CIndexDefinition IndexDefinition;
IndexDefinition.Open(Session);
IndexDefinition.DropIndex(TableName, IndexName);
```

## SYNCHRONIZING THE SCHEMA

One of the benefits of a database is that the definition of the data is separate from the code. As a result, the data can be accessible from many applications without having to plan for it. This also represents a challenge because the data and the code need to be synchronized. Unfortunately, there is no bulletproof method to enforce synchronization, but it is possible to ease the management of the data and its synchronization with the code.

Chapter 9 described dynamic accessors. These are the obvious choice when the layout of a table is unknown because they discover the columns at runtime. However, dynamic accessors can be burdensome because the code needs to check the column names all the time. The following sections explain how to minimize the risk of nonsynchronization between static accessors and data store tables.

### Checking Binding at Compile Time

One of the rules in software development is to check early and often, which in database/code synchronization translates into checking the binding at every compilation. Of course, this does not prevent any loss of synchronization after the software component has been released, but it is a convenient way to minimize risk.

One way to check is to define a token for the command line that specifies that the program should check its synchronization with the data store. We will use

_CheckDB for such a token. The WinMain function will then check for this token and call a special check function:

```
LPCTSTR lpszToken = FindOneOf(lpCmdLine, szTokens);
while (lpszToken != NULL)
{
   if (lstrcmpi(lpszToken, _T("UnregServer"))==0)
   {
      _Module.UpdateRegistryFromResource(IDR_Checkdb, FALSE);
      nRet = _Module.UnregisterServer(TRUE);
      bRun = FALSE;
      break;
   }
   if (lstrcmpi(lpszToken, _T("RegServer"))==0)
   {
      _Module.UpdateRegistryFromResource(IDR_Checkdb, TRUE);
      nRet = _Module.RegisterServer(TRUE);
      bRun = FALSE;
      break;
   }
   if (lstrcmpi(lpszToken, _T("CheckDB"))==0)
   {
      CheckDB();
      break;
   }
   lpszToken = FindOneOf(lpszToken, szTokens);
}
```

The CheckDB function can perform various checks. For example, the following code checks that class CdboMyTable can successfully bind with its table:

```
#define CHECK(expr) if(FAILED(expr)){printf (#expr);
printf("failed\n");}
HRESULT CheckDB()
{
   CdboMyTable MyTable;
   printf("-- start synchronization check\n");
   CHECK(MyTable.Open())
   printf("-- end synchronization check\n");
   return S_OK;
}
```

The final step is to add the check in the compiler by adding CheckDB in the command line of commands in the Project Settings dialog, as shown in Figure 14-4.

If the class fails to bind with the table, the build window of Visual C++ will display a message like the one on the next page.

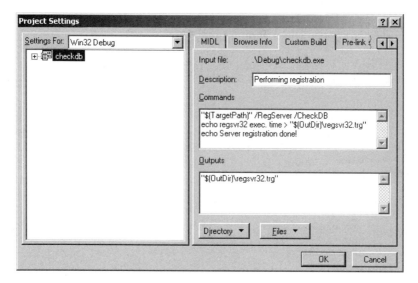

**Figure 14-4** Microsoft Visual C++ Project Settings with Synchronization Check

```
-------------------Configuration: checkdb - Win32 Debug--------------
Compiling...
checkdb.cpp
Linking...
Performing registration
-- start synchronization check
MyTable.Open()failed
-- end synchronization check
Server registration done!
```

Note that you can use this method outside development after the software is released. For example, you could write a simple diagnostic tool for administrators that displays the result of synchronization checks.

## Binding by Name

Until now, all bindings were by ordinal. That is, the columns were identified by their position in the list of columns rather than by name, which was not without problems. Consider a table with two columns: Column1 and Column2. The corresponding accessor class has the following binding:

```
BEGIN_COLUMN_MAP(CMyAccessor)
    COLUMN_ENTRY(1, m_Column1)
    COLUMN_ENTRY(2, m_Column2)
END_COLUMN_MAP()
```

| Ordinal 1 | Ordinal 2 |
|-----------|-----------|
| Column 1  | Column 2  |
|           |           |
|           |           |
|           |           |

| Ordinal 1 | Ordinal 2 |
|-----------|-----------|
| Column 2  | Column 1  |
|           |           |
|           |           |
|           |           |

**Figure 14-5** Table with Different Column Order

There is always the possibility that the table is recreated with columns in a different order. Figure 14-5 shows the table before and after the column swap. In each case it contains the same column but in a different order.

In many cases, the column swap will not have any impact. For example, if you use an SQL command such as

```
SELECT Column1, Column2 FROM TableName
```

the returned rowset will appear in the order defined in the command, not in the column order of the underlying table.

However, the user does not always specify the column order. For example, if you use class CTable or a command such as

```
SELECT * FROM TableName
```

the column order of the returned rowset will be the same as that in the underlying table. In this case, column binding by ordinal is dangerous because it is dependent on the table column order.

The solution is to bind by name instead of by ordinal. With this approach, the binding will be broken if a column name changes but not if the column is moved. The OLE DB consumer extensions provide a new accessor that binds by name, CAccessorByName, which should be used in place of CAccessor. Thus, for example, you might declare a variable of type

```
CTable<CAccessorByName<CMyAccessor> > var;
```

CAccessorByName works in conjunction with a new set of macros. As a rule, the name of the new macro corresponds to the name of an existing OLE DB consumer templates macro where COLUMN is replaced by NAMED_COLUMN. Table 14-5 summarizes these new macros. The new binding is

```
BEGIN_NAMED_COLUMN_MAP(CMyAccessor)
    NAMED_COLUMN_ENTRY(1, L"Column1", m_Column1)
    NAMED_COLUMN_ENTRY(2, L"Column2", m_Column2)
END_COLUMN_MAP()
```

**Table 14-5** Binding Macros with Column Name Support

| Macro | Description |
|---|---|
| BEGIN_NAMED_ACCESSOR_MAP | Similar to BEGIN_ACCESSOR_MAP with column name support |
| BEGIN_NAMED_COLUMN_MAP | Similar to BEGIN_COLUMN_MAP with column name support |
| _NAMED_COLUMN_ENTRY_CODE | Implements the code for a named column |
| NAMED_COLUMN_ENTRY_EX | Similar to COLUMN_ENTRY_EX; the second parameter represents the column name |
| NAMED_COLUMN_ENTRY_TYPE | Similar to COLUMN_ENTRY_TYPE; the second parameter represents the column name |
| NAMED_COLUMN_ENTRY_TYPE_SIZE | Similar to COLUMN_ENTRY_TYPE_SIZE; the second parameter represents the column name |
| NAMED_COLUMN_ENTRY | Similar to COLUMN_ENTRY; the second parameter represents the column name |
| NAMED_COLUMN_ENTRY_LENGTH | Similar to COLUMN_ENTRY_LENGTH; the second parameter represents the column name |
| NAMED_COLUMN_ENTRY_STATUS | Similar to COLUMN_ENTRY_STATUS; the second parameter represents the column name |
| NAMED_COLUMN_ENTRY_LENGTH_STATUS | Similar to COLUMN_ENTRY_LENGTH_STATUS; the second parameter represents the column name |

In addition to the column names, the named macros contain all the information in the regular OLE DB consumer templates macros. As a result, they are fully compatible with the OLE DB consumer templates. For example, if you declare a variable of type

```
CTable<CAccessor<CMyAccessor> > MyTable;
```

CAccessor will bind by ordinal and ignore the column names. On the other hand, if you declare a variable of type

```
CTable<CAccessorByName<CMyAccessor> >MyTable;
```

CAccessorByName will bind by name and ignore the ordinal.

## Creating Tables from the Code

The software product can have complete control over the data. In particular, it can be responsible for creating all the tables in the database. There are two ways to achieve this. First, the installation program can explicitly create the table, which requires that the installation program know the list of tables to create and their columns and properties. Second, the software package can create the tables after it is installed, either at once or on demand. In the on-demand scenario, each component is able to create the underlying table. Whenever the component performs some kind of database access, it checks whether the underlying table is present; if not, it creates the table from scratch.

The second method has three benefits. First, it simplifies the installation process since it does not have to create any tables. Second, only the necessary tables are created; if a component is never used, the underlying table is not created. Third, the software is "self-healing": If a table is inadvertently destroyed, the component will silently recreate it without having to reinstall software. As a note, it might be a good idea to alert the user or the administrator when creating new tables.

Components have two ways to create the underlying tables: via a DDL command or via the CTableDefinition class. If you bind your accessor classes by column name, you already define the name and type of each column. As a result, you can use CTableDefinition directly against the accessor class without having to duplicate the effort with CreateTableByAccessor.

CreateTableByAccessor gets the bindings from the accessor, transforms them into column information, and creates the table with the column information:

```
template <class T>
HRESULT CreateTableByAccessor (LPCTSTR szTableName,
   T & Accessor, int nAccessor = 0,
   DBPROPSET *pPropSet = NULL, ULONG cPropertySets = 0,
   DBID** out = NULL)
{
   DBBINDING*  pBindings = NULL;
   ULONG       nColumns;
   bool        bAuto;
   HRESULT     hr;
      // First time just get the number of entries by passing in
&nColumns
      T::_GetBindEntries(&nColumns, NULL, nAccessor, NULL);

      // Now allocate the binding structures
      ATLTRY(pBindings = new DBBINDING[nColumns]);
      if (pBindings == NULL)
         return E_OUTOFMEMORY;

      // Now get the bind entries
      StructInit <DBCOLUMNDESC>* pColumnDesc = NULL;
      OLECHAR** pNames = NULL;
      ATLTRY(pColumnDesc = new StructInit<DBCOLUMNDESC>[
         nColumns]);
      ATLTRY(pNames = new OLECHAR*[nColumns]);
```

```
        hr = T::_GetBindEntries(&nColumns, pBindings, nAccessor,
            &bAuto, NULL, pNames);
        for (ULONG i = 0; i < nColumns; i++)
        {
            DBTYPE wType = pBindings[i].wType;
            pColumnDesc[i].wType = wType;
            pColumnDesc[i].dbcid.eKind  = DBKIND_NAME;
            pColumnDesc[i].dbcid.uName.pwszName  = pNames[i];
            pColumnDesc[i].ulColumnSize = pBindings[i].cbMaxLen;
            if (wType == DBTYPE_STR || wType == DBTYPE_WSTR)
                pColumnDesc[i].ulColumnSize--;
            pColumnDesc[i].bPrecision = pBindings[i].bPrecision;
            pColumnDesc[i].bScale = pBindings[i].bScale;

        }
        hr = CreateTable(szTableName, pColumnDesc ,
            nColumns ,  pPropSet , cPropertySets ,
            out );
        delete [] pColumnDesc;
        delete [] pBindings;
        delete [] pNames;
        return hr;
    }
```

For example, if you declare the following accessor class:

```
class CdbomytableAccessor
{
public:
    LONG m_a;
    TCHAR m_b[11];
    DBTIMESTAMP m_c;

BEGIN_NAMED_COLUMN_MAP(CdbomytableAccessor)
    NAMED_COLUMN_ENTRY(0, L"a", m_a)
    NAMED_COLUMN_ENTRY(0, L"b",m_b)
    NAMED_COLUMN_ENTRY(0, L"c",m_c)
END_COLUMN_MAP()
};
```

you just write the following to create the corresponding table:

```
CdbomytableAccessor Accessor;
// Destroy the table if already present.
TableDefinition.DropTable("my_table");
// Create the table from the accessor information
hr = TableDefinition.CreateTableByAccessor("my_table", Accessor);
```

Even though this method is very practical, it also has limitations:

- The accessor must contain all the columns of the table.
- There is no type name. As a result, the data store chooses the closest type.
- No column property is specified; the data store chooses default column properties.

## SUMMARY

This chapter presented how to access the schema information with the OLE DB consumer templates class, explained how to change the schema with the OLE DB template extensions, and explained how to synchronize the different components with the database. It concluded with coverage of OLE DB for relational providers. The next two chapters will present two other types of provider: multidimensional and hierarchical.

# 15 OLAP

In previous chapters, the underlying assumption was that the data is tabular—in other words, it resides in a series of tables—which means that it is accessed through some kind of rowset object. However, OLE DB supports not only tabular data but *multidimensional* data as well, also called *online analytical processing*, or OLAP. This support, known as *OLE DB for OLAP*, was introduced with OLE DB 2.0.

Before reading on, it is important to understand that the OLE DB consumer templates do not support multidimensional data. You must use either the OLE DB extensions provided with this book or the raw OLE DB interfaces. This chapter assumes that you will be using the OLE DB extensions. In any case, the extensions needed for multidimensional data support are surprisingly small and straightforward to transform into raw OLE DB code.

OLAP by itself is a complex technology, and there is no way to cover it in one chapter. The simple introduction here focuses on how to *access* the data with OLE DB for OLAP. If you do not have any experience with OLAP, it is likely that the introduction provided in this chapter will be very fast.

## FROM TABULAR TO MULTIDIMENSIONAL DATA

In traditional tabular or relational data, the server manages a set of tables. On the consumer side, the programmer deals with a rowset. Simply speaking, both objects are two-dimensional arrays, the first dimension being the rows and the second being the columns. Figure 15-1, for example, shows a table or a rowset with three columns and four rows.

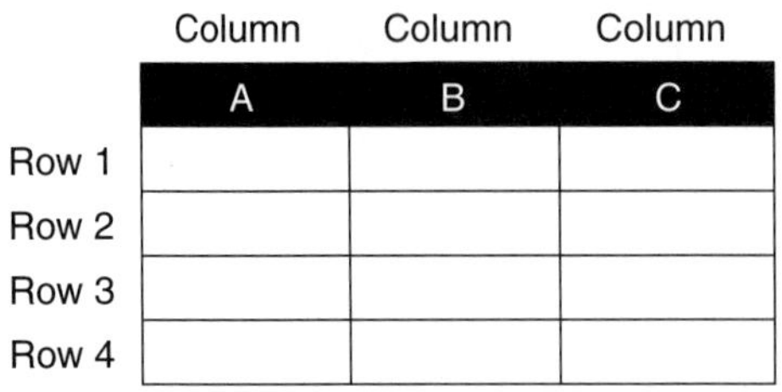

**Figure 15-1** Two-Dimensional Table or Rowset

The reality is a little more complex because rows and columns do not play a similar role: Columns have names and can be accessed directly, whereas rows are anonymous. As a result, you do not use tables and rowsets like regular two-dimensional rowsets.

Imagine a database that manages sales data: Each salesperson makes a certain number of sales in a given period. Table 15-1 represents a typical implementation as a table in a relational world. However, it is somewhat hard to read. An expert in relational databases might be used to it, but a naïve user might prefer the more natural representation of Table 15-2.

**Table 15-1** Sales Table—Database Version

| Salesperson | Date | Amount |
| --- | --- | --- |
| Albert | 1998 | 4 |
| Albert | 1999 | 5 |
| Bob | 1998 | 6 |
| Bob | 1999 | 2 |
| Charlie | 1998 | 5 |
| Charlie | 1999 | 8 |

**Table 15-2** Sales Table—Intuitive Version

| Salesperson | Date | |
| --- | --- | --- |
| | 1998 | 1999 |
| Albert | 4 | 5 |
| Bob | 6 | 2 |
| Charlie | 5 | 8 |

In real life, data can easily become more complicated. For example, the original table might have another column representing, say, the gender of the customer. In this case, an intuitive representation would be a three-dimensional object where the first dimension represents the salesperson, the second dimension represents the date, and the third dimension represents the customer gender. Because of its three dimensions, a more appropriate name for this object is *cube*, represented in Figure 15-2.

Evidently, there is no reason to stop at dimension three. One can imagine objects with four, five, or more dimensions. However, because we live in a three-dimensional world, objects can be graphically represented up to a dimension of three. For this reason, the name "cube" is appropriate for this object, whatever the dimension.

Whereas a tabular provider works on a series of tables, a multidimensional provider works on a series of cubes. Cubes can be implemented through a set of relational tables in a star schema. Another approach is to implement the cube natively.

While tables have a set of columns, cubes have one *axis* for each dimension. Figure 15-2 shows the three axes of the sales cube: salesperson, date, and gender.

An OLE DB rowset object is appropriate for tabular data, but multidimensional providers need a new COM object that grasps the multidimensional aspects. This is the *dataset* object, the only new COM object introduced by OLE DB for OLAP. Obviously, this object is central to OLE DB for OLAP. Datasets do not need the same dimensions as the underlying cube: They can be the result of one or several projections. For example, a dataset might represent the sales for a given gender, in which case there is no need for a gender axis.

The main difference between datasets and rowsets is that datasets do not have rows—indeed, a row does not make sense in the multidimensional world. Instead, datasets have *cells*, which represent items of data in the dataset, as shown in Figure 15-2. Contrary to rows, cells do not have columns but correspond to only one data point.

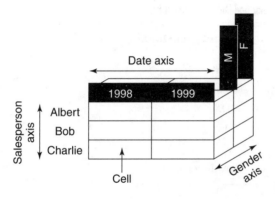

**Figure 15-2** Three-Dimensional Cube

SQL is standard for relational data, but multidimensional providers need a new language. *MDX*, or *multidimensional expression*, is Microsoft's attempt to establish such a standard. However, OLE DB for OLAP providers are not forced to use MDX and can employ their own custom language. MDX is very rich and powerful, but is not within the scope of this book. For more information, refer to the Microsoft documentation.

Figure 15-3 illustrates where MDX fits in multidimensional providers. Table 15-3 summarizes the differences between tabular and multidimensional providers.

OLE DB for OLAP aggressively reuses regular OLE DB objects. For example, data sources, sessions, errors, and commands behave the same way in both types of providers. OLE DB for OLAP introduces some additional properties, but they are used like any other OLE DB property. The following section explains how to use a multidimensional provider through OLE DB for OLAP. Since much of the code is similar to regular OLE DB, this chapter will focus on the area specific to OLAP.

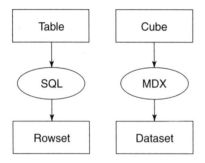

**Figure 15-3** MDX Transformation of Cubes into Datasets

**Table 15-3** Comparison of Tabular and Multidimensional Providers

| Tabular/Relational | Multidimensional |
|---|---|
| Table | Cube |
| Rowset | Dataset |
| SQL | MDX |
| Column | Axis |
| Row | Cell |
| Dimension = 2 | Any dimension |

## MULTIDIMENSIONAL SESSIONS AND COMMANDS

In some cases, CSession is not the appropriate class for manipulating multi-dimensional sessions. Indeed, the definition of the session type is slightly different for tabular providers and multidimensional providers: While IOpenRowset is mandatory for sessions of the former, it is only optional for the latter. CSession was written before OLE DB 2.0 and therefore assumes that the session supports IOpenRowset: It keeps a reference on an IOpenRowset interface:

```
CComPtr<IOpenRowset> m_spOpenRowset;
```

Since some multidimensional providers do not support this interface, we need a new session class. The solution is to keep a reference on an always-mandatory interface: IGetDataSource. CMDSession is the OLE DB extensions session class similar to CSession except for its class member:

```
CComPtr<IGetDataSource> m_spGetDataSource;
```

Moreover, CCommand opens with an instance of CSession, so we need a new command class that accepts an instance of CMDSession instead. This is CMDCommand, an OLE DB extensions class similar to CCommand except that its Open method accepts an instance of CMDSession.

```
// Create a command on the session and execute it
HRESULT Open(const CMDSession& session, LPCTSTR szCommand =NULL,
    DBPROPSET *pPropSet = NULL, LONG* pRowsAffected = NULL,
    REFGUID guidCommand = DBGUID_DEFAULT, bool bBind = true)
```

You can still use CSession and CCommand with multidimensional providers such as MS OLAP that support IOpenRowset. Conversely, you can use CMDSession and CMDCommand with tabular providers, since they always support IGetDataSource.

## DATASETS

An intuitive way to understand a dataset is to use the Cube Browser that comes with Microsoft OLAP manager. Other multidimensional providers might provide other tools.

Because cubes can have more than three dimensions, they are difficult to visualize. One common way to "see" them is to create a projection on two dimensions. As shown in Figure 15-4, the Cube Browser has two parts: The top shows all the dimensions; the bottom shows the projection on two axes (Time and Gender in

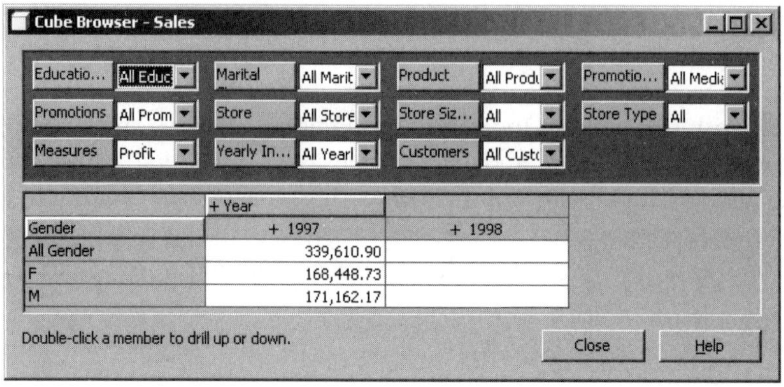

**Figure 15-4** Cube Browser

this example). The Cube Browser enables you to drag and drop dimensions to change the projection.

The dataset object is the only new COM object introduced by OLE DB for OLAP. The rest of this section explains the COM object and its associated C++ classes.

## The Dataset Object

As Figure 15-5 shows, the dataset object supports three interfaces:

- IMDDataset
- IMDRangeRowset
- IMDFind

IMDDataset, which is the main interface, gets axis information and cell data. IMDDataset is the only mandatory interface. IMDRangeRowset provides a convenient way to access a set of cells with a traditional rowset. This chapter ignores IMDFind.

## CDataset

The OLE DB extensions provide the CDataset class, which encapsulates the OLE DB dataset object. You use this class as you would the CRowset class. In particular, CDataset works in conjunction with an accessor class. For example, you might declare a dataset variable as

```
CCommand <CAccessor<CMyAccessor>, CDataSet> MyDataSet;
// or CMDCommand <CAccessor<CMyAccessor>, CDataSet> MyDataSet;
```

**Figure 15-5** The Dataset Object

CDataset is built to look like a rowset so that it can be used where a rowset is expected. In other words, it implements all the methods declared in CNoRowset. However, CDataset keeps a reference on an IMDDataset interface pointer, not a rowset object. Therefore, GetIID returns IID_IMDDataset.

Even though CDataset keeps a reference on an IMDDataset interface, it must have GetInterface and GetInterfacePtr methods that have the same return type as their rowset counterparts. This requires the use of reinterpret_cast:

```
IRowset* GetInterface() const
{
    return reinterpret_cast<IRowset*> (m_spDataset.p);
}
IRowset** GetInterfacePtr()
{
    return reinterpret_cast<IRowset**> (&m_spDataset);
}
```

CDataset has an m_pAccessor class member that points to the accessor in the same way CRowset does. You can set the accessor with the SetAccessor method.

## Working with Datasets

In working with a dataset, the first step is to get all of its metadata; this includes the number of axes and some information about each axis. The second step is to get the dataset data, including cell values and ranges. The following sections explore these steps.

## METADATA: AXIS INFORMATION

The m_cAxis class member holds the number of axes returned by OLE DB. Note, however, that OLE DB adds an additional axis, called the *slicer*, which holds the dimensions used for the projection—that is, all the cube dimensions that are not in another axis. The dataset represented by Table 15-2 has two axes. As an example, even though the dataset represented by Table 15-2 has two axes, the value of m_cAxis is 3:2 for the "real" corresponding axes plus 1 for the slicer.

The `m_AxisInfo` class member contains some axis information for each axis, including the slicer. It is an array of `MDAXISINFO` structures, each of which has the following definition:

```
typedef struct MDAXISINFO
{
    ULONG         cbSize;
    ULONG         iAxis;
    ULONG         cDimensions;
    ULONG         cCoordinates;
    ULONG *       rgcColumns;
    LPOLESTR *    rgpwszDimensionNames;
} MDAXISINFO
```

`cbSize` represents the size of the `MDAXISINFO` structure in bytes. `iAxis` represents the axis identifier (`MDAXIS_COLUMNS` for the first, `MDAXIS_ROWS` for the second, and so forth; the identifier of the slicer axis is `MDAXIS_SLICERS`).

For example, the dataset represented in Table 15-2 has the three `MDAXISINFO` structures. Their `iAxis` values are `MDAXIS_COLUMNS`, `MDAXIS_ROWS`, and `MDAXIS_SLICERS`.

`cCoordinates` represents the number of items of the axis. For example, the column axis in Table 15-2 has `cCoordinates = 2` and the row axis has `cCoordinates = 3`.

`rgcColumns` represents the number of columns for each dimension (see the section on axis rowsets).

`cDimensions` and `rgpwszDimensionNames` are used for multidimensional axes. See the section on axes with multiple dimensions for more information. There is no need to set `m_cAxis` and `m_AxisInfo` explicitly—CDataset does this automatically. Because `CDataset` is used as part of `CAccessorRowset`, `CAccessorRowset` calls the `BindFinished` method after the COM object has been successfully opened. The version of `CDataset::BindFinished` gets the axis information:

```
HRESULT BindFinished()
{
    return GetAxisInfo(&m_cAxis, &m_AxisInfo);
}
```

In turn, `GetAxisInfo` calls the OLE DB method that gets the axis information.

The `Close` method automatically frees the axis information:

```
void Close()
{
    if (m_spDataset)
    {
```

```
        if (m_AxisInfo)
        {
           m_spDataset->FreeAxisInfo(m_cAxis, m_AxisInfo);
           m_AxisInfo = NULL;
        }
        m_spDataset.Release();
    }
}
```

## Axis Navigation

An axis is nothing else than a rowset where each row represents a coordinate. Another name for an axis coordinate is *tuple*. Each row (or coordinate or tuple) includes the following columns:

- Tuple ordinal, which represents the ordinal of the tuple in the axis
- Member caption, which is the name of the coordinate
- Other pieces of information

For example, the dataset in Table 15-2 has two axes: date and salesperson. Table 15-4 is a simplified version of the rows of the first axis rowset. Table 15-5 corresponds to the salesperson axis.

### Hierarchies

In many cases, dimensions are organized into a hierarchy. This is a tree structure where the dimension members are the leaves. An example is shown in Figure 15-6.

**Table 15-4** Axis Rowset of the Date Axis

| Tuple Ordinal | Member Caption |
|---------------|----------------|
| 0             | 1998           |
| 1             | 1999           |

**Table 15-5** Axis Rowset of the Salesperson Axis

| Ordinal | Member Caption |
|---------|----------------|
| 0       | Albert         |
| 1       | Bob            |
| 2       | Charlie        |

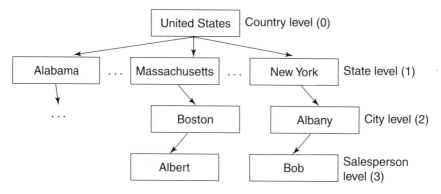

**Figure 15-6** Hierarchy Example

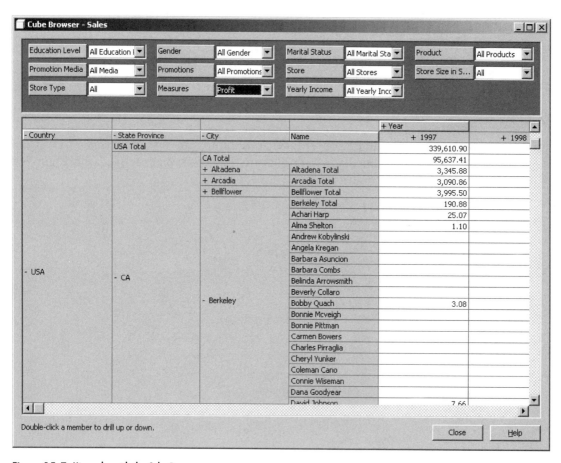

**Figure 15-7** Hierarchy with the Cube Browser

When the Cube Browser discovers a hierarchy, it displays a plus (+) sign next to the elements that can be expanded. Figure 15-7 shows the Cube Browser with an expanded salesperson dimension.

Although the concept of hierarchy is important in OLAP, it does not greatly affect OLE DB because this information is static. If fact, datasets do not depend on hierarchies; only axis coordinates do.

In the axis rowset, the m_LevelUniqueName class member represents the name of the level of the coordinate in the hierarchy—this name is "City" in the case of a city. The m_LevelNumber class member represents the depth of the level of the coordinate—in the case of a city, the level number is two.

### Using an Axis Rowset

The OLE DB templates provide two classes for axis navigation:

- CAxisRowset, the accessor rowset class; it is used like a table or command.
- CAxisAccessor, the accessor class. It has a template parameter for the dimension, 1 by default.

For example, you might declare a variable of type

```
CAxisRowset<CAccessor<CAxisAccessor<1> > > AxisRowset;
```

CAccessorRowset defines only one additional method, Open:

```
HRESULT Open(const CDataset& DataSet, DBCOUNTITEM iAxis,
    DBPROPSET* PropSets = NULL, ULONG cPropertySets = 1)
```

DataSet is the dataset that contains the axis; iAxis is the axis ordinal.

The following code shows the use of CAxisRowset and CAxisAccessor:

```
CAxisRowset<CAccessor<CAxisAccessor<1> > > AxisRowset;
// Open the column axis
hr = AxisRowset.Open(aDateset, MDAXIS_COLUMNS);
// use AxisRowset like a regular rowset
hr = AxisRowset.MoveFirst();
// etc
```

## Axes with Multiple Dimensions

Until now, it was implicit that each axis corresponded to one dimension—the column axis carried the time dimension; the row axis, the salesperson dimension. However, several dimensions can be on one axis, in which case the axis contains the Cartesian product of the dimension members, which is also called the *cross-join*. For example, if the values of a first dimension are {a, b, c} and the values of a second dimension are {A, B}, the values of the cross-join axis will be

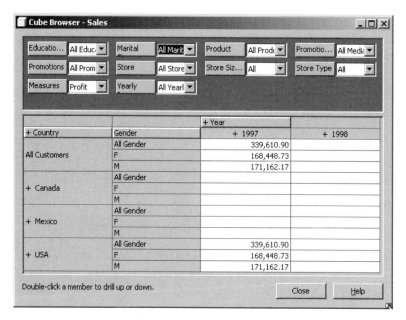

**Figure 15-8** The Row Axis as the Cross-Join between the Gender and the Salesperson Dimensions (Country Level)

{(a, A), (a, B), (b, A), (b, B), (c, A), (c, B)}. Figure 15-8 shows how the Cube Browser handles cross-joins: The row axis has two dimensions: salesperson and customer gender.

Having several dimensions on one axis does not affect the cell values. It is only a convenient projection. For example, it permits you to visualize more than two dimensions on a two-dimensional display.

## Axis Information with Multiple Dimensions

It is now time to go back to the `MDAXISINFO` structure to inspect its remaining fields. `cDimensions` represents the number of dimensions—for a single-dimension axis, it is 1. `rgpwszDimensionNames` is an array containing the name of each dimension—for example, the axis information for the row axis of the dataset represented in Figure 15-8 has `cDimensions = 2` and `rgpwsz DimensionNames = {"SalesPerson", "Gender"}`.

## Using CAxisAccessor with Multiple Dimensions

The template parameter of `CAxisAccessor` specifies the number of dimensions of the axis. It should be less than or equal to the actual number. Since most axes have a dimension of 1, the default parameter is 1.

A closer look at `CAxisAccessor` shows how it works:

```
template <ULONG AxisDimension = 1>
class CAxisAccessor
{
public:
   ULONG m_TupleOrdinal;
BEGIN_COLUMN_MAP(CAxisAccessor<AxisDimension>)
   COLUMN_ENTRY(1, m_TupleOrdinal)
   for (ULONG iAxis = 0; iAxis < AxisDimension; iAxis++)
   {
   COLUMN_ENTRY(2+ iAxis * 5, m_Columns[iAxis].m_MemberUniqueName)
   COLUMN_ENTRY(3+ iAxis * 5, m_Columns[iAxis].m_MemberCaption)
   COLUMN_ENTRY(4+ iAxis * 5, m_Columns[iAxis].m_LevelUniqueName)
   COLUMN_ENTRY(5+ iAxis * 5, m_Columns[iAxis].m_LevelNumber)
   COLUMN_ENTRY(6+ iAxis * 5, m_Columns[iAxis].m_DisplayInfo)
   }
END_COLUMN_MAP()
   CAxisColumns m_Columns[AxisDimension];
};
```

The important data is in the `m_Columns` array. It contains a set of `CAxisColumns`, a class that holds the actual data:

```
class CAxisColumns
{
public:
   TCHAR m_MemberUniqueName [512];
   TCHAR m_MemberCaption [512];
   TCHAR m_LevelUniqueName [512];
   LONG m_LevelNumber;
   ULONG m_DisplayInfo;
};
```

The size of `m_Columns` is the template parameter `AxisDimension`. Figure 15-9 shows the layout of an instance of `CAxisAccessor<2>`. Note that all the class members are bound in the accessor. As a result, `CAxisAccessor` holds and binds the information of all the axis dimensions.

Here is an example of `CAxisAccessor` with more than one dimension:

```
CAxisRowset<CAccessor<CAxisAccessor<2> > > AxisRowset;
// Open the column axis
hr = AxisRowset.Open(aDateset, MDAXIS_ROWS);
// use AxisRowset like a regular rowset
hr = AxisRowset.MoveFirst();
// the member ordinal is AxisRowset.m_TupleOrdinal
// AxisRowset.m_Columns[0] contains the values for the
// salesperson dimension
// AxisRowset.m_Columns[1] contains the values for the
// gender dimension
```

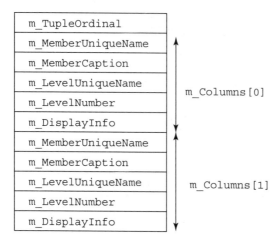

**Figure 15-9** Layout of `CAxisAccessor<2>`

# CELLS

Cells in datasets are different from rows in rowsets. Since datasets are multi-dimensional, there is no concept of navigation, first row or next row. As a result, you can jump from cell to cell. In addition, datasets need to identify each cell uniquely. Finally, cells do not have columns but relate to only one value, so they need a special kind of accessor.

## Cell Identification

Cell ordinals uniquely identify cells within the dataset, starting at zero for the cell corresponding to the first tuple of each axis. Ordinals initially increase along the first axis. When they reach the end of this axis, they increment along the second axis and increase along the first axis again. This mechanism continues for the remaining axes.

Table 15-6 shows ordinals for a two-dimensional dataset. Figure 15-10 shows ordinals for a three-dimensional dataset.

**Table 15-6** Cell Ordinals in a Two-Dimensional Dataset

| | Date | |
| Salesperson | 1998 | 1999 |
| --- | --- | --- |
| Albert | 0 | 1 |
| Bob | 2 | 3 |
| Charlie | 4 | 5 |

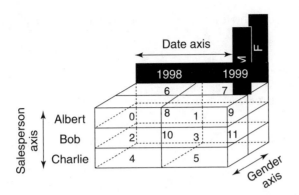

**Figure 15-10** Cell Ordinal in a Dataset

OLE DB does not provide any function to get the ordinal of a cell. However, this is relatively simple to do once you know the axes. CDataset keeps a reference on the axis information, so it can get the cell ordinal. Moreover, the GetCellOrdinal method returns the ordinal of a cell given a set of axis coordinates.

GetCellOrdinal assumes that the array of axis coordinates corresponds to the number of axes and that the coordinates are ordered. Here is its implementation:

```
ULONG GetCellOrdinal(ULONG pAxisOrdinal[])
{
    ATLASSERT(m_AxisInfo);
    ULONG Result = 0;
    ULONG Temp = 1;
    for (ULONG i = 0; i < m_cAxis; i++)
    {
        if (AxisInfo(i).iAxis != MDAXIS_SLICERS)
        {
            ATLASSERT(pAxisOrdinal[i] < AxisInfo(i).cCoordinates);
            Result += pAxisOrdinal[i] * Temp;
            Temp *= AxisInfo(i).cCoordinates;
        }
    }
    return Result;
}
```

For example, for a three-dimensional dataset, you call

```
ULONG Coordinates [] =
        {ColumnCoordinate, RowCoordinate, PageCoordinate};
CellOrdinal = DataSet.GetCellOrdinal(Coordinates);
```

However, it is illegal to call the following code because the number of coordinates is wrong:

```
ULONG Coordinates [] =
        {ColumnCoordinate, RowCoordinate};
CellOrdinal = dataset.GetCellOrdinal(Coordinates);
```

It is also illegal to call the following code because the coordinates are not in the right order:

```
ULONG Coordinates [] =
        {RowCoordinate, ColumnCoordinate, PageCoordinate};
CellOrdinal = dataset.GetCellOrdinal(Coordinates);
```

## Cell Accessors

Datasets are different from rowsets because the atomic data is the cell, not the row. However, both use the same accessor mechanism to get data. Each cell has three pieces of information attached to it. Each piece is a "column" in the accessor, but each accessor column corresponds to the same cell. In this context, the column of the accessor has nothing to do with the column of the cell itself. For example, Table 15-7 shows a dataset with column 1 and column 2:
Within these columns

- The value represents the actual value of the cell. It can be typed.
- The formatted value is a string representation of the value. It is useful for display.
- The ordinal is the ordinal of the cell in the dataset.

The accessor columns are fixed. There is no way to change them. Since it is likely that you will always use the same accessor, the OLE DB extensions provide a ready-to-use accessor class: CCellAccessor.

**Table 15-7** Dataset Columns

|  | Column 1 | | | Column 2 | | |
|---|---|---|---|---|---|---|
| **Row 1** | Value | Formatted value | Ordinal | Value | Formatted value | Ordinal |
| **Row 2** | Value | Formatted value | Ordinal | Value | Formatted value | Ordinal |

```
template <class TValueType = VARIANT>
class CCellAccessor
{
public:
    TValueType m_Value;
    TCHAR m_FormattedValue [512];
    LONG m_CellOrdinal;
BEGIN_COLUMN_MAP(CCellAccessor<TValueType>)
    COLUMN_ENTRY(1, m_Value)
    COLUMN_ENTRY(2, m_FormattedValue)
    COLUMN_ENTRY(3, m_CellOrdinal)
END_COLUMN_MAP()
};
```

CCellAccessor binds all three columns. The template parameter TValue Type represents the type of the value of each cell. For example, if you know that the cells contain doubles, use CCellAccessor<double>. On the other hand, if you do not know the type of the cells, either CCellAccessor<VARIANT> or CCellAccessor<> is a good choice.

CCellAccessor is only one of many choices among cell accessors. If binding all three columns is too expensive, you can create another accessor class that binds fewer columns. Additionally, you can bind more information, such as the status of the cell value. Since the accessor mechanism is the same for rowsets, details from the accessor chapter are still valid.

## Getting Cell Data

You can get the cell data by either ordinals or coordinates. The first GetCellData method gets the data at a given ordinal:

```
HRESULT GetCellData(DBORDINAL ulCell, int nAccessor = 0)
```

ulCell represents the cell ordinal and nAccessor represents the accessor index. In many cases, the cell will have only one accessor, and nAccessor = 0 will be an acceptable parameter.

The second method gets the cell data by coordinates:

```
HRESULT GetCellData (ULONG pAxisOrdinal[], int nAccessor = 0)
```

The coordinates have the same constraints as for the GetCellOrdinal method.
The following example shows how to get cell data with the two methods:

```
// get the cell data at ordinal 2
hr = Command.GetCellData (2);
// get the cell data at coordinates (2, 2)
ULONG Coordinates [] = {2, 2};
hr = Command.GetCellData(Coordinates);
```

The memory management rules that apply for rowsets also apply for datasets. For example, if the accessor binds a column by reference and specifies that it is client owned, the consumer should call `FreeRecordMemory` when finished with the data.

## Cell Ranges

The previous section explained how to get the data for one cell, but obviously getting data cell by cell can affect performance. A solution consists in retrieving several at once, using cell ranges.

A range contains all the cells in the largest sub-dataset between a starting and an ending ordinal. Figure 15-11 shows a dataset with 25 cells, with the starting ordinal as 6 and the ending ordinal as 18 and the cells in between in bold. The gray cells represent the largest rectangle in this interval. This is the range defined by `start = 6` and `end = 18`.

OLE DB offers two ways to get a range of cells. First, the OLE DB `GetCell Data` method allows several cells to be retrieved at once. Using this method directly can speed up data retrieval. Second, OLE DB offers another object: the range rowset. The following sections will explain the two methods.

| 0 | 1 | 2 | 3 | 4 |
| 5 | 6 | 7 | 8 | 9 |
| 10 | 11 | 12 | 13 | 14 |
| 15 | 16 | 17 | 18 | 19 |
| 20 | 21 | 22 | 23 | 24 |

**Figure 15-11**  Range of Cells

### Range Rowsets

A range rowset contains a set of rows, each row corresponding to a cell in a given range. For example, Table 15-8 represents the range rowset of the range from Figure 15-11. Note that the accessor of the range rowset is the same as the cell accessor.

**Table 15-8** Range Rowset of the Range in Figure 15-11

| Cell Value | Cell Formatted Value | Cell Ordinal |
|---|---|---|
| Value | Value | 6 |
| Value | Value | 7 |
| Value | Value | 8 |
| Value | Value | 11 |
| Value | Value | 12 |
| Value | Value | 13 |
| Value | Value | 16 |
| Value | Value | 17 |
| Value | Value | 18 |

The `CRangeRowset` class implements range rowsets. It is just another descendant of `CAccessorRowset`:

```
template <class TAccessor = CAccessor<CCellAccessor <> >,
      class TRowset = CRowset>
class CRangeRowset: public CAccessorRowset<TAccessor, TRowset>
```

By default, CRangeRowset has acceptable accessor and rowset parameters. It has only one additional method, Open().

```
HRESULT Open(CDataset DSet, ULONG ulStartCell = 0,
   ULONG ulEndCell = -1,    DBPROPSET* PropSets = NULL,
   ULONG cPropertySets = 1)
```

You can specify an optional property set that contains a set of rowset properties for the range rowset to open. Once open, the range rowset behaves just like any other rowset.

The following example shows how to use CRangeRowset.

```
CRangeRowset <> RangeRowset;
// The default template parameters will do just fine
hr = RangeRowset.Open (DataSet, 6, 18);
// Open the range between cells at ordinal 6 and 18.
hr = RangeRowset.MoveFirst();
// Navigate the RangeRowset like a regular rowset
while (hr == S_OK)
{
   hr = RangeRowset.MoveNext();
}
```

In particular, range rowsets can support setting data and deferred updates. In this respect, they behave like regular rowsets. In particular, you must specify what rowset interface you need when you open the range rowset. However, unlike rowsets, datasets cannot insert or delete rows, since doing so would be inconsistent with the axis structure. Thus, the range rowset cannot insert or delete rows either.

The optimizations described in Chapter 8 on rowsets apply for the range rowset as well. For example, you might use `CBulkRowset` or `CArrayRowset`. However, once you get the range rowset, you still have to call `MoveNext` repetitively. If this is too slow, OLE DB offers another method.

### Getting Cell Ranges

The OLE DB `GetCellData` method is more powerful than has been shown so far. It can get the whole range of data in the same way a range rowset does. However, you get the data all at once, so there is no need for repetitive calls to `MoveNext` and `GetData`. The signature of `GetCellData` is as follows:

```
HRESULT GetCellData(
    HACCESSOR    hAccessor,
    ULONG        ulStartCell,
    ULONG        ulEndCell,
    VOID *       pData);
```

where

- `hAccessor` is the cell accessor.
- `ulStartCell` and `ulEndCell` are the starting and ending cells, respectively.
- `pData` points to the buffer that receives the data.

It is critical that the buffer be large enough to hold all the cell data. The following example shows how to get a range of cells directly.

```
CCommand<CAccessor<CCellAccessor <> >, CDataset> Dataset;
hr = Command.Open(Session, SomeText);
CCellAccessor<> Values [13];
hr = Dataset.GetCellData(Dataset.m_pAccessor->GetHAccessor(0),
        6, 18, Values);
```

In summary, the OLE DB extensions offer three kind of access:

- Cell by cell
- Through a range rowset
- Through a range of cells

Each method has benefits and drawbacks, the main trade-off being performance versus ease of use and update support.

# USING MULTIDIMENSIONAL DATA WITH ROWSETS

Although the rowset object is not the most appropriate object for accessing a dataset, using it is a good idea if other parts of the system expect a rowset.

In this case, the OLAP engine "flattens" the dataset into a rowset. The flattening algorithm is well defined in the OLE DB documentation, and there is no way to change it. It is simple to apprehend, but there are many implementation details.

In the case of a two-dimensional dataset, the flattening operation is intuitive: The columns of the rowset contain the header for the row axis and the values of the column axis. Table 15-9 represents the rowset corresponding to the dataset from Table 15-2.

When the dimension of the dataset is greater than 2, the other axes are squeezed on the column axis. For example, if you consider the third dimension as a "depth" dimension, the flattening process rotates it so that it is inserted in the column dimension. For example, Table 15-10 represents a three-dimensional dataset as a rowset.

Using a dataset as a rowset involves two steps: First, replace CDataset by the appropriate rowset class, which is CRowset in most cases. Second, use an accessor class that can accept enough columns. A cell accessor is not appropriate because the rowset accesses a whole row instead of only a cell. CDynamic Accessor is a good candidate because it does not require any knowledge of the columns.

**Table 15-9**  Two-Dimensional Dataset as a Rowset

| [Salesperson] | [Date].[1998] | [Date].[1999] |
|---|---|---|
| Albert | 4 | 5 |
| Bob | 6 | 2 |
| Charlie | 5 | 8 |

**Table 15-10**  Three-Dimensional Dataset as a Rowset

| [Salesperson] | [1998].[Albany] | [1998].[Boston] | [1999].[Albany] | [1999].[Boston] |
|---|---|---|---|---|
| Albert | 2 | 2 | 3 | 2 |
| Bob | 4 | 2 | 0 | 2 |
| Charlie | 3 | 2 | 1 | 7 |

For example, if the dataset code is

```
CCommand<CAccessor<CCellAccessor <> >, CDataset> Dataset;
hr = Command.Open(Session, SomeText);
```

it can be replaced with

```
CCommand<CDynamicAccessor, CRowset> Rowset;
hr = Rowset.Open(Session, CommandText);
// the rest as usual
```

## OLAP SCHEMA

The previous chapter explained how to get the schema information of tabular providers. For example, it is possible to enumerate the tables in a given database and the columns in a given table. However, since multidimensional providers do not have tables and columns, the traditional schema is not appropriate. Instead, they define their own special schema objects such as cubes, dimensions, hierarchies, or levels. The OLE DB extensions provide a set of classes that encapsulate these schema objects in the same spirit as the traditional schema information.

## SUMMARY

This chapter provided a brief overview of the multidimensional concepts and their associated OLE DB extensions classes. OLE DB for OLAP is an exciting technology because it allows a complex data server to be accessed in a simple and intuitive way. The dataset was the only truly new concept introduced in this chapter.

# 16 Hierarchical Data

One of the goals of OLE DB is to access as much relevant data as possible. However, people rarely keep their personal data in tabular or multidimensional data stores. Instead, they use a series of files, Internet folders, email messages, notes, contacts, and appointments.

It does not matter whether a file is on a local drive, a local area network, or the Internet. The format of the document can be HTML or some other format like Word or Excel. Moreover, many products, such as Microsoft Outlook and Exchange, manage email and fax messages, contacts, appointments, and notes. Whatever the format, this kind of data is fundamentally different from tabular or multidimensional data.

First, it is inherently *hierarchical*: Each data item is part of a tree structure. For example, files are the leaves of the file system while directories are the nodes. This is true on a local system as well as on the Internet. In the same way, Microsoft Exchange folders contain a series of mail message, contact, or other folders.

Second, hierarchical folders are somewhat similar to rowsets because they represent a collection of rows. They are also different because they can hold items of different types and each type can have a different collection of columns. In other words, hierarchical folders are *not homogeneous*. For example, a directory contains both files and directories. While files have a size (the file type has a "size" column), directories do not.

Third, hierarchical data employs *direct binding*. In the previous chapters, we explored the different steps to get data, which follow:

- Open a data source.
- Open a session on the data source.

- Open a command on the session.
- Execute the command and traverse the rowset.

These steps are fine for a database programmer but excessively complicated for the average user. To get a Web page or a local file, you only have to enter an address (URL) and press "Enter." Hierarchical objects behave the same way: You can open them directly by name without using data sources, sessions, or commands. For the user, direct binding means that it is possible to click on a URL and get the underlying object.

Finally, hierarchical objects tend to be associated with *streams*. Consider a file: It has column values like its name, URL, and size, but the main information is its content. Think about an email message: It has a sender and a list of recipients, but the most important information is its text. The content of a row can be huge, but the stream allows you to read it chunk by chunk.

OLE DB 2.5 supports hierarchical providers. It comes with an *Internet publishing provider* that allows you to navigate files on the Internet as if they were on a local file system. You can enumerate the files of a directory, write files, and so forth. While Web pages are usually read-only documents, the Internet publishing

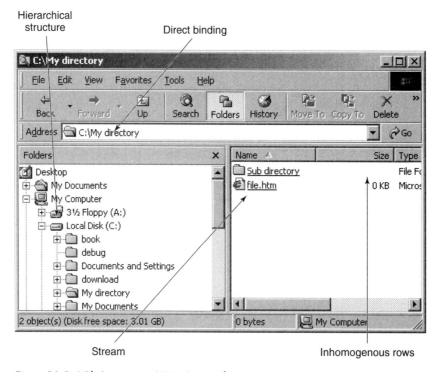

**Figure 16-1** A File System as an OLE DB 2.5 Provider

provider allows read and write operations. Since it always comes with OLE DB 2.5, this chapter will use it for its examples.

Figure 16-1 shows the file system with the four characteristics of hierarchical providers. While the Internet publishing provider does not expose the local drive, the mechanisms are the same.

Before going further, it is important to understand that traditional relational providers *could* emulate hierarchical providers. For example, you could implement hierarchical structures with a parent/child table. You could also simulate a variable number of columns with the use of NULL columns. However, since this kind of implementation is inherently difficult and inefficient, it is better to use a true hierarchical provider. Hierarchical *providers* are different from the hierarchical *rowsets* described in Chapter 13. Hierarchical rowsets use chapters to *simulate* a parent/child relationship, but the data still lies in a series of tables.

The OLE DB consumer templates do not support OLE DB 2.5, so this chapter employs the OLE DB extensions classes. As usual, you can go through the C++ code to better understand the OLE DB interfaces.

## OBJECT OVERVIEW

The OLE DB extensions provide three classes—CRow, CRowFolder, and CStream — that are explained in the following paragraphs.

CRow implements access to the row object, which is at the center of hierarchical providers. It has a list of columns you can read and write and defines operations like *copy, move,* and *delete*. Rows are not supposed to be useful by themselves, but usually are to be used in conjunction with other objects.

CRowFolder implements access to the *row folder* object, which represents a collection of child rows. In reality, Microsoft does not use the term "row folder" because this is a regular OLE DB rowset. However, I use "row folder" because it defines what the object is and what domain it applies to. The main purpose of the row folder object is to enumerate its children. Row folder objects are also row objects, so what applies to rows also applies to folders, such as copying, moving, or deleting through CRow.

CStream implements access to the *stream* object, whose main purpose is to read and write a sequence of bytes. Streams are also rows and can be copied, moved, or deleted through CRow.

It is important to understand that these three classes represent only a *way* to access an object of the underlying provider. For example, the file system/Internet defines two "real" objects: directories and files. You can access a directory as a row and query its column values or perform copy, move, and delete operations; or you can access a directory as a row folder and navigate its children. Similarly, you can access a file as a row and query its column values or perform copy, move, and delete operations; or you can access a file as a stream and read or write its content.

## Direct Binding

Direct binding allows you to open an object directly, which means without a data source, a session, or a command. With direct binding, objects can open themselves directly with a URL. The three OLE DB 2.5 classes support direct binding. They have an `Open` method with the following declaration:

```
HRESULT Open(LPTSTR szURL, DBBINDURLFLAG Flag = ... etc);
```

where

- `szURL` is the URL of the object to open. It follows the conventions defined for URLs.
- `Flag` is a URL binding flag that describes the access to the object.

The OLE DB extensions provide a default that you can override. `Flag` can have many different values, which we will discover as needed. Table 16-1 contains the most common.

## Working with Direct Binding

When you open an object from a URL, the object first creates a *root binder* object. This is a well-known object provided with MDAC. The object then calls the `Bind` function on the root binder object.

**Table 16-1** Common URL Binding Flags

| Symbol | Description |
| --- | --- |
| DBBINDURLFLAG_READ | Open the object in read-only mode |
| DBBINDURLFLAG_WRITE | Open the object in write-only mode |
| DBBINDURLFLAG_READWRITE | Open the object in read-write mode |
| DBBINDURLFLAG_SHARE_DENY_READ | Deny read access to others |
| DBBINDURLFLAG_SHARE_DENY_WRITE | Deny write access to others |
| DBBINDURLFLAG_SHARE_EXCLUSIVE | Deny all access to others |
| DBBINDURLFLAG_SHARE_DENY_NONE | Deny no access to others |
| DBBINDURLFLAG_ASYNCHRONOUS | Open the object in asynchronous mode |

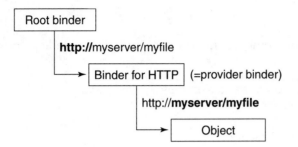

**Figure 16-2** Direct Binding Architecture

```
{
    CComPtr<IBindResource> RootBinder;
    HRESULT hr = RootBinder.CoCreateInstance(CLSID_RootBinder);
    //...
    hr = RootBinder->Bind(NULL, T2W(szName), Flag,
            // more parameters);
    //...
}
```

When the root binder object gets the URL, it parses it until it can determine the type of protocol. For example, if you pass *http://myserver/myfile*, the root binder needs only "*http://*" to determine that the protocol is HTTP. It then creates a binder for the particular protocol, also called a *provider binder*, and transmits the call to this provider. When the provider binder receives the URL, it decodes it in a particular fashion and creates the corresponding instance. Figure 16-2 summarizes this architecture.

## THE ROW OBJECT

The row object is the fundamental object of hierarchical providers. Class CRow implements support for rows and has some similarities with CAccessorRowset. In particular, because rows can get column values, CRow always works with an accessor class. It is declared as

```
template <class TRowAccessor>
class CRow: public TRowAccessor
```

As we will see later, rows need a special kind of accessor. For now, we will use CDynamicRowAccessor as the accessor class.

## Opening a Row

CRow has two Open methods. The first is a classic direct binding Open method:

```
HRESULT Open(LPTSTR szName, DBBINDURLFLAG Flag =
    DBBINDURLFLAG_READ, DBPROPSET* pPropSet = NULL,
    ULONG nPropertySets = 1,bool bGetColumns = true)
```

For example, you might write

```
CRow<CDynamicRowAccessor> Row;
hr = Row.Open("http://myserver/myfile");
//or
hr = Row.Open(someotherURL, DBBINDURLFLAG_READWRITE, &propset);
```

The bGetColumns parameter specifies whether to get the column values when opening the object. The section on data exchange will give more details on this.

In a sense, the URL is the equivalent of the absolute path of the row object. CRow offers another Open method that accept a relative path:

```
HRESULT Open(CRow& Row, LPTSTR szName, DBBINDURLFLAG Flag =
    DBBINDURLFLAG_READ, bool bGetColumns = true)
```

The Row parameter represents the parent row; szName is the relative path. This method does not accept any properties. Indeed, the new row inherits its properties from the parent row. The following example shows how to open a row with a relative path:

```
CRow<CDynamicRowAccessor> Row;
CRow<CDynamicRowAccessor> ChildRow;
hr = Row.Open ("http://myserver/dir");
hr = ChildRow.Open (Row, "subrow");
// is equivalent to:
hr = ChildRow.Open("http://myserver/dir/subrow");
```

## Creating a Row

It is also possible to create a row the same way you create files. CRow has two Create methods that work like the Open methods. One accepts a URL, while the other accepts a relative path. The first Create method is declared as

```
HRESULT Create(LPTSTR szName, DBBINDURLFLAG Flag =
    DBBINDURLFLAG_OPENIFEXISTS|DBBINDURLFLAG_READWRITE,
    DBPROPSET* pPropSet = NULL, ULONG nPropertySets = 1)
```

For example, you can create a row by calling

```
CRow<CDynamicRowAccessor> Row;
hr = Row.Create("http://myserver/myfile");
```

`Flag` represents the URL binding flag. It is a combination of the usual flags (see Table 16-1) and those in Table 16-2. The second `Create` method is declared as

```
HRESULT Create(CRow& Row, LPTSTR szName, DBBINDURLFLAG dwFlags =
    DBBINDURLFLAG_READWRITE)
```

For example, you can create a row by calling

```
CRow<CDynamicRowAccessor> Row;
CRow<CDynamicRowAccessor> ChildRow;
hr = Row.Open ("http://myserver/dir");
hr = ChildRow.Create (Row, "subrow");
```

## Getting and Setting Column Values

Like rowsets, rows have columns with values. Imagine a mechanism for getting row data that is similar to the rowset technique: Create an accessor from a collection of column bindings and then get and set the data. For a rowset, the accessor mechanism makes sense because you define the accessor once and use it multiple times (once per row). However, unlike rowsets, rows represent only one row, for which the accessor mechanism is very cumbersome. As a result, rows define a different simpler method to get data.

To get the column values, you simply call `IRow::GetColumns`:

```
HRESULT STDMETHODCALLTYPE GetColumns(
DBORDINAL cColumns,
DBCOLUMNACCESS __RPC_FAR rgColumns[  ])
```

**Table 16-2** Row Creation Flags

| Symbol | Description |
| --- | --- |
| DBBINDURLFLAG_OVERWRITE | If there is a row at the specified location, overwrite it |
| DBBINDURLFLAG_OPENIFEXISTS | If there is a row at the specified location, open it instead of creating a new one |
| DBBINDURLFLAG_ISSTRUCTUREDDOCUMENT | Create a structured document |

cColumns represents the number of columns to get, while rgColumns contains the cColumns DBCOLUMNACCESS structures. DBCOLUMNACCESS contains the information for one column and is defined as

```
typedef struct tagDBCOLUMNACCESS {
void *         pData;       // Pointer to buffer that receives the data
DBID           columnid;    // Column ID
DBLENGTH       cbDataLen;   // Length of the returned data
DBSTATUS       dwStatus;    // Status of the returned data
DBLENGTH       cbMaxLen;    // Length of the buffer
DB_DWRESERVE   dwReserved;  // Reserved
DBTYPE         wType;       // Type of the data
BYTE           bPrecision;  // Numeric precision
BYTE           bScale;      // Numeric scale
}   DBCOLUMNACCESS;
```

Although this method is very straightforward, it is completely different from the rowset binding model. Fortunately, CRow enables sharing code between rowset and row bindings. One of the important differences between the two is that the rowset binds by column ordinal while the row binds by column name. If you define an accessor that binds by both column name and column ordinal, it is possible to use it in both rowsets and rows.

The OLE DB extensions introduce the concept of row accessor, which, in addition to the traditional accessor methods, implements the following method:

```
HRESULT GetColumnAccess(ULONG* pColumns, int nAccessor,
   DBCOLUMNACCESS *pColumnAccess ,
   DBCOLUMNACCESS_COMPLEMENT *pColumnAccess2)
```

Like traditional accessors, row accessors support multiple accessors. For the accessor at index nAccessor, pColumns receives the number of bound columns. If pColumnAccess is not NULL, it should contain an array of pColumns DBCOLUMN ACCESS. GetColumnAccess is responsible for filling these structures. Because the rowset and row binding models are different, we need some more information, which we get from DBCOLUMNACCESS_COMPLEMENT.

```
typedef struct tagDBCOLUMNACCESS_COMPLEMENT
{
   DBPART dwPart;
   DBLENGTH *pLength;
   DBSTATUS *pStatus;
}   DBCOLUMNACCESS_COMPLEMENT;
```

dwPart holds the parts that are bound. If, for example, the accessor binds only the value and the length, it will be DBPART_VALUE|DBPART_LENGTH.

`pLength` and `pStatus` represent a pointer to the length and the status, respectively. They are useful for writing these values back to the row object if necessary.

`CRowAccessor` is an adaptation of `CAccessor` that implements the row accessor operations. For example,

```
CTable<CAccessor<CMyAccessor> > MyTable;
```

is replaced with

```
CRow<CRowAccessor <CMyAccessor> > MyRow;
```

The only requirement of `CRowAccessor` is that the corresponding accessor class (for example, `CMyAccessor`) bind columns by name. For more information about this, see Chapter 14.

`CDynamicRowAccessor` is an adaptation of `CDynamicAccessor` that implements row accessor operations. It gets the column names dynamically.

`GetColumns` gets the column values:

```
HRESULT GetColumns (int nAccessor = 0)
```

For example,

```
CRow<CDynamicRowAccessor> Row;
//Get the row
hr = Row.GetColumns();
```

Because rows correspond to only one set of column values, it makes sense to get these values when you open a row. The `bGetColumns` parameter of the `Open` methods specifies whether to get the column values when opening a row. It is true by default, as illustrated by the following example:

```
CRow<CDynamicRowAccessor> Row;
hr = Row.Open(szURL);
// Equivalent to
hr = Row.Open(szURL, DBBINDURLFLAG_READ, NULL, 0, true);
// Equivalent to
hr = Row.Open(szURL, DBBINDURLFLAG_READ, NULL, 0, false);
if (SUCCEEDED (hr))
   hr = Row.GetColumn();
```

When you open a row, the provider always retrieves the column values and caches them whether or not you call `GetColumn`. You can override this behavior by specifying the `DBBINDURLFLAG_DELAYFETCHCOLUMNS` URL binding flag. In this case, the provider will get the columns only when they are explicitly asked for.

## Scoped Operations

OLE DB 2.5 defines three *scoped operations* on rows:

- Copying
- Moving
- Deleting

These are called "scoped" because they apply to the row as well as to its children. For example, if you delete a row, you delete its children as well. After all, how can the provider do otherwise?

The most intuitive way to understand scoped operations is to play with Windows Explorer and copy, move, and delete files and directories. A hierarchical provider operates the same way.

### Copying a Row

CRow defines a Copy method to copy itself to another row:

```
HRESULT Copy(LPCTSTR szDestURL, DBCOPYFLAGS dwCopyFlags = 0,
    LPCTSTR szSourceURL = _T(""),
    IAuthenticate * Authenticate  = NULL)
```

You need to specify the destination of the row when you copy it. Imagine that you want to perform the copy operation illustrated in Figure 16-3.

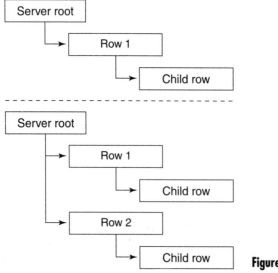

**Figure 16-3** Copying a Row

The destination row is *http://myserver/row2*; the corresponding code is

```
hr = Row.Open("http://myserver/row1");
hr = Row.Copy("http://myserver/row2");
```

Note that the destination does not need to be on the same server or even on same provider.

The `Copy` method has some additional, optional parameters:

- `dwCopyFlags` represents the copy flags. It is one of the values in Table 16-3.
- `szSourceURL` is the name of the child row to copy. By default, it is `""`, which indicates the current row. If you specify a different string, it will be interpreted as a child row.

For example, if you want to copy a row named *http://myserver/row/childrow*, the first method opens the child row directly:

```
hr = Row.Open("http://myserver/row/childrow");
hr = Row.Copy("somewhereelse");
```

The second method opens the parent row and specifies the child row in the source URL:

```
hr = Row.Open("http://myserver/row");
hr = Row.Copy("somewhereelse", 0, "childrow");
```

**Table 16-3** Row Copy Flags

| Symbol | Description |
| --- | --- |
| DBCOPY_ALLOW_EMULATION | Provider can emulate the copy operation with a download and an upload if needed |
| DBCOPY_ASYNC | Copy operation is asynchronous |
| DBCOPY_ATOMIC | Copy operation is atomic in the transactional sense: Either all rows copy successfully or none do |
| DBCOPY_NON_RECURSIVE | Copy the current row but not its children |
| DBCOPY_REPLACE_EXISTING | If there is a row at the destination, replace it with the source row |

## Moving a Row

CRow declares the Move method as

```
HRESULT Move(LPCTSTR szDestURL, DBMOVEFLAGS dwMoveFlags = 0,
    LPCTSTR szSourceURL = _T(""),
    IAuthenticate * Authenticate  = NULL)
```

Moving a row is very similar to copying one. The difference is that the source row is deleted at the end of the operation. Figure 16-4 illustrates a move operation.

The corresponding code is

```
hr = Row.Open("http://myserver/row1");
hr = Row.Move("http://myserver/row2");
```

dwMoveFlags represents the copy flag, which is one of those in Table 16-4. szSourceURL represents the name of the child row to move. As in the Copy method, it is "" by default, which indicates the current row. A different string is interpreted as a child row. As a result,

```
hr = Row.Open("http://myserver/row/childrow");
hr = Row.Move("somewhereelse");
```

is equivalent to

```
hr = Row.Open("http://myserver/row");
hr = Row.Move("somewhereelse", 0, "childrow");
```

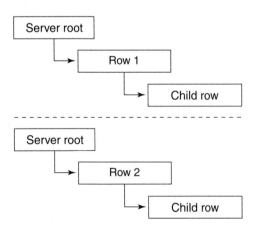

**Figure 16-4** Moving a Row

**Table 16-4**  Row Move Flags

| Symbol | Description |
|---|---|
| DBMOVE_ALLOW_EMULATION | Provider can emulate the operation with an upload and a download |
| DBMOVE_ASYNC | Move operation is asynchronous |
| DBMOVE_ATOMIC | Move operation is atomic |
| DBMOVE_DONT_UPDATE_LINKS | Forbid the server to update links |
| DBMOVE_REPLACE_EXISTING | If there is a row at the destination, replace it with the source row |

**Table 16-5**  Row Delete Flags

| Symbol | Description |
|---|---|
| DBDELETE_ASYNC | Delete the row asynchronously |
| DBDELETE_ATOMIC | Delete operation is atomic |

### Deleting a Row

To delete a row, call

```
HRESULT Delete (LPCTSTR szURL = _T(""),
   DBDELETEFLAGS dwDeleteFlags = 0)
```

The following sample demonstrates how to delete the row at a given URL:

```
hr = Row.Open(URL);
hr = Row.Delete();
```

Optionally, you can specify one of the row delete flags. dwDeleteFlags can be a combination of the values in Table 16-5. For example, to delete a row asynchronously, write:

```
hr = Row.Open(URL);
hr = Row.Delete(_T(""),DBDELETE_ASYNC);
```

The Delete method accepts the relative path name of the row to delete. By default, it is "", which indicates the current row. You can also use the path name. The following example shows how to delete the row at *http://myserver/row/childrow*.

```
hr = Row.Open("http://myserver/row");
hr = Row.Delete("childrow");
// equivalent to
hr = Row.Open("http://myserver/row/childrow");
hr = Row.Delete();
```

# DOCUMENT MODEL

In some cases, the rows represent a *document*. For example, with the Internet publishing provider, each HTML file is a document. Microsoft Office documents are another example, and there are many others. Providers that support documents present rows with a series of columns predefined by OLE DB, each with a well-defined DBID. Class CResourceAccessor binds these columns both for a row and for a rowset. It is handy to access document rows.

For example, you might declare a row type such as

```
CRow<CRowAccessor<CResourceAccessor> > MyRow;
```

CResourceAccessor is defined as follows:

```
class CResourceAccessor
{
public:
    TCHAR m_ParseName [512];
    TCHAR m_ParentName [512];
    TCHAR m_AbsoluteParseName [512];
    BOOL m_IsHidden;
    BOOL m_IsReadOnly ;
    TCHAR m_ContentType [512];
    TCHAR m_ContentClass[512];
    TCHAR m_ContentLanguage [512];
    DBTIMESTAMP m_CreationTime;
    DBTIMESTAMP m_LastAccessTime;
    DBTIMESTAMP m_LastWriteTime;
    ULARGE_INTEGER m_StreamSize;
    BOOL m_IsCollection;
    BOOL m_IsStructuredDocument;
    TCHAR m_DefaultDocument [512];
    TCHAR m_DisplayName [512];
    BOOL m_IsRoot;
BEGIN_NAMED_COLUMN_MAP (CResourceAccessor)
    DBID_COLUMN_ENTRY(1, DBROWCOL_PARSENAME, m_ParseName)
    DBID_COLUMN_ENTRY(2, DBROWCOL_PARENTNAME, m_ParentName)
    DBID_COLUMN_ENTRY(3, DBROWCOL_ABSOLUTEPARSENAME,
        m_AbsoluteParseName)
    DBID_COLUMN_ENTRY(4, DBROWCOL_ISHIDDEN, m_IsHidden)
    DBID_COLUMN_ENTRY(5, DBROWCOL_ISREADONLY, m_IsReadOnly)
    DBID_COLUMN_ENTRY(6, DBROWCOL_CONTENTTYPE, m_ContentType)
```

```
    DBID_COLUMN_ENTRY(7, DBROWCOL_CONTENTCLASS, m_ContentClass)
    DBID_COLUMN_ENTRY(8, DBROWCOL_CONTENTLANGUAGE,
      m_ContentLanguage)
    DBID_COLUMN_ENTRY(9, DBROWCOL_CREATIONTIME, m_CreationTime)
    DBID_COLUMN_ENTRY(10, DBROWCOL_LASTACCESSTIME,
      m_LastAccessTime)
    DBID_COLUMN_ENTRY(11, DBROWCOL_LASTWRITETIME, m_LastWriteTime)
    DBID_COLUMN_ENTRY(12, DBROWCOL_STREAMSIZE, m_StreamSize)
    DBID_COLUMN_ENTRY(13, DBROWCOL_ISCOLLECTION, m_IsCollection)
    DBID_COLUMN_ENTRY(14, DBROWCOL_ISSTRUCTUREDDOCUMENT,
      m_IsStructuredDocument)
    DBID_COLUMN_ENTRY(15, DBROWCOL_DEFAULTDOCUMENT,
      m_DefaultDocument)
    DBID_COLUMN_ENTRY(16, DBROWCOL_DISPLAYNAME, m_DisplayName)
    DBID_COLUMN_ENTRY(17, DBROWCOL_ISROOT, m_IsRoot) END_COLUMN_MAP()
};
```

`m_ParseName` represents the relative name of the document, while `m_Parent Name` is the absolute name of the parent. Together, they form `m_Absolute ParseName`, examples, of which include

- `m_ParseName`= "myfile.htm"

- `m_ParentName`= "http://myserver/"

- `m_AbsoluteParseName`= "http://myserver/myfile.htm"

Each document has attributes: `m_IsHidden` specifies whether the document is hidden (for example, system files), and `m_IsReadOnly` indicates whether the document is read only. `m_IsReadOnly` can be useful for choosing an appropriate bind URL flag to open the document.

Documents can have a type, a class, and a language (`m_ContentType`, `m_ContentClass`, and `m_ContentLanguage`). They also have three associated time stamps: `m_CreationTime` represents the date and time the document was created; `m_LastWriteTime` represents the last time somebody wrote in it; and `m_LastAccessTime` represents the last time somebody accessed it. Note that it is possible to access the document without writing into it.

As a result, we have

```
m_CreationTime <= m_LastWriteTime <= m_LastAccessTime
```

When a document has an attached stream, `m_StreamSize` represents the stream size. Since this is a 64-bit integer, there is no 4-gigabyte limit.

`m_IsCollection` specifies whether the document can have child rows. It will always be false for files and will always be true for directories regardless of whether a directory actually has children.

m_IsStructuredDocument specifies whether the document is structured. Office documents are examples of structured documents.

Some rows have an associated default document (m_DefaultDocument). For example, Web directories usually default to a file. Thus *http://myserver* might default to *http://myserver/default.htm*.

The display name (m_DisplayName) is a friendly name used for display. For example, file *myfile.htm* might have the friendly name "information for next meeting."

Finally, m_IsRoot specifies whether the document is at the root of the server. For example, *http://myserver* corresponds to a root document while *http://myserver/myfile* does not.

## ROW FOLDER OBJECT

Some row objects can have children. However, CRow itself does not provide any way to enumerate them. For this we have another class, CRowFolder, which can enumerate the child rows of a given row. CRowFolder is implemented as a regular rowset in which each row handle corresponds to one child row object. In Figure 16-5, a parent row has two child row objects named "a" and "b." The corresponding row folder thus has one row for a and one row for b.

Since a row folder contains a set of rows, a natural name for the corresponding class would be CRowset. However, since this name is already taken for the "regular" rowset, the OLE DB extensions supply a new one: CRowFolder. The OLE DB extensions implement this object as a regular rowset accessor object,

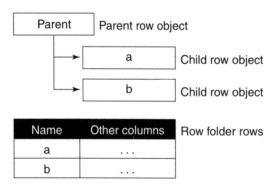

**Figure 16-5** Child Row Objects and the Corresponding Row Folder

which means, in C++, that it is a descendant of `CAccessorRowset`. In a sense, `CRowFolder` is at the same level as `CTable` and `CCommand`. It is declared as

```
template <class TAccessor , class TRowset = CRowset>
class CRowFolder :
    public CAccessorRowset<TAccessor, TRowset>
```

For example, you could declare the following row folders:

```
CRowFolder<CAccessor<CResourceAccessor> > Folder;
CRowFolder<CDynamicAccessor, CRowset > Folder2;
```

You use `CRowFolder` like `CCommand` or `CTable`. The only difference is in how to open or create it.

## Opening and Creating a Row Folder

Opening and creating a row folder is very similar to opening and creating a row. After all, they might represent the same underlying object. You can either call `Open` to open an already created object or call `Create` to create one. Also, you can specify an absolute or a relative path. This section explores the different cases.

To open a row folder from a URL, you need to call the following method:

```
HRESULT Open(LPTSTR szName, DBBINDURLFLAG Flag =
    DBBINDURLFLAG_READ, DBPROPSET* pPropSet = NULL,
    ULONG nPropertySets = 1)
```

For example, you might write

```
CRowFolder<CAccessor<CResourceAccessor> > RowFolder;
hr = RowFolder.Open(_T("http://myserver/directory"));
```

As with rows, you can open a row folder as a child of a row with a relative path by calling

```
template <class TRow>
HRESULT Open(TRow& Row, LPCTSTR szSubDir = NULL,
    DBPROPSET* pPropSet = NULL, ULONG nPropertySets=1)
```

The `szSubDir` parameter represents the relative path of the row folder. If it is `NULL`, the row folder and row represent the same underlying object. For example, you might write

```
CRow< CRowAccessor<CResourceAccessor> > Row;
hr Row.Open(_T("http://myserver/directory");
CRowFolder<CAccessor<CResourceAccessor> > RowFolder;
//Open http://myserver/directory/subdirectory:
hr = RowFolder.Open(Row, _T("subdirectory"));
//Open http://myserver/directory:
hr = RowFolder.Open(Row);
```

It is also possible to create a row folder from an absolute or a relative path. Although it is very similar to creating a row, the object created might be different. With the Internet publishing provider, for example, CRow will create a file while CRowFolder will create a directory.

To create a row folder from an absolute path, call

```
HRESULT Create(LPTSTR szName, DBBINDURLFLAG Flag =
    DBBINDURLFLAG_OPENIFEXISTS|DBBINDURLFLAG_READWRITE,
    DBPROPSET* pPropSet = NULL, ULONG nPropertySets=1)
```

For example:

```
CRowFolder<CAccessor<CResourceAccessor> > RowFolder;
hr = RowFolder.Create(_T("http://myserver/directory"));
```

The URL binding flag can have one of the usual values. In addition, it can contain the DBBINDURLFLAG_COLLECTION flag, which indicates that the object to be created is a collection (folder).

To create a row folder with a relative path, call

```
template <class TRow>
HRESULT Create(TRow& Row, LPCTSTR szName, DBBINDURLFLAG dwFlags
    = DBBINDURLFLAG_COLLECTION|DBBINDURLFLAG_OPENIFEXISTS,
    DBPROPSET* pPropSet = NULL, ULONG nPropertySets=1)
```

For example:

```
CRow< CRowAccessor<CResourceAccessor> > Row;
hr = Row.Open(_T("http://myserver/directory");
CRowFolder<CAccessor<CResourceAccessor> > RowFolder;
//Create http://myserver/directory/subdirectory:
hr = RowFolder.Create(Row, _T("subdirectory"));
```

## Enumerating Children

Each row handle in the rowset of the row folder represents a child row, which you can navigate as you would a regular rowset. For example, if a row has two children, a and b, its row folder object will have two rows, one for row a and one for row b.

When the row folder has a current row (for example, after you call `MoveFirst`), you can open the row object that corresponds to it. The `CRow` method is declared as

```
HRESULT Open(const CRowset& Rowset, bool bGetColumns = true)
```

Figure 16-6 illustrates the row/row folder architecture. The following example shows one way to enumerate the children of a row:

```
CRow<CAccessor<CResourceAccessor> > ParentRow;
hr = ParentRow.Open(..);
CRowFolder<CAccessor<CResourceAccessor> > RowFolder;
hr = RowFolder.Open(ParentRow);
hr = RowFolder.MoveFirst();
CRow<CAccessor<CResourceAccessor> > RowA;
hr = RowA.Open(RowFolder);
CRow<CAccessor<CResourceAccessor> > RowB;
hr = RowFolder.MoveNext();
hr = RowB.Open(RowFolder);
```

Another way is to get the URL of the child row and open the row with it. The benefit of this method is that you can specify URL binding flags and properties when opening the child row. The previous example then becomes

```
CRow<CAccessor<CResourceAccessor> > ParentRow;
hr = ParentRow.Open(..);
CRowFolder<CAccessor<CResourceAccessor> > RowFolder;
hr = RowFolder.Open(ParentRow);
hr = RowFolder.MoveFirst();
CRow<CAccessor<CResourceAccessor> > RowA;
hr = RowA.Open(RowFolder.m_AbsoluteParseName);
CRow<CAccessor<CResourceAccessor> > RowB;
hr = RowFolder.MoveNext();
hr = RowB.Open(RowFolder.m_AbsoluteParseName);
```

Obviously, this method works only when row folders can bind the absolute parse name.

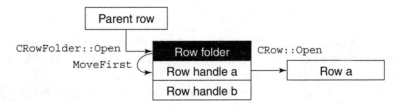

**Figure 16-6** Row and Row Folder Architecture

# STREAMS

Many row objects are associated with a stream object. For example, a file object has a stream that contains the actual file data. Similarly, an email can have a stream that contains its text. OLE DB 2.5 streams are very similar to BLOBs in that they can contain a large amount of data and the preferred access interface is ISequential Stream. If you understand BLOBs, manipulating OLE DB 2.5 streams will be very similar. Class CStream implements the stream object.

There are two steps in using a stream: opening it and reading or writing bytes into it.

## Opening a Stream

There are two ways to open a stream. The first is to open the corresponding row and then open the stream with it. It does not matter how the row was opened: You can use an absolute path or a relative path, and you can open it from a row folder.

The following example demonstrates this technique:

```
CRow <CRowAccessor <CResourceAccessor> > Row;
hr = Row.Open(szURL);
CStream Stream
hr = Stream.Open(Row);
```

By default, the row downloads the content of the stream at open time. However, you can override this behavior by specifying the DBBINDURLFLAG_DELAYFETCH STREAM URL binding flag.

The second method is to open a stream directly from a URL. The Open method has the following signature:

```
HRESULT Open(LPTSTR szName, DBBINDURLFLAG Flag =
    DBBINDURLFLAG_READWRITE, DBPROPSET* pPropSet = NULL,
    ULONG nPropertySets = 1)
```

with which the previous example becomes

```
CStream Stream;
hr = Stream.Open(szURL);
```

This is simpler, but it does not give access to the row methods. For example, you cannot move or copy the stream directly, but must get its associated row object first.

In any case, you can open a row from a stream with the following method:

```
HRESULT Open(const CStream& Stream, bool bGetColumns = true)
```

For example:

```
CStream Stream;
hr = Stream.Open(szURL);
CRow <CRowAccessor <CResourceAccessor> > Row;
hr = Row.Open(Stream);
```

To create a stream, you call the `Create` method:

```
HRESULT Create(LPTSTR szName, DBBINDURLFLAG Flag =
    DBBINDURLFLAG_OPENIFEXISTS|DBBINDURLFLAG_READWRITE,
    DBPROPSET* pPropSet = NULL, ULONG nPropertySets=1)
```

The following example shows how to create and open a stream from a URL:

```
CStream Stream;
hr = Stream.Create(URL);
```

In all cases, we opened the default stream of the row. `CStream` does not offer any method to open nondefault streams.

## Reading and Writing in a Stream

`CStream` provides `Read` and `Write` methods to read and write in the stream. These are straight encapsulations of the corresponding `ISequentialStream` methods (for more information, refer to Chapter 11).

```
HRESULT Read(void *pv, ULONG cb, ULONG *pcbRead)
```

and

```
HRESULT Write(const void *pv, ULONG cb, ULONG *pcbWritten)
```

The following example shows how to read data from a stream object:

```
char text [1234];
ULONG ActuallyRead;
hr = Stream.Read(text, sizeof(text), & ActuallyRead);
```

Once you are finished with the stream, you can either call `Close` to release the underlying object or wait for the destructor of `CStream` to do it for you.

## SUMMARY

This chapter described how to access hierarchical providers through OLE DB. The OLE DB extensions provide three classes that give access to the underlying objects: `CRow`, `CRowFolder`, and `CStream`.

## EPILOGUE

This book has described OLE DB and the OLE DB consumer templates. Hopefully by now, you can understand the benefits of OLE DB: It provides fast access to a wide variety of data sources. The OLE DB templates provide something C++ programmers crave: full control and great flexibility.

But, OLE DB is also an evolving technology. In fact, wherever there is data, one will find OLE DB. As I finish this book, Microsoft is releasing OLE DB 2.6 with XML support. Watch for more convergence in this area. In addition, Visual Studio 7 should bring some improvements on the template side. The version 7 preview shows how C++ attributes facilitate the development of consumer code, but the release might bring other enhancements.

Finally, while the new MSIL architecture introduces some interesting concepts, such as cross language development and garbage collection, OLE DB should stay with COM. Visual studio 7 should also come with a new library, ATL server, which facilitates the development of ISAPI solutions. Together with the OLE DB consumer templates, it should offer the best way to develop very high-performance Web sites and services.

# Advanced C++ Techniques

The OLE DB consumer templates use some "advanced" features of C++, including multiple inheritance, templates, and local types. While this is a delight for advanced programmers, it can be a little bit confusing for beginners. Thus, it might be a good idea to review these more advanced techniques before diving into the heart of the C++ library.

## Inheriting from a Template Parameter

To inherit from a template parameter, you might write something like

```
template <class T>
class CMyClass : public T
{
    void MyMethod();
    int m_MyClassMember;
};
```

In this example, `CMyClass` inherits all the class members and methods of `T`, so if we have two classes, `A` and `B`,

```
Class A
{
    void AMethod();
    int m_AClassMember;
};
Class B
{
    void BMethod();
    int m_BClassMember;
};
```

Declaring a type `CMyClass<A>` is equivalent to having an imaginary class, `CMyClass_A`, defined as

```
Class CMyClass_A: public A
{
   void MyMethod();
   int m_MyClassMember;
}
```

As a result, `CMyClass<A>` will unfold as

```
   void AMethod();
   int m_AClassMember;
   void MyMethod();
   int m_MyClassMember;
```

while `CMyClass<B>` will unfold as

```
   void BMethod();
   int m_BClassMember;
   void MyMethod();
   int m_MyMember;
```

Template parameter inheritance is illustrated in Figure A-1.

## Default Template Parameters

With default template parameters, if we have a class defined as

```
template <class T = CDefaultParameter>
class CMyClass
{
};
```

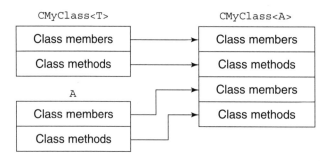

**Figure A-1** Inheriting from a Template Parameter

writing

```
CMyClass<>
```

is equivalent to writing

```
CMyClass< CDefaultParameter >
```

While this does not seem hard to figure out, it becomes more difficult when combined with inheritance from a template parameter. For example, if we have a class defined as

```
template <class T = CDefaultParameter>
class CMyClass : public T
{
};
```

an instance of `CMyClass<>` will actually "silently" inherit from `CDefault Parameter`.

## Type Definition Overloading

The ability to declare types, as opposed to classes, is one of my favorite C++ features because it enables the programmer to build nice flexible architectures. It is also possible to override a global type definition with a type definition local to a class. The following example will clarify this point.

Suppose we have the following class:

```
class class1
{
   static int f()
   {
      return 1;
   }
}
```

We can use this in a global `typedef` as follows:

```
typedef class1 mytypedef;
```

Thus, any class declared after this type definition can use the `mytypedef`. For example, such a class could be

```
Class CTest1
{
   int test1()
   {
      return mytypedef::f();
   }
};
```

In this context, a call to `test1` returns 1. In addition, a class can declare a local `typedef`, that is, one whose scope is local to the class. Such a class might look like

```
class CTest2
{
    typedef class2 mytypedef;
    int test2()
    {
        return mytypedef::f();
    }
};
```

where `class2` is defined as

```
class class2
{
    static int f()
    {
        return 2;
    }
}
```

In this case, the local type definition overrides the global `typedef`. As a result, a call to `test2` is forwarded to `class2`. In other words, `test2()` returns 2. This is also true if the `typedef` is inherited.

Putting all the techniques together, we have the following scenario:

```
template <class T = CTest2>
class CMyClass : public T
{
    int test()
    {
        return mytypedef::f();
    }
};
```

What does `CMyClass<>::test()` return? The first two techniques tell us that `CMyClass<>` inherits from `CTest2`. Since `CTest2` redefines `mytypedef` as `class2`, `CMyClass<>` uses `class2`'s version of `f` as well. As a result, `CMyClass<>::test()` returns 2.

# Appendix

# B  OLE DB Types and Conversions

The following OLE DB data types identify the types of the columns in a rowset.

DBTYPE_I1: a 1-byte signed integer; the corresponding C type is signed char.

DBTYPE_UI1: a 1-byte unsigned integer; the corresponding C type is BYTE.

DBTYPE_I2: a 2-byte signed integer; the corresponding C type is SHORT.

DBTYPE_UI2: a 2-byte unsigned integer; the corresponding C type is unsigned short.

DBTYPE_I4: a 4-byte signed integer; the corresponding C type is LONG.

DBTYPE_UI4: a 4-byte unsigned integer; the corresponding C type is unsigned long.

DBTYPE_I8: am 8-byte signed integer; the corresponding C type is LARGE_INTEGER.

DBTYPE_UI8: an 8-byte unsigned integer; the corresponding C type is ULARGE_INTEGER.

DBTYPE_R4: a single-precision floating-point value; the corresponding C type is float.

DBTYPE_R8: a double-precision floating-point value; the corresponding C type is double.

DBTYPE_BOOL: a boolean stored as a VARIANT_BOOL.

DBTYPE_ERROR: an error code; the corresponding C type is SCODE.

DBTYPE_STR: a single-byte string; the corresponding C type is CHAR[].

DBTYPE_WSTR: a double-byte string; the corresponding C type is WCHAR[].

DBTYPE_BSTR: a double-byte string with the length stored in the string; the corresponding C type is BSTR.

DBTYPE_BYTES: an array of bytes; the corresponding C type is BYTE[].

DBTYPE_DATE: a date stored as a DATE.

DBTYPE_DBDATE: a date stored as a DBDATE.

DBTYPE_DBTIME: a time stored as a DBTIME.

DBTYPE_DBTIMESTAMP: a date and time stored as a DBTIMESTAMP.

DBTYPE_FILETIME: a date and time stored as a FILETIME.

DBTYPE_GUID: a 128-bit identifier; the corresponding C type is GUID.

DBTYPE_CY: a currency value; the corresponding C type is LARGE_INTEGER.

DBTYPE_DECIMAL: a decimal value; the corresponding C type is DECIMAL.

DBTYPE_NUMERIC: a numeric value; the corresponding C type is DB_NUMERIC.

DBTYPE_VARNUMERIC: a variable-length numeric value; the corresponding C type is DB_VARNUMERIC.

DBTYPE_VARIANT: an OLE automation VARIANT value.

DBTYPE_PROPVARIANT: an OLE automation PROPVARIANT value.

DBTYPE_IDISPATCH: a pointer to an IDispatch interface.

DBTYPE_IUNKNOWN: a pointer to an IUnknown interface.

OLE DB comes with a data conversion library. The different providers are not required to use it, but most of them do because there is no point in replicating the effort of writing it. For this reason, it is safe to assume that the providers offer the same conversions.

## CONVERSION TABLE

The following table summarizes the conversions. The first column contains the source types; the first row, the destination.

| From: \ To: | I1, I2, UI1, UI2 | I4, UI4 | I9, UI8 | R4 | R8 | BOOL | ERROR | STR | BSTR, WSTR | BYTES | DATE | DBDATE | DBTIME | DBTIMESTAMP | FILETIME | GUID | CY | DECIMAL | NUMERIC | VARNUMERIC | VARIANT | PROPVARIANT | IDispatch | IUnknown |
|---|---|---|---|---|---|---|---|---|---|---|---|---|---|---|---|---|---|---|---|---|---|---|---|---|
| I1 | Y | Y | Y | Y | Y | Y |  | Y | Y |  | Y | Y | Y | Y |  |  | Y | Y | Y | Y | Y |  |  |  |
| UI1 | Y | Y | Y | Y | Y | Y |  | Y | Y |  | Y | Y | Y | Y |  |  | Y | Y | Y | Y | Y | Y |  |  |
| I2 | Y | Y | Y | Y | Y | Y |  | Y | Y |  | Y | Y | Y | Y |  |  | Y | Y | Y | Y | Y | Y |  |  |
| UI2 | Y | Y | Y | Y | Y | Y |  | Y | Y |  | Y | Y | Y | Y |  |  | Y | Y | Y | Y | Y | Y |  |  |
| I4 | Y | Y | Y | Y | Y | Y |  | Y | Y | Y | Y | Y | Y | Y |  |  | Y | Y | Y | Y | Y | Y |  |  |
| UI4 | Y | Y | Y | Y | Y | Y |  | Y | Y | Y | Y | Y | Y | Y |  |  | Y | Y | Y | Y | Y | Y |  |  |
| I8 | Y | Y | Y | Y | Y | Y |  | Y | Y | Y |  |  |  |  | Y |  | Y | Y |  |  | Y | Y |  |  |
| UI8 | Y | Y | Y | Y | Y | Y |  | Y | Y | Y |  |  |  |  | Y |  | Y | Y |  |  | Y | Y |  |  |
| R4 | Y | Y | Y | Y | Y | Y |  | Y | Y |  | Y | Y | Y |  |  |  | Y | Y | Y | Y | Y | Y |  |  |
| R8 | Y | Y | Y | Y | Y | Y |  | Y | Y |  | Y | Y | Y | Y |  |  | Y | Y | Y | Y | Y | Y |  |  |
| BOOL | Y | Y | Y | Y | Y | Y |  | Y | Y |  | Y |  |  |  |  |  | Y | Y | Y | Y | Y | Y |  |  |
| ERROR |  |  |  |  |  |  | Y | Y |  |  |  |  |  |  |  |  |  |  |  |  | Y |  |  |  |
| STR | Y | Y | Y | Y | Y | Y |  | Y | Y | Y | Y | Y | Y | Y | Y | Y | Y | Y | Y | Y | Y | Y |  |  |
| WSTR | Y | Y | Y | Y | Y | Y |  | Y | Y | Y | Y | Y | Y | Y | Y | Y | Y | Y | Y | Y | Y | Y |  |  |
| BSTR | Y | Y | Y | Y | Y | Y |  | Y | Y | Y | Y | Y | Y | Y | Y | Y | Y | Y | Y | Y | Y | Y |  |  |
| BYTES |  | Y | Y |  |  |  |  | Y | Y | Y |  |  |  |  |  | Y |  |  |  |  | Y | Y |  |  |
| DATE | Y |  |  | Y | Y | Y |  | Y | Y | Y | Y | Y | Y | Y | Y |  |  |  |  |  | Y | Y |  |  |
| DBDATE |  |  |  |  |  |  |  | Y | Y |  | Y | Y | Y | Y | Y |  |  |  |  |  | Y |  |  |  |
| DBTIME |  |  |  |  |  |  |  | Y | Y |  | Y | Y | Y | Y | Y |  |  |  |  |  | Y |  |  |  |
| STAMP |  |  |  |  |  |  |  | Y | Y |  | Y | Y | Y | Y | Y |  |  |  |  |  | Y |  |  |  |
| FILETIME |  | Y |  |  |  |  |  | Y | Y |  | Y | Y | Y | Y | Y |  |  |  |  |  | Y | Y |  |  |
| GUID |  |  |  |  |  |  |  | Y | Y | Y |  |  |  |  |  | Y |  |  |  |  | Y | Y |  |  |
| CY | Y |  |  | Y | Y | Y |  | Y | Y |  |  |  |  |  |  |  | Y | Y | Y | Y | Y | Y |  |  |
| DECIMAL | Y |  |  | Y | Y | Y |  | Y | Y |  |  | Y | Y | Y |  |  | Y | Y | Y | Y | Y |  |  |  |
| NUMERIC | Y |  |  | Y | Y | Y |  | Y | Y |  |  |  |  |  |  |  | Y | Y | Y | Y | Y |  |  |  |
| VARNUMERIC | Y |  |  | Y | Y | Y |  | Y | Y |  |  |  |  |  |  |  | Y | Y | Y | Y | Y |  |  |  |
| VARIANT | Y |  |  | Y | Y | Y | Y | Y | Y | Y | Y | Y | Y | Y | Y | Y | Y | Y | Y | Y | Y | Y | Y | Y |
| PROPVARIANT | Y |  |  | Y | Y | Y | Y | Y | Y | Y | Y | Y | Y | Y | Y | Y | Y | Y | Y | Y | Y | Y | Y | Y |
| IDispatch | Y |  |  | Y | Y | Y | Y | Y | Y | Y | Y | Y | Y | Y | Y | Y | Y | Y | Y | Y | Y | Y | Y | Y |
| IUnknown |  |  |  |  |  |  |  |  |  |  |  |  |  |  |  |  |  |  |  |  | Y |  | Y | Y |

# Index

# Also Available from Addison-Wesley

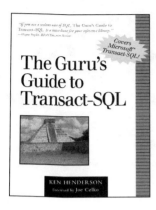

## The Guru's Guide to Transact-SQL
Ken Henderson

Since its introduction more than a decade ago, the Microsoft SQL Server query language, Transact-SQL, has become increasingly popular and more powerful. The current version sports advanced features such as OLE Automation support, cross-platform querying facilities, and full-text search management. This book is the consummate guide to Microsoft Transact-SQL. From data type nuances to complex statistical computations to the bevy of undocumented features in the language, *The Guru's Guide to Transact-SQL* imparts the knowledge you need to become a virtuoso of the language as quickly as possible. This book contains the information, explanations, and advice needed to master Transact-SQL and develop the best possible Transact-SQL code. Some 600 code examples not only illustrate important concepts and best practices, but also provide working Transact-SQL code that can be incorporated into your own real-world DBMS applications.

0-201-61576-2 • Paperback • 576 pages • ©2000

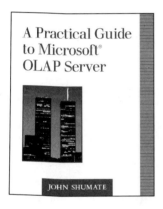

## A Practical Guide to Microsoft® OLAP Server
John Shumate

With the introduction of Microsoft's OLAP Services, Online Analytical Processing (OLAP) technology has become a major force in today's marketplace. OLAP, which enables multidimensional databases for sophisticated decision support, is a technology that IT and database professionals simply need to know. *A Practical Guide to Microsoft® OLAP Server* introduces you to OLAP technology and leads you step-by-step through the process of deploying an OLAP server, focusing particularly on Microsoft's OLAP Services. This book explains the basic concepts underlying OLAP, compares various OLAP products, and describes Microsoft's OLAP Services architecture. In addition, it enumerates the development lifecycle of an OLAP Services application from planning and design through installation and administration, discussing the goals and approaches for each phase and task.

0-201-48557-5 • Paperback • 432 pages • ©2000

## Developing Applications Using Outlook 2000, CDO, Exchange, and Visual Basic
Raffaele Piemonte and Scott Jamison

Written for IT developers who build collaborative and workflow applications, this book provides a comprehensive reference to working with Microsoft's powerful collaborative development environment, including Outlook 2000, Exchange Server, Visual Basic, and the Collaboration Data Objects (CDO) Library. It demonstrates ways in which these technologies can be tied together into effective business solutions—from small-scale groupware to large-scale enterprisewide systems. *Developing Applications Using Outlook 2000, CDO, Exchange, and Visual Basic* offers an overview of the Microsoft collaborative landscape, and then examines each element of that environment in detail. Numerous examples showcase the applications made possible with these technologies.

0-201-61575-4 • Paperback • 592 pages • ©2000

# Register
## Your Book

at www.aw.com/cseng/register

You may be eligible to receive:

- Advance notice of forthcoming editions of the book
- Related book recommendations
- Chapter excerpts and supplements of forthcoming titles
- Information about special contests and promotions throughout the year
- Notices and reminders about author appearances, tradeshows, and online chats with special guests

## Contact us

If you are interested in writing a book or reviewing manuscripts prior to publication, please write to us at:

Editorial Department
Addison-Wesley Professional
75 Arlington Street, Suite 300
Boston, MA 02116 USA
Email: AWPro@aw.com

Addison-Wesley

Visit us on the Web: http://www.aw.com/cseng